Saint
Petersburg

A GUIDE TO THE ARCHITECTURE

BIBLIOPOLIS
SAINT PETERSBURG
1994

Photographs by
Kira Zharinova
Vladimir Sobolev
Vladimir Melnikov
Translated from the Russian by
Yelena Kazey
Layout by
Nadezhda Lakatosh

ISBN 5-7435-0071-1

CONTENTS

INTRODUCTION

Among the many poetical names applied to St.Petersburg the most common are «Northern Venice» and «Northern Palmyra».

It has been called «Venice» because the latter city encompasses a number of islands in the Venetian Lagoon, Adriatic Sea; Petersburg is likewise divided into numerous islands by the Neva, Fontanka and other rivers and canals.

It has been called «Palmyra» because on its discovery this ancient capital became world famous for the perfection of its classical proportions; similarly, Petersburg presents a perfect combination of logical spacial composition and linear street layout with the wide openings of squares, tall verticals of its towers and belfries, figured railings, arch-shaped bridges and granite embankments, all elements joined together to form a single work of art.

This is the city that stands out for its architectural ensembles. People who created them were not only architects but poets as well; they managed to combine columns and portals, arches and cupolas, Baroque lavishness and Classical austerity to produce the impression of perfect harmony. The names of Rossi and Rastrelli are the first to be mentioned among them. Others, Zakharov, Quarenghi, Thomas-de-Thomon, Vallin de la Mothe, possesed no less individuality and exhibited great tact towards their predecessors. Stakenschneider's architectural suite served to harmonize the multi-style products of eclectism. Lidval and Suzor, masters of Art-Nouveau, were the first to introduce elaborate decoration and refined facade design in the architecture of apartment houses. However scarce the examples, Constructivism has also left a notable trace in the city architecture.

There are different ways of getting to know the city, if not just seeing its main sights. There are various kinds of guide-books, including universal, professional, architectural ones, etc.

The book you are holding is not a guide-book in the strict sence of the word. It does not lead you anywhere, nor does it suggest any itinerary; it does not provide you with the chronological sequence of events. Rather, it makes you stop to have a look around, muse at the sight that has caught your eye and get to know the main facts about it.

The purpose of the book is to tell you about the place you have found yourself in, in terms of its artistic and historical value. Such guide book might be refered to as topological.

The city has been divided into seven zones that are given conventional names, the division being based on the city's 18th-century layout. The central, Admiralty, part enclosed between the Neva and Fontanka, is especially rich in architectural monuments; it was along the Fontanka River that the most prominent ensembles are centered, including that of the central squares.

Some city part have been designated according to the «artistic dominant», though they include a broader space, as shown on the scheme (the Field of Mars, New Holland, etc.).

Nina Vasilevskaya,
Yelena Vasilevskaya

CENTRAL PART OF THE CITY
Between the Neva
and Fontanka River

Dvortsovaya (Palace) Square

The Palace Square ensemble is of great historical and architectural value and takes up an important place in the spatial composition of central Petersburg. Several generations of outstanding architects had been working on the ensemble for several centuries.

Palace Square came into being in the middle of the 18th century, when the Winter Palace was put up (1754—62).

C.Rossi contributed greatly to the formation of the Palace Square ensemble. In 1819—29 he put up the grand building of the General Staff here, in place of the houses built in the 1780s. He also erected the building housing the Ministries, uniting the two structures into a single whole by a grand triumphal arch thrown across Bolshaya Morskaya Street.

In 1837—43 the architect Briullov put up the building of the Guards Corps Headquarters, that gave shape to the eastern side of the square, and in 1846 the corner part of the General Staff building facing Nevsky Prospekt was

Palace Square

completed, which added the final stroke to the formation of the ensemble.

Masterful arrangement of the ensemble, proportionality of different architectural volumes and unity of proportions, rhythm and module create an ensemble of buildings executed in different styles, making Palace Square one of the most beautiful places in Petersburg.

1
THE WINTER PALACE
Dvortsovaya (Palace) Embankment, 38
1754—62. Architect B.Rastrelli

The Winter Palace is one of the most important architectural monuments in Petersburg, as well as the compositional center of the territory including the largest city's ensembles. It belongs to the greatest achievements of Russian and world architecture of the 18th century, both from the point of view of art and that of urban design.

The history of the construction is quite interesting. During Peter I's reign it was prohibited to allot land to people having no naval rank in the place now occupied by the palace. So Peter the Great, who wanted to build a palace for himself there, got a building permit as Peter Alekseyev, a shipbuilder. The first wooden Winter Palace was erected on the bank of the Zimniaya Kanavka (Winter Canal) in 1711. In 1719—20 the second, stone Winter Palace, was built on the site of the modern Hermitage Theater to a design by G.Mattarnovi, where Peter I moved with his family from his Summer Palace. In 1726—27. it was considerably enlarged.

In 1732 the architect B.Rastrelli began the construction of the third Winter Palace facing the Neva and Palace Square.

In 1754—62 he rebuilt it radically and created a new monumental building—the fourth Winter Palace existing now, which by far exceeds all the previous ones both in size and in the splendor of ornamentation. It is an outstanding example of the 18th-century Baroque architecture, created, in Rastrelli's own words, «exclusively to glorify Russia».

The palace was designed as a closed quadrangle with a spacious inner court. Its facades face the Neva, the Admiralty and Palace Square; in the center of the square Rastrelli planned to put up an equestrian statue of Peter I.

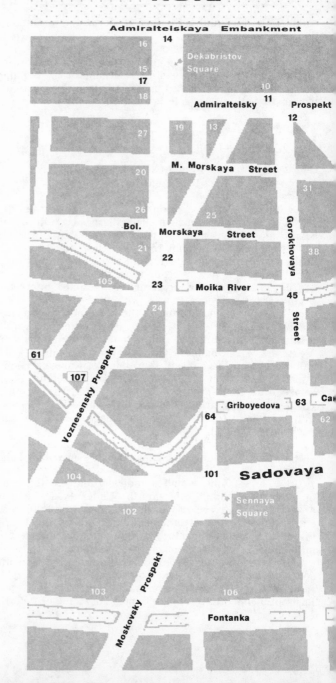

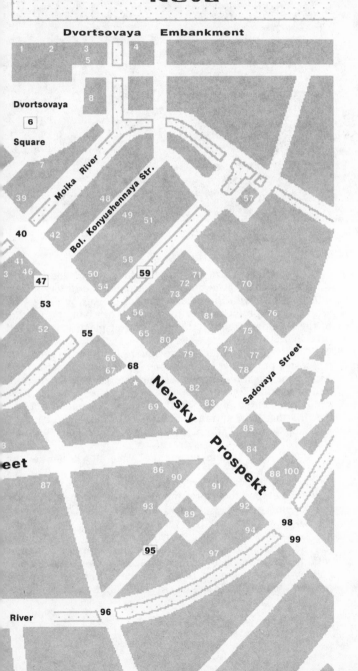

The Winter Palace (No 1)

The immense size of the building (more than 1000 rooms) and each of the façades, designed in a different way, in accordance with the peculiarities of the surrounding cityscape, sharp projections of the rizalits, the changing rhythm of the columns create the impression of plastic power, and grandeur.

The main façade facing the square is rather lengthy, but it doesn't produce a monotonous impression. In its central part there are three arches leading into the spacious court, and protruding forward stepwise.

In the center of the northern façade facing the Neva there is the main entrance that leads to the Ambassadorial (Jordan) Staircase, where the suite of royal halls took its start.

The western façade facing the Admiralty is flanked by powerful projections.

On each façade the columns are arranged in a different way—sometimes they form bunches at the corners, at other times being arranged at equal intervals. The balustrade of the roof with decorative vases and statues makes the building outline still more intricate.

The lintels of the two thousand windows are ornamented with masks, mascarones and cartouches. The smartness and holiday-like appearance of the palace is enhanced by the color of the walls, that makes the columns stand out for their whiteness.

The interiors of the palace are no less grand. According to Rastrelli's own words, «everything in the palace is decorated with great lavishness».

After 1762 work on the inner decoration and renovation of the palace was during fifty years carried on by such outstanding masters as Yu.Velten, J.-B.Vallin de la Mothe, A.Rinaldi, I.Starov, D.Quarenghi, A.Montferrand, C.Rossi.

Since the 1760s the Winter Palace had been the Russian emperor's residence. In the Winter Palace the solemn appearance of the emperors took place, as well as receptions, balls and other ceremonies. The Treasury housed royal regalia (the crown, scepter and orb), lots of jewelry and relics.

The main entrance to the palace is the Jordan Staircase facing the Dvortsovaya (Palace) Embankment (through this entrance members of the royal family and higher clergy went out to the Neva for going through a special rite of water sanctification during the holiday of Christening; the ceremony took place in a special pavilion called «Jordan», hence the name).

In 1837 a disastrous fire, that lasted more than thirty hours, destroyed all the splendid decor of the Winter Palace. After the fire only the walls and the vaults remained (works of art, furniture and other valuables were saved). To restore the palace a special commission was set up headed by the Minister of the Court Prince P.Volkonsky, which included the architects A.Briullov, V.Stasov, A.Staubert, engineers M.Clerk and I.Krol, A.Gotman. General P.Kleinmichel supervised the works. The palace was restored to the designs by V.Stasov and A.Briullov in the record term — during just two years. About 8 to 10 thousand workers were daily employed on the construction site. To commemorate the restoration works a gold medal was coined with an inscription reading: «Diligence overcomes everything». General Kleinmichel was awarded the title of a count. Some of the halls were restored as much close to the original as possible; other rooms were decorated to the designs newly done. Of great artistic value is the decoration of the St.George Hall, the Gallery of the War of 1812, the Jordan Staircase, the Small Avant-Salle, the Peter, Alexander and White Halls, and others.

During the restoration works fire-proof metal constructions were used for the floors and ceilings, as well as for spanning large bays.

In 1892—94 the delapidated sculptures on the parapets

and pediments of the palace, made of limestone, were replaced by hollow ones, made of sheet brass.

After the members of the People's Will society assassined Alexander II (1881), Alexander III moved his place of residence to Gatchina, and the Winter Palace was used only on some especially solemn occasions. When Nicholas II ascended the throne (1894), the royal family returned to the Winter Palace (the former chambers of Nicholas I on the ground floor were redecorated in the Art-Nouveau style); however, in 1904 the royal residence was moved to Tsarskoye Selo (Tsar's Village).

Since July 1917 the Winter Palace had been the residence of the Provisional Government, which resided in the former chambers of Nicholas II. During the October Revolution the Winter Palace was taken by storm by the revolutionary soldiers and workers.

At present the Winter Palace houses the Hermitage museum, which is one of the largest in the world.

Dvortsovaya (Palace) Embankment

This is the oldest embankment in the city. It was built up from the Admiralty as far as the Marble Palace in the late 1730s. The wooden embankment was replaced with a granite one in 1763—67. The steep bridges (1760s), curved outlines of the descents to the water with granite benches lend variety to the austerity of the granite walls.

2
THE SMALL HERMITAGE
Dvortsovaya Embankment, 36
1764—75. Architect J.-B.Vallin de la Mothe

The Small Hermitage is one of a set of buildings comprising a single whole with the Winter Palace. It was built with the purpose of housing a fine arts collection.

The façade facing the Neva is notable for the lavishness and refinement of its architectural forms. It boasts of a monumental six-column portico and decorative sculpture—the statues of Flora and Pomona, as well as the sculptural group on top of the attic. The Small Hermitage is connected with the Old Hermitage building by means of a suspension garden, which has been preserved up to now.

Of big artistic value are also the interiors of the halls facing the Neva, especially that of the White (Pavilion) Hall with two tiers of windows, where A.Stakenschneider managed to combine elements of Arabic and Renaissance architecture.

The Small Hermitage (No 2)   *The Old Hermitage (No 3)*

3
THE OLD HERMITAGE
Dvortsovaya Embankment, 34
1771—87. Architect Yu.Velten

For the construction of the Old Hermitage the foundations and walls of the former houses, that had stood there since early 18th century, were used. In the 19th century the building got the name of the Old Hermitage and was turned into a depository for objects of art.

The façade facing the embankment is decorated in the early classical style. The decoration being rather modest, the building serves as a link between the smart Small Hermitage and the Winter Palace, and the classically austere Hermitage Theater.

The Hermitage Theater (No 4)

When the building was reconstructed in 1851—59, the architect Stakenschneider changed the interior decoration only, preserving the façade in general intact.

The main staircase of white Italian marble and Olonetsk porphyry is remarkable. Its name, Sovetskaya, dates back to the second half of the 19th century, when members of the State Council (Sovet) were to go up the staircase to reach the room where the sittings were held.

Adjacent to the building of the Old Hermitage are the so-called Raphael Loggias—a gallery running along the Zimniaya Kanavka Embankment (1783—94, architect Quarenghi), decorated with copies of murals by Raphael and his pupils in the Vatican Palace in Rome.

4
THE HERMITAGE THEATER
Dvortsovaya Embankment, 32
1783—87. Architect G.Quarenghi

The Hermitage Theater building is the last in the set of buildings connected with the Winter Palace by means of a number of arches and passages. The famous arch over the Zimniaya Kanavka erected by Yu.Velten makes this integral architectural complex especially picturesque.

The first play was staged here in 1785, even before the decoration of the building was finally completed. The seats for the spectators are arranged in a semicircle. The walls are decorated with columns and niches with sculptures. The foyer was decorated in 1904 by the architect L.Benois.

Royal opera and drama companies from Italy, France, and Russia performed in the Hermitage Theater.

5
THE NEW HERMITAGE
Millionnaya Street, 35
1839—52. Architect L. von Klenze

The monumental building of the New Hermitage was put up especially to house the ever-increasing collections of the objects of arts, that had previously been stored in the Small and Old Hermitages. It was the first museum building in Russia. The layout of the interior, the lighting arrangements in some halls were meant to expose pictures and other objects most favorably.

The main façade of the New Hermitage faces Millionnaya Street. The portico is decorated with the figures of ten Atlantes that were cut from monolithic gray granite to a model by A.Terebenev. Sculpture plays a big part in the composition of the facades, emphasizing the

The New Hermitage (No 5)

purpose to which the building was put up. It includes the statues of artists, cast from an alloy of zinc with tin, granite germs at the windows, terra-cotta decorations over the first floor windows with the emblems of different arts.

The New Hermitage interiors are decorated with painting, stucco moulding and gilding. Construction was carried on to a design by Klenze, but under the supervision and with the participation of V.Stasov and N.Yefimov.

6

THE ALEXANDER COLUMN
Dvortsovaya Square
1830—34. Architect A.Montferrand

The Alexander Column was erected to commemorate Russia's victory over Napoleon in the War of 1812 and put up in the center of Palace Square.

During two years in the Piuterlak quarries near Vyborg a granite monolith 30m long and 7m thick was being cut out. About four hundred workers were hewing and polishing the rock, which was later brought to Petersburg. Montferrand commissioned a twenty-year-old, talented, self-taught technician, Yakovlev by name, to organize all the works and deliver the column to the capital by sea. Meanwhile 1250 pine piles 6 m long were being driven into the ground in the square as a foundation; granite blocks 0.5m thick were laid to form the pedestal.

In August 1832 the column was raised and installed on the pedestal, with crowds of people attending the ceremony. Two thousand soldiers and four hundred workers took part in the operation. Thanks to the original system of scaffoldings and winches, developed by the engineer A.Betancourt, it took only two hours to lift the column on to its pedestal.

The final decor of the column was done after it had been put up. It is 25.58m high and is not in any way fastened to its foundation; due to accurate calculations it is held in its place by its own weight (more than 600 tons). On the whole, the monument is 47.5m high including the pedestal and the statue of the angel. It is the highest triumphal column in the world.

The Alexander Column is the compositional center of Palace Square. The pedestal is decorated with bronze reliefs representing allegorical armored figures by sculptors

I.Leppe and P.Svintsov to a design by G.B.Scotti. The column is topped with a figure of an angel having a cross in his hand, treading upon a snake (sculptor B.Orlovsky). The angel has the likeness to Alexander I.

The ceremonial opening of the monument took place on August 30, 1834. To commemorate this event a memorial medal was coined.

7
THE GENERAL STAFF BUILDINGS
Dvortsovaya Square, 6—10
1819—29. Architect C.Rossi

In the south Palace Square is bound by a grand building, erected to house the General Staff and two ministries those of foreign affairs and finance.

The building consists of two parts of great length united into a single whole by monumental arches thrown over Bolshaya Morskaya Street. One of them is spreading over the exit to the square, while the other one lends the final stroke to the whole ensemble on the side of Nevsky Prospekt. Rossi managed to make use of the curved outline of the southern boundary of the square. The two buildings opposite the Winter Palace enlarge the space in front of its façade by their semicircular layout. The architect's skill is manifested in the manner he was combining the classical forms of the new building with the lavish decoration of the Winter Palace. He achieved this by dividing the General Staff façade into two tiers, similar to the Winter Palace; the lower one, at the same time, serves as a socle for Corinthian columns. The stucco moulding on the frieze, simple lintels, as well as the sculpture make the building especially monumental.

It was not easy to arrange the façade of the longest building in contemporary Europe (about 600 m) in such a simple and expressive way. Rossi skilfully solved the task accentuating the central part by means of a majestic arch, that was conceived as a monument to the Patriotic War of 1812. The arch is decorated with imitations of Russian armor and flying Glories, and topped with Victory driving a six-horse chariot. The sculptural details of the arch and the chariot are chased from sheet copper to the models by the sculptors S.Pimenov and V.Demuth-Malinovsky.

On the first floor of the left wing some interiors have

remained made to a designs by Rossi. Among them are the
Blue Hall and the home church illuminated by overhead
lights.

8

THE GUARDS CORPS HEADQUARTERS
Dvortsovaya Square, 2
Architect A.Briullov

The Headquarters building bounds the Palace Square in the
east. The site was built up as early as the early 18th
century. Here the house belonging to the famous engineer
and designer A.Nartov was located, that was later owned by
A.Bruce. In the late 18th century Bruce's house was taken
over by the Treasury, and during th reign of Paul I a vast
building of an *exerzierhaus* (manège) was put up here.

The present building is rather well-proportioned. Its
main façade decorated with a portico with 12 Ionic columns
closes the perspective of the square. Briullov managed to
link the new building with the surrounding ones and thus
complete the ensemble of Palace Square.

9

THE PALACE BRIDGE
over the Neva to Birzhevaya Square

The first pontoon bridge was erected in 1828 to a design
by the engineer P.Basin. The permanent bridge was built in
1912—16 (engineer A.Pshenitsky). It is a metal five-span
bridge. During the drawing mechanism construction the
problem of creating a three-hinge arch was solved for the
first time in the world. The supports are made of concrete
and faced with granite. The cast-iron railings were put up in
1939 (architect L.Noskov, sculptor I.Krestovsky). The
bridge is 260m long and 27.7m wide.

10

THE ADMIRALTY
Admiralteisky (Admiralty) Prospekt, 1
1806—23. Architect A.Zakharov

The Main Admiralty building is an outstanding sample of
Russian and world architecture, a major achievement of the

early classical art. The Admiralty is the architectural and compositional center of St.Petersburg. Three main thoroughfares of the city converge here — Nevsky Prospekt, Voznesensky (Resurrection) Prospekt and Gorokhovaya Street.

The building was assuming its present aspect during a whole century. The first Admiralty was founded in 1704 as

The General Staff buildings
(No 7)

The Admiralty
(No 10)

a shipbuilding yard, to a design of Peter I himself. One-story clay-walled structures were arranged in the form of the Russian letter П; in the south the territory was fortified by an earthen rampart and bastions. The yard was surrounded by an inner moat. The building housed warehouses, workshops, as well as different admiralty departments; the yard held covered slips for constructing sailing vessels.

The new, stone building of the Admiralty was erected in 1732—38 to a design by A.Korobov. It was built in the same place and retained the former layout and general outline. In the center, above the gates, a well-proportioned tower went up 72 m high, topped by a gilt spire which has remained there up to the present.

In the early 19th century, when the center of the city could boast of grand architectural ensembles, it became necessary to radically rebuild the Admiralty. The fortification structures were demolished. In 1806—23 the third Admiralty (the present one) was erected to a design by the great Russian architect A.Zakharov, that was to commemorate the naval power and victories of the Russian fleet. The grand structure (its main façade being 407 m long) consists of two П-shaped buildings — the outer and the inner ones; a canal used to run between them, that was later filled up. The first of them housed administrative establishments, the Department of Marine and River Transport of Russia; the second housed industrial workshops. The central part of the main building is topped with a tower having a weather-vane in the form of a ship on its top, that has become the symbol of the city.

Zakharov repeated the motif of the arch cutting through the central part of the building in the façades of the two symmetrical pavilions facing the Neva and completing the eastern and western wings. The regular segmentation rhythm makes the Admiralty look like a single whole. The Admiralty building is an example of architectural and sculptural synthesis. Zakharov enlisted the best contemporary Russian sculptors with Th.Shchedrin at the head. The main high-relief *The Establishment of a Fleet in Russia* (sculptor I.Terebenev) in the tower attic is linked with the *raison d'être* of the building—navigation and shipbuilding. The relief represents Neptune who is handing Peter I the trident—a symbol of power over the sea. The lateral parts of the relief are filled with the figures of Tritons and Nymphs engaged in the shipbuilding works or saluting the ships already launched. The sculptural decoration of the tower is especially rich and interesting. On both sides of the main arch there are sculptural groups representing Nymphs carrying the Globe; at the corners of the tower attic stand the statues of Alexander the Great, Achilles, Ajax and Pyrrhus (sculptor Th.Shchedrin). The statues above the upper colonnade of the tower symbolize the four seasons of the year, four elements of nature, four

main winds, there are Isis, the patroness of shipbuilding,
and Urania, the Muse of Astronomy among them. Sculptors
S.Pimenov, V.Demuth-Malinovsky and A.Anisimov also took
part in the works.

The new Admiralty building put up by Zakharov
entailed big work on the re-decoration of Palace and Senate
Squares.

Shipbuilding in the Admiralty went on till 1844. Later
only some departments concerned with the Navy remained
in the building, and since 1925 the Admiralty houses the
Higher Naval Engineering School.

11
THE ALEXANDER GARDEN

Up to the middle of the 18th century the territory to the
south of the Admiralty was called the Admiralty Lawn. The
Admiralty Lawn used to be a place for military exercise and
public merry-making.

In the second half of the 18th century the southern part
of the Lawn was built up, and before the main façade of the
Admiralty there was formed Admiralty Square. In 1872—
74 a garden was planted here, and the trees spread to
occupy the largest part of the square. The garden, named
after Emperor Alexander, was laid out to a design by the
gardener and botanist E.Regel. In front of the Admiralty in
1876—77 a fountain was set up (architects A.Geschwend,
N.Benois). In 1887 a bust of the poet V.Zhukovsky was put
up on the territory adjoining Palace Square (sculptor
V.Kreitan), in 1892 a monument to N.Przhevalsky, explorer
of the Central Asia, was set up opposite it (sculptor
I.Schreder). Near the fountain bronze busts of the composer
M.Glinka, the writer N.Gogol, and the poet M.Lermontov
were set up in the 1890s (sculptors V.Pashchenko and
V.Kreitan).

In the early 1920s the garden was reconstructed. In the
period of the blockade not a single tree was cut down in
the garden; however, it suffered big damages because of
the shelling and bombing. During the first post-war years it
was fully restored and put in order. In the western part of
the garden facing St. Isaac's Cathedral, a rosary was laid
out (architect D.Ripp).

12
THE FORMER HOUSE
OF THE PROVINCIAL ADMINISTRATION
Admiralteisky Prospekt, 6/2
1788—90. Architect G.Quarenghi

The house was originally built for I.Fitinhoff, the President of the Medical Board. The building is decorated with a monumental colonnade taking up the two upper stories. The arch in the center of the façade facing Gorokhovaya Street served as an entrance into the yard.

In 1804 the house was acquired by the Treasury for accommodating provincial administrative offices and the interior were rebuilt by the architect A.Mikhailov the 1st; in the late 19th and early 20th century the building housed the city administration; in 1917—18 there was the All-Russian Extraordinary Commission headed by F.Dzerzhinsky.

*The Lobanov-
Rostovsky
house (No 13)*

13
THE LOBANOV-ROSTOVSKY HOUSE
Admiralteisky Prospekt, 12
1817—20. Architect A.Montferrand. Lions of white marble by the sculptor L.Triscorni

The Admiralty is faced by the main façade of a monumental building, occupying the triangular plot between Voznesensky Prospekt and St. Isaac's Square.

The center of the main façade is accentuated with an 8-column portico, raised to the first-floor level. The main entrance is emphasized by means of arcade with a high porch and the figures of white marble lions on both sides of it made in Italy in 1810.

In the second half of the 19th—early 20th century the building belonged to the Military Department.

Dekabristov (Decembrist's) Square

This square came into being due to the construction of the granite embankment along the Neva and the piers for the only pontoon bridge (1727), connecting the city center with Vasilyevsky Island.

In the 1760s the square got the name of Senatskaya Square. It was here that the Senate—one of the highest bodies of power in Russia—was transferred from Vasilyevsky Island.

Later, after the monument to Peter I was opened in 1782, the square was named after him on the order of Catherine II; the name, however, did not survive. After the new building of the Synod and Senate was erected in 1829—34 to a design by C.Rossi, the name of Senatskaya Square was restored.

In 1804—7 G.Quarenghi put up the building of the Manège. The ensemble was completed after the construction of St. Isaac's Cathedral was finished in 1858: the enormous mass of the cathedral bounded the square in the south.

In the 1840s the Konnogvardeisky Boulevard was laid out in place of the Admiralty Canal.

On December 14, 1825, an important historical event took place in Senatskaya Square.

At the foot of the monument to Peter I the rebellious troops lined up, headed by noblemen, members of the underground North Society who were intended to overthrow the autocratic regime. On the whole there were about three thousand rebels in the square, that were surrounded by the troops devoted to the tsar. The uprising was suppressed.

On the 100th anniversary of the uprising Senatskaya Square was renamed Dekabristov (Decembrists') Square.

14

THE BRONZE HORSEMAN (MONUMENT TO PETER I)
Dekabristov (Decembrists') Square
1768—82. Sculptor E.-M.Falconet

In Senatskaya Square the first monument in our city was erected—that to Peter I, the founder of Petersburg. This monument, that was commemorated by Pushkin in his poem *The Bronze Horseman*, is one of the best samples of the world monumental sculpture, one of the symbols of Petersburg.

The French sculptor E.-M.Falconet was employed to make the sketches for the monument; he had especially come to Russia to do the work. It took him three years (1768—70) to make the model of the equestrian statue. The head of Peter I was performed by Falconet's pupil — M.-A. Collot.

The pedestal was performed to a design by the architect Yu.Velten. The enormous granite boulder (called Thunderstone) that served as the foundation, was discovered in 1768 on the shore of the Gulf of Finland, in the vicinity of the Lakhta village. It took nine months to deliver the enormous monolith, weighting 1,600 tons, to the construction site. Four hundred people, using special devices, were first transporting it by land, and further—by water, on a barge built especially for this purpose.

Catherine II herself went to inspect the stone and the transportation device for a few times and to commemorate the endeavor ordered to coin a gold medal with an inscription reading: «This was a deed of daring. January 20, 1770».

In October 1770 the rock was put into its place; however, it was only 12 years later that the monument was opened. The size of the monolith was decreased considerably in the process of working on it.

The great size of the model made the casters feel afraid. The casting that began in 1775, nearly ended in a catastrophe. Molten copper began to pour out of a crack that appeared in the mold. The caster Ye.Khailov who was in charge of the works repaired the damage with a risk to his life and completed the casting.

Sculptor F.Gordeyev directed the process of putting up the monument. It was he who moulded the snake trampled by the horse, that serves as a support for the statue.

The ceremony of the opening took place on August 7, 1782. On each side of the pedestal there is an inscription done in Russian and in Latin reading: «To Peter the First—Catherine the Second».

The Bronze Horseman, a monument remarkable for its perfect composition and masterful workmanship, is an integral part of the ensemble of central Petersburg. The author himself interpreted the symbolic meaning of the rearing horseman. «The monument will be simple,—he wrote.—I shall limit myself to the statue of this hero, and I am treating him neither as a great marshal, nor as a victor, though he was both. More important is his creative personality, that of the benefactor of the whole country, and it is this personality that is to be shown to the people. My tsar is not holding any warder; he is stretching his benefactory arm over the country that he is trying to 'break in'. He is going up to the top of the rock that serves as a pedestal—this is the symbol of the hardships that he had to overcome... He overcame them by the persistence of genius... In other words, this is a monument to Russia and its Transformer».

15
THE BUILDINGS OF THE SENATE AND SYNOD
Dekabristov (Decembrist's) Square, 1—3
1829—34. Architect C.Rossi
Now the Russian State Historical Archives

Senatskaya Square took its final architectural shape when a new building for the supreme governmental bodies of Russia—the Senate and the Synod—was erected in place of the former buildings to a project by the architect C.Rossi. When putting up this building Rossi evidently took account of the Admiralty building already existing on the opposite side of the square and retained similar proportions.

The compositional center of the main façade facing the square is the archway to Galernaya Street. Rossi decorated the central part with double columns and abundant sculptures—isolated figures of geniuses, plastic frieze and the sculptural group symbolizing Justice and Piety on top of the arch (sculptors S.Pimenov, V.Demuth-Malinovsky, P.Sokolov and others), thus importing the arch somewhat Baroque exuberance.

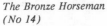

The Bronze Horseman
(No 14)

La Valle's house
(No 16)

The entrances to the building are solemnly decorated by granite stairs and ramps that are laid out symmetrically in relation to the arch. They enrich the composition and create intensive interplay of light and shade on the façade. A rounded corner with eight columns links the façade to the Neva embankment.

The buildings of the Senate and Synod (No 15)

16

LA VALLE'S HOUSE
Krasnogo Flota Embankment, 4
1800s. Architect Thomas de Thomon
Now the Russian State Historical Archives

The house that was put up in the 1720s and belonged to
A.Menshikov changed its owners and was rebuilt several
times.

In the early 1800s the façade and part of the rooms in
the house were changed on the order of the new owner,
Countess A.La Valle.

In the early 19th century this building was occupied by
S.Trubetskoi, the Decembrist, whose wife, nee Yekaterina La
Valle, was the first of the Decembrists' wives to follow her
husband into exile to Siberia. It was here that the
Decembrists' gatherings took place, including that on the
eve of the uprising. In the 1820s A.Griboyedov,
P.Viazemsky, V.Zhukovsky visited the literary salon of
A.La Valle. Here Pushkin read aloud his *Boris Godunov* on
May 16, 1828, in the presence of A.Griboyedov and
A.Mitskevich. And in the same house, at the ball, on
February 16, 1840, the quarrel between M.Lermontov and
E. de Barant broke out, that ended in a duel and
Lermontov's exile from the city.

17

THE COLUMNS WITH STATUES OF VICTORY
Konnogvardeisky Boulevard
1845—46

The statues were cast to a model by Ch.Rauch in Berlin.
Friederich Wilhelm of Prussia gave them as a present to
Nicholas I. Monolithic columns are made of gray granite.

18

MANÈGE
Konnogvardeisky Boulevard, 2
1804—7. Architect G.Quarenghi
Now the Central Exhibition Hall

Senatskaya Square gives start to Konnogvardeisky (Horse
guards) Boulevard, that got its name from the horse guards

barracks located there. The boulevard originated after 1842, when part of the Admiralty canal, connecting the Admiralty with the «New Holland» was inclosed into a pipe and buried underground.

Alongside the boulevard the side façade of the Manège of the Horse Guards Regiment is stretching. The architect was fully aware of the important part the building was to

Manege (No 18)

play in the city architecture. The main façade facing the square has more elaborate decoration, whereas the side ones are much simpler.

The main façade boasts of a grand and austere portico, topped by a pediment. On both sides of the portico there are sculptures representing the Dioscur brothers done in marble. They were made in Italy by P.Triscorni and delivered into Russia in 1817. They were made after the model of the antique statues put up before the Quirinal Palace in Rome.

Isaakiyevskaya (St. Isaac's) Square

St.Isaac's Square was the last of the central squares to take shape in Petersburg.

It was started in the 1730s—1740s. It was then named Torgovaya Square. Its overall design and appearance took shape mainly during the construction of St.Isaac's Cathedral.

To a design by A.Montferrand the house of Duke Lobanov-Rostovsky was erected next to the cathedral in 1817—20, which was later occupied by the Military Department.

In 1839—44 A.Stakenschneider erected the Mariinsky Palace in the square. In 1844—51 N.Yefimov went on working on the architectural ensemble putting up two houses for the Ministry of State Property on both sides of the square. The two buildings are similar in design, which gave the square a unified architectural pattern.

In 1856—59 a monument to Nicholas I was erected there. After that the square was called Nikolayevskaya for a rather short period of time. Then it was named Mariinskaya (after the Mariinsky Palace). But soon it was given the name Isaakiyevskaya (St.Isaac's), the name which it is called up to this time.

19
ST.ISAAC'S CATHEDRAL
1818—58. Architect A.Montferrand

St.Isaac's Cathedral is a remarkable monument of Russian architecture. This grand structure filled up the space of the Senate Square, and gave rise to a new square as well. Alongside with the Peter and Paul's Cathedral and the Admiralty it became an important architectural landmark in the city outline. The golden dome of St.Isaac's can be seen from any part of the city, and in clear weather—even from the suburbs.

The history of the construction began in 1710, when the first wooden church was put up in honor of St.Isaac of Dalmatia; it was on St.Isaac's day, according to the Orthodox calendar, that Peter I was born. The present Cathedral is the fourth existed on the place. In the early 19th century a contest was arranged for the best project of a new cathedral, in which the most well-known architects took part. In 1818 Alexander I approved a project submitted by A.Montferrand, a talented drawer who had just arrived from Paris; however, he had had but little experience in architecture.

The cathedral took forty years to build. Three years after the construction had been started it came to a halt because of a number of mistakes made in the project and during the performance of works. A special commission was formed including notable Russian architects. In 1825 the construction was resumed according to the corrected project. When putting up such a gigantic structure a lot of complicated engineering problems were to be solved for the first time. In 1828, even before the walls were erected, installation of the 48 monolithic columns was started, that were to form the porticoes, each weighing about 110 tons. The ideas of A.Betancourt, an engineer, made it possible to raise the 67-ton granite columns to the height of 40 m and install them around the dome drum.

St.Isaac's Cathedral is one of the largest domed structures in the world. The building, being rectangular in its layout, rose 101.5 m high. Having the area of 4 thousand square meters, the Cathedral can hold up to 12 thousand people.

The dome is of an original construction, practically including three domes, placed one over other.

The cathedral, faced with light-gray marble from Olonetsk, was completed by 1842; however, it took sixteen years more to decorate the interior. A lot of valuable materials were used, among them lazurite, malachite, porphyry, all kinds of marbles. Casting, followed by gilding was also widely used. The walls and vaults of the cathedral bear paintings and mosaic works made by well-known Russian artists—C.Briullov, F.Bruni, P.Basin, P.Shebuyev and others. On the whole more than 200 artists took part in the works. The great plafond of the big dome with the area of more than 700 square meters was painted by C.Briullov.

Both inside and outside the cathedral is decorated with sculptures made to the designs by I.Vitali, N.Pimenov, A.Loganovsky, P.Klodt and others. It was for the first time that the galvanoplastics method developed by B.Yakoby was used for making monumental sculptures.

The cathedral, that stands out for its grandeur, was sanctified in 1858 and became the main church in St.Petersburg.

20
MIATLEV'S HOUSE
Isaakiyevskaya (St.Isaac's) Square
1760s. Architect unknown

Miatlev's House is the oldest building in the square, that is an integral part of the whole ensemble. This three-story building with decorative bas-relief panels was partly rebuilt in the early 19th century.

Its first owner was L.Naryshkin. In the late 18th—early 19th century D.Diderot, G.de Stael, the German criticist A.Schlegel all stayed here one time or another during their visits to Petersburg. In the early 19th century the house was bought by the statesman and amateur poet I.Miatlev (hence the name); his literary salon was attended by such outstanding Russian poets as A.Pushkin, P.Viazemsky, V.Zhukovsky, M.Lermontov and other men of letters.

In the early 1920s the building housed the Saint-Petersburg Scientific and Historical Society, that was concerned with the study and preservation of the historical and cultural sites of the city; in 1923—26 it was taken over by the State Institute of Artistic Culture.

A lot of well-known artists belonging to Russian Avant-guarde of the 1920s were associated with the Institute, among them K.Malevich, M.Matiushin, V.Tatlin, P.Filonov, and others.

21
THE HOUSES OF THE MINISTRY OF STATE PROPERTY
Isaakiyevskaya Square, 4 and 13
1844—53. Architect N.Yefimov
Now the N.Vavilov Research Institute for Plant-growing

The two symmetrical buildings were put up in the square in front of the Mariinsky Palace to comply with the needs of urban design and to fill up the architectural space of the grand square, that assumed a special importance and appearance after the construction of the palace and St.Isaac's Cathedral.

In the decoration of both buildings the architectural motifs of the Renaissance can be traced. Compositionally the buildings counterbalance each other.

St. Isaac's Cathedral
(No 19)

The monument to Nicholas I
(No 22)

22
THE MONUMENT TO NICHOLAS I
Isaakiyevskaya Square
1856—59. Architect A.Montferrand. Sculptor P.Klodt

In 1856—59 a monument to Emperor Nicholas I was put up in the center of St.Isaac's Square.

The pedestal of the monument, that consists of three parts of different kinds of marble (dark-gray, red and light-gray) is decorated with allegorical statues of Justice, Faith, and Wisdom (sculptor R.Salemann), as well as four bas-reliefs depicting the emperor's endeavors (sculptor N.Ramazanov). The state coat-of-arms in bronze is placed between the statues, with an inscription below reading: «To All-Russian Emperor Nicholas I. 1859». The equestrian statue performed by the well-known sculptor P.Klodt has only two points of support.

The monument became an organic part of St.Isaac's Square. The stylistics of the monument is characterized by the combination of realistic images (the emperor's statue and the bas-reliefs) with allegorical figures and attributes, as well as fanciful, almost Baroque forms of the pedestal, all typical for the middle 19th century.

23
THE BLUE BRIDGE
over the Moika, in front of the Mariinsky Palace

The Blue Bridge, which is the broadest in Petersburg, is part of St.Isaac's Square. The first wooden drawbridge was built in 1737, to be replaced in 1818 by a new one, with a cast-iron arch and granite facing (architect V.Heste). In 1842—44 the bridge was widened to assume its present size. In 1930 the cast-iron part of the arch was replaced with a hingeless arch of reinforced concrete (engineers V.Chebotariov and O.Bugayeva). The bridge is 35m long and 99.9m wide.

24
THE MARIINSKY PALACE
Isaakiyevskaya Square, 6
1839—44. Architect A.Stakenschneider
Now the City's Administration building

The palace was built for Nicholas I's daughter Grand Duchess Maria Nikolayevna. It was the first big work by the architect. The façade is designed on classical principles; its center is accentuated by a portico with a bulky attic and open arcade of the main entrance, supporting a balcony with six big vases.

The Mariinsky Palace (No 24)

During the construction a few technological innovations were introduced, among them fire-proof spans across metal beams, metal rafters, earthenware vaults, etc.

Artistically the palace interiors are of interest. Having taken the layout of the Tavrichesky (Taurida) Palace for a model (architect I.Starov, 1783—90) and developed it Stakenschneider created a suite of halls that was not parallel to the main façade, but went back, along the central axis of the building. It is the only suite of such kind known in Russian 19th-century architecture. The suite is opened by a vestibule leading to the central Rotunda. It is decorated with 32 columns, spanned with a cupola and illuminated from above. In 1906—7 a spacious Hall for the State Council Sittings was set up in place of the former winter garden, to a design by L.Benois. In 1884 the palace was acquired into the Treasury and came to accommodate the State Council; after the February revolution of 1917 it used to be the residence of the Provisional Government.

25
THE ASTORIA HOTEL
Bolshaya Morskaya Street, 39
1911—12. Architect F.Lidval

The Astoria building completed the ensemble of St.Isaac's Square. Having six stories and garret it is higher than all the other buildings in the square. The lower stories are faced with granite. The building's modest decoration (oval garlanded medallions cut out in granite, masks over the windows, embossed vases) is in harmony with the simple architecture of the facade. The interiors (vestibule, main staircase, big banquet hall, etc.) were decorated in the Art-Nouveau style, in combination with some elements of Classicism.

Before 1917 Astoria was considered the best hotel in Russia. At present the neighboring building of the former Angleterre Hotel has become part of the Astoria complex. It was built in the early 19th century, architect unknown, and suffered many reconstructions. In one of the rooms the life of S.Yesenin, the poet, ended tragically on December 27, 1925.

In 1987—90 both buildings underwent capital reconstruction carried on by a Finnish building firm.

The Astoria Hotel (No 25)

26
THE GERMAN EMBASSY BUILDING
Isaakiyevskaya Square, 11
1911—12. Architect P.Behrens
Now St.-Petersburg Tourist Company

The building designed for the German Embassy was erected to a design by the outstanding German architect P.Behrens shortly before the First World War and is a sample of Neoclassicism. Its façade is done in solid half-columns of granite blocks. The building was topped with a bulky equestrian group that was thrown down by the crowd during the manifestation occasioned by the declaration of war.

27
A DWELLING HOUSE
Isaakiyevskaya Square, 5
1843. Architect G.Bosse
Now the Research Institute for Theater, Music and Cinematography

The house erected in 1843 was later, in the 1870s, rebuilt by the architect K.Schulz.

In the 1920s this building housed the Institute of the History of Arts where well-known scientists and writers worked, such as Yu.Tynianov, V.Zubov, B.Asafyev, V.Shklovsky, K.Chukovsky. At present it houses the research department of the Institute for Theater, Music and Cinematography. There is also a permanent exhibition of musical instruments.

Nevsky Prospekt

This is Petersburg's central thoroughfare, laid during the first years of the city's existence; it had originally been just a cutting in the forest connecting the Admiralty with the old Novgorod Road and had followed the present Ligovsky Prospekt. In the 1710s the cutting was extended as far as the Alexander Nevsky Monastery, that had just been established. Thus the length of the thorougfare reached more than 4km. Later the cutting was paved and got the name of Bolshaya (Big) Perspektiva, which was in the late 18th century renamed to Nevsky Prospekt; it became the city's main street.

In the first half of the 18th century palaces and country estate residences were being built in Nevsky Prospekt. The fine ensembles alternated with ordinary buildings constituting «a solid façade». The interplay of different architectural device, ensembles taking turns with vistas opening along the Moika and Fontanka rivers, Griboyedov

Nevsky Prospekt

Canal, Bolshaya and Malaya Morskaya, Mikhailovskaya and Sadovaya streets, makes Nevsky Prospekt an excellent sample of urban design. Since 1776, by the order of the Commission for Construction, only stone buildings had been erected in the prospekt. Since the second half of the 19th century Nevsky had become both commercial and business city center; new banks and company offices were put up, as well as trade and apartment houses. In the stretch from the Admiralty up to the Fontanka River (19th-century city borderline) classical features predominate. The section beyond the Fontanka took shape in the second half of the 19th century.

28
WAWELBERG'S HOUSE. THE TRADING BANK
Nevsky Prospekt, 7/9
1911—12. Architect M.Peretiatkovich
Now the Aeroflot Agency

Among the public buildings that were being erected in Petersburg in the late 19th—early 20th century the bank buildings take up a special place. During a short term a few of them were put up, mainly in the city center; Wawelberg's House (Saint Petersburg Trading Bank) among them.

In the decoration some features of the Italian Renaissance architecture can be traced (the loggias, window shapes, arcade of the ground floor remind of the Palace of Doges in Venice). The original sculptural decoration was performed by V.Kozlov and L.Dietrich. The façades are faced with dark-gray granite brought from Sweden. The rusticated columns, pilasters, bas-reliefs and cartouches are made of the same material. Peretiatkovich did not strive to achieve stylistic unity with the neighboring buildings, which is also characteristic of other architects working in Nevsky Prospekt in the 1900s—1910s.

The spacious operation hall inside is decorated with columns and pilasters faced with yellow artificial marble as well as a carved plafond with caissons.

29
A DWELLING HOUSE
Nevsky Prospekt, 11
Rebuilt in 1898. Architect L.Benois

30
SAFONOV'S AND WEIMAR'S HOUSES
Nevsky Prospekt, 8, 10
1760s. Architect A.Kvasov

The houses have remained without any significant changes.

31
GOLITSYNA'S HOUSE
Malaya Morskaya Street, 10
1770s. Architect unknown

The house that had belonged to Princess N.Golitsyna (the house of «the Queen of Spades») was in 1839 rebuilt by A.Thon for the War Minister A.Chernyshov.

32
SCHOOL No 210
Nevsky Prospekt, 14
1939. Architect B.Rubanenko

The building has become an organic part of the prospekt due to its purely classical forms. The author of the project had a double task façing him; on the one hand he had to build on a small lot, on the other—to find a design for the façade that would harmonize with the surrounding buildings and, at the same time, single it out among the dwelling houses.

The architectural forms of the facade are a bit enlarged. It is divided into three tiers. The construction was carried on by high-speed methods and completed in 54 days.

In 1962 memorial plaque was put up next to the inscription that had remained here since 1941: «Citizen! During shelling this side of the street is most dangerous». This is a reminder of the days of blockade of 1941—44.

33
CHICHERIN'S HOUSE
Nevsky Prospekt, 15
1768—71. Architect unknown. Rebuilt in 1858 by N.Grebenka

The house was built on the site of the Palace of Empress Yelizaveta Petrovna. This palace-type building is very important architecturally, as its façades face three streets. The two-tier colonnades give it a solemn outlook. The interiors retain some fragments of the 18th-century decoration.

The house is historically linked with many developments in the cultural life of the city. In 1780—83 the architect G.Quarenghi lived here. In the late 18th century there was housed the first musical club in Petersburg. In the early 19th century on the ground floor there was a well-known printing-house and bookstore of A.Pluchard, P.Talon's restaurant, which Pushkin used to frequent. Also, the publishers of the *Otechestvennye Zapiski* journal was located here, edited by P.Svinyin; N.Grech, the writer and editor of the *Syn Otechestva* journal, lived here as well.

In the second half of the 19th century the building housed the Noble Assembly; literary parties and concerts were held here (in 1878—79 F.Dostoyevsky took part in them).

In 1919—22 the building housed the famous House of Arts, established on the initiative of K.Chukovsky and M.Gorky.

34
CHAPLIN'S HOUSE
Nevsky Prospekt, 13
First quarter of the 19th century. Architect V.Beretti

It is a dwelling house typical for the early 19th-century Russian Classicism.

35
THE AZOV-DON TRADING BANK
Bolshaya Morskaya Street, 3-5
1907—13. Architect F.Lidval
Now Long-distance Telephone Exchange

In 1907 the Azov-Don Bank Board bought house № 5 in Bolshaya Morskaya Street; on this site the architect F.Lidval erected a new bank building. After the construction was completed the bank bought the adjoining house No 3. Lidval faced a new task—he had to combine both buildings into a single whole. The facades of the buildings have individual designs. In the decoration elements of Classicism and Art-Nouveau are combined. Sculpture is widely used, there is a sculptural frieze carved at the ground floor level, as well as oval medallions and other details (sculptor V.Kuznetsov). Reinforced concrete constructions were used in the works, that made it possible to develop a light framework and span spacious interiors.

Wawelberg's house
(No 28)

The Azov-Don Traiding Bank
(No 35)

36
THE RUSSIAN TRADING AND INDUSTRIAL BANK
Bolshaya Morskaya Street, 15
1912—14. Architect M.Peretiatkovich

37
THE INSTITUTE OF TECHNOLOGICAL DESIGN
Bolshaya Morskaya Street, 18
1915. Architects L.Benois, F.Lidval, completed in 1930—34, architects L.Rudnev, Ya.Svirsky

38
THE FABERGÉ HOUSE
Bolshaya Morskaya, 24
Rebuilt in 1899—1900. Architect K.Schmidt

*The Russian Traiding
and Industrial Bank (No 36)*

*The Faberge House
(No 38)*

39
KOTOMIN'S HOUSE
Nevsky Prospekt, 18
1812—15. Architect V.Stasov
Now the Literaturnoye Café and Old Books Shop

Kotomin's House is one of the most interesting samples of
dwelling houses built in classical style. The building
assumed its present-day appearance after radical
reconstruction, during which the two lower stories were
united with a single Doric order. The building is topped
with an impressive cornice on corbels, with rosettes and
bas-reliefs between them.

During the recent restoration works the lateral loggias with colonnades were rebuilt. The Literaturnoye Café was opened in 1985 in the part of the building which had formerly housed the Wolf and Beranger's confectionery famous in old times. It was here that on January 27, 1837, A.Pushkin had a meeting with K.Danzas, his second. From

Kotomin's house (No 39)

here they proceeded to the place of the duel. The confectionery was also frequented by M.Lermontov, I.Chernyshevsky, T.Shevchenko, and others. Here the meeting between F.Dostoyevsky and M.Butashevich-Petrashevsky took place, that marked the beginning of the writer's participation in the well-known political society.

40
THE NARODNY BRIDGE
over the Moika along Nevsky Prospekt
1806—8

The first wooden drawbridge was put up in 1730. In 1735 it was rebuilt and named the Green Bridge, according to its color. In the early 19th century the architect V.Heste developed a project for a series of similar original metallic bridges, consisting of separate cast-iron sections, bolted to form a span. This bridge was the first to be build to this design. In 1908 the lanterns were put up (architect L.Ilyin), and in 1951 and 1967 the architectural decoration restored. The bridge is 39.8m long and 38.5m wide.

The Stroganov Palace (No 41) and the Dutch Church (No 42)

41
THE STROGANOV PALACE
Nevsky Prospekt, 17
1752—54. Architect B.Rastrelli
Now the Russian Museum branch

The Stroganov Palace is located at the crossing of Nevsky Prospekt and the Moika River embankment. Unlike the estate-type palaces popular in those times, the Stroganov Palace faces the Nevsky Prospekt with its main façade.

On the ground floor there are auxiliary rooms and the vestibule in front of the main staircase. The exterior and the layout of the building are a brilliant example of the Russian Baroque style.

The palace's façades facing Nevsky Prospekt and the embankment are different in composition. The Nevsky facade is more impressive; it is accentuated with columns standing on rusticated foundations, as well as with sculptural decorations in the shape of lion masks, caryatides, Cupid figures. The decorative effect is enhanced by wrought-iron open-work railings under the first floor windows.

The center of the façade facing the Moika is emphasized by a four-column portico topped by a triangular pediment. Originally the building could be entered only from the courtyard.

From that time the hall has remained with two tiers of windows, which was decorated to the drawings of Rastrelli. The hall retains a ceiling painting made by G.Valeriani, one of the best decorators of the 18th-century Russia.

In the late 18th century the palace belonged to Count A.Stroganov, who was an outstanding patron of arts and the Academy of Arts President. Stroganov supported his former serf, the talented architect A.Voronikhin, whose first work was to become the interior reconstruction of the Stroganov Palace in 1793. Due to the reconstruction a number of the first-floor interiors were redecorated in the classical style. Among them of special interest are the Corner and Arabesque Rooms, as well as the Mineral Study. The Stroganov Palace was frequented by famous contemporary writers, poets and composers, among them D.Fonvizin, G.Derzhavin, I.Krylov, N.Gnedich, D.Bortniansky and others. The palace housed one of the best art collection in Russia.

The palace belonged to the Stroganovs up to 1917. After the revolution the art collections were transferred to the Hermitage.

At present restoration works are carried on in the palace.

42
THE DUTCH CHURCH
Nevsky Prospekt, 20
1831—33. Architect P.Jacquot
Now the Blok Library

Most of the churches in Nevsky Prospekt were erected away from the Prospekt, in the back of spacious lots. Only the dwelling houses that belonged to churches opened on the street. In the Dutch Church building the church proper and the dwelling houses comprise one large structure lined exactly along the prospekt border. The church hall is singled out by a four-column portico and topped with a discreet cupola. The high relief in the pediment tympanum (angels' figures) emphasizes the purpose the building served. The lateral wing façades have semicircular windows forming a kind of a continuous arcade. In the central part of the building the original interior decoration has remained.

43
THE RAZUMOVSKY PALACE
The Moika Embankment, 48
1762—66. Architect L.Kokorinov, J.-B.Vallin de la Mothe
Now the Pedagogical University

In terms of its layout the Razumovsky Palace belongs to the few remaining country-estates in the city, dating back to the first half of the 18th century, which were typically erected in the back of the lots and had regular gardens. Stylistically it is a sample of the transition period from Baroque to Classicism.

In the 1730s B.Rastrelli built a wooden palace for Count Levenvolde on the site. In the 1760s it was dismantled and the construction of a new, stone palace, was started to a design by A.Kokorinov, followed by J.-B.Vallin de la Mothe. The palace underwent a number of reconstructions. It acquired its present appearance in 1831—34.

The central part of the building, dominating the whole composition, is characteristically emphasized, whereas the whole ensemble with its lateral wings is symmetrical in its layout. In the sculptural decoration of the façade finely outlined bas-reliefs are predominant.

Of interest is the design of the garden façade, with its protruding rizalits, a colonnade of Corinthian order and stucco moulding imitating the main façade motifs. From Kazanskaya Street side the site is fenced with a railing made to a design by A.Voronikhin.

In 1798 the palace was given over to the Treasury. First a Foundling Hospital was established here, later to be succeeded by the Nikolayevsky Women's Orphanage Institute.

The Razumovsky Palace (No 43)

44

STEGELMANN'S HOUSE
The Moika Embankment, 50
1750—53. Architect B.Rastrelli. Rebuilt after 1764.
Architect unknown
THE BUILDING OF THE FOUNDLING HOSPITAL
The Moika Embankment, 52
Rebuilt in 1839—43. Architect P.Pavlov
Now the Pedagogical University

In the 1750s a spacious lot on the Moika Embankment
adjoining Razumovsky's estate belonged to a rich merchant,
the court supplier G.Ch.Stegelmann. In 1750—53 the
architect B.Rastrelli built a large two-story house for him,
placed back in the lot, with two symmetrical wings flanking
the main courtyard.

In 1764 the house was taken over by the Treasury and
in the following years largely rebuilt to acquire the early
classical appearance. The central rizalit of the main façade
was decorated with pilasters, and the ground floor
segmented by apertures, with columns set in them. The
plastic decor is enriched by stucco moulding garlands in
the niches and decorative vases. The reconstructions that
followed greatly changed the appearance of the estate: the
main building and lateral wings have been raised,

Stegelmann's House and Razumovsky's Palace joined together by means of a new building, and an annex had appeared on the garden side. In the late 18th century Razumovsky's and Stegelmann's palaces were handed over to the Foundling Hospital and later—to the Nikolayevsky Orphanage Institute.

One more building of the former Foundling Hospital, that with a six-column portico on its façade, was rebuilt in the late classical style. In front of it in 1868 a bronze bust of I.Betskoi was put up, who was the founder of the Foundling Hospital and other similar establishments in Russia (sculptor N.Lavretsky).

Next stands the building of the former School for the Deaf-and-Dumb; its main façade faces Gorokhovaya Street, 18. It was rebuilt in 1844—47 by the architect P.Plavov.

The building of the Pokrovsky (Intercession) Church of the Orphanage Institute (the Moika Embankment, 48) was put up in 1829—34 (architect D.Quadri, since 1832—P.Plavov) and is a monument of the Empire style. All the buildings are occupied by the Russian Pedagogical University.

In 1961 a monument to K.Ushinsky was put up in front of Razumovsky's Palace (sculptor V.Lishev, architect V.Yakovlev).

45
THE RED BRIDGE
over the Moika along Gorokhovaya Street
1808—14. Architect V.Heste

One of the four similar metal bridges over the Moika river, that has preserved its original appearance.

The bridge is 42m long, 16.8m wide.

46
THE MERTENS FIRM
Nevsky Prospekt, 21
1911—12. Architect M.Lialevich
Now the Fashions

F.Mertens owned a big firm trading in furs and fur articles that was active in Petersburg in 1841; he bought the house No 21. After demolishing it architect M.Lialevich erected a monumental building which came to house the firm's shop, working facilities and workshops.

Three glassed arches cut through the façade to the fourth floor level. The glazed surface is intersected by the horizontal lines of the spans between the floors. Key-stones above the arches in the shape of enormous volutes are decorated with female figures (sculptor V.Kuznetsov).

The house is a typical example of a firm building designed in the classical style of the early 20th century.

47

THE DWELLING HOUSE OF THE CLERGY
OF THE CATHEDRAL OF OUR LADY OF KAZAN
Nevsky Prospekt, 25
1813—17. Architect V.Stasov

48

THE TRADING HOUSE
OF THE GUARDS ECONOMIC SOCIETY
Bolshaya Koniushennaya Street, 21—23
1908—9. Architects E.Virrich, S.Krichinsky and others
Now a department store

The large territory that is now occupied by a department store, had in the 18th century belonged to A.Volynsky, one of the leading public figures of Peter's period. He was accused of participating in a conspiracy and executed in 1740. A lane connecting the Bolshaya Koniushennaya street with the Moika Embankment was named after Volynsky.

In 1907 the Guards Economic Society acquired the lot, and in 1908 the construction of the Trading House was started. It should be noted that ferro-concrete structures were used for the construction, which was in those times a novelty in Russian building. The exterior and interior decoration reflected the interest to Russian classical architecture, characteristic of the 1910s; it is manifested in the use of order columns, pilasters, as well as the thin spire on top of the corner rotunda.

The design of the layout and spacial arrangement of the building are its strongest points. The spans do not divide it into storeys, but rather into galleries running around its perimeter and resting upon the columns raising up to the second floor level. The vacant space inside is saturated with air and light.

49
THE FINNISH CHURCH
Bolshaya Koniushennaya Street, 6a
1803—5. Architect G.Paulson

In 1733 a site for constructing a praying house for the Swedes and Finns living in Petersburg was allotted in Bolshaya Koniushennaya Street to the order of Tsarina Anna Ioannovna.

The Finnish Church (No 49)

In 1803—5 a new stone Finnish church was built on the site called the St.Maria Church. In the late 19th century the church underwent reconstruction involving changing the interior spacing and partial remodelling the façades (architects K.Anderson, later—L.Benois). In the 1920s interior reconstruction was undertaken, that divided the whole volume into three stories.

50

THE LUTHERAN CHURCH OF ST. PETER AND PAUL
Nevsky Prospekt, 22—24

1832—38. Architect A.Briullov

The buildings of the former Lutheran Church front Nevsky Prospekt section between Bolshaya and Malaya Koniushennaya Streets.

The first kirk was built here in 1730. The spacial and compositional arrangement of the ensemble, with the church building positioned at the back of the lot and the two dwelling houses symmetrically on both sides of it, was retained during the construction of a new church. The architecture is Romanesque, which is not characteristic for Petersburg. The main façade is slit by the portal arch. On the first floor the motif of an open loggia was used. Two three-tier turrets over the corners of the façade, which is in itself rather short, give an impression of an upwards urge. Behind the church there is the building of the school that is the oldest in the city, and dates back to 1710. The building of the Peterschule (erected by M.Hoffmann in 1760—62 in Baroque style) was later rebuilt, in 1876 and 1915.

Among the students of the school were C.Rossi, the architect, M.Musorgsky, the composer, and scientists K.Raukhfus, V.Junker, P.Lesgaft and others.

51

THE SWEDISH CHURCH OF ST.CATHERINE
Malaya Koniushennaya Street, 1

1863—67. Architect K.Anderson

The church is located at the street frontline. It is considered to have some Romanesque features due to its tripartite façade, accentuated portal and a big rose-window.

52

THE CATHEDRAL OF OUR LADY OF KAZAN
Kazanskaya Square, 2

Architect V.Voronikhin

53
THE MONUMENTS
TO M.KUTUZOV AND BARKLAY DE TOLLI
Sculptor B.Orlovsky, architect V.Stasov

The Cathedral of Our Lady of Kazan is an outstanding example of the early 19th-century Russian architecture. It was erected on the site of a small stone church to hold the ancient icon of Our Lady of Kazan, and was named after it.

In 1800 Emperor Paul I issued an order for a cathedral to be built after the model of St.Peter's Cathedral in Rome. The design was entrusted to A.Voronikhin, who had formerly been Count Stroganov's serf, later to become the professor of architecture in the Academy of Arts.

The foundation was laid a year later, during the reign of Alexander I (he laid the first stone into it); the cathedral took ten years to build. It was planned in the shape of the Latin Cross. Voronikhin had a difficult task to solve. The matter was that according to the church canons the altar was to face eastwards, hence the main entrance and the façade faced westwards. Thus Nevsky Prospekt was to front the side façade of the cathedral, and not the main one. Voronikhin solved the problem supplying the cathedral with a grand semicircular colonnade opening on the prospekt, that added to its beauty. Moreover, the cathedral as well as the colonnade were elevated on to a granite socle with wide staircases. The wings of the colonnade that formed a square in front of the cathedral have monumental portals at the ends, simultaneously serving as passageways. Voronikhin intended to erect a similar colonnade facing south; however, the Patriotic War of 1812 that had just broken out prevented him from doing it.

The well-proportioned, light cupola on a high drum, reaching the height of 62 m, crowns the central part of the building and counterbalances the colonnade, spreading horizontally. This was the first cupola in the world to be built of ferro-concrete structures.

The facing of the building, the pilasters, columns as well as elements of sculptural decoration were made of light-yellow stone quarried on the Pudost' river, in the vicinity of Petersburg.

The Cathedral of Our Lady of Kazan is one of the top achievements of high classical architecture and a brilliant example of the arts synthesis. Best sculptors and artists were enlisted to decorate it. Sculpture plays a special part here. The niches of the northern portico enclose bronze statues of historic and mythological heroes, those of Duke Vladimir and St. Alexander Nevsky (sculptor S.Pimenov), John the Baptist (sculptor I.Martos), apostle Andrew (sculptor Demuth-Malinovsky). The relief over the eastern passageway representing Moses making water gush from the rock was performed by the sculptor I.Martos, that over the western one, called *Raising of the Bronze Serpent* was

The Cathedral of Our Lady of Kazan. The monuments to M.Kutuzov and M.Barklay de Tolley (Nos 52, 53)

made by I.Prokofyev. The frieze in the church apse attic depicting the Entrance into Jerusalem was performed by J.Rachette. In 1805—6 the folds of the northern door were cast of bronze, that were an imitation of the famous Doors of Heaven of the Baptistry in Florence by the 15th-century sculptor Lorenzo Ghiberti.

In decorating the interiors alongside with sculptors many outstanding artists took part, such as V.Borovikovsky, V.Shebuyev, O.Kiprensky, A.Yegorov, A.Ivanov and others. They painted the iconostasis and other parts of the cathedral.

The interior represents a grand three-nave hall. Majestic

colonnades of 56 Corinthian columns cut out of the monoliths of pink Finnish granite, topped with bronze capitals are mainly responsible for the artistic effect produced.

The monumental cast-iron railing of exquisite design embraces a small square in front of the main, western entrance to the cathedral. It was laid out to the design of Voronikhin, and is a good addition to the cathedral

The Cathedral of Our Lady of Kazan.
Interior (No 52)

ensemble. The public garden set up there in 1935—36 is decorated with a granite fountain (1809, architect Thomas de Thomon), transferred here from the Tsarskoselskaya road in 1934.

The public garden facing Nevsky Prospekt was laid out in the late 19th century. Although built before the Patriotic War of 1812, the cathedral became the War Memorial, a pantheon of Russian glory. It was after a ceremonial public prayer said here that M.Kutuzov set out for the Army in the Field. And it was here that the remains of the great marshal were brought in 1813. He is buried in the crypt of the northern chapel of the cathedral. It was also here that the numerous Patriotic War trophies were brought, including keys of the European cities that had surrendered to the Russian Army, the captured banners, standarts, as well as Marshal Davout's baton.

The importance of the Cathedral of Our Lady of Kazan as a memorial to the heroes of the Patriotic War was still more emphasized when the monuments to Field-Marshals M.Kutuzov and Barclay de Tolli were put up in front of it in 1837.

Singer Company house (No 54)

The Kazansky Bridge (No 55) and Engelhart's house (No 56)

54
THE SINGER COMPANY HOUSE
Nevsky Prospekt, 28
1902—4. Architect P.Suzor
Now the House of Books

Opposite the Cathedral of Our Lady of Kazan rises a building with a corner tower that was originally built for the Singer shareholding society. During its construction the latest achievements of Russian building technology were being used: steel framework, filled with brick-work on mortar, and ferro-concrete structures.

The first two stories are faced with red polished granite, the next three ones — with gray hammered granite, and the upper one—with gray polished granite.

The Singer Company was eager to get the licence to put up a skyscraper. However, the city administration did not deviate from the law regulating the height of buildings in the capital; they just gave a permission to complete the building with a cupola-tower, topped with a globe.

Enormous show-windows, their outlines and proportions, as well as the abundance of stylized decorative sculpture on the façades (sculptors A.Adamson and A.Ober) are all typical of the Art-Nouveau style.

At present the building houses one of the largest bookshops in the country—the House of Books, as well as a number of publishing companies.

55

THE KAZANSKY BRIDGE
over the Griboyedov Canal, along Nevsky Prospekt
1765—66. Engineers V.Nazimov and I.Golenishchev-Kutuzov

This is the second widest bridge in Petersburg (following the Blue Bridge). As well as the latter one, it is part of a square.

The bridge is 18.8m long and 95m wide.

56

ENGELHARDT'S HOUSE
Nevsky Prospekt, 30
1759—61. Architect B.Rastrelli. Capitally rebuilt in 1829—30. Architect P.Jacquot
Now the Small Hall of the Philharmonic Society

This building, originally put up by B.Rastrelli, later underwent a number of reconstructions and has traditionally been the center of Petersburg's musical life. Since early 19th century it accommodated the Russian Philharmonic Society. After the architect P.Jacquot rebuilt it for V.Engelhardt, a rich patron of arts, the building became the capital's main concert hall. Here F.Liszt and H.Berlioz, M.Glinka and A.Rubinstein, R.Wagner and J.Strauss performed. This place was often visited by A.Pushkin. It was also popular as a place for holding masquerades. Some episodes from Lermontov's drama *Masquerade* take place in Engelhardt's mansion.

The building was damaged by an aviation bomb in 1941, and was one of the first to be restored. Later it was reconstructed to include the vestibule of the Nevsky Prospekt underground station.

57
THE CHURCH OF CHRIST'S RESURRECTION (THE SAVIOR ON BLOOD)
Griboyedov Canal, 2a
1887—1907. Architects A.Parland and I.Makarov

From the Kazansky bridge, in Griboyedov Canal perspective the Church of Christ's Resurrection (sometimes called The Savior on Blood) can be seen. It was put up to commemorate the tsar-martyr on the site where on March 1, 1881, I.Grinevitsky, a member of the People's Will society, mortally wounded Emperor Alexander II. The church was put up with the money collected all over Russia.

The Ressurection Church
(No 57)

The Mutual Credit Society
(No 58)

Architecturally it revives the traditions of the 17th-century Russian church-building. In particular, the compositional techniques and shapes were used similar to those characteristic of the fámous Pokrovsky Cathedral (Church of St. Basil the Blessed), that stands in Red Square in Moscow.

The church stands out for its complicated and picturesque outline, as well as rich and multicolored decoration. The façades are faced with glazed shaped brick and ceramic tiles as well as decorated with mosaic panels. In the decor of interiors Italian marbles and Russian semiprecious stones are used. The church is of interest as a kind of an architectural accent in classical surroundings. Moreover, the interior is unique, boasting of the mosaic panels made in Frolovs' workshop to the originals by outstanding Russian artists, including V.Vasnetsov, M.Nesterov, A.Riabushkin and others.

This is the largest mosaic ensemble existing on the church facades and interior walls.

58
THE HOUSE OF THE MUTUAL CREDIT SOCIETY
Griboyedov Canal, 13
1888—90. Architect P.Suzor
Now the Petersburg office of the State Bank

The building stands out among the surrounding ones for its size and grand decoration. The author strived to make it look like a palace; for this purpose he introduced into the façade composition the motif of richly dressed rizalits and topped the central part of the building with a cupola. A low attic with a sculptural group serves as a transition from the façade wall to the cupola. Between the first and second floors there is a composition representing a triumphal arch decorated with columns and sculptures. The design of the wrought-iron gates and open-work window railings is exquisite.

59
THE ITALIAN BRIDGE
over the Griboyedov Canal to Italian Street
1955. Architect V.Vasilkovsky, engineer A.Guttsait

The first footbridge was erected in 1896 (engineer L.Kolonitsyn); in 1937 it was rebuilt, and in 1955—built anew. It can boast of a high-level artistic work. Making use of the 19th-century traditions the architect managed to create a new type of classical decor of the railing and the standard lamps. Their smooth curve fits very well into the canal's perspective.

This one-span footbrige is 21 m long and 3 m wide.

The Bank Bridge (No 60)

60
THE BANK BRIDGE
over the Griboyedov Canal,
near the former Assignation Bank
1825—26. Engineer G.Traitteur

This is one of six suspension bridges over the Griboyedov Canal. It is decorated with four cast-iron gryphons (sculptor P.Sokolov).

The bridge is 25.2 m long and 1.9 m wide.

61
THE LION BRIDGE
over the Griboyedov Canal
to Malaya Podyacheskaya Street
1825—26. Engeneers G.Traitteur and V.Khristianovich.
Sculptor P.Sokolov

A suspension footbridge with four cast-iron lions. In 1954
the railings and lanterns were restored (architect A.Rotach).
   The bridge is 27.6 m long and 2,2 m wide.

The Stone Bridge (No 63)

62
GRABBE'S HOUSE
Griboyedov Canal, 40/26
Middle of the 18th century. Architect unknown. In 1834
the fourth story added

It is one of the few remaining samples of the apartment
houses for «average citizens» of the middle of the 18th
century. The main façade facing the canal stands out for the

wealth of decoration, including the Corinthian pilasters and sophisticated lintels, the ornamentation filling up the whole wall surface.

63
THE STONE BRIDGE
over the Griboyedov Canal along Gorokhovaya Street
1776. Engineers V.Nazimov and I.Borisov

The first wooden bridge was built in 1752. The modern bridge has one span. It is made of stone and faced with granite.
  The bridge is 19.7m long and 13.9m wide.

64
THE DEMIDOV BRIDGE
over the Griboyedov Canal along Demidov Lane
1834—35. Engineer E.Adam

The first wooden bridge was built in 1776. The present cast-iron bridge has one span, and a slanting tubing arch. In 1854—55 the lanterns and railings were restored (architect A.Rotach).
  The bridge is 33m long and 16.1m wide.

65
THE POLISH ROMAN-CATHOLIC CHURCH
OF ST.CATHERINE
Nevsky Prospekt, 32—34
1762—83. Architects J.-B.Vallin de la Mothe and A.Rinaldi

During construction the architects used the design of 1739 made by D.Trezzini; according to the latter the church was placed at the back of the lot. It is linked with Nevsky Prospekt by means of the two dwelling houses flanking it. The church belongs to the best samples of the transitional period between Baroque and classical styles; it is a grand building with a powerful cupola, Evangelists' figures on a high parapet and a grand arched portal.

St. Catherine's Catholic Church (No 65)

Here the Polish King S.Poniatovsky was buried, as well as the French General J.Moreau who fought the war against Napoleon on the Russian side.

66
THE SILVER STALLS
Nevsky Prospekt, 31—38

67
THE CITY DUMA (COUNCIL)
Dumskaya Street, 1

The buildings of the City Duma and the Silver Stalls, that date back one and a half centuries ago are a unique and original architectural monument. The multi-tier clock tower erected next to the Duma building in 1799—1804 by D.Ferrari in imitation of West-European town-halls is the dominant point of the main part of the prospekt. It has a discreet classical outline and is stationed on a protruding corner, thus being visible from long distances.

An old trade center with an open arcade adjoins the tower from the right—it is the Silver Stalls built in 1784—87 to a design by G.Quarenghi on the site of the wooden stalls that had belonged to silver traders and had been burned down.

The City Duma (No 67)

The City Duma building faces Dumskaya Street. It was erected simultaneously with the Silver Stalls, but in 1847—52 it was rebuilt by the architects N.Yefimov and L.Bonstedt.

The Duma not only accommodated the institutions of local government. In the hall there the concerts of the Russian Musical Society and the Free Musical School took place, as well as the lectures of the Free University and literary evenings, with the participation of F.Dostoyevsky, A.Blok, S.Yesenin and others.

68
THE PORTICO IN PERINNAYA LINE
Nevsky Prospekt, 33a
1802—6. Architect L.Rusca

The Gostiny Dvor was in need of new rooms, so additional rows of stalls were put up next to it. In 1797—98 a new building with an open arcade was erected along the Perinnaya Line, parallel to the western Gostiny Dvor façade. In 1802—6 L.Rusca decorated the butt-end of the façade with a portico. Later, in 1830s, when the Mikhailovsky Palace ensemble was taking shape, C.Rossi laid a new, Mikhailovskaya Street, leading to Nevsky Prospekt; the portico nicely closed the street's perspective.

The building in Perinnaya Line and the portico were dismantled because of the underground line construction. In 1972 the portico was restored as an important architectural element at Nevsky Prospekt crossing.

69
THE GOSTINY DVOR
Nevsky Prospekt, 35
1757—beginning of the works to a design by B.Rastrelli; 1761—85, architect J.-B.Vallin de la Moth; 1886—87, architect A.Benois
Now a Department Store

The building occupies a large area between Sadovaya Street, Nevsky Prospekt, and Lomonosov Street. It is a rectangular two-story structure with a big inner courtyard. The façades are about one kilometer long along the perimeter. The building consists of numerous similar arcades.

The corners are cut off and decorated with a kind of porticoes. The main entrance facing Nevsky Prospekt is also marked out with a portico. At the top, all along the perimeter runs a light balustrade.

The building is strictly classical in its outline. Construction went on for 24 years and was completed in 1785. The building became a model for the similar type of structures in provinces. In the late 19th century it was redecorated to a design by A.Benois.

The Gostiny Dvor (No 69)

The Mikhailovskaya Square Ensemble

Characteristic of the early 19th-century construction in Petersburg was a tendency to create whole ensembles of streets and squares.

The Mikhailovskaya Square ensemble performed to a project by C.Rossi is the best example of this principle being put into practice. It was possible to basically change the layout of the whole area because until the 1820s only part of it was built up. The Mikhailovsky Palace became the architectural dominant and compositional center of the square. As for the latter, it plays the secondary part; this idea is emphasized by the discreet façade designs of the dwelling houses framing it on three sides. C.Rossi intended to build in the square in a way that would make it a single whole. The architect made designs for the façades of all the houses. However, they were completed by other architects.

From the square to Nevsky Prospekt Mikhailovskaya Street was laid. Rossi intended to put up similar buildings on both sides of the street. The street perspective, that opened the view over the Mikhailovsky Palace, was to be closed by the Perinnaya Line portico in Nevsky Prospekt.

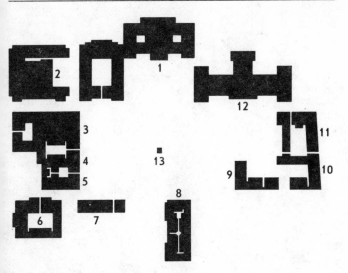

The Mikhailovskaya Square ensemble

1. The Mikhailovsky Palace (No 70);
2. The Bnois Building;
3. The Mikhailovsky Theater (No 71);
4. KHGGolenishchev-Kutuzov's house (No 72);
5. Jacquots' house (No 73);
6. The Jesuit's Order house;
7. St. Catherine's Church clergy house;
8. The Noble Assembly (No 79);
9. Vielgorsky's house (No 74);
10. Yakovleva's house (No 78);
11. Commandant's office (No 77);
12. The Ethnography Museum (No 76);
13. The Monument to A.Pushkin (No 81)

70
THE MIKHAILOVSKY PALACE
Inzhenernaya Street, 4/2
1819—25. Architect C.Rossi
Now the Russian Museum Department

The palace was build for Grand Duke Mikhail Pavlovich, the junior son of Paul I. In the ensemble of buildings framing the square the palace is architecturally dominant.

The Russian Museum (No 70)

The layout is of the country estate type, which is typical for Russian Classicism. The main building is placed in the back of the front yard of the *cour d'honneur* type.

The lateral wings are located symmetrically on both sides of the yard. The front yard is separated from the square by a cast-iron railing with three gates. It is one of the nicest railings in the city and adds to the beauty of the square.

The main façade is singled out by a portico and Corinthian columns, raised on to the ground floor arcade. The portico has a pediment and a splendid frieze made up of 44 bas-reliefs by sculptor V.Demuth-Malinovsky. A wide staircase with figures of lions and curved ramps lead to the entrance. The symmetrical projections with more discreet decoration emphasize the grandeur of the façade.

The opposite, northern façade opening on the Mikhailovsky Garden is more lyrical in appearance. The main decorative element here is a majestic loggia with a colonnade and a wide staircase; it goes very well with the large lawn and alleys of the garden.

The sculptural elements of the façades were performed by S.Pimenov and V.Demuth-Malinovsky. The same sculptors took part in the works on the interior, as well as the artists G. and P.Scotti, A.Vighi, B.Medici, F.Brullo, as well as modelers, engravers and parquet layers.

After Mikhail Pavlovich died in 1849 his widow, Grand Duchess Yelena Pavlovna (1806—73) owned the palace. Her salon was frequented by many outstanding Russian men of culture and liberal-minded statesmen. The last to own the palace was Grand Duchess Yekaterina Mikhailovna. In 1895 it was transferred into possession of the Treasury with the purpose of arranging a museum in it. The reconstruction works were headed by the architect V.Svinyin. Only part of the interiors retained their original decoration.

The most lavish halls were redecorated. Only the White Column Hall and some other rooms, as well as the vestibule and the main staircase remained unchanged.

In 1898 the Imperial Museum of Russian Art of Alexander III was opened in the palace.

At present the Russian Museum possesses the largest collections of Russian fine arts, as well as applied and popular art. It holds the masterpieces of Old Russian Art, as well as the painting and sculpture of the 18th—20th centuries.

The museum collections grew with time; in order to provide new space and arrange exhibitions the western wing of the museum was erected on the corner of Inzhenernaya Street and the Griboyedov Canal.

The building was designed in the classical style by the architects L.Benois and S.Ovsiannikov (1910—12). The foundation was laid in 1914, but the building was completed in post-revolutionary time.

71
THE MIKHAILOVSKY THEATER
Mikhailovskaya Square, 1
1831—33. To a design by C.Rossi. 1859—60, architect
A.Kavos
Now the Musorgsky Theater of Opera and Ballet

The Mikhailovsky Theater building is outwardly similar to
the dwelling houses in the square; all the façades were
designed by C.Rossi. The architect did not single out the
theater in order to provide for the integral, ensemble-like
appearance of the square. The height of the theater, the
rhythm of the window openings, the façade decorations
almost fully coincide with those of the dwelling houses.

The interior layout was designed by A.Briullov. The hall
used to be of a horse-shoe shape. The seats were arranged
in four circles, leaning on thin cast-iron columns and
corbels. Briullov made use of such lightened supports
instead of the bulky columns that had been originally
proposed. During the reconstruction A.Kavos changed the
interior layout and decoration, enlarging the hall and
adding one more tier.

The Mikhailovsky Theater was opened in 1833 and was
mainly used for concert performances. Since the 1870s and
up to 1917 a permanent French company performed here,
that was considered to be one of the best ones in Europe.
In 1918 the Maly Theater of Opera and Ballet was opened,
that became known for its daring experiments in the field
of performing. In 1990 it was named after M.Musorgsky.

72
GOLENISHCHEV-KUTUZOV'S HOUSE
Mikhailovskaya Square, 3
1820s. Architect C.Rossi

In 1822 the site next to the theater was allotted to
Leutenant-General Golenishchev-Kutuzov. The main façade
of his house faces the square. Some rooms have retained
their interiors with rich stucco moulding.

In the 1830s M.Vielgorsky lived in the house. In 1837
he moved—first into Jacquot's house, then into the house
on the opposite side of the square.

The Musorgsky Theater of Opera and Ballet (No 71)

73
JACQUOT'S HOUSE
Mikhailovskaya Square, 5
1820s. Architect C.Rossi

In 1822 the site was given as a present to the court
jewellers, brothers F. and I.Segin. Later it was taken over by
the architect P.Jacquot. Outwardly it is similar to the
building of the Mikhailovsky Theater. Of interest is the
three-tier gallery in the courtyard consisting of bulky Doric
colonnades placed one over the other.

In 1911 the famous literary and artistic café called Stray
Dog was opened in the cellar of Jacquot's house, that
existed till 1915. In the Stray Dog one of the domineering
ideas of the early 20th century was realized—that of the
synthesis of arts: poetry, music, painting and theater. Here
artists of the new schools came together. Poetical, musical
and dramatic evenings were arranged and lectures
delivered. The café was frequented by A.Akhmatova,
N.Gumilev, O.Mandelstam, M.Kuzmin, V.Meyerhold,
M.Dobuzhinsky, S.Sudeikin and others.

74
VIELGORSKY'S HOUSE
Mikhailovskaya Square, 4
1830—32. Architect A.Bolotov, to a design by C.Rossi
Now a gymnasium attached to the Russian Museum

Vielgorsky's house is an architectural monument of late Classicism, similar to Jacquot's house opposite it.

In the 1830s the widow of N.Karamzin, the historian, lived in the house; A.Pushkin was a frequent visitor here. Since 1844 the brothers, Counts Mikhail and Matvei Vielgorsky had lived in the house; they were musicians and outstanding contributors in this field, the founders of the Russian Musical and Symphonic Societies. Mikhail was one of the closest friends of Pushkin (after the poet's death he was appointed one of the guardians over his children and property). Since the 1820s many prominent personalities in Russian cultural life got together in his salon. It was visited by V.Zhukovsky, P.Viazemsky, N.Gogol, C.Briullov and others; in the musical evenings many the prominent musicians took part.

75
A SCHOOL BUILDING
Mikhailovskaya Square, 2
1930s. Architect N.Trotsky; rebuilt in 1947, architect A. Kedrinsky

The Ethnography Museum (No 76)

76
THE MUSEUM OF ETHNOGRAPHY
Inzhenernaya Street, 4/1
1900—11. Architect V.Svinyin

The building came into being as a result of the reconstruction of the eastern wing of the Mikhailovsky Palace. The architect used the techniques and motifs of Russian Classicism in his design in order to achieve stylistic unity of the new building and the palace.

The construction works lasted for a long time. The vestibule and the spacious Marble Hall are faced with Olonetsk marbles. The sculptural frieze is performed by the sculptors M.Kharlamov and V.Bogatyriov.

The Museum of Ethnography that originally used to be a Russian Museum department, in 1934 became independent. Its rich collections offer interesting ethnographic information on the peoples inhabiting this country.

77
THE COMMANDANT'S OFFICE
Sadovaya Street, 3
1824—26. Architect C.Rossi

78
YAKOVLEV'S HOUSE
Sadovaya Street, 5
1830s. Architect C.Rossi
Now a dwelling house

79
THE NOBLE ASSEMBLY BUILDING
Mikhailovskaya Street, 1
1834—39. Architect P.Jacquot, to a design by C.Rossi
Now the Shostakovich Petersburg Philharmonic Society

The Noble Assembly building takes up an important place in the Mikhailovskaya Square ensemble.

P.Jacquot designed the main three-tier hall, which is now the Philharmonic concert hall and stands out for its

The monument to A.Pushkin (No 81)

The Noble Assembly building (No 79)

high acoustic qualities. The hall is decorated with Corinthian columns faced with white artificial marble. The butt-end walls are cut with wide arched apertures with columns and decorated with pilasters. In 1899—1901 the fourth story was added, the main staircase and vestibule renovated and the actors' dressing rooms redecorated (architect A.Maksimov, to a design by V.Schreter).

The Petersburg Philharmonic Society was founded in 1921, and in 1975 it was named after D.Shostakovich. During the blockade, on August 9, 1942, the famous 7th Symphony by Shostakovich was performed here (conducted by K.Eliasberg).

80
THE EUROPE HOTEL
Mikhailovskaya Street, 2/7
1873—75. Architect L.Fontana

The Europe Hotel is one of the best hotels in Petersburg. The comfortable hotel lavishly decorated in the eclectic style was erected on the site of the former G.Kleie hotel and a rooming-house. The new interiors in the Art-Nouveau style were performed in 1905 to a design by K.McKensen and in 1908—14—to those by Lidval. In 1908 the fifth story was added, where in 1910 the famous Roof restaurant was opened, with a summer hall and a garden. In 1988—91 the hotel was fully reconstructed to meet the modern requirements.

81
THE MONUMENT TO PUSHKIN
Mikhailovskaya Square
1957. Sculptor M.Anikushin, architect V.Petrov

82
THE ARMENIAN CHURCH
Nevsky Prospekt, 40—42
1771—80. Architect Yu.Velten

The Armenian Church belongs to the early classical period. In the façade decoration sculpture is widely used. The main

The Europe Hotel (No 80)

entrance is marked with a portico crowned with a triangular pediment.

During the construction the compositional device was used characteristic of all the churches in the prospekt. The church building is placed in the back of the lot, in the gap between two dwelling houses that are cited along the prospekt borderline.

The Armenian Church   *The Passage (No 83)*
(No 82)

83
THE PASSAGE
Nevsky Prospekt, 48
1846—48. Architect R.Zheliazevich
Now the Passage department store. The Komissarzhevskaya Drama Theater

The Golitsyn Gallery in Moscow served as a model for the Passage. Arrangement of the trading rooms is original: they run along both sides of a glass-covered gallery linking two parallel streets, the light coming from above. The department store occupied the ground and the first floors; the second floor was made suitable for living. In the basement they traded in wines and foodstuffs, in the shops fashionable clothes, jewelry, etc. were sold. There were also a confectionery, coffee-shops, anatomical museum, various panoramas, dioramas and other entertainments.

In 1899—90 engineer S.Kozlov reconstructed the Passage and changed its interior layout; he added the third floor and wide glass show-windows in the ground and first floors. The concert hall that had existed in the old Passage remained unchanged (the entrance to it was from Italianskaya Street). Since the middle of the 19th century concerts were given here, public lectures delivered and literary readings held. In 1904—6 it used to house a drama theater directed by V.Komissarzhevskaya.

84
YELISEYEV'S HOUSE
Nevsky Prospekt, 56
1901—3. Architect G.Baranovsky
Now the Comedy Theater and Food Store

While rebuilding the Company building for Yeliseyev, the merchant, G.Baranovsky designed part of the façades in the classical style, whereas the trading hall was decorated in the Art-Nouveau style. On both sides of a gigantic window the architect placed large allegorical figures of Trade and Industry (sculptor A.Adamson).

Sadovaya Street

One of the major thoroughfares in the city center is stretching for almost 5km, from the Field of Mars as far as Repin Square. The name dates from the 1730s when the street was fringing the estates situated along the Fontanka banks. Starting as a grand thoroughfare it turns businesslike after crossing Nevsky with its large shops, offices and educational establishments. After crossing Voznesensky Prospekt it becomes a densely built-up housing district.

Yeliseyev's house (No 84)

85

THE FOUR COLONNADE HOUSE
Sadovaya Street, 12

1750—60. Architect L.Kokorinov (?). 1809, architects
L.Rusca and S.Bernikov
Now the Molodezhny Cinema and the Shanghai restaurant

86

THE VORONTSOV PALACE
Sadovaya Street, 26

1749—57. Architect B.Rastrelli
Now the Suvorov Military School

The Palace of M.Vorontsov is a sample of the mid-18th
century rich city estate. The main three-story building with
inner court is sited in the back of the area. Two
symmetrical wings are moved to the forefront and placed at
the pavement borderline. The main courtyard in front of the
building is separated from the street by an open-work
railing made to a design by Rastrelli.

In the decoration of the central part of the main
building Rastrelli used his favorite motif of doubled

pilasters and columns. This device creates the light and shade interplay on the wall surface, cut through by wide windows with figured lintels.

In the late 18th century an Orthodox Church and a Catholic Chapel of the Maltese Knights were built. The Maltese Capella adjoining the main building on the garden side is considered to be one of Quarenghi's finest works. Its interior decoration has remained intact—the painting, sculpture, stucco moulding and artificial marble facing.

In 1810 the palace came to house the Pages Corps—a privileged military educational establishment in Russia.

87
THE APRAKSIN DVOR
Sadovaya Street, 28—30

This is a complex of shops and warehouses. In 1818 a project for symmetrical building in stone was conceived by the architect A.Moduit. By 1870 forty-five trading facilities had been put up.

The Vorontsov Palace (No 86)

The Apraksin Dvor (No 87)

88
THE ASSIGNATION BANK
Sadovaya Street, 21
1783—90. Architect G.Quarenghi
Now the Economics and Finance University

The Assignation Bank building located between the
Sadovaya Street and the Griboyedov Canal occupies a
prominent place among the monuments of the 18th-century

The Assignation Bank viewed from the Griboyedov Canal (No 88)

Russian architecture. In designing the layout and framing the general concept of the building Quarenghi had developed the compositional devices that later came to be widely applied in the palace and estate-house construction. The main building is placed in the back of the front courtyard, which is separated from Sadovaya Street by a cast-iron railing on granite piles topped with balls. It is a three-story building with a six-column portico; the pediment is decorated with statues. The former warehouses envelop the main building and the front courtyard, forming a horseshoe around them.

The fence facing the Griboyedov Canal was put up in 1817 to a design by the architect L.Rusca.

The vestibule and main staircase have retained the original late 18th-century decor. In the garden, in front of the building, a monument to G.Quarenghi was erected to commemorate his 150th death anniversary.

The Assignation Bank (No 88)

The Ostrovskogo Square
1816—34. Architect C.Rossi

In the 18th century Petersburg expanded mostly along the Neva banks and in the adjoining quarters. It was here that construction was characterized by utmost compositional unity. Consequently, many territories were re-designed anew. C.Rossi continued to play an important part in fulfilling these tasks. Thus, he wholly re-developed the Anichkov Palace estate and the adjoining territory between Nevsky Prospect and Chernyshov Lane (the estate itself used to spread from the Fontanka as far as Sadovaya Street in the 18th century).

When the Public Library was built on the corner of Nevsky Prospekt and Sadovaya Street Rossi suggested laying out a square dominated by the building of a theater. The final version implied creating passage behind the theater formed by two grand buildings and a semicircular at the Chernyshov Bridge. This connection between the two squares (Ostrovskogo and Chernyshov) and the resulting street between them was a major achievement of the talented architect.

89
THE ALEXANDRINSKY THEATER
Ostrovskogo Square,2
1828—32. Architect C.Rossi

The Alexandrinsky Theater building is one of the outstanding samples of Russian Classicism. Its main façade facing Nevsky Prospekt, plays the main part in the ensemble of the square.

The rusticated walls of the ground floor serve as a kind of a socle for the majestic colonnades decorating the façades. The six-column colonnade of the main facade stands out clearly against the wall placed further backwards. The traditional protruding classical portico is here replaced with an impressive loggia. Sculpture plays the major part in the facade decoration. The semicircular niches hold the figures of the Muses—Terpsichore and Melpomene. The attic decorated with the figures of the Glories is crowned with Apollo's carriage that was chased from sheet copper to a model by S.Pimenov. In sculptural decoration of the building V.Demuth-Malinovsky and A.Triscorni also took part. In the hall the decorative gilt carving of the tsar's box and those next to the stage has remained that was performed in the second half of the 19th century. The ceremonial opening of the theater was held on August 6, 1832.

90
THE COMPLEX OF THE RUSSIAN NATIONAL LIBRARY BUILDINGS
Ostrovskogo Square, 1
The main building: 1796—1801. Architect Y.Sokolov
The new building: 1828—34. Architect C.Rossi
The third building: 1896—1901. Architect Ye.Vorotilov

The three Russian National Library buildings are an integral part of the Ostrovskogo Square ensemble. The oldest is the building opening on Sadovaya Street, Nevsky Prospekt and Ostrovskogo Square. In 1828—34 a new one was put up next to it. With all respect to his predecessor and revealing architectural talant Rossi made the old façade facing the square part of the new building. In the façade design he used the motifs Sokolov had used: shallow niches ending in a semicircle in the bottom story and the Ionic order in the upper ones. The façade is decorated with colonnade of 18 columns; between them stand the sculptural images of the scientists, philosophers and poets of the past (sculptors S.Pimenov, V.Demuth-Malinovsky and others). The whole building is united by a newly-built attic with the statue of Minerva on top of it (sculptor V.Demuth-Malinovsky). As the library expanded the third building was added to it in the late 19th century; it retained the outlines that were close to the classical aura of the whole architectural complex.

Of the interiors that have remained intact in the old building the Gothic Room (The Faust Study) is of interest (architect I.Gornostayev, 1857). The decor of the room reproduces a typical decor of the 15th-century library chamber.

The library was officially opened in 1814. Many outstanding representatives of Russian culture worked here. It possesses unique collections of ancient manuscripts and printed books and is one of the largest general-purpose libraries in the world.

91
THE MONUMENT TO CATHERINE II
Ostrovskogo Square
1873. Sculptor M.Mikeshin

The monument to Catherine the Great was put up in the public garden in front of the Alexandrinsky Theater in

The Alexandrinsky Theater (No 89)

1873. Sculptors M.Chizhov and A.Opekushin, as well as architect D.Grimm assisted in carrying out M.Mikeshin's project. The statue stands on a high figured pedestal made of gray polished Serdobolsk granite. The figures of outstanding Russian statesmen of the second half of the 19th century surround the pedestal, including those of G.Potiomkin-Tavrichesky, A.Orlov, A.Bezborodko, I.Betskoi, Ye.Dashkova, A.Suvorov, P.Rumiantsev-Zadunaisky, G.Derzhavin, V.Chichagov, and many others. The socle of the pedestal carries a plaque with a dedication inscription decorated with emblems of Science, Arts and Law.

92
THE ANICHKOV PALACE PAVILIONS
1816—18. Architect C.Rossi

During the reconstruction of the Anichkov estate two one-story pavilions were built to the west of the palace; they became an integral part of the square ensemble. Their

The monument to Catherine II (No 91)

façades stand out for their fine proportions, which is due to the relatively large windows and Ionic columns. Skilful use is made of sculpture, which is placed in small hollows between the columns and represents Old Russian warriors, as well as of plastic bas-reliefs (sculptor S.Pimenov).

93
THE CITY CREDIT SOCIETY BUILDING
Ostrovskogo Square, 9
1876. Architect V.Schreter
THE HOUSE IN RUSSIAN STYLE
Ostrovskogo Square, 7
1877—79. Architect N.Basin

94
THE ANICHKOV PALACE
Nevsky Prospekt, 39
1741—50. Architects M.Zemtsov and G.Dmitriyev; completed in 1754, architect B.Rastrelli
Now the Palace of Youth's Art

On the corner of Nevsky Prospekt and the Fontanka Embankment the large Anichkov Palace complex is located.

Both the palace and the bridge were named after Leutenant-Colonel M.Anichkov who supervised the building of the first wooden bridge.

In 1741 the construction of a vast country estate with a palace was started near the Anichkov Bridge. The palace's main façade did not look at Nevsky Prospekt that did not yet at that time play the part of the main street; the estate itself opened on the Fontanka. In the center of the front courtyard a swimming pool was set up connected with the Fontanka by means of a canal. The three-story palace designed in Baroque style stood out for its lavish exterior. The regular garden was decorated with pavilions, summer-houses and garden sculpture. After the construction had been completed Empress Elizabeth gave it as a gift to her favorite Count A.Razumovsky.

In the later years the palace changed its owners a few times, in the result of which the building itself suffered

Russian National Library (No 90)

The Anichkov Palace (No 94)

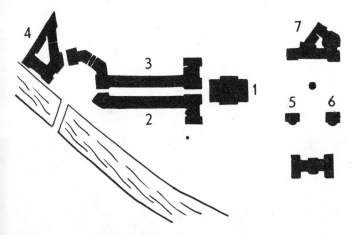

The Ostrovskogo Square ensemble

1. The Alexandrinsky Theater (No 89);
2. The Theater Administration (No 95);
3. Ministry of People's Education (No 95);
4. Ministry of Home Affairs;
5,6. The Anichkov Palace pavilions (No 92);
7. Russian National Library (No 90)

many reconstructions and renovations. In the 1770s the palace was bought by Catherine II and given as a present to Duke G.Potiomkin.

In 1778—79 the architect I.Starov reconstructed the palace in Classicism style changing the façade decor. In the early 19th century G.Quarenghi erected a monumental «Cabinet» building opening on the Fontanka and Nevsky Prospekt and having a colonnade that shut out the view of the palace's main façade from the Fontanka. During the 19th century such architects as L.Rusca, C.Rossi, K.Rachau and M.Nessmacher contributed to the renovation of the palace.

In 1817—18 the architect C.Rossi undertook large-scale reconstruction works on the palace interiors and drastically changed the layout of the whole estate decreasing the garden size. He put up metal railing round the garden and erected two pavilions. He also designed the outbuildings adjoining the palace on the garden side.

Zodchego Rossi Street (No 95)

The Chernyshev Bridge (No 96)

In the early 19th century the palace, which was taken over by the Treasury, accommodated His Majesty's, the Emperors' Cabinet. In the middle of the 1860s Grand Duke Alexander Alexandrovich (the future Emperor) became the owner of the palace. In 1881—94 the Anichkov Palace was the residence of Alexander III, to be owned later by his widow Maria Fiodorovna.

From 1918 up to 1935 the palace housed the Museum of the City's History.

In 1936—37 the palace again underwent large-scale renovation to house the Palace of Young Pioneers (architects A.Gegello and D.Krichevsky). In 1987 a theater building was put up in the back of the garden (architects I.Noakh, N.Kulikova).

95
THE ZODCHEGO ROSSI STREET

The Zodchego Rossi Street is made up of two architecturally identical buildings, that of the Theater Administration (No 2), now the Vaganova Choreographic School, and that of the Ministry of People's Education (No 1/3). Lomonosova Square became a continuation of one of the buildings and is included into the street ensemble. In the Fontanka Embankment there is another house, the Ministry of Foreign Affairs (No 57), put up to a design by C.Rossi, that is also part of the Lomonosova Square ensemble.

The whole set of buildings was not completed in Rossi's lifetime and in place of the part of the Theater Administration Building an apartment house was erected in the 19th century that interfered with the unity of the ensemble.

The Anichkov Bridge (No 98)

96

THE LOMONOSOV (CHERNYSHOV) BRIDGE
over the Fontanka to the Lomonosov Square
1785—87

The bridge was one of the six similar tower bridges over the Fontanka, of which two have remained—the Lomonosov and the Staro-Kalinkin bridges. It has three spans. Four pavilion-towers were erected on piers. In 1925 granite obelisk-lanterns were put up on the abutments (architect I.Fomin).

The bridge is 63m long and 14.7m wide.

97
KOCHNEVA'S HOUSE
Fontanka Embankment, 41
1805—8. Architect L.Rusca

The house is typical of the 18th—19th-century city architecture. In the inner wing the plafonds and murals by D.Scotti have remained, as well as the sculptural friezes by I.Terebenev. Kocheva's house is one of the best samples of the early 19th-century civil engineering.

98
THE ANICHKOV BRIDGE
over the Fontanka along Nevsky Prospekt
Around 1783—85

A stone bridge of a standard model. Reconstructed in 1841 (engineers I.Buttats and others, architect K.Sheppel).
The bridge is 54.6m long and 37.9m wide.

99
THE SCULPTURAL GROUPS 'Taming the Horse'
Anichkov Bridge
1842—50. Sculptor P.Klodt

The four equestrian statues placed at the Anichkov Bridge corners can be viewed as separate monuments. They symbolize man's struggle with natural elements and conquering them. The city on the Neva, being subject to frequent floods, has to conquer the water element, too, and so these groups came to be a kind of a symbol of Petersburg. Originally they had intended to put them up on the Neva bank, in front of the Admiralty. Later, when the bridge construction was started, Klodt suggested decorating it with these sculptures. They are to be viewed counter-clockwise, beginning from the Anichkov Palace corner. Their story did not go on smoothly. In 1842 they were given as a gift to the King of Prussia. New casts were made in 1843; however, in 1846 two of them were sent to Naples. And only in 1850 Klodt made two more casts.
    During the Great Patriotic War the statues were buried in the Anichkov garden. They were re-installed in 1945.

100
THE NARYSHKIN PALACE (THE SHUVALOV PALACE)
Fontanka Embankment, 21
1790s. Architect unknown. Rebuilt in 1844—46. Architect
B.Simon and N.Yefimov
Now the House of Peace and Friendship with the Peoples of
Foreign Countries

In the 1790s the mansion for Countess Vorontsova was
erected on the Fontanka near the Anichkov Bridge. In the
early 19th century her house was bought by the Court

Sculptural groups
decorating
the Anichkov Bridge
(No 99)

Ober-Jagdtmeister D.Naryshkin. In 1821—22 he added an
attachment to the building which housed a large dancing-
hall decorated with reliefs devoted to the subjects of the
Trojan War and plafonds painted by D.Scotti, as well as the
«museum» room.

In 1844—46 the palace was taken over by Countess
S.Shuvalova (hence its second name). The façade was
reconstructed in the Renaissance style, and the interiors
redecorated. Of most interest among them are the vestibule
and main staircase, as well as the Golden, Blue and Red

reception-rooms. The doors and windows in the Golden Reception-room are framed with twisted columns ornamented with gilt Cupids; the tent-vault is decorated with stucco moulding and painting. The Red Reception-room spanned by a semicircular vault is decorated with dark polished walnut.

In the 1820s Naryshkin's Palace was a place well known in Petersburg. The balls and receptions there were attended by the flower of the society. The palace was frequented by P.Viazemsky, V.Zhukovsky, A.Pushkin and others.

The Shuvalov Palace (No 100)

In 1918 the Museum of the Mode of Life was opened here. In 1925 the rich Shuvalovs' collections were transferred to the Hermitage and other museums.

During the Second World War the building suffered severe damage: it was hit by a bomb that destroyed the dancing-hall and the plafond. However, as early as in autumn of 1942 the restoration works began that were completed in 1950.

Sennaya (Hay) Square

The square originated in the 1730s. Since the 1740s it had been the place where hay was traded, hence the name. Until the early 19th century it had been one of the least comfortable districts populated by poor people. In the second half of the 19th century a number of apartment houses were put up there. In the 1940s—1950s the square was expanded.

The Sennaya Square.
The Guard house of the Sennoi Market (on the left) (No 101)

101
THE GUARD-HOUSE OF THE SENNOI MARKET
Sadovaya Street, 37
1818—20. Architect V.Beretti

This is a typical sample of classical architecture that played a major part in the ensemble of the square.

102
THE YUSUPOV GARDEN
1790s

This is an example of a landscape garden. In the back of the garden the Yusupov Palace stands, renovated in the same period by G.Quarenghi.

103
THE YUSUPOV PALACE
Fontanka Embankment, 115
1790s. Architect G.Quarenghi
Now the Institute for the Railway Transport Engineers

As early as 1724 a wooden house facing the Fontanka river was put up on the lot that belonged to Yusupov. In the middle of the 18th century it was substituted by a stone palace designed in Baroque style. In the regular garden figured ponds and canals were dug, parterres and flower gardens laid out. During the reconstruction of the palace G.Quarenghi developed a new, landscape garden.

Along the borderline of the Fontanka Embankment, which by that time had already been clad with granite, two more wings were erected, connected by a gateway arch. Quarenghi designed the inner courtyard in a semicircular form, thus playing down the main façade being parallel to the embankment line. He preserved the walls of the old house, introducing loggias on the façade and decorating it with a six-column portico supporting a balcony on the garden side. The estate changed its appearance completely and acquired a new artistic outlook. In 1810 the palace came to house the Institute for the Railway Engineers, one of the oldest educational establishments in Petersburg.

104
THE BUILDING OF THE CITY OFFICES
Sadovaya Street, 55
1907. Architect A.Lishnevsky

It was designed in Art-Nouveau style, with some motifs of medieval architecture introduced.

105
THE BUILDING OF THE
RUSSIAN-AMERICAN TRADING COMPANY
Moika Embankment, 72

Reconstructed to house a pawnshop by the architect
G.Baranovsky in 1809

In 1824 K.Ryleyev, a Decemberist, came to live here. The
house was frequented by the writers collaborating in the
Poliarnaya Zvezda (Polar Star) almanac, including
A.Pushkin, I.Krylov, V.Zhukovsky, S.Baratynsky and others.

Kitner's house (No 107)

106
OLENIN'S HOUSE
Fontanka Embankment, 101
Late 18th century. Architect unknown

107
KITNER'S HOUSE
Voznesensky Prospekt, 23
Late 19th century. Architect I.Kitner

Marsovo Pole (The Field of Mars)

In the early 18th century there used to be a bog on the site of the Field, which gave start to two rivers—the Mya (Moika) and Krikusha (Griboyedov Canal). Peter I ordered

Marsovo Pole (The Field of Mars)

to drain the place. After the two rivers had been connected and the Lebiazhya Kanavka (Swan Canal) laid, a spacious meadow was formed, that got the name of the Big or Poteshnoye (Amusement) Pole (in the days of court festivals amusement fireworks were held here; military parades and public merry-making took place here too. The Field was also called Tsaritsyn (Tsarina's) Meadow, after the palace of

Catherine I that was located here. By the early 19th century the field got its final name of Mars.

In the 18th—19th centuries the magnificent buildings were put up that faces the Field of Mars and formed a single ensemble with it (the Mramorny (Marble) Palace, houses of N.Saltykov and I.Betskoi, Pavlovsky (Paul) Regiment barracks and Adamini's house).

After the revolution of 1917 the Field of Mars was no more used as a parade-ground. In 1917—19 in the center of the Field a memorial was erected to those who had fallen in the revolutionary struggle (architect L.Rudnev).

Here are the graves of the participants of the February and October revolutions, the Civil War, as well as those of the outstanding Soviet statesmen. Over the common graves a low wall of granite blocks was erected. It bears dedicative inscriptions. In 1920—23 a regular garden was laid out in the Field that transformed the whole ensemble. In 1957 the Eternal Fire was lit in the center of the Memorial, the first one in this country.

108
THE MRAMORNY (MARBLE) PALACE
Millionnaya Street, 5/1
1768—85. Architect A.Rinaldi
Now a Branch of the Russian Museum

The Marble Palace is one of the outstanding samples of early Classic architecture. Unlike the majority of Petersburg buildings it is faced with natural materials—granite and marble. This is what gave the Palace its name.

The building is notable for its discreet decor and strict forms. Both in the exterior and interior, many decorative elements are faced with marble of 32 kinds, the shades chosen with extreme precision and delicacy. The façade's central part is topped with an attic decorated with two statues and compositions of armor performed by the famous Russian sculptor F. Shubin. After the palace had been rebuilt in the middle of the 19th century (architect A.Briullov), original decoration remained on the main staircase and the first tier of the Marble Hall walls, bearing bas-reliefs by F.Shubin and M.Kozlovsky. The front court-yard is on Millionnaya Street and the Neva sides fenced with a forged railing supported by pillars of pink granite with white marble vases. It connects the palace with the outbuilding (1780—87, architect P.Yegorov; rebuilt in 1844—47 by A.Briullov). The outbuilding façade facing the garden is decorated with a unique plastic frieze devoted to the subject of *Horse in the Service of Man* (sculptor P.Klodt), which is 2m high.

The Marble Palace (No 108)

At first the palace was owned by Count G.Orlov. After his death in 1783 the palace was acquired into the Treasury. It used to be the residence of S.Poniatovsky, the last king of Rech Pospolita. Later, up to 1917, it was owned by several Grand Dukes in succession.

Since 1937 the palace had housed the Branch of the Central Lenin Museum; in 1991 it was transferred into the possession of the Russian Museum.

109
BETSKOI'S HOUSE
Dvortsovaya Embankment, 2
1780s. Architect J.-B.Vallin de la Mothe
Now the University of Culture

Next comes the house that had once belonged to the well-known Russian educationalist I.Betskoi (in 1764—94

Betskoi was the President of the Academy of Arts, he was also the author of the reforms concerned with school). It is one of the interesting samples of the late 18th-century Russian architecture. The house was partly rebuilt, but its original outward appearance is well known from the 18th—19th-century drawings and engravings. The façade opening on the Field of Mars was two stories high and had corner towers. There was a hanging garden in the house. In the 1830s, during the reconstruction (architect V.Stasov), the third story was added, and the gardens eliminated.

In 1791—96 I.Krylov, a famous fabulist, lived here. The building also housed the printing works where the *Spectator* and *Saint-Petersburg Mercury* magazines were printed.

110
SALTYKOV'S HOUSE
Dvortsovaya Embankment, 4
1784—88. Architect G.Quarenghi. Rebuilt in 1818, architect C.Rossi
Now the University of Culture

Saltykov's house plays a major part in the Field of Mars ensemble. The building runs along the perimeter of the site and has an inner court. The façade facing the Neva has retained its original appearance, with only slight introduces. The interiors have partly retained the decoration typical of the 1820s—1850s architecture. The White Hall stands out for its sophisticated and rich decoration, its columns being topped with sculptured figures.

Saltykov's house is one of the buildings connected with the life of prominent Russian men of culture. In the 1820s it used to be the residence of the Austrian Ambassador Count Fikelmon. The salon of his wife, D.Fikelmon, who was Kutuzov's grand-daughter, and that of her mother, Ye.Khitrovo, was frequented by A.Pushkin.

111
THE ALLEGORICAL STATUE OF A. SUVOROV
Suvorov Square
1801. Sculptor M.Kozlovsky, architect A.Voronikhin

The monument to the great Russian generalissimo A.Suvorov is one of the finest ones created in Russia in the

18th century, due to its brilliant composition and masterfully chosen silhouette.

The sculptor created an allegorical image of a military leader representing him as Mars, the God of War. On the altar placed beside the figure there lie the Crowns of Naples and Sardinia and the Papal tiara, which are covered with a shield with the Russian coat-of-arms on it. This allegory is to remind us of the protection of Italy from Napoleon by the Russian troops under Suvorov's command. The round pedestal is decorated with a bronze bas-relief by the sculptor F.Gordeyev. In 1801 the monument was put up in the Field of Mars; however, in 1818, it was transferred to the square newly laid out by C.Rossi and named after Suvorov.

The statue of A.Suvorov (No 111)

112
THE PAVLOVSKY (PAUL) REGIMENT BARRACKS
Field of Mars, 1
1817—19. Architect V.Stasov
Now the Lenenergo building

The barracks building that takes up more than half of the extensive block formed by the Field of Mars, Millionnaya Street and the Moika river gave final shape to the spacious city square where military drills and parades were held. The lengthy façade is decorated with three porticoes. The central twelve-column portico is not topped with a pediment, as are the flanking ones, but with a stepped attic that is richly decorated with sculpture. The façade facing Millionnaya Street also had a portico with Doric columns. The sculptural panels representing military attributes (armor and weapons) emphasize the building's purpose.

The barracks belong to the most perfect and artistically expressive structures created during the flowering of Classicism.

113
ADAMINI'S HOUSE
Field of Mars, 7
1823—27. Architect D.Adamini

The Adamini House, that was named after its architect, continues the barracks' line and plays a major part in the formation of the Field's western border. The portico on the façade facing the Moika river closes the Griboyedov Canal perspective when viewed from Nevsky Prospekt. The rounded house corner is decorated with pilasters, while the façades have porticos and a plastic frieze of griffins and ornaments.

The Pavlovsky Regiment Barracks (No 112)

Adamini's house (No 113)

The house is famous in the history of Russian culture. In the 1820s P.Shilling lived here, who invented the electromagnetic telegraph. In 1914—19 the cellar of the Adamini house gave shelter to the artistic club called the Comedians' Halt, which was one of the centers of Petersburg cultural life. It was visited by A.Block, V.Meyerhold, A.Akhmatova, M.Kuzmin, V.Mayakovsky and others. The cellar walls were painted by artists S.Sudeikin, B.Grigoryev, A.Yakovlev (the paintings have not remained).

In 1942 the house was badly damaged when it was directly hit by a bomb; however, during just a few years following the war this valuable sample of classical architecture was restored in its original form.

114
THE KANTEMIR PALACE
Dvortsovaya Embankment, 8
1721—27. Architect B.Rastrelli

This was the first work by Rastrelli in Petersburg. Its walls became part of the existing building—a mansion that had belonged to a timber-merchant Gromov (1875—77, architect K.Rachau).

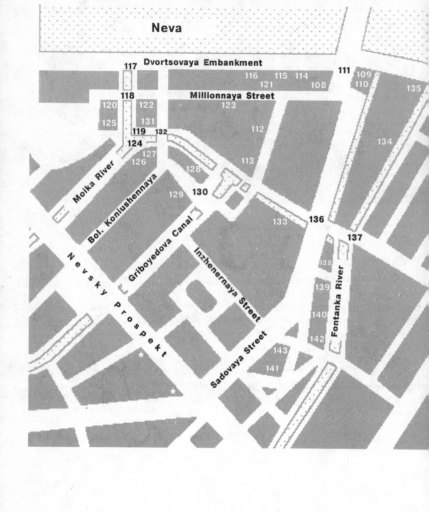

115
THE NOVO-MIKHAILOVSKY PALACE
Dvortsovaya Embankment, 18
1857—61. Architect A.Stakenschneider
Now a Research Institute of the Academy of Sciences

The Novo-Mikhailovsky Palace was built for Grand Duke Mikhail Nikolayevich, son of Nicholas I, on the piece of land that in the 18th century belonged to the Counts Sheremetevs. The palace occupied the space between the

The Novo-Mikhailovsky Palace (No 115)

embankment and Millionnaya Street. The main façade facing the embankment is grand and impressive; Stakenschneider achieved the effect by using Baroque and Renaissance architectural forms, including porticoes and Corinthian columns of Carrara marble, as well as the terra-cotta sculpture (sculptor D.Jensen). The columns are impressively completes with caryatides that are supporting the entableture. The façade opening on Millionnaya Street is discreetly designed and reminds of an apartment-house.

The interior decoration includes stucco moulding, wall painting, artificial marble facing, leather upholstery of the walls, valuable kinds of wood, decorative sculptural panels.

116
THE PALACE
OF GRAND DUKE VLADIMIR ALEKSANDROVICH
Dvortsovaya Embankment, 26
1867—72. Architect A.Rezanov
Now the House of Scientists

The palace belonged to the son of Alexander II, Grand Duke Vladimir Aleksandrovich. The building forms a whole with the continuous line along the embankment. The lobby at the entrance in the center of the main façade facing the Neva is made of the Bremen sandstone. It projects into the street taking up the whole pavement.

The reception rooms are decorated in different styles. The main staircase is faced with artificial marble; its walls are from floor to ceiling decorated with stucco moulding and sculptured figures against golden background. The plafond *The Genius of Arts on the Neva Banks* was painted by V.Vereshchagin. The main reception room is designed in the Renaissance style, and the dining room next to it—in Gothic style. In decorating the two-tier dancing hall Rezanov used the Rococo motifs, while the banquet hall is designed in Russian style. The suite of the main halls that run parallel to the Neva is completed by a small boudoir decorated in Moresque style.

117
THE HERMITAGE BRIDGE
Over the Zimniaya Kanavka (Winter Canal)
along the Dvortsovaya Embankment
1763—66. The first granite bridge in Petersburg

118
THE PERVY ZIMNY (FIRST WINTER) BRIDGE
over the Zimniaya Kanavka along Millionnaya Street
1783—84. Engineer T.Nasonov

The construction of the bridge and the granite embankments along the Zimniaya Kanavka twenty years

after the Hermitage Bridge had been build created a unified
architectural ensemble.

The bridges over the Winter Canal (Nos 117, 118, 119)

119
THE VTOROI ZIMNY (SECOND WINTER) BRIDGE
over the Zimniaya Kanavka at the confluence
with the Moika River
1962—64. Engineer V.Ksenofontov, architect L.Noskov

The new bridge is similar to the two old ones built over the
Zinniaya Kanavka 200 years ago, thus completing the
ensemble of bridges that have become so typical for
Petersburg architecture.

120

THE BUILDING OF THE CENTRAL NAVAL ARCHIVES
Millionnaya Street, 36

1883—86. Architect M.Messmacher

Was built in the Italian Renaissance style for specially the State Council Archives.

121

BARIATINSKY'S HOUSE
Millionnaya Street, 21

1720—1730s.   Architect   unknown.   1830s—rebuilt, architect L.Charlemagne

It is a good sample of a classical façade without any architectural order. The artistic effect is due to a good proportion between different parts and elements of the facade. In the 19th—early 20th century the building was reconstructed for its new owners—the Bariatinsky family (architects P.Sadovnikov, I.Kitner, B.Vorotilov).

122

ABAMELEK-LAZAREV'S HOUSES
Millionnaya Street, 22—24

The house No 22 was erected in 1735—37 for Count F.Apraksin; in 1904 it was bought by Duke S.Abamelek-Lazarev, who later, in 1911, added the house No 24 to it.

The part of the house opening on the Moika was in 1913—15 rebuilt by the architect I.Fomin. In No 22 the 18th-century interiors have remained.

The façade of the house facing the Moika was designed by Ye.Vorotilov (Nos 21—23). It imitates the façade of the Armenian Church (Nevsky Prospekt, 40). In the interior decoration marble, sculpture and wall painting are widely used.

123
THE MAIN PHARMACY
Millionnaya Street, 4
1732. Architect D.Trezzini. Rebuilt in 1789—96, architect G.Quarenghi
Now the Energia Publishers

The Main Pharmacy (No 123)

The main façade facing Millionnaya Street was decorated with four Corinthian semi-columns and a triangular pediment; the façade opening on Aptekarsky Lane has four Corinthian pilasters. Having used a grand order uniting the ground and first floors Quarenghi imparted the whole building a monumental appearance.

124
THE PEVCHESKY (SINGER) BRIDGE
**over the Moika along the Dvortsovaya Square
towards the Capella**
1839—40. Engineer Ye.Adam

The third widest bridge in Petersburg. The bridge is 24m long and 72m wide.

125
ARAKCHEYEV'S HOUSE
Moika Embankment, 35
1800s. Architect F.Demertsev

A typical 19th-century dwelling house, strictly classical in style.

The Capella (No 126)

126
THE CAPELLA
Moika Embankment, 20
1887—9. Architect L.Benois

The building is designed in Neo-Classical style. It is separated from the embankment by a cast-iron railing. At present it houses the Glinka Academic Capella; the concert hall is famous for its splendid acoustics.

127
VOLKONSKY'S HOUSE
Moika Embankment, 12
18th century. Architect unknown
Now the Pushkin's Memorial Museum

The large three-story Volkonsky's house is connected with Pushkin's name. On the first floor here the poet had

Volkonsky's house (No 127)

lived from October 1836 and up to the day of his tragic death.

The building was put up in the 1720s, and reconstructed in the late 18th and early 19th centuries. Its façade was designed in a way characteristic of early Classicism. On January 23, 1837 Pushkin departed from here for his duel with Dantes. The news about his deadly wound immediately spread all over Petersburg. Pushkin's friends—A.Turgenev, V.Zhukovsky, the Viazemskys, doctor V.Dahl—came to visit him. People from all over the capital

gathered near Volkonsky's house. Zhukovsky put out the
bulletins on the door of the poet's flat telling about the
state of his health. At 2.45 p.m., on January 29, Pushkin
died. In 1925 an exhibition devoted to his life and work
was opened in the flat, and in 1937, in commemoration of
the 100th anniversary since his death, a memorial museum
was opened there.

In 1950 a monument was erected in the courtyard
(sculptor N.Dydykin).

In 1982—87 the house was completely restored, and
new expositions were set up in the museum.

128
THE BUILDING OF THE STABLE DEPARTMENT
Koniushennaya Square, 1
1817—23. Architect V.Stasov

The Stable Department building is a sample of Empire
style. Stasov reconstructed the former building preserving
its complex configuration, the foundation and walls. The
central, dominating church structure has two-story wings
adjoining it. Their strict rhythm is interrupted by pavilions
with loggias. Due to the enormous length of its façade the
building plays a major part in the ensemble of the square.

The church façade is ornamented with the bas-reliefs
Carrying of the Cross and *The Entrance into Jerusalem* by
V.Demuth-Malinovsky.

The Stable Department (No 128)

Koniushennaya Square

In the church on February 1, 1837, the funeral service over Pushkin was held; on February 3, at night, the coffin with the body was secretly removed from the church to the Sviatogorsky monastery.

At present the Koniushennaya Church is an active Orthodox church.

129
THE KONIUSHENNY (STABLE) MUSEUM
Koniushennaya Square, 4
1857—60. Architect P.Sadovnikov

The Stable Museum was in charge of the Court Stable Department and was designed for storing carriages. The building was performed in Neo-Baroque style. The main façade is decorated with 15 carved oak gates, terra-cotta vases (sculptor D.Jensen) and intricate relief lintels. The ground floor was designed for storing the imperial family's carriages. On the first floor old carriages were stored. In order to lift the carriages in to the first floor a pente douse was erected on the court side provided with a hoisting gear. In 1917 the museum became a Hermitage Department; in 1922 it was liquidated, and the funds transferred to the collections of the Hermitage and the palaces of the town of Pushkin.

130
THE MALY KONIUSHENNY BRIDGE
over the Griboyedov Canal near its estuary
from the Moika
1829—30. Engineers Ye.Adam and V.Traitteur

The first wooden bridge had existed till 1716. In the
process of replacing the latter, as the neighboring Theater
Bridge, with cast-iron ones the engineers connected them
and erected an imitation bridge span on the stable side,
thus creating a single architectural composition. This
bridge ensemble is unique and is considered to be a
masterpiece of bridge-building. In 1952 the standard
lamps, lanterns and railings were restored.
    The bridge is about 33m long and 15.6m wide.

131
THE KRUGLY (ROUND) MARKET
Moika Embankment, 3
1790s. Architect G.Quarenghi

The Round Market is one of the few remaining private
markets that were erected in each of the city districts in the
18th—19th centuries; the market concerned was located in
the Admiralty district. Later the building was disfigured by
several reconstructions and additions; however, the 19th-
century drawings and investigations on site made it
possible to restore the original shape of the building.

132
THE BOLSHOI KONIUSHENNY BRIDGE
over the Moika River, connects Moshkov
and Konniushenny Lanes
1828. Engineer Ye.Adam

The first wooden bridge was erected in 1753. The slanted
hingeless arch was constructed of tubings. In 1955 part of
the pier bodies and the above-arch brick filling were
replaced by a ferro-concrete hinged arch that bore all the
transport loading; this made it possible to preserve the
bridge as an architectural monument and a sample of

excellent building technology. In 1961 the cast-iron lanterns and railing were restored.

The bridge is 28.8m long and 11.6m wide.

The Small Koniushenny Bridge (No 130)

133
THE MIKHAILOVSKY GARDEN PAVILION
1825. Architect C.Rossi

The small pavilion-cum-pier is located in the Mikhailovsky Garden on the Moika bank. Two rectangular rooms are connected by a colonnade of loosely standing columns; on passing through you get on to a semicircular terrace opening on the garden. The interior retains the original ceiling painting. The granite terraced pier in front of the pavilion is fenced with an iron railing cast to a drawing by C.Rossi.

In 1959 the banks of the Moika river were strengthened with a low supporting wall faced with granite.

134
THE SUMMER GARDENS

The Summer Gardens are almost of the same age as the city itself. It might date back to the early 1704, when on the order of Peter I they started to bring saplings of various trees, flower seeds, marble statues, columns. etc. to Petersburg from all parts of Russia and Europe. As early as

Mikhailovsky Garden Pavilion (No 133)

1707 much of the work on laying out the gardens, planting the trees and setting up the fountains had been completed. It was a regular garden with a geometrical pattern of crossing alleys and with trimmed shrubs, the statues and fountains symmetrically arranged (to a design of the gardener J.Roosen, followed by I.Surmin). In the early 18th century the Summer Gardens occupied a much larger territory, beginning from the Neva bank and almost reaching Nevsky Prospekt. Originally the Summer Gardens fountains were provided with water by special mechanisms from the Bezymiannaya (Nameless) River, that consequently got the name of the Fontanka (Fountain) River. Later to improve the water supply the Ligovsky Canal was set up that ended in a pool dug especially for this purpose. By pipes laid along the street that was consequently called Basseinaya (Pool) Street—the present Nekrasov Street—water was fed into the water-tower, and hence into the fountains. This water-pipe, the first in Petersburg, was put into operation in 1725.

In the 1720s the Lebiazhya (Swan) Kanavka was laid

The Summer Gardens (No 134)

that separated the Summer Gardens from the Field of Mars; the Mya (Moika) River was made deeper and connected with the Fontanka. Thus the Summer Gardens surrounded by the Neva, Fontanka, Moika and Lebiazhya Kanavka became an island.

The Summer Palace of Peter I was small and not suited for large receptions; so in summer court festivities and receptions were held in the garden alleys. Dinners were given in the galleries on the Neva bank built especially for this purpose. There were many other entertainments in the garden, including pavilions, a grotto, curvy paths, a maze, etc. The contemporaries left a lot of descriptions testifying of its extraordinary beauty and wealth. Peter I took special care of acquiring the sculptures that were not only to decorate the garden, but to glorify the transformations he was introducing into the state system. According to the tsar's directions statues were bought or ordered in Europe, especially in Venice, famous for its sculptors. At present among the 250 sculptures decorating the garden there are about 90 statues and busts that make up a genuinely unique collection of Italian Baroque sculpture, performed by P.Baratta, D.Bonazza, F.Cabianca and others. Among them there are allegorical images of the professions most respected by Peter I, such as Architecture and Navigation. Some of the statues, including Justice, Abundance, Charity and Truth personify essential components of wise government. Glory, Minerva and Belonna glorify military valor. The *Peace and Abundance* sculptural group is an allegory of the Nistadt peace treaty concluded between Russia and Sweden (1721); Peter I ordered it from P.Baratta especially for the Summer Gardens. In the early 18th century the famous statue of Taurida Venus also stood there; it is now displayed in the Hermitage. On the order of Peter I the statue was bought in Rome. However, due to the ban on the export of antiquities they could not bring it into Russia. The tsar offered the Pope to exchange the statue for the relic of St.Bridget from Revel (Tallinn). The exchange was accomplished and in 1720 Venus was installed in the Summer Gardens. Later it was transferred to the Taurida Palace, hence the name.

The terrible storm and flood of 1777 caused the Summer Gardens irreparable damage: the fountain system was wrecked, many statues were lost or damaged, the maze destroyed, a lot of trees pulled out. After this disaster the former decoration was never restored, and the Imperial summer residence was moved to the suburbs. In the first half of the 19th century the Gardens became open to the public (with the exclusion of the «common people»).

In 1773—86 the famous railing was put up on the side facing the Neva (architects Yu.Velten, P.Yegorov). Much has been written about its perfect proportions, austere outline combined with airy transparency, harmony and beauty; legends have been made up about it.

In 1826 the Coffee-house was erected in the back of the Summer Gardens on the site of the grotto to a design by C.Rossi, in 1827 the Tea-house was built not far from it by L.Charlemagne. In 1855 the monument to the fabulist

I.Krylov was put up on the voluntary donations (sculptor P.Klodt); it was the first monument to a man of letters to be erected in Russia. In the southern part of the garden a pond has remained from the Peter's times; it is connected with the Fontanka and Lebiazhya Kanavka by means of pipes, so it has running water in it. In 1839 a vase of pink porphyry was installed on a pedestal beside it, performed in the town of Elfdahlen and given as a present to Nicholas I by Swedish king Charles XIV.

On the Moika side the Summer Gardens are fenced by a low cast-iron railing (architect L.Charlemagne, 1826); it is ornamented with bas-reliefs representing Medusa Gorgona.

135
THE SUMMER PALACE OF PETER I
Summer Gardens
1710—14. Architect D.Trezzini

The Summer Palace is the oldest stone building in Petersburg. It is built in Baroque style of the period of Peter the Great. In the decor of the palace architects A.Schluter, N.Michetti, M.Zemtsov took part. The facade of this low building with a sloping roof is decorated with a narrow ornamental frieze and bas-reliefs on mythological subjects glorifying Russia's victory in the Northern War. Most

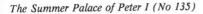

The Summer Palace of Peter I (No 135)

valuable in the interiors are the plafonds painted with oil on canvas, as well as the carved oak panels and tiled stoves.

After the death of Peter I the members of the Imperial family and courtiers lived in the palace. In the middle of the 18th century it was leased to high court officials. Since the 1840s the palace had been vacant.

Due to this its layout and decoration did not suffer any significant alterations. Since 1934 the Summer Palace has housed the Museum of History and Mode of Life devoted to the epoch of Peter I.

136
THE PERVY (FIRST) SADOVY BRIDGE
over the Moika along Sadovaya Street
1835—36. Engineers P.Basin and others

Cast-iron railings and standard lamps made up of lance shieves were executed in 1910—13.

The bridge is 33.3m long and 20.4m wide.

137
THE FIRST INZHENERNY (ENGINEER) BRIDGE
over Moika at its estuary from the Fontanka
1824—25. Engineer N.Basin

One-spane arch bridge. The cast-iron railing is made of darts joined together by horizontal rods. The pillars represent the so-called «lictor wisps» (the power symbol of lictors, special guards in Rome); they carry crossed swords and shields. The pillars are austere and delicate at the same time; their presence is also technologically justified, as they add too the stability of the whole structure.

The bridge is 27.3m long and 9.5m wide.

THE SECOND INZHENERNY (ENGINEER) BRIDGE
over Voskresensky Canal—has not remained—on the right Fontanka bank near Engineers' Castle. False bridge
1824—26. Engineers P.Basin and E.Cleiperon. Standard lamps and lanterns—architect A.Rotach

138
THE ENGINEERS' (MIKHAILOVSKY) CASTLE
Sadovaya Street, 2
1797—1800. Architect V.Brenna

The Mikhailovsky Castle stands on the Moika and Fontanka embankments. It was built by Paul I on the site of the Summer Palace of the Empress Yelizaveta Petrovna and was named in honor of Archangel Michael, whom the Emperor considered to be his patron. The foundation was laid in February 1797, the Emperor ordered the construction to be finished that very year. Consequently the work continued day and night; from 2.5 to 6 thousand people were engaged every day. The castle was completed by November 1800, and in January 1801 the imperial family moved into it.

The Mikhailovsky Castle ensemble is one of the most outstanding ones in the history of Petersburg. Its somewhat severe and mysterious appearance is inspired by Romanticism. The castle is cardinally different from the contemporary classical buildings. Some of its features manifest the influence of the Italian Renaissance architecture as well as that of the French Classicism and Gothic. None of the four façades repeats the other. The castle is rectangular in plan with an octagonal courtyard. The northern façade, resembling a country-house opens on the Moika and the Summer Gardens. The wide front staircase leading into the garden is decorated with the statues of Heracles and Flora. It raises majestically to the colonnade that is supporting the open first floor terrace. The main, southern façade that faces the square where parades used to take place, looks emphatically monumental. The grand row of columns and gigantic obelisks remind one of the Louvre colonnade and the Saint-Denis Gates in Paris. The front entrance leads into the courtyard. The massive portico with a heavy pediment is ornamented with a bas-relief *History Puts Down into Its Tables the Glory of Russia* (sculptor P.Stadgi).

The castle surrounded by rivers in all sides, as well as by canals with draw-bridges seemed impregnable. However, on the night of March 12, 1801, only 40 days after he had moved in, Paul I was killed in his bedroom by conspirators.

After his death the imperial family left the castle that for a long time after that remained vacant. Only in 1819 it was handed over to the School of Military Engineers, whence the new name. Consequently some changes took place; the canals on both sides were filled up, fortifications and the draw-bridge pulled down. Some palace interiors were destroyed or changed in the reconstruction process; the furniture, sculpture and paintings were removed to the

The First Sadovy Bridge (No 136)

Mramorny (Marble) and Winter Palaces the year Paul I died. However, part of the interiors retained their original decor. The general layout remained unchanged; rooms of elaborate configuration prevailed, including round, oval, polygonal and rectangular ones, with niches. Best preserved are the main staircase, Throne Hall, Raphael Gallery, Oval Hall and the church. In the finishing of the castle the sculptors P.Stadgi, Thibaud, P.Triscorini, as the well as the painters D.Scotti, A.Vighi and others took part.

F.Dostoyevsky boarded in the school in 1838—41 the and studied for two years more. In different periods of time many outstanding Russian writers, scientists and generals were students here as well.

139
THE MONUMENT TO PETER I
(in front of the Mikhailovsky Castle)
1800. Sculptor B.Rastrelli

The Mikhailovsky Castle is so naturally linked with its surroundings that the necessity of developing the ensemble became self-evident. In front of the southern façade there

The monument to Peter I in front of the Engineers' Castle (No 139)

spread Connetable Square. In 1800, simultaneously with the completion of the Castle a monument to Peter I was erected in it. The idea of commemorating the founder of Petersburg belonged to Empress Anna Ioannovna; in the 1720s she ordered B.Rastrelli, father of a well-known architect, to make a model for the first equestrian statue to be put up in Russia. The statue was cast only in 1747, but even then it was not mounted until after a long period of time.

Peter I is represented as a Roman triumpher. The marble pedestal bears an inscription: «To Grandfather from Grandson 1800». The bronze bas-reliefs are by the sculptors M.Kozlovsky, I.Terebenev and V.Demuth-Malinovsky.

140
THE MIKHAILOVSKY CASTLE PAVILIONS
Inzhenernaya Street, 8, 10
Architect V.Brenna

Inzhenernaya Street that was continued to C.Rossi's concept
is on both sides faced by twin pavilions that used to
accommodate the Castle Guards and formed a passageway
towards the entrance. The façades have retained their
original appearance. Against the terra-cotta background of
the walls the graceful arched colonnades stand out, raised
on to high rusticated socles. The raised panels placed
above semicircular window were performed by the sculptor
F.Gordeyev.

141
THE MIKHAILOVSKY MANÈGE
AND STABLE BUILDING
Manezhnaya (Manege) Square, 6, 10
1798—1800. Architect V.Brenna

Having completed the Mikhailovsky Castle ensemble
C.Rossi went in the 1820s to redesign all the city quarters
adjoining it. An alley was laid in the square that got the
name of the Klenovaya (Maple) alley; it continued the
perspective as far as Manezhnaya Square. C.Rossi
transformed the square itself. He rebuilt the southern, butt-
end façades of the Manège and the stables on both its sides
in the austere, grand classical manner, thus creating a
uniform composition. Strict proportions are emphasized by
sculptural decor—the bas-reliefs representing armor,
swords and shields and oak branches.

142
THE CIRCUS
Fontanka Embankment, 3
1877. Architect V.Kenel

First wooden circuses appeared in Russia in the early 19th
century. The first stationary stone circus was built in 1877
on the initiative of G.Cineselli, who was the head of the
circus family on tour in Petersburg. The architect took into

consideration a specific nature of a circus performance; it had a spherical cupola and a manège, 13m in diameter.

In 1928 a unique Museum of the Circus Art began to function here, the number of the exhibits being more than 30 thousand.

The Mikhailovsky Manege (No 141)

143
THE SHUVALOV PALACE
Italianskaya Street, 25
1753—55. Architect S.Chevakinsky
Now the House of Sanitary Education

Representations of the Palace of I.Shuvalov, the famous Russian patron of arts of the 18th century, in its original form are well known. The estate occupied the area between Italianskaya Street and Nevsky Prospekt. Contemporaries considered it to be an outstanding edifice. The palace housed the picture gallery of Shuvalov.

In the late 18th—19th centuries the palace was partly altered. However, in spite of the reconstructions it remains a good sample of the transitional period from Baroque to Classicism. The features typical for Baroque (such as the risalits on the façade that create the interplay of light and shade) are combined with typically classical devices (such as the use of shallow panels and rusticating the risalit corners from top to bottom). All the decorative details of the façade are exquisitely drawn; the façade itself is very well proportioned. Inside original decor of the vestibule has remained, as well as of some rooms in the first floor.

144
POLOVTSOV'S HOUSE
Bolshaya Morskaya Street, 52
1835—36. Architect A.Pel
Now the House of Architects

In the middle of the 18th century the house belonged to Count G.Golovin, and in the first half of the 19th century it was owned by S.Gagarin. In the early 1860s it was taken over by senator A.Polovtsov, who was the chairman of the Russian Historical Society.

The façade of the house with a semicircular bay-window has retained its late-classical appearance. The interior decoration and partly the layout suffered large alterations. A number of rooms were redecorated by the architects N.Briullov in the 1870s and M.Messmacher in 1880—1890s. The interiors created in different periods and styles are performed with great skill. The Golden Hall is faced with many kinds of marble (architect Messmacher). The Oak Hall is decorated with carving and a splendid fireplace with two sculptures of Florentine work. The Oak Hall adjoins the Bronze Hall designed for ceremonial receptions and dinners. In its decoration various kinds of marble and malachite, stucco moulding and bronze ornaments, mirrors and wall-carpets were used. In many rooms marble fireplaces, carved doors and stucco moulding have remained intact.

145
DEMIDOV'S MANSION
Bolshaya Morskaya Street, 43
2nd half of the 1830s. Architect A.Montferrand

The mansion of a wealthy manufacturer P.Demidov is one of the first buildings in which Montferrand departed from the classical tradition; he decorated each story of the façade with an order, which is typical of the Italian Renaissance architecture, and combined this with Baroque motifs. The first story is decorated with marble caryatides and vases, the second—with winged Glories supporting a cartouche with the owner's coat-of-arms (sculptor T.Jacque). The magnificent mansion of the palazzo type, designed in the Renaissance-Baroque style stood out for its originality in the contemporary surroundings. The lot bought by Demidov was small and had to be built up very densely; beyond the façade two narrow well-yards that served for lighting purposes and were typical for Petersburg architecture were concealed. The reception rooms surrounded the yard along the perimeter. Such ring-shaped suite of rooms came to be widely used in the 19th-century mansions. This device made it possible to create an impressive suite in spite of the small size of the lot. In decorating the interiors as well as the façade Montferrand used valuable materials; gilt bronze, malachite, different kinds of marble.

146
GAGARINA'S HOUSE
Bolshaya Morskaya Street, 45
1840s. Architect A.Montferrand
Now the House of Composers

Until the early 1870s the house of Duchess B.Gagarina had belonged to P.Demidov. The building manifests some new features—both in the layout and in the decoration of the façades. In search for a more economical and convenient design Montferrand abandoned the idea of symmetrical layout; the main building is an ordinary one-story house, a three-story wing adjoining it on the left. In order to play down the asymmetry the upper part of the left-hand building is moved backwards; a terrace is arranged above the first story, its balustrade being decorated with sculpture. The asymmetrical composition of the mansion and Renaissance motifs in the façade decoration all suggest of a gradual transition from Classicism to Neo-Renaissance. The remaining interior decor (oak panels, marble fireplaces, carved doors) belong to the 1890s.

147
NABOKOV'S HOUSE ·
Bolshaya Morskaya Street, 47
1900—1. Architect M.F.Geisler

In this house Vladimir Nabokov, a prominent Russian writer, was born and had lived before he emigrated abroad. The house has an interesting history. It was built in the

Demidov's mansion (No 145)

1730s to a standard design. Its first owners were the Maslov family. During the 18th—19th centuries it had changed several owners and had belonged to the most prominent people of their time, including Engelgardt, the Yusupov family Khitrovo, Lobanov-Rostovsky. Each of them had introduced some changes to suit his own tastes, until it was bought by Rogov, a high government official. The building had lost its classical image. Further it was purchased by A.Polovtsov and finally—by I.Rukavishnikov,

Nabokov's grandfather, for his daughter Yelena, who later married V.Nabokov. The house underwent capital reconstruction in Art-Nouveau style.

In his novel *Other Shores* V.Nabokov wrote: «At Morskaya 47 we had a three-story mansion of pink granite with a colored mosaic strip over the upper windows. I was born there—in the last ... room, on the third floor—where there used to be a cache with mother's jewelery. Ustin, the

Nabokov's house (No 147)

doorman, was the one who personally lead people to it through all the rooms in November 1917...»

The house has retained this appearance. The mosaic frieze was performed in the workshops of V.Frolov, author of the mosaics in the Ressurection Cathedral (Savior on the Blood); the large stained-glass window was produced by E.Tode Firm in Riga. The interiors show combination of styles, which is characteristic of Art-Nouveau, including Baroque, antique style and French Renaissance.

148

THE BEZBORODKO PALACE
Pochtamtskaya Street, 7
1780s. Architect unknown
Now the Popov Central Communications Museum

In 1781 A.Bezborodko, who headed several departments, the Post Department among them, acquired two stone houses in the neighborhood of the General Post Office. He joined both houses to build a palace, which is rather discreet in its outward appearance, but finely decorated inside.

The interiors performed to the drawings by G.Quarenghi have been partly preserved. The dancing hall with Corinthian columns, painted plafond and stucco moulding is one of the best samples of the classical interior architecture. In 1829 the building was acquired by the Post Department, and in the 1870s the façades were redecorated in Renaissance style, which altered their original appearance considerably.

149

THE GENERAL POST OFFICE
Pochtamtskaya Street, 9
1782—89. Architect N.Lvov

In the façade composition the architect repeated the scheme characteristic of Russian Classicism. He marked out the risalits in each of the three façade centers and decorated them with four-column porticoes topped with pediments. In 1859 an arch was erected over the street, and a closed gallery upon it, that connected the two buildings at the second story level. Originally the building had a spacious inner courtyard that was in 1903 spanned with a glass ceiling and converted into the central operation hall.

150

NIKOLAYEVSKY (BLAGOVESHCHENSKY) BRIDGE
over the Neva to Vasilyevsky Island
1843—50. Architect A.Briullov. Engineer S.Kerbedz

It is the first permanent bridge over the Neva and the last to be made of cast-iron (later only steel structures were

B o l s h a y a   N e v a

150

Krasnogo Flota

Embankment

158 157 156 155
159

154 153

151

Truda
Square

Galernaya Street

152

Konnoqvardeisky Boulevard

169

River

Prospekt

180

Pochtamtskaya Street
148

149

160

147 146 145

161

Moika

Bol. Morskaya Street
144

Dekabristov Street

163 162

River

Pryazhka

176

177

178

179

Maklina

Prospekt

171

170

Rimskogo-

164

165
166

Korsakova

Griboedova

Prospekt

Canal

172

5

167

Fontanka   River

173

Lermontovsky

168

Sadovaya

Voznesensky Prospekt

Street

Moskovsky Prospekt

174

used). The authors of the design and the bridge builders created a new construction of bridge spans in the form of lattice trusses. The seven gently sloped arches increasing in size towards the middle of the bridge create an expressive architectural rhythm. It is worth mentioning that the

The Bezborodko Palace (No 148)

construction of the bridge was notable for its accuracy and precision of performance. The joints between the cast-iron blocks were filled with lead padding. When in 1930 compete reconstruction of the bridge was undertaken to a project by G.Peredery and the arches were dismantled neither rust nor a fleck of dust was found in the joints. The bridge is 298.2m long and 20.3m wide.

151
THE NIKOLAYEVSKY PALACE
Truda (Labour) Square, 4
1853—61. Architect A.Stakenschneider

The building of the palace for Grand Duke Nikolai Nikolayevich—son of Nicholas I—was connected with the construction of the first permanent bridge over the Neva and building up of the newly formed Blagoveshchenskaya

(Annunciation) Square. Part of the block between the Galernaya (Galley) Street and Konnogvardeisky (Horse Guards) Boulevard was at that time occupied by the marine barracks. They were dismantled and on the site the

The Nikolayevsky Palace (No 151)

construction of the palace began, that was to play a major part in the city's architectural image and become a dominant in the architecture of Blagoveshchenskaya Square. This richly decorated building of considerable size is placed at a distance from the pavement border. In front of it the front courtyard was laid out fenced with a cast-iron railing. The façades are a typical sample of the Neo-Renaissance style. Variations in the decaration of different stories and gradual diminution of the order elements, from the bottom and upwards produce a specific artistic effect; the palace looks larger than it actually is. When decorating the interiors Stakenschneider used different styles giving preference to Renaissance and Baroque. The main staircase decorated with columns of gray granite with white marble bases and capitals is one of the most interesting works by Stakenschneider, as well as in the Russian 19th century-architecture.

In 1894 the Nikolayevsky Palace came to house the Kseninsky Boarding Shcool—a closed educational establishment for girls from noble families founded by Emperor Alexander III in honor of his elder daughter Grand Duchess Kseniya Alexandrovna. In 1917 the building was taken over by the Trade Unions Council.

152
KOCHUBEI'S HOUSE
Konnogvardeisky Boulevard, 7
Rebuilt in 1853—54. Architect D.Bosset
Now the Institute of Beauty

The house was built on the site of a former spinning mill and radically reconstructed for Duke M.Kochubei in the Italian Renaissance style, with wide arched windows and rusticated walls.

Inside many interiors have remained that are of high artistic value. The main halls were decorated to the drawings by Bosset in the Baroque and Rococo styles. The styles were wide spread in the mansions of the Petersburg aristocracy in the middle of the 19th century.

In the 1860s the house was taken over by the merchant Rodonaki and up to 1917 remained in the ownership of his descendants.

Krasnogo Flota (Red Fleet) Embankment

The embankment (formerly named English) was erected in 1767—88. It stands out for the stylistic unity of the three-story building stannding in it. Its peculiarity is the lack of passages into the courtyard—they are all arranged from Galernaya Street.

153
VORONTSOV-DASHKOV'S HOUSE
Krasnogo Flota Embankment, 10
1736—38. Architect unknown
Now an office building

The house was built for A.Naryshkin, Head of the Office for the Construction of Imperial Houses and Gardens, and rebuilt in the 1770s (architect unknown). In the 19th century it belonged to the Vorontsov-Dashkov family. It is a typical example of a rich mansion of the early Classicism period. The protruding portico distinguishes the house from the surrounding buildings and enriches the austere façade decor. The interiors have retained the painted panels, marble fireplaces, wooden doors and *dessus-de-port* of the late 18th century.

154
THE BUILDING OF THE FOREIGN COLLEGIA
Krasnogo Flota Embankment, 32
1782—83. Architect G.Quarenghi

It is the place where D.Fonvizin, A.Griboyedov, A.Pushkin were in the military service.

155
RUMIANTSEV'S HOUSE
Krasnogo Flota Embankment, 44
18th century. Rebuilt in 1826—27, architect V.Glinka

The house belonged to the outstanding statesman, scientist and collector N.Rumiantsev. The great collection of books, manuscripts and works of arts formed the so-called Rumiantsev Museum. In 1861 it was transferred to Moscow to become later the basis for the State Lenin Library.

156
THE ENGLISH CHURCH
Krasnogo Flota Embankment, 56
1814—15. Architect G.Quarenghi. Rebuilt in 1876, architect F.Boltengagen
Now the City Excursion Bureau

157
STIEGLITZ'S MANSION
Krasnogo Flota Embankment, 66—68
1859—62. Architect A.Krakau

The mansion that had belonged to the baron, well-known banker and famous patron of arts A.L.Stieglitz and later—to

Grand Duke Pavel Aleksandrovich, stands out among the other buildings at the end of the Angliyskaya Embankment. Having acquired two lots on the most fashionable embankment of Petersburg Stieglitz gave orders to put up a large new mansion with the façade in Renaissance style. Krakau united two dwelling houses into a single whole. One of them was erected in 1716 and was the first stone building on the embankment. The architect made the mansion look like a monumental palazzo. It is a two-story building, and still is much higher than the neighboring

Vorontsov-Dashkov's house (No 153)

three-story building. The bottom story walls are deeply rusticated, and the plastering of the upper story imitates decor with trimmed stone.

The vestibule and white marble staircase are ornamented in Italian Baroque style. In the decor of the reception halls damask drapery, gilt stucco moulding and carving were used. The Big Reception Room is decorated with caryatides; in the concert hall sculptural portraits of composers are set in oval medallions. Designs for the painted panels *Four Seasons of the Year* were made by the famous Russian artist F.Bruni.

158
DEMIDOV'S HOUSE (GAUSCH'S HOUSE)
Krasnogo Flota Embankment, 74/2
1737—38. Architect M.Zemtsov

Rebuilt in 1826—38 and acquired classical appearance; the façade is orderless. Only the first and second story vaults have remained from the original interiors. In the early 20th century the house belonged to the artist L.Gausch.

The Bobrinsky Palace (No 159)

159
THE BOBRINSKY PALACE
Galernaya Street, 58—60
1790s. Architect L.Rusca. Interiors, 1822—25, architect A.Mikhailov the 2nd
Now a faculty of the Petersburg University

The layout of the area between Galernaya Street, and the Krustein and Admiralteisky Canals is characteristic of the city estate of the late 18th century. In front of the palace there was a front courtyard framed by out-buildings. The courtyard entrance from Galernaya Street is decorated with monumental gates with busts on pylons. On the Krustein Canal side a small garden adjoins the palace. The main building façades are more richly decorated. The wall separating the garden from the embankment is decorated

New Holland
(No 160)

with sculptures. On the corner of the wall a small garden pavilion was erected.

Artistically most interesting among the interiors are the main staircase, Red Reception Room, White and dancing halls. In the White Hall an excellent wall painting has remained, made supposedly by D.Scotti.

160
THE NEW HOLLAND
Moika Embankment, 103
1766—80. Architects S.Chevakinsky and J.-B.Vallin de la Mothe

The erection of the ensemble is due to the development of Petersburg as a shipbuilding center on the Baltic Sea. The small island that was long back, in Peter's times, called New Holland, was formed after the Admiralteisky and Kriukov Canals had been dug. In 1732—40 the first wooden warehouses for storing timber for shipbuilding purposes were built here (architect I.Korobov). In 1765 Chevakinsky developed a new version of warehouses that was actually implemented. The façades and the monumental arch over the canal leading into the island's interior were designed by Vallin de la Mothe.

The construction of new warehouses went on till the late 1780s, but was not completed even then. The building on the Admiralteisky and Kriukov Canals banks was put up as late as 1848—49, due to the construction of a bridge over the Neva and improvements carried on the adjoining areas.

The Tuscanian columns of the magnificent portal, strictly classical in their proportions, are made of blocks of trimmed granite. The rusticated walls are characteristic for early Classicism. The architects manifested much skill in designing the spatial and façade composition of a building for utilitarian purposes.

161
THE POTSELUYEV BRIDGE
over the Moika to Glinka Street
1803—16. Architect Heste

It was built in place of a foot-bridge that had existed since 1738. The architectural image is made complete by four obelisks with lanterns on corbels. The bridge got its name from the tavern located nearly and owned by the merchant Potseluyev.

The bridge is 41.5m long and 23.5m wide.

162
THE YUSUPOV PALACE
Moika Embankment, 94
1760s. Architect J.-B.Vallin de la Mothe. Rebuilt in the 1830s, architect A.Mikhailov the 2nd

In 1760 another story was added to the original small two-story house and it was enlarged. The center of the main façade is marked out by a six-column portico that united the two lower stories; the third story remained an attic. In the course of the following reconstruction a wing was added to the old house parallel to the embankment; it contained gala halls of striking grandeur. The dancing hall and the White Columns Hall stand out especially for their beauty. The refined simplicity of the dancing hall, which is decorated with artificial marble, is in contrast with the lavish decoration of the White Columns Hall. The gilt chandeliers of delicate work made of papier-mache, sculptural insets and wall-painting enhance the architectural effect of the hall decorated with a colonnade. In the 1910s part of the ground floor rooms were redecorated by the architects A.Vaitens and A.Beloborodov, as well as the artists N.Tyrsa and V.Konashevich, who made use for the interior decorating motifs typical for Russian Classicism.

Since 1830 the palace was owned by Prince N.Yusupov, one of the richest men in Russia. On the night of December 17, 1916, the monarchist conspirators killed G.Rasputin here.

163
BARON A.FITTINHOFF'S HOUSE
Moika Embankment, 100
1856. Architect K.Anderson

Teatralnaya (Theater) Square

In the middle of the 18th century the spacious vacant land adjoining the Kriukov Canal was called Karuselnaya (Roundabout) Square. Entertaining performances were often arranged here. On the painted scaffoldings comedians performed, and behind the show-booths there spread a row of roundabouts and swings.

In 1777—83 a theater building was erected in Karuselnaya Square to a design by the theater artist L.Tischbein by the architect F.V. von Baur and military engineer M.Dedenev. The Bolshoi (Big) or Kamenny (Stone) Theater, as it was sometimes called, was designed for

Fittinhofs house (No 163)

performing comedies, tragedies, operas, concerts and masquerades. For a long time it was the largest theater building not only in Russia, but in Europe as well. Until the middle of the 19th century the Imperial Court Company had performed here. The theater stage saw the first nights of the operas *Ivan Susanin* by M.Glinka (1836) and *Ruslan and Liudmila* (1842). In 1891—96 the present building of the Conservatoire was put up in place of the dismantled theater, which was the first musical educational establishment in Russia, founded by A.Rubinstein in 1862.

In the 1820s Karuselnaya Square was renamed Teatralnaya Square. Opposite the Conservatoire there is the Mariinsky Opera and Ballet Theater opened in 1860.

In Teatralnaya Square, to commemorate different periods of Russian musical history, monuments to two great Russian composers were erected—to M.Glinka and N.Rimsky-Korsakov.

164
THE MARIINSKY THEATER
Teatralnaya Square, 1

1859. Architect A.Kavos. Rebuilt in 1883—96, architect V.Schreter

165
THE RIMSKY-KORSAKOV CONSERVATOIRE
Teatralnaya Square, 3

1891—96. Architect V.Nicol

166
THE MONUMENT TO M.GLINKA
Teatralnaya Square

1906. Sculptor R.Bach. Architect A.Bach
THE MONUMENT TO N.RIMSKY-KORSAKOV
Teatralnaya Square

1952. Sculptors V.Ingal and V.Bogoliubov

The Mariinsky Theater (No 164)

The St. Nicholas' Navy Cathedral
(No 167)

167
THE ST.NICHOLAS NAVAL CATHEDRAL
Nikolskaya (Nicholas) Square
1753—62. Architect S.Chevakinsky

The five-domed two-story cathedral decorated with clusters of columns and numerous sculptures placed on high pedestals, is one of the best architectural monuments of Petersburg.

Into the decorative design of the façades Chevakinsky introduced a new motif never used by his contemporaries and borrowed from old Russian architecture: all protruding corners of the building are provided with three-column clusters, the central column set at the very corner, contrary to all architectural canons. The wide expressive entembleture belt also serves the same purpose—to enhance the decorative effect of the façades. In decorating the interior of the lower and upper churches Chevakinsky manifested exceptional capabilities and inventiveness. Architecturally he was most successful in designing the upper church; it is full of air and light and is remarkable for the iconostasis which is perfectly designed and carved, as well as for the canopy over the altar. The colonnade decorating the iconostasis is notable for its classical forms and proportions. The four-tier belfry standing separately on the canal bank is one of the best achievements in the Russian 18th-century architecture. The three bottom tiers of the belfry are decorated with columns, whereas the upper tier is designed as a drum topped with a small cupola and a thin graceful spire.

In the composition of the belfry the architect made use of the contrast between the concave wall surface of the bottom tiers and the two upper tiers which are circular in plan. The belfry gives an impression of being part of the canal perspective and its embankments.

When putting up the cathedral Chevakinsky also manifested his great capabilities as an urban designer. He erected the building on the axis of a large thoroughfare. The cathedral closes the Glinka Street perspective and dominates in the ensemble of the square, limited by the embankments of the two canals crossing it at a right angle.

168
THE NIKOLSKY MARKET
Sadovaya Street, 62
Architect unknown

169
THE PALACE
OF GRAND DUKE ALEKSEI ALEKSANDROVICH
Moika Embankment, 122
1880s. Architect M.Messmacher
Now the building of the Institute of Russian Literature (the Pushkin House)

A large territory on the corner of Angliysky (English) Prospekt (Maklin Prospekt) and the Moika Embankment remained vacant as long as the 1840s. In the 1840s a small stone house was put up here that in the 1880s became a property of Admiral-General Aleksei Aleksandrovich, brother of Alexander III. After that the house was drastically rebuilt. The main building that has an asymmetrical layout, a picturesque outline with turrets and is lavishly decorated (which is characteristic of eclecticism), is placed at the back of the front courtyard. In his desire to enrich the exterior Messmacher introduced rectangular, oval and semicircular windows with lintels of different design, decorative columns and pilasters, balustrade with sculptural busts, etc. The front courtyard is separated from the embankment by a metal wrought-iron fence with monograms. The gates are decorated with wrought-iron lanterns, windows and balconies have open-work railings.

The interiors vary in style; the dining room with an enormous fireplace to a design by Adamson and the study upholstered with leather are designed in English Renaissance style, the walls and plafond in the next hall—in Rococo style.

The construction of the new palace with outbuildings, stables and a spacious garden gave rise to a new Alexeyevskaya Street (now Pisarev Street) that connected the Moika Embankment with Dekabristov Street.

Kolomna

The name originated in the first half of the 18th century. There are several versions concerning its origin: it could come from the settlers who had arrived from the Kolomenskoye settlement in the vicinity of Moscow; it might be the corrupted version for the «colony». The layout of the district was developed in the 1730s by P.Yeropkin. Up to the middle of the 19th century Kolomna had been the outskirts of Petersburg inhabited by petty clerks and merchants. It was mostly built up with apartment houses.

Turgeneva Square is the central point of Kolomna. In 1798—1812 the Church of Intercession was put up here to a design by V.Starov (has not remained); around it a square was formed that got the name of Pokrovskaya Square.

170
THE ALARCHIN BRIDGE
over the Griboyedov Canal along Maklina Prospekt
1780s

The bridge is made of stone, with wooden parts replaced with metal ones. In 1953 and 1969 the granite obelisks with lanterns were restored (architect A.Rotach).

The bridge is 35.3m long and 15.8m wide.

171
A DWELLING HOUSE
Griboyedov Canal Embankment, 71
1888. Architect P.Suzor

172
THE MALY (SMALL) KALINKIN BRIDGE
over the Griboyedov Canal along Sadovaya Street
1783. Engineer I.Borisov

A three-span bridge with stone piers. Made wider in 1907—8. In 1952 the lanterns were restored.
   The bridge is 23.3m long and 16.2m wide.

A dwelling house (No 171)

173
A DWELLING HOUSE
Fontanka Embankment, 159/9
1910—12. Architect A.Bubyr

174
THE EGYPTIAN (PALL) BRIDGE
over the Fontanka along Lermontovsky Prospekt
1825—26; 1955. Architects P.Areshev and V.Vasilkovsky

It is a suspension one-span bridge on chains. The columns were ornamented with Egyptian hieroglyphs. At the entrance cast-iron Sphinxes were set. In 1905 the bridge collapsed when a House Guards squadron was crossing it. After that a wooden bridge was erected in the vicinity of

The Egyptian Bridge (No 174)

Usachev Lane. In 1955 the present one-span metal bridge was built to a design by the architects P.Areshev and V.Vasilkovsky. The original figures of Sphinxes were installed, as well as new obelisks with lanterns.
The bridge is 65.6m long and 27m wide.

175

THE STARO-KALINKIN (OLD KALINKIN) BRIDGE
over the Fontanka along Staro-Peterhofsky Prospekt
1785—87

It is one of the two stone bridges over the Fontanka (the other one being the Lomonosov Bridge) that have retained their original appearance. The bridge was partly reconstructed in 1792—93. The stone towers designed for fastening the chains and bridge raising were preserved for purely decorative purposes. Architecturally the Staro-Kalinkin Bridge is one of the finest in the city and testifies to the high level of bridge-building in the 18th-century Russia. The bridge is 65.6m long and 30m wide.

The Priazhka River

Left tributary of the Moika

Up to 1753 had borne the name of the Chukhonskaya river. The name of the area—Priazhka—from *priast* (to spin) comes from the spinning mills that were located in Kolomna. Construction on the river banks started in the late 18th century.

176

A ROOMING-HOUSE
Priazka Embankment, 34b
1904—5. Architect A.Uspensky

177

A ROOMING-HOUSE
Priazhka Embankment, 40
1910—11. Architect V.Fridlein

178

SUKHANOVA'S HOUSE
Priazhka Embankment, 50

179
A ROOMING-HOUSE
Priazhka Embankment, 66
1896. Architect V.Rozinsky

A rooming house (No 176)

180
A.BLOK'S MEMORIAL MUSEUM
Dekabristov Street, 57

A.Blok liked this remote city district. He spent the last nine years of his life here (from 1917 until 1921). First he occupied an apartment on the third floor; in 1920 he moved into an apartment on the first floor.

It was in this house that the poet worked on his *Punishment*, the poems *The Scythians* and *The Twelve* were also written here.

In 1980 a museum was opened here to commemorate his 100th birthday anniversary.

«LITEINY» PART OF THE CITY
Between the Fontanka,
Obvodny Canal and Moscovsky Prospekt

The Kutuzov Embankment

The Kutuzov Embankment (formerly Gagarinskaya, later Frantsuzskaya (French) continues the Palace Embankment as far as the Liteiny Bridge and resembles it in appearance. The granite parapets alternate with curved descents to the water. Its construction began in 1764. The embankment took its present shape in the second half of the 19th century, when most of the houses were rebuilt.

181
THE PRACHECHNY BRIDGE
over the Fontanka from the Dvortsovaya Embankment
to the Kutuzova Embankment
1766—79. Engineer T.Nasonov

The bridge got its name from the neighboring Laundries of the Court. It is a three-span stone bridge, one of the first bridges in Peterburg. It forms a single ensemble with the Verkhne-Lebiazhy Bridge over the Lebiazhya Kanavka and the Summer Palace railing.

The Prachechny Bridge (No 181)

182
BAUR'S HOUSE
Kutuzova Embankment, 36
1781—84. Architect Yu.Velten

A typical 18th-century house. When it was put up the
embankment did not yet exist, so the facade protrudes
beyond the street frontline.

183
THE KUSHELEV-BEZBORODKO MANSIONS
Gagarinskaya Street, 1/24, 3
1857—58.   Architect   R.Heinrichsen.   1840s.   Architect
G.Bosse. 1857—62. Architect E.Schmidt

The   two   mansions   located   at   the   beginning   of
Gagarinskaya Street form a sort of microensemble. They
had   formerly   belonged   to   brothers,   Counts   G.   and
N.Kushelev-Bezborodko.   They   were   sons   of   Alexander
Andreyevich   Bezborodko,   an   influencial   high   official
under Catherine II. The house of Grigory Alexandrovich
is   facing   the   Kutuzova   Embankment.   During   the
reconstruction   by   R.Heinrichsen   the   three-story   house
retained its classical proportions. The facade, however,
was redecorated in the style typical of the 19th-century
Petersburg   Neo-Renaissance;   the   first   story   was
rusticated, the second and third ones acquired pilasters;
whereas   the   second   story   housing   reception   halls   was
ornamented with sculptural bas-reliefs.

The   mansion   of   Nikolai   Alexandrovich   was   also
designed   in   the   Renaissance   style.   The   semicircular
windows on the first floor have order pillars separating
them; those on the upper floor have germs. The side wings
are set back at the upper floor level to give place to open
terraces and accentuate the central volume of the building.
The façade is clad with Ruscol marble almost all over. This
was a unique case in the architecture of Petersburg; almost
overall marble facing of the façades was only used in the
Marble Palace and St.Isaac's Cathedral.

Some   ornamental   forms   (lion   masks,   pilaster   capitals,
entrance   gate)   were   made   of   cast   iron.   The   interior
decoration that has in part remained is rather exquisite; it
combines different styles and includes numerous caryatides,
stucco moulding, carved oak, stamped leather, etc.

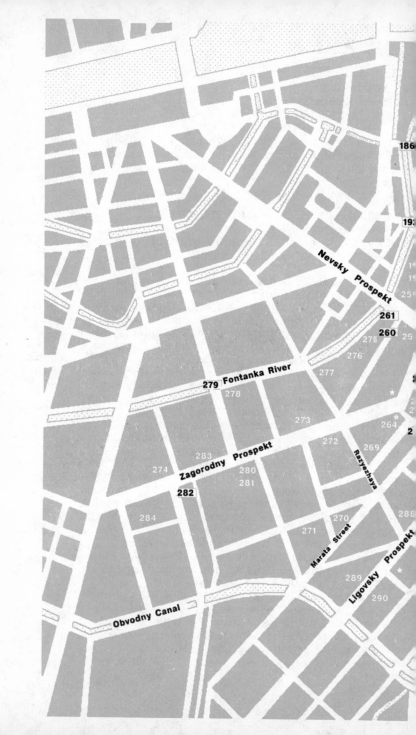

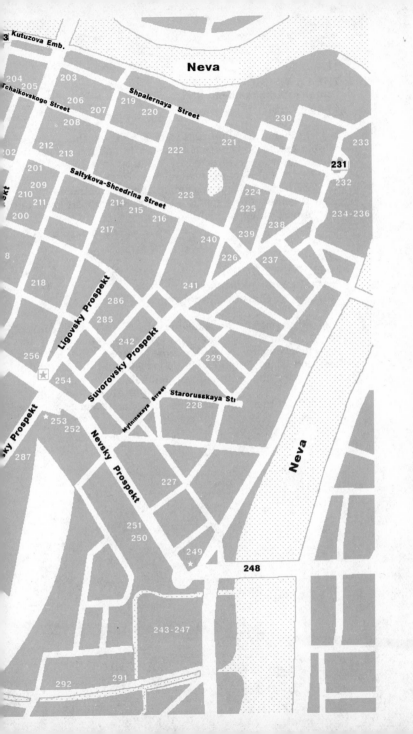

184
THE LAW SCHOOL
Fontanka Embankment, 6
1780s. Architect unknown

In 1835 the building was redesigned by the architect
A.Melnikov to house a school; in 1836 and the 1840s the
interiors were reconstructed by V.Stasov; in 1893—95 and
1909—10 considerable alterations were introduced into
the façade by P.Suzor (including the new entrance in the
portico center, the stepped attic and the cupolas over the
central part of the façade).

185
MIZHUYEV'S HOUSE
Fontanka Embankment, 26
1804—6. Architect A.Zakharov

This is an interesting example of an early 19th-century
block of flats. The plot takes up the space from the
Fontanka and up to the Mokhovaya Street. The façade is
designed in the Empire style. Alongside with the traditional
portico carrying a triangular pediment, the building has
symmetrical tripartite windows on the upper floors and a
rounded corner, which is a new motif in the civic

Baur's house (No 182)

The Panteleimonovsky Bridge (No 186)

architecture of the period. The layout of the interiors running along the embankment is typical for the 19th-century dwelling houses, with the reception halls opening on the street and the less important rooms overlooking the courtyard.

186

THE PANTELEIMONOVSKY BRIDGE
over Fontanka to Panteleimonovskaya Street

1907—14. Engineer A.Pshenitsky, architect L.Ilyin. In the 1950s the standard lamps were restored—architect A.Rotach

The first wooden bridge on piles was erected in the 1780s; in 1823—24 it was replaced by a suspension chain bridge to a design of the engineer G.Traitteur. It was the first suspension bridge to be erected in Petersburg (further came the Egyptian, Bank and Lion Bridges). Traitteur designed open-work cast-iron pylons that went very well with the graceful outline of the chains; the whole exquisite silhouette of the Panteleimonovsky Bridge supported Traitteur's idea that «chain bridges possess such lightness and elegance which cannot be attained in other construction systems».

In 1905, after the Egyptian Bridge had collapsed, the

Panteleimonovsky Bridge was dismantled for safety reasons; three years later a new bridge was erected, that has remained till now and proved to be as elegant as its predecessor, though built in another style. Its decoration was completed in 1910 in the classical traditions of the bridges built «under the supervision of C.Rossi». The author, architect L.Ilyin, made use of classical motifs— palmettes, lion masks, sheilds, etc. The Panteleimonovsky Bridge is a good contribution to the ensemble of bridges, big and small, in the vicinity of the Engineers' Castle, Summer Gardens and Field of Mars.

187
THE PARTIKULIARNAYA (CIVIL) SHIPYARD (SOLIANOI GORODOK)
On the left Fontanka bank, opposite the Summer Gardens, between Panteleimonovskaya and Gangutskaya Streets and Solianoi (Salt) Lane
1715—22. Architects G.Mattarnovi (up to 1719), N.Herbel and D.Trezzini

In the shipyard small craft were constructed for *particularny* (civil) purposes. On the territory barracks, offices, and a drugstore were located, as well as stone tar-works put up by D.Trezzini. Of the 18th-century buildings only St.Panteleimon's Church has remained. In the 1760s— 1780s the so-called Solianoi Gorodok (Salt City) was formed here, based on salt- and wine-stores. In the 1870s different civic buildings were put up, the most well known being Baron A.Stieglitz School of Technical Drawing and the Museum.

188
ST.PANTELEIMON'S CHURCH
Solianoi Lane, 17
1735—39. Architect I.Korobov

St.Panteleimon's Church was designed to commemorate the glory of the Russian fleet. St.Panteleimon's commemoration day coincided with the dates of the two major naval victories of Russia in the Northern War—the Battle at Gangut (Hanko; 1714) and at Grengam (1720). In both battles only rowing ships took part that were mostly built at the Particuliarny Shipyard. In the early 20th century memorial plaques were placed on the church façade listing all the army units that took part in the battle at Gangut.

The church building is a typical sample of the so-called «Baroque of Annesperiod». Characteristic of the style are bright, two-color buildings with an intricate outline, high roofs and pediments of sophisticated design, flat-looking façades with figured window framings and pilasters in piers. Churches in those times had the so-called «ship-like» layout: the belfry, the main domed part and the connecting refectory were arranged along one long axis. The tiered belfry was typically topped with a spire, whereas the faceted dome with a lantern was supported by a bulky octahedral drum.

The memorial church has generally retained its original shape, though some alterations were introduced with time. The interior decoration and marble bas-reliefs on the facade were done in the 19th century (sculptor A.Loganovsky).

189
THE CENTRAL SCHOOL OF TECHNICAL DRAWING
1879—81. Architect A.Krakau, R.Gedike
MUSEUM OF BARON STIEGLITZ
1885—95. Architect M.Messmacher
Solianoi Lane, 13, 15
Now the Mukhina Higher School of Arts and Industrial Design

Two buildings were put up on the territory of the former Solianoi City to house the school and museum established in Petersburg by Baron A.Stieglitz. The building of the museum of applied arts designed for teaching purposes was put up by the first Director of the School, Professor of Architecture M.Messmacher. The museum has something in common with St.Mark's Library in Venice in its appearance. Due to the relatively small size of the plot it has a very compact layout, with two little courtyards for lighting purposes. Most part of the building is taken up by an exhibition hall (its area exceeding 1 thousand square meters), spanned by a glass dome. Two-tier arcades run along the perimeter of the hall, which imitates an Italian palazzo of the Renaissance. The composition of the museum collection influenced its interior layout. On the ground floor the objects of Byzantine, Gothic, Italian and Old Russian art were exhibited; the first floor housed the Venetian Hall, Raphael's Hall and Loggias, works of French, English and Flemish art. The interior of each hall was decorated in accordance with the style of the objects exhibited. Skillful craftsmanship and wealth of the interior decoration, that the students of the school contributed to as well, all make the museum one of the most interesting architectural samples of the late 19th century.

The building of the school proper has a more discreet design. The central part of the main façade with a small loggia at the second floor level juts out forcefully. Columns and walls are rusticated. Of most interest among the interior rooms is the reading hall ornamented with carving.

St. Panteleimon's Church (No 188)

A dwelling house (No 190)

190
A DWELLING HOUSE
Panteleimonovskaya Street, 7
1911—13. Architect M.Lialevich

191
RATKOV-ROZHNOV'S HOUSE
Panteleimonovskaya Street, 13—15
1898—1900. Architect P.Suzor

Ratkov-Rozhnov's house stands out among the undistinguished buildings in Panteleimonovskaya Street for its size, high monumental arch, the show-windows in the lower stories and a vista of bay-windows. It was put up in the late 19th century for the great house-owner and city mayor V.Ratkov-Rozhnov. When working on the design Suzor manifested his talent of a bold innovator. He enlarged the traditional arch leading into the courtyard until it reached immense proportions, cutting through the façades it goes up to the third floor level. In this way he managed to link the courtyard space with that of the street, breaking the tradition of contraposing the inner courtyard to the main façade that was characteristic of the Petersburg architecture. The façades facing the yard are as rich in decoration as the main one, overlooking the street; while the bay-windows stretching into the back of the yard create an impressive vista opening up through the arch. Stylistically the building is a typical sample of Suzor's work. The architect applied horizontal rustic-work to the lower part of the building, thus emphasizing its solidness; he also introduced massive rectangular bay-windows, thus creating an expressive rhythm of volumes in the street's perspective, as well as decorative figured pediments enlivening the building's outline. Ratkov-Rozhnov's house accumulates in a way the achievements of the 19th-century eclecticism and predicts architectural innovations of the coming century.

192
THE BELINSKY BRIDGE
over Fontanka to Belinsky Street

This is one of the seven similar tower bridges over the Fontanka, of which two have remained. Rebuilt in 1859. All superstructures have been pulled down to make space for the traffic.
The bridge is 59m long and 19.1m wide.

193

THE CHURCH OF STS SIMEON AND ANNE
Mokhovaya Street, 46

1731—34. Architect M.Zemtsov. Rebuilt in 1869—72. Architect G.Winterhalter

This is one of few remaining samples of the early 18th-century architecture in Petersburg. However, not only 18th-century features can be traced in its forms, but Old-Russian compositional devices as well. The central volume topped with an octahedral drum is adjoined by a one-story refectory and a multi-tier belfry.

In the early 19th century a stone chapel was built on Mokhovaya Street corner, and a vestry was attached to the northern church wall.

194

THE SHEREMETEV PALACE
Fontanka Embankment, 34

1750—55. Architects S.Chevakinsky and F.Argunov

This spacious lot on the Fontanka bank, not far from Nevsky Prospekt, was in 1712 granted to Field Marshal Sheremetev by Peter I. Sheremetev built a small wooden house here, on whose site in the 1730s—1740s a large stone palace was erected.

The Sheremetev Palace, called the Fountain House, combines in its design characteristics of all periods in the construction of Petersburg, ranging from Peter's times and up to the early 20th century. Each period coincided with the interior reconstructions to suit the tastes of new owners and the current fashion.

In terms of its layout and general composition Sheremetiev's residence was close to other estate palaces put up on the Fontanka banks in the 18th century. The palace was erected at the back of the plot, its main façade facing the river. Beyond the palace there was a regular garden that spread as far as Liteiny Prospekt. In the garden a grotto, the Hermitage pavilion and summer-houses were built (architect F.Argunov) that have not survived.

Later Chevakinsky added one more story to the palace. Outwardly it combines some features of the architecture of the Peter I period (well-balanced and distinct segmentation, flattened façade decoration) with Baroque elements that are easily traced in the stucco moulding (sculptured heads, capitals of intricate design ornamented with lion masks and decorative compositions).

Interior reception halls located on the first floor in suites running along the main and garden façades underwent

The Sheremetev Palace (No 194)

many reconstructions. Such famous architects of the period as I.Starov, G.Quarenghi, A.Voronikhin took part in the design development. In 1837—40 interior decoration was altered by the architect I.Corsini. To his design an openwork cast-iron fence was put up in front of the building. In 1867 a one-story outbuilding was erected in the front courtyard provided with gates decorated with the coat-of-arms of Counts Sheremetevs (architect N.Benois). In the early 1910s the grotto and gates overlooking Liteiny Prospekt were pulled down; some rooming houses and shops were built on the site instead.

The Fountain House had for almost two centuries belonged to the Sheremetev family. And all the time it had been one of the cultural centers of Petersburg; the names and lives of many prominent men were linked with the house. At different time it was visited by V.Zhukovsky, A.Turgenev, M.Glinka, A.Pushkin, O.Kiprensky, M.Balakirev and others. It was here that the famous serf actress P.Zhemchugova was performing before Emperor Paul I; later she became Count N.Sheremetyev's wife. Besides, in the late 19th century the palace used to house the Old Russian Writing Fans Society, of which many well-known historians, linguists and philosophers were members.

In 1918 Count S.Sheremetev, the last owner of the palace, handed the building and its abundant collections over to the Soviet authorities. The Museum of Everyday Life was opened there that existed till 1931. Later the palace housed the Institute for Arctic Studies.

In 1990 the palace was handed over to the Museum of Performing Arts.

It should be noted that the Fountain House story is also linked with the name of A.Akhmatova. For many years she used to live in the former garden outbuilding, where in 1989 a memorial museum was opened.

195
THE CATHERINE BOARDING SCHOOL
FOR YOUNG LADIES OF NOBLE BIRTH
Fontanka Embankment, 36
1804—7. Architect G.Quarenghi
Now the Department of the Russian National Library

In the 18th century the Italian Palace was located on the site, that was in the 1800s transferred into the possession of the Catherine Boarding School for Young Ladies of Noble Birth, for the daughters of gentlemen by birth to be educated there. A new building, the present one, was put up on the site to house the Boarding School; it was designed in classical forms and stood out for its clear and simple outline. The main building is adjoined by two protruding wings (partly reconstructed by the architect D.Quadri in 1823—25). The central part is decorated with an arched risalit and an eight-column portico. Two ramps are approaching it.

Interior decoration is also marked for its simplicity; the main entrance hall was linked to a wide corridor, with classrooms on both sides of it. The left-hand wing housed a large two-tier hall with wooden columns, stuccoed and painted.

The Yekaterininsky Boarding School (No 195)

Liteiny Prospekt

Formation of the so-called Liteiny (Foundry) part of the prospekt is linked with the establishment of the Ordnance Department (early 18th century) and laying of the foundry on the left Neva bank, close to the present Liteiny Bridge (1711); next to the foundry houses for workers were built. Liteiny Street (later Prospekt) became the main one in the settlement, its one end set against the foundry itself, the other one reaching Nevsky Prospekt. In the 1850s the foundry was demolished, which made it possible to extend the prospekt as far as the Neva; the pontoon bridge was transferred here to link the prospekt to the Vyborgsky District. The overall lenght of Liteiny Prospekt is over 1.5km. Architecturally it took shape mostly in the second half of the 19th century and stands out for the variety of styles. Liteiny is approached by Shpalernaya (Tapestry) Street (called so because tapestry used to be manufactured here), Zakharievskaya, Tchaikovskogo, Furshtatskaya, Saltykova-Shchedrina (former Kirochnaya), Nekrasova (former Basseinaya), Belinskogo (former Simeonovskaya) and Zhukovskogo streets. All the streets, as well as the prospekt were being built up intensively in the 19th century with mansions and apartment houses.

196
«THE NEW PASSAGE»
Liteiny Prospekt, 57
1912. Architect N.Vasilyev
Now a book-shop and an exhibition hall

This long two-story building with portals and piers faced with gray granite, and large show-windows was designed in Art-Nouveau style popular in the early 20th-century architecture. In the construction ferro-concrete beams, pillars and ribbed floors were used.

197

THE MARIINSKAYA HOSPITAL
Liteiny Prospekt, 56
1803—5. Architect G.Quarenghi

The hospital building is located on the territory of the Italian Garden that was laid out in the early 18th century and had belonged to the tsar's family. The garden took up a large plot that spread from the Fontanka Embankment up to the Znamenskaya Street.

In 1803—5 a hospital was put up here to commemorate the 100th city anniversary, that got the name of Mariinskaya Hospital. It takes up a large territory and includes several buildings. The main building and the side wings face Liteiny Prospekt. A monumental cast-iron fence separates the front courtyard from the prospekt.

The hospital building is designed in austere, laconic, characteristically classical forms. The elongated main building approached by two ramps is decorated with an eight-column portico.

Interior layout is simple and rational, corresponding to the purpose of the building.

198
YUSUPOVA'S MANSION
Liteiny Prospekt, 42
1852—58. Architect L.Bonstedt
Now the Lecture Hall of the Znaniye (Knowledge) Society

The mansion of Duchess Z.Yusupova is one of the most notable works by L.Bonstedt. The architect strived to attain originality and freshness in the façade design. The decoration is an obvious imitation of the early 18th-century German and Austrian Baroque motifs. It is notable for the abundance of somewhat heavy decorative elements. Of special interest is the fact that the façade is clad all over with Bremen limestone brought from Germany. Such overall facing is a rare case in Petersburg. Only very rich owners could afford it. Architectural works of such sort were considered most fashionable and luxurious. When writing about the newly built mansion contemporaries noted with admiration the «grand forms and proportions between the parts and the whole... combined with the latest approach to the antique style. The mat, whitish coloring of the walls, the interplay of light and shade in sunny weather and artful performance of all architectural details all add to the grandeur of the design». The interiors decorated with artificial marble, stucco moulding, gilding and painting were noted for the same grandeur (ceiling painting, medallions designed by the artists N.Maikov, K.Paul; stucco moulding by T.Dylev, and the rich sculptural decor performed in Triscorni's workshop).

In the 1900s the building housed the Theater Club where A.Block used read his poems; in 1908—31 the Distorting Mirror Theater performed here, and in 1949 it was handed over to the Znaniye Society.

199
PASHKOV'S HOUSE
(the House of the Apanage Department)
Liteiny Prospekt, 39
1841—44. Architect G.Bosse

In 1848 the house was bought by Count A.Orlov, Head of the Gendarmery, and was in 1857 sold to the Apanage Department. The house was partly rebuilt by the architect A.Rezanov.

In the façade composition he departs from Classicism—although the lintels design and the portico marking the central part of the façade do go back to the classical canons. However, the shape of the portico, rusticated walls and powerful entablature are the manifestation of a new stylistic device, strange to Russian Classicism and going back to Italian Renaissance. Most part of the walls was left unstuccoed. It was a new architectural device consciously used by the author. The natural texture of red brickwork was set off by the stuccoed elements and the granite of the socle. Pashkov's house was the first among the Petersburg mansions where bare brickwork was used. It was a rational innovation, beginning of the «brick style», which came to be widely used in the late 19th-century architecture.

After 1917 the mansion housed various offices. It is this building that is spoken about in the famous poem by N.Nekrasov *Reflections at the Main Entrance*. A bust of Nekrasov was put up in the public garden near the house (1922, sculptor V.Lishev).

200
THE NEKRASOV HOUSE
Liteiny Prospekt, 36
1781—82. A story added in 1858. Architect unknown

In this house N.Nekrasov, the famous Russian poet, lived from 1857 up to 1877, as well as A.Dobroliubov (in 1858—59). During the twenty years Nekrasov's flat in Liteiny Prospekt used to be the center of Russian democratic literature. It housed the editorial offices of two prominent magazines: *Sovremennik* (Contemporary), and *Otechestvennyie Zapiski* (Notes of Fatherland, that succeeded the previous one after it was closed down). One of Nekrasov's co-editors was Saltykov-Shchedrin, a prominent Russian satyrical writer. In 1946 a memorial museum was opened in Nekrasov's flat.

201
THE BUILDING OF THE FORMER
OFFICERS' ASSEMBLY
Liteiny Prospekt, 20
1895—98. Military engineers V.Gauder and A.Danchenko; works were supervised by the military engineer N.Smirnov
Now the House of Officers

The House of Officers building is an architectural monument of the late 19th century. In the façade decoration some elements of Old Russian architecture were used. The tent-like corner turret is one of the prominent points in Liteiny Prospekt panorama. The house has retained most of its rich interior decoration. Until 1917 the building had housed the Army and Naval Officers' Assembly, and until 1914 meetings of the members of the Military Knowledge Zealots Society took place there.

202
TUPIKOV'S HOUSE
Liteiny Prospekt, 21/14
Rebuilt in 1876. Architect Yu.Duten (?)
Now an apartment house

The house at the corner of Panteleimonovskaya Street and Liteiny Prospekt was rebuilt for merchant A.M.Tupikov in the eclectic style. All the decorative motifs for the façades were borrowed from ancient originals; however, considerable modifications were introduced. The façade is almost all over covered with horizontal rustic-work and an intricate ornament; false arcades include column supported by consoles in the shape of small dragons; the minor arcades in the upper part remind us of the Romanesque and the bay-windows having tent-like tops—of Old Russian architecture. Among the plastic elements the griffins are remarkable—they are holding heraldic shields with the warder of Mercury, God of Trade, on them. The bay-windows are topped with peacock figures, their tails spread, symbolizing home comforts and prosperity.

In 1918 the Kolos Publishers was opened in the building, and in 1919 the Free Philosophic Organization (Volphil) was established here. Among the founders were A.Blok and A.Bely, the poets, R.Ivanov-Razumnik and Ye.Lundberg, the critics, L.Shestov and A.Steinberg, the philosophers, the artist K.Petrov-Vodkin, stage manager V.Meyerhold and others. At the Volphil meetings, disputes and literary evenings were arranged; lectures were delivered by well-known philosophers, critics and authors. The Organization gave start to the people who were to become prominent in Russian literature. The school of philosophers existed till 1924. In 1926 the Kolos Publishers was closed down. In 1927—37 S.Marshak, a well-known children's author and poet lived in the house.

203
AN ADMINISTRATIVE BUILDING
Liteiny Prospekt, 4
1931—32. Architects A.Gegello, N.Trotsky, A.Ol and others

204
KOKOSHKIN'S HOUSE
Tchaikovskogo Street, 4
The first quarters of the 19th century. Architect unknown

This is a sample of a small dwelling house of the early 19th century. Remarkable are the columns at the corner; this is a device used in Russian classical architecture to decorate buildings standing at the crossroads. Inside, of interest is the design of the main staircase spanned with a wooden dome and ornamented with pilasters. The light comes from above, through a window in the dome.

205
BUTURLINA'S MANSION
Tchaikovskogo Street, 10
1857—60. Architect G.Bosse

Buturlina's house erected in the Neo-Baroque style plays an important part in the urban design as it anchors up the vista of Mokhovaya Street. The «second Baroque» architecture came to be one of the most widespread in Petersburg and its suburbs in the middle of the 19th century.

Most popular were stylizations imitating Rastrelli, Chevakinsky and their contemporaries. Buturlina's mansion is one of the best examples of such style. The central part of the façade topped with a semicircular pediment is somewhat set back. At the first floor level there is an open terrace with an open-work fence. In façade decoration Bosse made wide use of sculpture, plastic elements, pilasters and columns.

206
KELCH'S MANSION
Tchaikovskogo Street, 28

1896—1903. Architect V.Schene and V.Chagin, with the assistance of K.Schmidt

The mansion of A.Kelch differs from other buildings in Tchaikovskogo Street. The lavish two-story facade is designed in French Renaissance style, whereas the three-story courtyard facade is made in the Gothic style. The facade overlooking the street is clad with pale yellow and pink limestone. The attic is topped with a high tent-like roof. The courtyard is architecturally no less important and complete than the street facade. It is anchored up with an outbuilding that has marble sculpture put up its Gothic Pavilion. There is a Gothic arch over the courtyard entrance; the courtyard facades of the main building are designed in the same style.

The interiors stand out for their lavish and fanciful decoration including sculpture, carving, stucco moulding, painted insets in Watteau style that fill up the whole wall and ceiling space. Alongside with the Renaissance and Gothic elements Rococo motifs were used.

207
KOCHUBEI'S HOUSE
Tchaikovskogo Street, 30

1844. Architect R.Kuzmin. 1845—46. Architect G.Bosse
Now the administrative center of Dzerzhinsky District

The facade is performed in Italian Renaissance style; it has wide archways, the ground floor walls are rusticated, while the first floor windows are arranged pairwise and enveloped by wide arches from above. The facade is complete with a massive cornice typical of the 14th—15th century Italian architecture.

The one-story gallery adjacent to the main building was used as a winter garden and designed in neo-Renaissance style as well.

Outwardly, the building is quite simple, which runs contrary to the lavish interior decoration. The facade is clad with Pudost limestone.

After the house was in the 1880s taken over by a prominent manufacturer Yu.Nechayev-Maltsev it was redecorated by the architect L.Benois.

Among the remaining interiors noteworthy is the big concert hall; its walls, ceiling and the scene portal are ornamented with Rococo stucco moulding of exquisite design. The ceiling painting depicting Aurora was done by the artist G.Semiradsky.

208
KOCHUBEI'S HOUSE
Fuhrstadtskaya Street, 24
1908—9. Architect R.Melzer
Now a children's polyclinics

The house of Prince V.Kochubei, designed in Art-Nouveau style, is one of the most typical works by Melzer, one of the adherents of this style. He was quite original in his treatment of the main façade, providing it with three risalits. The right-hand risalit is cut through by an archway up to the second floor level and decorated with a metal lantern in the vault. Art-Nouveau decorative motifs are widely used in the façade design; they include wall facing of white ceramic tiles, figured metal lattices and majolica panels depicting garlands and flower baskets. The outbuildings, likewise faced with ceramic tiles, form a closed courtyard with a small garden.

209
SPASO-PREOBRAZHENSKY (TRANSFIGURATION) CATHEDRAL
Preobrazhenskaya Square, 1
1827—29. Architect V.Stasov

The story of the cathedral is linked with one of the oldest army units in Russia—the Life Guards of the Preobrazhensky Regiment formed in 1687 by Peter I. In the early 18th century the regiment was quartered on the site of the present square. It was here that in 1741 the regiment took the oath of fidelity to Elizabeth, daughter of Peter I. To commemorate this event and express her gratitude to the loyal Guards she ordered to put up a large stone church on the site in the name of Our Lord's Transfiguration.

Construction works were started in 1743 by the architect M.Zemtsov and finished in 1754 by D.Trezzini.

This was the first five-dome church in the capital. In the early 19th century it was awarded with the honorary name of the Cathedral of the Whole Guard Corps. After the fire of 1825 it was decided to restore the cathedral imparting it

Spaso-Preobrazhensky Cathedral (No 209)

a monumental air characteristic of high Classicism. The cathedral was reconstructed by V.Stasov. The closely grouped central and side domes are rising above the main volume of the church, imparting it an austere and magnificent appearance. The western façade with its four-column portico is especially impressive. Overlooking Panteleimonovskaya Street, it contributes to the grandeur of the vista. The carved wooden iconostasis and the altar canopy were made to a design by V.Stasov, and the icons were pained by V.Shebuyev, A.Yegorov and A.Ivanov.

Completion of the restoration works coincided with the victorious end of the Russian-Turkish War (1828—29). To commemorate this event the cathedral was surrounded with a fence made of the barrels of captured Turkish guns linked by chains. Up to 1917 the Transfiguration Cathedral was a kind of a museum devoted to the victories of the Preobrazhensky Regiment, that was considered the leading one among the imperial troops. Various trophies, regiment relics and banners were kept here. However, after the revolution all the relics were removed from the cathedral. At present one of the sacred relics of Old Petersburg is kept here—the icon of Our Savior; according to the legend, it was this icon that Peter I had used to bless the foundation of the city.

210
MURUSI'S HOUSE
Liteiny Prospekt, 24/27
1874—76. Architects A.Serebryakov, P.Shestov
Now an apartment house

This great apartment house was originally built for Prince Murusi. The bulky five-story edifice has three equally imposing façades, and its silhouette with protruding bay-windows and high roofs dominates the neighboring houses.

Murusi's house is one of the unique samples of application of Moresque motifs in the decoration of a house. Though the façade decoration includes lots of eastern architectural elements, in terms of its layout and composition it is a typical apartment house of the eclectic style. While the façades were designed in Moresque style, the interiors were mostly decorated in Rococo style. Decoration in the reception rooms of the first and second floors includes gilt stucco moulding, sculpture, ceiling painting, damask wall upholstering, carved marble and oak panels. The first floor was occupied by the owner of the house, A.Murusi. The house had a winter garden, a fountain, water heating system, running water supply; all main staircases were decorated with mirrors, clocks and carpets. In 1890 the house was taken over by O.Rein.

In Murusi's house many prominent representatives of Russian intelligentsia rented flats, among them were philosophers and men of letters, lawyers and economists, military men and scholars.

From 1899 up to 1913 the flat on the fourth, and later on the second floor, was rented by D.Merezhkovsky and Z.Gippius. The Merezhkovsky's salon was one of the major cultural centers of Petersburg at the period. It was frequented by A.Blok, A.Bely and many famous poets. The salon was visited by the poet V.Pyast, who lived in the same house, as well as other poets-symbolists and artists from the World of Art group and philosophers. Merezhkovsky

Murusi's house (No 210)

initiated the Religious and Philosophical Society (1902) there that brought together writers, artists, philosophers, public leaders and the clergy. In 1911 the Poets' Workshop circle used to hold its meetings in Pyast's flat; it was a new literary circle headed by N.Gumiliov and S.Gorodetsky, that included young poets, A.Akhmatova, O.Mandelstam and V.Narbut among them.

After 1917 most part of the tenants moved elsewhere. In 1918 it was decided to accommodate a studio for young translators here. In the winter 1919 the studio moved into the House of Arts (Moika, 59), while in Murusi's house N.Gumiliov established the House of Poets (1921), which was a kind of a literary club. In August 1921 Gumiliov was arrested and executed, while most of the writers and poets left the country altogether.

In the 1920—1930s the house suffered considerable alterations: all the large flats and rooms were divided with partitions into smaller ones. Gradually all decoration was damaged or lost. However, the literary traditions remained. It was here that the outstanding poet, Nobel Prize winner, I.Brodsky had lived there for more than twenty years (1949—72), in apartment 28.

211

BULATOV'S HOUSE
Ryleyeva Street, 1
1807—15. Architect unknown. Left part was attached in 1838. Architect A.Gemilian

In 1877 the architect V.Lvov attached the House of the Society for Supporting the Poor (Spasskaya Street, 3—Artilleriysky Lane, 6) to Bulatov's house. In 1890 the architect N.Melnikov expanded the house along the lane and finally, in 1899 the architect V.Prussakov raised the house No 3 in Spasskaya Street introducing alterations into the façade. Such is the story of Bulatov's house throughout the last century.

212

THE LUTHERAN CHURCH OF ST.ANNE
Saltykova-Shchedrina Street, 8
1775—79. Architect Yu.Velten
Now the Spartak cinema-house

Most expressive is the northern façade facing the Fuhrstadtskaya Street, which was originally the main one. It is decorated with Ionic columns arranged in a loose semicircle. The building is topped with a spherical dome on a circular drum decorated with paired columns. By its composition and architectural forms the Church of St.Anne is close to the Armenian church in Nevsky Prospekt and the Lutheran Church of St.Catherine in Bolshoi Prospekt of Vasilyevsky Island. It is no wonder, because the both were designed by Yu.Velten.

213
AN APARTMENT HOUSE
Saltykova-Shchedrina Street, 6
1908—9. Architect Van der Guht

214
AN APARTMENT HOUSE
Saltykova-Shchedrina Street, 32—34
1899—1900. Architect P.Suzor

An apartment house
(No 213)

An apartment house
(No 214)

215
THE BARRACKS OF THE PREOBRAZHENSKY
REGIMENT
Saltykova-Shchedrina Street, 31—37
1802—7. Architect F.Volkov

When laying out and building up Petersburg in the 18th
century a problem arose concerned with the allocation of

the army quarters in the city. Barracks were put up to a standard design developed by Volkov in classical traditions.

The main place in the barrack complex is taken up by the former hospital building located at the back of the front courtyard. Due to its size the building becomes the structural center of the whole ensemble and anchors up Potiomkinskaya Street vista.

The whole complex is of architectural interest because it presents one of the first attempts made in Petersburg to built up a large city block according to a ready-made compositional design.

216
THE CLINICAL INSTITUTE
Saltykova-Shchedrina Street, 41
1878—85.   Architect   R.Gedike.   1896—8.   Architect P.Balinsky

217
MIASNIKOV'S HOUSE
Vosstaniya Street, 45
1857—59. Architect A.Gemilian

Typical sample of neo-Baroque style.

218
THE ROMAN-CATHOLIC CHURCH
OF THE FRENCH EMBASSY
Kovensky Lane, 7
1908—9. Architect L.Benois and M.Peretiatkovich

The building of the church was designed in the Middle Age architectural proportions. The main façade is clad with roughly hewn granite blocks. The façade design is asymmetrical: the two-tier tetrahedral bell-tower, being part of the main building, is perceived as a separate volume. On the opposite corner there is a similar small turret. The portal of the main entrance representing an arch with columns is rather impressive. The main church room is on the upper floor. It is decorated with Gothic columns; light comes from tall windows cut in the longitudinal walls.

219
THE CHURCH OF ALL THE MOURNFUL
Shpalernaya Street, 35a
1817—18. Architect L.Rusca

The church is of interest as a domed structure designed in Russian late-classical style. The main façade overlooking Shpalernaya Street is decorated with a six-column portico, the plain walls have sculptured reliefs over the windows. The spacious church hall represents a rotunda made up of artificial marble columns that are supporting the dome (20m in diameter).

220
THE BARRACKS AND MANÈGE OF THE HORSE GUARDS REGIMENT
Shpalernaya Street, 41/43
1800—6. Architect L.Rusca

In the barrack complex of interest is the main building located in Shpalernaya Street. The interior layout and outward appearance of this strictly symmetrical building are characteristic of classical architecture. The façade is decorated with a powerful eight-column portico supported by the ground floor arcade. On both sides of it are the statues of Mars and Belonna, his spouse.

The complex also includes the former manège; its façade ornamented with paired rusticated columns overlooks Potiomkinskaya Street.

221
THE TAVRICHESKY (TAURIDA) PALACE
Shpalernaya Street, 47
1783—89. Architect I.Starov

The palace was put up by Catherine II for her favorite, Prince G.Potiomkin-Tavrichesky, in strictly classical style. The composition is markedly clear and simple. The two-story building is topped with a flat dome in the center, supported by a low drum; one-story galleries are linking it with the two-story side wings. The main entrance is marked with a monumental six-column portico. Plain walls, devoid

of any decoration are cut through by tall windows. A low
fence separates the front courtyard from the street; it was
put up in 1792—93 to a design by the architect F.Volkov.
Refined discreetness and simplicity of the façades was in
sharp contrast with the grandeur of interior decoration. The
palace was designed for holding lavish receptions.
Especially impressive is the rotunda generously ornamented
with stucco moulding, that follows the main entrance-hall
and is joined to the White Column Hall by means of a wide

The Taurida Palace (No 221)

doorway. The hall was followed by a winter garden, an open
double colonnade separating them; in 1906 the garden was
turned into a sitting hall of the State Düma (Council).
Reception room, the Picture Hall, the Gobelin Sitting Room,
the Chinese Hall have partly retained their authentic
decoration. Originally the Taurida Palace had overlooked
the Neva; there had been a canal running from the palace
to the river and ending in a harbor, that had existed till the
middle of the 19th century. Beyond the palace a spacious

landscape garden was laid out, while the newly-laid Tavricheskaya and Potiomkinskaya (Potiomkin) Streets confine the ensemble in the east and west.

After Potiomkin's death the palace was taken over by the Treasury and became one of the favorite places of residence of Catherine II. During the reign of Paul I the palace was turned into the barracks of the Horse Guards Regiment, and all the belongings were removed to the Mikhailovsky Palace. In 1802—4 the palace was restored anew (architect L.Rusca); the interiors underwent considerable alterations. In 1906—17 the State Duma was sitting in the palace; consequently, some of the rooms were reconstructed (architect P.Shestov). During the February Revolution the Provisional Goverment and the Executive Committee of the Soviets of Workers' and Soldiers' Deputies resided in the palace. In the 1930s it housed the All-Union Agricultural Communist University, later—the Higher Communist Party School.

222

THE HOUSE OF THE GARDENER OF THE TAURIDA PALACE
Potiomkinskaya Street, 2
1793—94. Architect F.Volkov

The house is an integral part of the palace ensemble; it was built for the gardener V.Guld, who was developing the layout of the Tavrichesky garden. The main two-story building decorated with a four-column portico is placed at the back of the plot; two one-story wings are set forth and topped with small turrets. The garden façade is decorated with a protruding semi-rotunda with a balcony over it. According to its overall design the house is a typical sample of Russian country estate architecure of the second half of the 19th century.

223

THE TAVRICHESKY (TAURIDA) GARDEN
Saltykova-Shchedrina Street, 50
1783—89. Architect I.Starov, gardener V.Guld

The Taurida Garden was laid out on the territory of Potiomkin's estate and is one of the best samples of a city landscape park. In spite of the flat relief Guld managed to achieve landscape variety by building artificial hills and bridges, as well as digging canals and ponds with islands in them. In the 19th—20th centuries the garden was partly redesigned. In 1896 the fence was put up. Since the 19th century the Taurida Garden has been a traditional place for children's recreation. In 1954 it got the name of the City Children's Park. In 1962 a monument to the «Young Heroes, defenders of the City of Lenin» was opened on the pond bank (sculptors I.Kostiukhin and V.Novikov); it was put up with the money collected by children.

The Taurida Garden (No 223)

224
THE TOWER OF VIACHESLAV IVANOV
Tavricheskaya (Taurida) Street, 35
1903—5. Engineer M.Kondratyev

The house with a tower on the corner of Tavricheskaya and Tverskaya streets is a typical Petersburg apartment house of the early 20th century. First such houses appeared on the site in the early 19th century. Originally they were built of wood, later of brick; and only by the end of the century tall stone buildings appeared there. There is nothing remarkable about the house design. The tower and three tiers of open-work balcony railings accentuate the house corner, the wings extending along the two adjacent streets—which is characteristic of the Petersburg eclectic style of the period. It became famous since late 1905, when the poet Viacheslav Ivanov together with his wife, L.D.Zinovyeva-Annibal moved into the flat on the fifth towered story.

Many outstanding works of art were first voiced there, and many a poet got their inspiration. Perhaps it is in such sites of Petersburg that the magic of the city is contained. It was here that N.Gumiliov had for the first time brought the

The Viacheslav Ivanov Tower
(No 224)

A dwelling house
(No 225)

young Anya Gorenko—the future great Anna Akhmatova. It was here that in 1910 V.Meyerhold had first staged Calderon's *Worship of the Cross* translated K.Balmont.

A year later, in 1906, Y.Zvantseva's Art Studio was accommodated on the ground floor. She invited adherents of Art-Nouveau tendencies as teachers, who were mostly members of the World of Art group. L.Bakst gave painting lessons and M.Dobuzhinsky provide instruction in drawing. The meeting with Bakst had played a major part in Mark Chagall life. The school stayed in the house till 1909. In 1918, however, on Lunacharsky's direction the Petrograd Arts school once again came to stay on the ground floor of the building; it used to be called «Shablovsky's school» by the name of its founder and long-term director

Ya.Shablovsky. In 1934 the school was turned into the Serov Art School and in 1961 it moved into a house in the vicinity of Smolny.

As for the «tower» society, it had existed till 1912, when V.Ivanov left abroad and the friends stopped meeting.

225
A DWELLING HOUSE
Tavricheskaya Street, 17
1900s. Architect A.Khrenov

226
A DWELLING HOUSE
Tavricheskaya Street, 5
1908—9. Architect A.Khrenov

227
A DWELLING HOUSE
Perekupnoi Lane, 9
1903. Architect F.Lumberg

A dwelling house (No 226)

A dwelling house (No 227)

A dwelling house (No 228)
A dwelling house (No 229)

228
A DWELLING HOUSE
Starorusskaya Street, 5
1915. Architect I.Yakovlev

229
A DWELLING HOUSE
Mytninskaya Street, 5/2
1908. Architect D.Kryzhanovsky

230
KIKIN'S MANSION
Stavropolsky Lane, 9
1714—20. Architect unknown

The building was put up for the Admiralty Counsellor A.Kikin. It is a sample of the Baroque of Peter's period. In general layout and appearance it is similar to the Great Palace in Peterhoff. In 1718—27 it had housed Peter's Chamber of Curiosities (*Kunstkammer*) and his private library. During the 19th century the building underwent a number of reconstructions. In 1956 it was restored in its original shape (architect I.Benois).

Kikin's mansion (No 230)

The Smolny ensemble

The Smolny ensemble includes a number of structures put up at different time. This territory on the Neva bank, opposite the Nienschanz Fortress put up by the Swedes in the 17th century, was allotted for the tar-yard (Smolianoi dvor); tar was stored and smelted there for the needs of the Admiralty. The name of Smolny (tar) was henceforth used for the territory, though the tar-works ceased to exist in the first half of the 18th century. In the mid-18th century a construction of the Smolny ensemble was started on the site. The oldest here are the buildings of the Voskresensky (Resurrection) Novodevichiy Convent, or the Smolny Convent, as it was known among the citizens. Construction works began in 1748, performed to a design by B.Rastrelli. Cells for the nuns were built later.

The second to be built was the Alexandrovsky Boarding School for Girls (1765—75, architect Yu.Velten); it was intended for educating girls from middle-class families.

The square that took shape in front of the convent was in 1923 named after B.Rastrelli.

To the south of the Smolny Convent the Smolny Boarding School for Young Ladies of Noble Birth was erected in 1806—8; it was designed in Russian Empire style by D.Quarenghi. This building added considerably to the size of the whole ensemble completing architecturally one of the city outskirts. It used to house the first educational institution in Russia for girls of noble birth. In 1917 the Smolny Broading School became the revolutionary headquarters. It was here that Lenin resided during the uprising. The building also accommodated the Central Committee of the Bolsheviks' Party and the Petrograd Soviet of the Workers' and Peasants' Deputies. In the 1920s a regular garden was laid out in front of it. In 1927 a monument to Lenin was put up at the main entrance (sculptor V.Kozlov, architects V.Shchuko and V.Gelfreich).

From the Smolny propylaea a view opens on Proletarskoi Dictatury (Proletarian Dictaorship) Square. In the 1970s it was connected with Rastrelli Square by means of a wide esplanade. On it eastern side the building of the former orphanage has remained (1903, architect V.Veis).

Opposite the propylaea the House for Political Education was built in 1974 (architects D.Goldgor, G.Vasilyev and T.Shivinskaya).

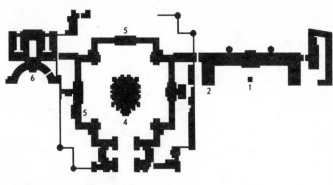

The Smolny ensemble

231
THE SMOLNY CONVENT CATHEDRAL
Rastrelli Square, 3/1
1748—64. Architect B.Rastrelli
Now the Concert and Exhibition Hall

The Smolny Convent Cathedral is a brilliant sample of Russian architecture of the mid-18th century, and one of the best works by Rastrelli. This is one of the outstanding achievements in world architecture, for its perfect proportions, exquisite painting and expressive composition. The cathedral tends to dominate the neighboring buildings. It can be seen from afar, from Shpalernaya Street and Suvorovsky Prospekt; it is especially impressive when viewed from the opposite Neva bank.

Intricate facade design, abundant decorative sculpture and stucco moulding, clusters of columns at the corners and richly ornamented lintels are all typical of Baroque architecture. The lower part of the cathedral divided into two tiers is topped with the high drum of the central dome. It has well-proportioned towers of four belfries adjoining it.

All this make the cathedral soar upwards, as it were, producing the impression of dynamics and plasticity. The contraposition of blue wall, white stucco moulding and the gold of the domes makes it look especially picturesque.

In 1764 construction works came to a halt. The belfry that was to be 140m high and was to be put up in front of the cathedral, according to Rastrelli's design, was never erected. Construction was completed and interior decoration performed as late as 1832—35 to a design by V.Stasov, however, it was done in another style—Classicism. It was also to Stasov's design that the open-work railing at the entrance was put up.

232
THE BUILDINGS OF THE SMOLNY CONVENT
1749—64. Architect B.Rastrelli

The convent buildings, laid out in a square and including the cells, refectory and other structures, were, according to Rastrelli, to form an exclusive cross-shaped polygon. The cathedral was to be placed in the center. The four tower-churches were situated inside the corners of the square; the main facades facing the courtyard represented two-tier arcades. A major part in the facade decoration is played by Rastrelli's favorite paired half-columns that create the interplay of light and shade, as well as plastic and cast-iron ornaments.

Construction of the buildings was started at the same time as the Cathedral, but was several times suspended. The buildings flanking the main entrance were put up later, in 1832—35, by V.Stasov in the late classical style; it was renovated in the 1860s by the architect P.Tamansky. The latter was striving to make the buildings resemble Rastrelli's style in appearance; so he redecorated the facades accordingly, adding the stucco moulding in Baroque style. Of interest is the remaining interior decoration which equally stands out for its rich stucco moulding. The whole complex of the Smolny Convent buildings is distinguished for the completeness of conception and outward expressiveness.

In 1764, shortly after the convent had got the official status, part of its buildings were taken up by the school for girls of noble birth. The convent proper, which occupied only a small part of the territory, was abolished in 1797.

The Smolny Cathedral (No 231)

233
ALEXANDROVSKY BOARDING SCHOOL
Smolnogo Street, 3
1765—75. Architect Yu.Velten

The grand building of the Alexandrovsky Boarding School is located to the north of the main part of the Smolny ensemble, on the Neva bank. It stands out for its daring and original composition. The spacious three-story structure consists of several rectangular buildings that form three inner courtyards. These buildings, in their turn, are joined into a single whole by means of the main, semicircular one. The façades are typical of early Classicism. The ground floor is rusticated, while the façades are ornamented with panels and niches. The central part of the main building is marked out by means of a minor risalit with four pilasters. The façade overlooking the Neva is more richly decorated.

During the reconstruction of 1821 (architect D.Quadri) the building did not suffer any outward changes; the renovation involved only interiors.

234
THE SMOLNY BOARDING SCHOOL
1806—8. Architect D.Quarenghi

The Smolny building was designed to house the most privileged closed educational institution for the nobility— the Institute for Young Ladies of Noble Birth, founded as early as 1764. Architecturally it embodies the main features of high Classicism: monumental forms, accuracy of design and laconic proportionality. Its central part is accentuated with an Ionic portico topped with a pediment. Protruding side wings outline the front courtyard.

Interior layout is simple and rational. It is characteristic of the educational institutions that were being put up in the 18th—early 19th centuries. Class-room and dormitories are arranged on both sides of wide long corridors. Artistically of most interest is the large two-tier Assembly Hall. The hall space is divided into three parts by columns. In wall decoration Quarenghi made use of a plastic frieze and the figure of the flying Glory placed over the entrance. The ceiling in side bays is ornamented with rosettes inclosed in caissons. The Smolny Assembly Hall is one of the best samples of reception halls in Russian classical architecture.

The Smolny Boarding School (No 234)

The Smolny building is linked with the revolutionary events. In August 1917 the All-Union Central Executive Committee and the Petrograd Soviet moved here from the Taurida Palace. It was here that the Military Revolutionary Committee was residing that was in the head of the revolutionary uprising. In Smolny the first Soviet government had been sitting before it moved to Moscow in 1918. The memorial rooms where Lenin used to live and work have been turned into a museum. Smolny used to be the revolutionary headquarters where Bolshevik meetings and conferences took place. Since 1918 it used to house the Regional and City Committees of the CPSU.

235
THE SMOLNY PROPYLAEA
1923. Architects V.Shchuko and V.Gelfriech

The propylaea flanking the main entrance to the Smolny territory are one of the first architectural works of the Soviet period. They were designed in classical style and formed an integral part of the ensemble, binding as they do semicircular Proletarskoi Diktatury (Proletarian Dictatorship) Square and the adjacent garden with the Smolny building. The propylaea consist of two pavilions with five-column porticoes and are on both sides of the central garden alley.

236
THE MONUMENT TO LENIN
(IN FRONT OF THE SMOLNY)
1927. Sculptor V.Kozlov

The monument was erected to commemorate the tenth anniversary of the October revolution and is one of Lenin's first sculptural portrayals.

Suvorovsky Prospekt
(between Nevsky Prospekt and Smolny)

This is one of the largest thoroughfares in the central part of the city. Up to 1900 it used to be called Slonovaya (Elephant) Street, since an elephant menagerie was located here.

The street got its present name in honor of Generalissimo A.Suvorov.

237
THE LAND FORCES HOSPITAL
Suvorovsky Prospekt, 63
1835—40. Architect A.Staubert
Now the Regional Military Hospital

Suvorovsky Prospekt

238
A DWELLING HOUSE
Suvorovsky Prospekt, 56
1953. Architect I.Fomin and others

This is a typical sample of the so-called «Stalin style» in architecture and reliefs.

239

THE MARIINSKY BOARDING SCHOOL FOR YOUNG LADIES
Saltykova-Shchedrina Street, 54
1835—37. Architect A.Stakenschneider
Built in the austere forms of late classicism

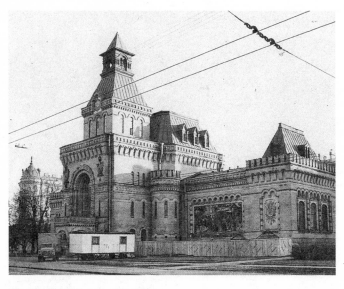

The Suvorov Museum (No 240)

240

THE SUVOROV MUSEUM
Saltykova-Shchedrina Street, 43
1901—4. Architect A.Gogin and G.Grimm

The main façade carries mosaic panels called *Suvorov's Departure for the Italian Campaign of 1799* (artist A.Shabunin) and *Suvorov's March over the Alps* (artist A.Popov). The building proper is designed in the neo-Russian style; it has high roof, a tent-like turret and was especially put up to house the museum. The exhibition includes Suvorov's personal belongings, his portraits and military awards.

241
THE GENERAL HEADQUARTERS ACADEMY
Suvorovsky Prospekt, 32
1901. Architect A.Gogin

242
A DWELLING HOUSE
Suvorovsky Prospekt, 12
1936. Architects A.Ol and Ye.Kholmogorov

Alexander Nevsky Lavra ensemble

Alexander Nevsky Lavra ensemble is located at the end of
Nevsky Prospekt, between Alexander Nevsky Square and
the Obvodny Canal, at the confluence of the Monastyrka
and Neva rivers; it is considered to be one of the largest
architectural ensembles in Petersburg. It was founded by
Peter I in 1710 as the Monastery of the Holy Trinity and
Saint Grand Duke Alexander Nevsky in honor of the victory
over the Swedes won in 1240. In 1712—13 the first
wooden Annunciation Church was put up on the left bank
of the Monastyrka (or Chiornaya) River, and in 1717
construction of the monastery buildings in stone was
started. In 1724 the remains of Alexander Nevsky were on
Peter's order transferred from the city of Vladimir to the
Blagoveshchenskaya (Annunciation) Church, newly built of
stone (in 1790 the silver shrine with the relics was
transferred to the Holy Trinity Cathedral).

Peter I assigned utmost importance to the monastery.
The monastery trained priests of high rank for the
Orthodox Church. In 1720 printing-works were established
in the monastery, in 1721 a Slovenian school for middle-
class children was opened followed, in 1726, by the
Slavonic, Greek and Latin Seminary and, further, by the
Theological Academy as a higher educational establishment
of the Moscow Partriarchy, and the Theological Seminary as
a secondary religious school (both opened in 1809).

In 1797 the monastery got the lavra status. Most part of
the territory is taken up by the Metropolitant Garden and
the cemeteries: the Lazarevskoye (18th-century Necropolis),
Tikhvinskoye (Necropolis of the Men of Arts) and
Nikolskoye (founded in 1861) cemeteries.

Many outstanding Russian men of culture, statesmen,

military and public leaders were buried here. After the revolution, in 1918, the monastery was closed down; many of the historical relics and works of art were transferred to the Hermitage, Russian Museum and other places. In 1923 a Necropolis-Museum was established on part of the territory (since 1939 called the Museum of City Sculpture).

Construction works went on all through the 19th century; thus the Baroque elements of the Peter's epoch were blended with the mid-18th century Baroque as well as with the late 18th-century classical forms. Though the buildings were erected by different architects and at various time, they all form a single whole.

The first design of the ensemble approved by Peter I was developed by D.Trezzini in 1715. The two-story monastery buildings were flanking the cathedral and overlooked the garden and the Neva embankment. Construction works started by Trezzini were continued by the architect T.Schwertfeger who introduced some changes into the original design. All the subsequent architects of the lavra followed the same plan, with slight modifications. Schwertfeger developed the design for the first Holy Trinity Cathedral; however, he did not manage to carry the construction up to the end. In 1741—1750s D.Trezzini completed the Fiodorovskaya Church and the Fiodorovsky building started by Schwertfeger. In 1755 the architect M.Rastorguyev developed a design for several one- and two-story buildings (the Metropolitan House, the Seminary building and the Prosforny House). The ensemble was completed by I.Starov, who was the author of the Holy Trinity Cathedral (1776—90). While directing the construction works he was at the same time renovating the adjacent territory, having formed thereby a new square (named after Alexander Nevsky). He enclosed the square within a semicircle of stone walls and erected a gate-church and two houses at the entrance, thus linking the lavra ensemble with Nevsky Prospekt. The Holy Trinity Cathedral completed one of the oldest city ensembles.

243
THE ANNUNCIATION CHURCH
1717—22

This is the oldest building in the lavra ensemble. It was put up in early Russian Baroque style and has retained the original façade decoration; it also served as a model for the later constructions—those of the Fiodorovskaya Church and the corner towers in the monastery square. In 1764—65 an outbuilding with a flight of stairs leading into the upper, two-tier Alexander Nevsky Church was erected to a design by M.Rastorguyev. The Annunciation Church was a burial-place for the 18th-century Russian statesmen. The inscription on one of the tombstones reads: «Here lies Suvorov».

The Annunciation Church (No 243)

244
THE HOLY TRINITY CATHEDRAL
1776—90. Architect I.Starov

The cathedral is the compositional center of the Alexander Nevsky Lavra designed in early classical austere forms. The main entrance is marked with a six-column portico flanked by two bell-towers. Alongside with the grand dome on a tall

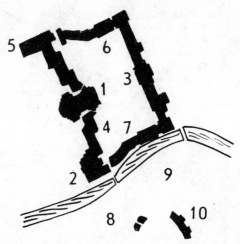

The Alexander Nevsky Lavra ensemble

1. The Holy Trinity Cathedral (No 244);
2. The Annunciation Church (No 243);
3. The Metropolitan House (No 245);
4. The Dukhovskoi House;
5. The Fiodorovsky House;
6. The Seminarsky House;
7. The Prosforny House;
8. The Lazarevskoye Cemetery (No 246);
9. The Tikhvinskoye Cemetery (No 247);
10. The Shelter

drum they dominate the whole composition. The façades are decorated with pilasters and panels. Over the entrance there are bas-reliefs by the well-known 18th-century sculptor F.Shubin. Two bow-shaped galleries cut by arches link the cathedral to the Fiodorovsky and the Dukhovskoi buildings.

The cathedral interior, cross-shaped in plan, is divided into three naves by bulky pylons. Columns with gilt capitals, statues of the saints on the main nave entablatures (sculptor F.Shubin), painting of the cupola and vaults (originally performed by F.Danilov later to be replaced with new painting after G.Quarenghi's design), marble iconostasis and fine design of the gilt bronze holy gates— all contribute to the grandeur of the interior decoration.

Inside the cathedral the relics of Alexander Nevsky are kept. A silver shrine with lavish decoration was made in 1753 of the first silver obtained from the Altai mountains and was designed especially to hold Alexander's relics, it is now exhibited in the Hermitage.

The Holy Trinity Cathedral viewed from the south (No 244)

245

THE METROPOLITAN HOUSE
1756—58. Architect M.Rastorguyev

The Metropolitan House is the second in importance after the Holy Trinity Cathedral. According to a project by Rastorguyev, who had developed the design for the monastery buildings, the Metropolitan House was to be located in the center of the western side of the square, along the same axis as the cathedral. Originally the bishop's chambers represented a two-story building; one-story wings connected it with the corner turrets that were rebuilt in the mid-19th century. The façades of the house stand out among other lavra buildings for their lavish decoration characteristic of Baroque. Columns and pilasters, figured lintels create a lively interplay of light and shade. The corner turrets erected in 1772—74 remined of the Annunciation and Fiodorovskaya churches in their appearance. Each is topped with a high cylindrical drum and a slightly elongated cupola. Beyond the Mitropolitan House there is a regular garden with pavilions in it; during the 19th and 20th centuries its size was reduced considerably and is now delineated by the Monastyrka river.

246

THE LAZAREVSKOYE CEMETERY
(18th-century Necropolis)

The Lazarevskoye Cemetery, which is the oldest in the lavra, came into being as early as Peter's times. It got its name from the St.Lazarus Church that was put up in 1717 next to the Annunciation Church (rebuilt in 1835—36 by the architect L.Tiblen). The cemetery became a burial-place for many statesmen, members of aristocratic families, as well as men of culture and science. On the territory, that has become a necropolis-museum, more than a thousand tombstones and memorials have been preserved performed by I.Vitali, I.Martos, V.Demuth-Malinovsky, M.Kozlovsky and other prominent sculptors and architects. Here is the grave of M.Lomonosov, the great Russian scientist. In 1923 the cemetery was turned into a preserve, and in the 1930s the remains of some outstanding men of the 18th century, as well as some valuable tombstones were transferred here because of the liquidation of some of the city cemeteries.

247
THE TIKHVINSKOYE CEMETERY
(19th-century Necropolis)

The Tikhvinskoye Cemetery was opened in 1823 and now is a necropolis-museum of the men of arts. In the 19th—early 20th centuries it was considered to be the most aristocratic cemetery in Petersburg. Here outstanding scholars, artists, writers, poets, actors and composers are buried.

In the 1930s many prominent Russian men of science and culture were buried anew in the Necropolis, and their tombstones transferred from other city cemeteries. Since 1935 it has been part of the Museum of City Sculpture.

The third—Nikolskoye—cemetery, that is located to the east of the cathedral, came into being in 1861. Alongside with the others it has retained the tombstones of many outstanding men of Russian culture and science.

248
THE ALEXANDER NEVSKY BRIDGE
over the Neva to Malaya Okhta
1965. Engineer A.Yevdonin, architect A.Zhuk

This is the longest bridge in Petersburg. It is made of ferro-concrete and consists of seven spans (the central span is drawn and has two leaves). The bridge is of major importance for the urban design. It served as a link between the two stylistically different districts—the old district of Alexander Nevsky Lavra and the newly built Malaya Okhta district. The authors introduced a lot of novel technologies during the construction (such as ferro-concrete shells used as piers and hydraulic drive for bridge-drawing). Formation of under-bridge spaces was also considered a success; they made it possible to arrange transport passages on two levels. The bridge architecture is inferior to the engineering design. The Petersburg bridges are said to be either «suspended over the waters» or surge upwards with their arched span.

The Alexander Nevsky Bridge is rather flat; it seems to lack the curved rhythm of the lower beam outline (which is present in the Lieutenant Schmidt Bridge, for example). The dullness of decorative design is also manifested in the repeated rhythm of the numerous lanterns that are far from being refined.

The bridge (together with the ramp) is 909.5m long and 35m wide.

The Alexander Nevsky Bridge (No 248)

249
THE MOSCOW HOTEL
Alexander Nevsky Square, 2
1974—77. Architects E.Goldgor, V.Shcherbin and L.Varshavskaya

The architects took account of the Alexander Nevsky Bridge that had been erected ten years before, especially the transport passage in the square before it. This seven-story complex fits well into the overall panorama, alongside with the new buildings on the right Neva bank.

250
AN APARTMENT HOUSE
Nevsky Prospekt, 147
1905—6. Architect P.Batuev

Characteristic of Art-Nouveau style.

251
A DWELLING HOUSE
Nevsky Prospekt, 141
1936. Architect A.Lishnevsky

One of the few samples of Constructivism in Petersburg architecture.

An apartment house (No 250)

252
A DWELLING HOUSE
Nevsky Prospekt, 95
1912. Architect L.Kharlamov

A typical sample of Art-Nouveau style.

253
THE NIKOLAYEVSKY (NOW MOSKOVSKY)
RAILWAY STATION
Vosstaniya Square, 2
1851. Architect K.Thon

The Nikolayevsky Railway Station was the second (after the Vitebsky Station) to be built in Petersburg, and in Russia in the whole. Due to the railway construction started in 1836, buildings for utilitarian purposes began to be put up in the old, historical districts. The intersection of Nevsky and Ligovsky prospekts was chosen as a site for a railway station. Construction of the monumental station building gave rise to a new spacious square, that got the name of

The Moskovsky Railway Station (No 253)

Znamenskaya. The façade was designed in Renaissance style; town-halls of West-European cities served as a model. The main façade also includes a clock-tower marking the central entrance. In 1909 a monument to Alexander III by sculptor P.Trubetskoi was put up in the square in front of the station. In the 1930s the monument was dismantled and is now kept in the Russian Museum. In the 1950s and 1967 the entrance and waiting halls were redecorated by the architect V.Kuznetsov; on the Ligovsky side a new building was added, as well as the vestibule of the Vosstaniya Square underground station.

254
THE OKTIABRSKAYA HOTEL
Nevsky Prospekt, 188; Ligovsky Prospekt, 10
1847. Architect A.Gemilian. In 1900 the sixth story added, architect A.Khrenov

The main hotel building is on Nevsky and Ligovsky prospekts corner. Since 1977 the hotel has had two branches. One of them is at Ligovsky Prospekt, 43—45. the Moskovskaya Hotel, built in 1902—4 by the architect G.Gavrilov. At No 41 there used to be a rooming house of Grechkova. In 1957 the house was included into the hotel complex. The other branch is at Vosstaniya Street, 2/116 (the former Severnaya Hotel, before 1932—the Hermitage Hotel), erected in 1841 by the architect A.Gemilian.

Pushkinskaya Street

between Nevsky Prospekt

and Kuznechny Lane.

Laid in the 1870s

In 1875 the street used to have the name of Novaya (New), further—Alexandrovskaya Street, and a year later—Kompaneiskaya Street. The street was laid out on the lands that belonged to the Maltsev and Co firm. It was the case of a so-called «private» street, that were in the late 19th century laid with the money of prominent landowners—Counts Shuvalovs, Orlovs, Baron von Hildebrandt, Baroness Ikskul and others.

Architecturally ten houses are prominent, built to a design by P.Suzor (No 1, 2, 3, 5, 6, 7, 12, 13, 14, 16). They stand out for heir fanciful façade decoration, combined with rational interior layout. Writers and artists rented flats readily in such new comfortable houses. Here lived G.Miasoyedov, the artist, K.Staniukovich, the writer, as well as Fiodor Shaliapin. In 1881 the street got the name of Pushkin.

In 1884 a monument to Pushkin was put up in the public garden here (sculptor A.Opekushin, architect N.Benois).

255
YUSUPOVA'S HOUSE
Nevsky Prospekt, 86
1820s. Architect M.Ovsiannikov, rebuilt in the 1830s, architect G.Fossati
Now the House of the Men of Art

In the late 18th century the plots beyond the Fontanka along Nevsky Prospekt were built up with small stone and

Pushkinskaya Street

wooden houses. It was only since the 19th century that construction of large dwelling houses was started, that are now predominant here. Yusupova's house was erected on the site of a small estate with a garden that had existed here in the 18th century. During the 19th century the building was several times reconstructed. Several rooms have retained the decoration of the early 19th century.

The grand, elevated six-column portico, sculptured bas-reliefs and ornamentation, the general design make this building stand out among the other dwelling houses put up here in the late 19th century.

256
THE COLISEUM CINEMA
Nevsky Prospekt, 100
1867. Architect M.Makarov

257
THE PARISIANA CINEMA
Nevsky Prospekt, 80
1913. Architect M.Lialevich

258
THE TITAN CINEMA
Nevsky Prospekt, 47.
Rebuilt in 1871

Until 1924 the building used to house the famous Palkin's restaurant. It was visited by N.Leskov, P.Tchaikovsky, A.Chekhov, A.Blok. The same building used to house printing-works of A.Genshel, where the *Grazhdanin* (Citizen) magazine was printed with F.Dostoyevsky as editor.

259
SUKHOZANET'S HOUSE
Nevsky Prospekt, 70
1820s. Architect D.Quadri. Built for general I.Sukhozanet, hero of the war with Napoleon in 1812. Interiors decorated in 1835—38 by the architects D.Visconti and S.Shustov. Façade redecorated in 1864—66, architect I.Strom
Now the House of Journalists

The façade is designed in classical forms, lacking order columns and pilasters. Part of the interiors have remained,

The Titan Cinema (No 258)

of superb decoration and great artistic value. The interiors are ornamented with ceiling painting, stucco moulding, cannelated pilasters, etc.

Sukhozanet's house
(No 259)

A dwelling house
(No 260)

260
A DWELLING HOUSE
Troitskaya Street, 4
1904. Architect A.Khrenov

261
THE BELOSELSKY-BELOZERSKY PALACE
Nevsky Prospekt, 41
1800. Architect F.Demertsev. Rebuilt in 1846—48, architect A.Stakenschneider, sculptor D.Fensen

The palace was put up on the order of Prince K.Beloselsky-Belozersky. It was the first sample of neo-Baroque architecture in Petersburg, and one of the first ones in

Russia. Its façades are designed in the 18th-century Russian Baroque style. Stakenschneider took the Stroganov Palace for a model, that had been put up by B.Rastrelli and located on a similar site—Nevsky Prospekt and the Moika corner. Stakenschneider's palace, that imitates Rastrelli's general outlines, constitutes an organic part of the Nevsky panorama and has become a dominant point of the prospekt beyond the Fontanka. The palace was considered one of the finest private houses in the capital, both by its lavish outward decoration and by the grandeur of its interiors.

A whole range of Baroque artistic devices was made use of in the palace decoration, including porticoes with columns and pilasters, oval-shaped windows, lintels of intricate design, Atlantes, etc. The bright, three-colored façades add to the festive impression of the palace architecture. The Atlantes made to the models of sculptor D.Fensen are quite a felicitous stilization. Contemporaries considered the palace to be a perfect work of art and called Stakenschneider «successor to Count Rastrelli's exquisite taste and art».

Beginning from 1884 the palace had belonged to Sergei Alexandrovich, brother of Alexander III. Consequently, some interiors were reconstructed to suit the new owners tastes. The palace interiors have mostly remained intact and are of considerable artistic value. The wide main staircase leading into the first floor has an open-work railing of wrought iron, while its walls are decorated with pilasters and caryatides. The palace has an intricate interior layout. To facilitate communication Stakenschneider devised a whole system of corridors, interior staircases, etc. Reception halls are lavishly decorated with stucco moulding, painting, gold carving, mirrors and damask upholstery.

262
ST.NICHOLAS' DISSENTERS' CHURCH
Marata Street, 24a
1820—26. Architect A.Melnikov

Architectural monument of late Classicism. The building, cross-shaped in floor plan, is stationed on a stylobate, which is approached by a wide staircase on the square side.

A wide cornice is dividing the main column into two tiers. The main entrance is accentuated by a six-column

The Beloselsky-Belozersky Palace (No 261)

portico. The upper tier is decorated with colonnades. The whole building is topped with a monumental dome

F.Dostoyevsky's Memorial Museum (No 263)

supported by a tetrahedral drum. The interior design stands out for its originality. Instead of a drum that is traditional for church architecture, the sail-shaped vaults are supporting a rotunda-colonnade that constitutes the second story. The interior is decorated with Corinthian columns, plastic cornices and caissons.

During the reconstruction of 1934 the interior was divided by partitions and the loggia glazed, to suit the needs of the Arctic Museum.

263
F.DOSTOYEVSKY MEMORIAL MUSEUM
Dostoyevsky Street, 2/5

Dostoyevsky had stayed in this house during two periods: for a few months in 1846, and for the last years of his life—from 1878 until January 1881. Here in 1971 a memorial museum was opened that illuminates the life and work of the great Russian author.

264
THE KUZNECHNY MARKET
Kuznechny Lane, 3
1925—27. Architects S.Ovsiannikov and A.Pronin

Vladimirsky
and Zagorodny Prospekts

Liteiny, Vladimirsky and Zagorodny Prospekts form yet another arch-shaped thoroughfare, as if following the Fontanka outlines, that had in the 18th century been located outside the city boundaries.

Vladimirsky Prospekt that continues Liteiny, changes its direction slightly at the square of the same name; the next section is called Zagorodny Prospekt, the name dating from the 18th century when the «zagorodny» (out-of-town) road was passing here that ran around the city which lay within the Fontanka borderline.

265
OUR LADY OF VLADIMIR CHURCH
Vladimirsky Prospekt, 20

1761—69. Architect D.Trezzini(?). Three-tier belfry—1783, architect G.Quarenghi; in 1848 the architect L.Rusca added the fourth tier. In 1831 the architect A.Melnikov built a stone vestibule

In the 18th century the site of the present church got the name of the Dvortsovaya (Palace) settlement. Land was allotted here to court officials. The church built here played a major part in the urban design. Not only does the

Our Lady of Vladimir Church (No 265)

building anchor Zagorodny Prospekt vista and represent a dominant point in the whole district built up with apartment houses; it has also lead to redesigning adjacent areas and gave rise to a new square (Vladimirskaya Square).

The five-dome church designed in Baroque continues the traditions laid down by Rastrelli and Chevakinsky. Similar to St.Nicholas Cathedral, it has two stories. The vestibule with staircases leading into the second story is a link between the main volume and the refectory. It was erected in the 19th century and is a typical sample of classical architecture.

In the upper church a carved iconostasis has been preserved, which is one of the most interesting samples of this kind, dating back to the mid 18th-century. In 1864 a public garden was laid out beside the church building.

After the building had been returned into the possession of the Orthodox Church works were started on restoration and renovation of the interiors, which are still going on.

266
OTKRYTY (OPEN) THEATER
Vladimirsky Prospekt, 12
1826—28. Architect A.Mikhailov the 2nd

The building was originally put up as Korsakovs' mansion. In the 1840s the present theater hall and small foyer were added. In the 1860s the building used to house the Merchants' Club. The main façade is decorated with a projection carrying a colonnade and pilasters, joining the two stories together. The theater stands out for its strict classical forms among the apartment houses that were put up in Vladimirsky Prospekt in the late 19th century.

267
NIKONOV'S HOUSE
Kolokolnaya Street, 11
1900s. Architect N.Nikonov

268
A DWELLING HOUSE
Stremiannaya Street, 11
1907. Architects N.Vasiliev and A.Bubyr

Piat Uglov (The Five Corners)

A peculiar architectural ensemble at the crossing of Zagorodny Prospekt, Razyezzhaya, Rubinshtein and Lomonosov streets

It originated in the 1760s. The dominant point is the house No 11, Zagorodny Prospekt, topped with a turret (1913, architect A.Lishnevsky)

269
THE YAMSKOI (COACHMEN) MARKET
Marata Street, 53
1817—19. Architect I.Starov
Now a second-hand furniture store

This is sample of classical architecture. The building which is triangular in floor plan has an inner courtyard and is enclosed with columns, instead of the arches typical of Petersburg trading stalls.

*Nikonov's house
(No 267)*

*A dwelling house
(No 268)*

270
MEYER'S HOUSE
Marata Street, 66
Architect V.Schreter

271
BAZHANOV'S HOUSE
Marata Street, 72
1907—8. Architect P.Aleshin
Now the Chekhov Library

The house was erected for merchant F.Bazhanov in Art-
Nouveau style. The asymmetrical façade clad with Finnish
granite is cut through by windows of various shapes and
decorated with an ornamental frieze. The interiors are

Piat Uglov
(Five Corners)

Meyer's house
(No 270)

lavishly decorated with carved oak panels, majolica, tiles
and stucco moulding. A majolica fireplace made to Vrubel's
design after the Russian epic *Volga and Mikula* has been
preserved. The dining room walls were decorated with
painted panels by N.Roerich.

272
A DWELLING HOUSE
Zagorodny Prospekt, 28

In this house N.Rimsky-Korsakov, the composer, used to live. His flat was one of the centers of musical life in Petersburg. Musical evenings were arranged there, where A.Glazunov, A.Skriabin, I.Stravinsky used to play their latest pieces. F.Shaliapin also took part in these evenings, the flat was frequented by M.Vrubel, the artist.

Since 1971 the flat has been the Rimsky-Korsakov Memorial Museum.

273
A DWELLING HOUSE
Zagorodny Prospekt, 27
1914—16. Architects B.Velikovsky and A.Rozenberg

The house was built in neo-classical style. It belonged to the owner of famous porcelain works, I.Kuznetsov.

274
DEPARTMENT OF THE OBUKHOVSKAYA HOSPITAL
Zagorodny Prospekt, 47
1836—39. Architect P.Pavlov

Being located at Zagorodny Prospekt and Vvedensky Canal intersection the building is of an original design. It consists of two wings joined into a single whole by the round turret at the corner, spanned with a flat cupola. In façade decoration classical forms were used.

275
KARLOVA'S HOUSE
Fontanka Embankment, 46
1760s. Rebuilt in the 1840s, architect V.Langwagen

Until 1917 the house used to belong to Countess Karlova. In the early 18th century it used to be the summer residence of A.Kormedon, who had for some time been at the head of the Office for Construction. In the 1840s the house was reconstructed to suit the needs of the new owner—Adjutant-General N.Zinovyev. The third story was built over the wings of the building, so that the central part became lower. The façade is decorated in Baroque way. Some interiors have retained their original decoration (columns, painted ceilings, stucco moulding), dating back to the 1st quarter of the 19th century.

Tolstoy's house (No 276)

276
TOLSTOY'S HOUSE
Fontanka Embankment, 52—54
1910—12. Architect F.Lidval

The house of Count M.Tolstoy is an illustrative example of the Art-Nouveau architecture in St.Petersburg. Small-sized plots in the early 20th-century Petersburg gave rise to multi-storied houses with well-courtyards. Huge Tolstoy's house fit very well into the plot of intricate shape between

the Fontanka and Rubinstein Street. Its wings are cut
through with wide archways three stories high. The archway
vaults have wrought-iron lanterns of fine design, hanging
down from them. In façade decoration the architect made
use of oval-shaped windows, plastic ornaments, combination
of plaster of different colors and textures with brick and
hewn limestone—all characteristic of Art-Nouveau style.
The courtyard façades are as expressive and elaborate as
the street ones.

Merchant Yeliseyev's house (No 277)

277
MERCHANT YELISEYEV'S HOUSE
Fontanka Embankment, 64
1889—90. Architect G.Baranovsky

The façade is lavishly decorated with terra-cotta moulding.
The general design of the building is in Italian Renaissance
style.

278
THE BARRACKS OF THE LOCAL TROOPS
Fontanka Embankment, 90

The construction began in 1787, on the site of the Glebov Dom estate. In 1798—1803 the building was reconstructed to house the barracks, architect F.Volkov(?).

The Barracks of the Local Troops (No 278)

279
THE SEMIONOVSKY BRIDGE
over the Fontanka, along Gorokhovaya Street

This is one of the first seven stone bridges across the Fontanka. In 1788 it was reconstructed according to the standard design. In 1856—57 the bridge turrets were dismantled, and the spans provided with metal beams (the first bridge of the type built in Petersburg).

The bridge is 54.7m long and 19.5m wide.

280

THE SEMIONOVSKY REGIMENT
BARRACKS AND DRILL-GROUND
Zvenigorodskaya Street, Pionerskaya Square
1798—1800. Architects F.Volkov and F.Demertsov

The Semionovsky Regiment was transferred to Petersburg
from Semionovsky settlement near Moscow in 1723 and
occupied a spacious territory beyond the Fontanka. In
1816 the League for Salvation, the first revolutionary
organization in Russia, was founded in the officers' barracks
here, in the flat of the brothers Muravyiov-Apostols. Many
Decemberists used to serve in the Semionovsky Regiment.
In 1849 the execution of the members of the Petrashevsky
Circle was to take place on the drill-ground here. At the
last moment it was substituted for hard labor. Among the
condemned was F.Dostoyevsky. In 1881 the members of
the Peoples' Will underground organization were put to
death here. They took part in the attempt upon the life of
Alexander II. In the 1880s the drill-ground was turned into
an hippodrome, and in 1893 the first Russian cycle track
was opened here. In the 1950s a square was formed here
(Pionerskaya Square). In 1959 a monument to the writer
A.Griboyedov was erected in the square (sculptor V.Lishev).

281

THE THEATER FOR YOUNG SPECTATORS
Pionerskaya Square, 1
1962. Architect A.Zhuk

The theater building is in the same axis with Gorokhovaya
Street, whose vista is anchored by the Admiralty spire. This
was a rather felicitous choice, for the architect took account
of the traditions of urban design in Petersburg, its radial
streets concluded by tall dominants.

282

THE VITEBSKY (TSARSKOSELSKY) RAILWAY STATION
Zagorodny Prospekt, 52
1904. Architects S.Brzhozovsky and S.Minash

In 1837 a wooden building of the first Russian railway
station was erected in Petersburg. In the same year the first

train in Russia covered the distance between Petersburg to Tsarskoye Selo. In 1849—52 the first stone station building was put up (architect K.Thon). The present station is designed in Art-Nouveau style. The asymmetrical structure is spanned with an original glass cupola. The decoration of this utility building includes a clock tower, large semicircular windows and ornamental bas-reliefs.

The Vitebsky Railway Station (No 282)

283
A DWELLING HOUSE
Zagorodny Prospekt, 45/13
1906. Architect I.Moshinsky

284
A DWELLING HOUSE
Klinsky Lane, 17/19
1912—13. Engineer A.Zakharov. Majolika made in P.Vaulin's workshop

285
THE OCTIABRSKY CONCERT HALL
Ligovsky Prospekt, 6
1967. Architects V.Kamensky, T.Verzhbitsky and A.Zhuk

In front of the building there is the *October* sculptural group by A.Matveyev.

A dwelling house (No 283)   *A dwelling house (No 284)*

286
PRINCE OLDENBURG'S CHILDREN'S HOSPITAL
Ligovsky Prospekt, 8
1869. Architect C.Kavos
Now the Rauchfus Children's Hospital

287
AN APARTMENT HOUSE
Ligovsky Prospekt, 44
1910—11. Architects S.Galenzovsky and I.Pretro

Typical sample of the Petersburg Art-Nouveau style.

288
A DWELLING HOUSE
Ligovsky Prospekt, 105
1977—78. Architect E.Kondratovich

Of interest is the façade with triangular bay-windows. There is a book shop on the ground floor.

The Oktiabrsky Concert Hall (No 285)

289
AN APARTMENT HOUSE
Ligovsky Prospekt, 125
1906. Architect A.Lishnevsky

Typical sample of Art-Nouveau style.

290
THE CHURCH OF THE HOLY CROSS
Ligovsky Prospekt, 128
1810—12 (belfry), architect A.Postnikov. 1848—51, architect Y.Dimmert

The church was put up on the site that had in the 18th century belonged to the Moscow Coachmen's Settlement. In the early 19th century a many-tier belfry was attached to the 18th-century stone church, the two chapels connected with it by a semicircular colonnade. The belfry is topped with a spire and decorated with columns and sculpture.The church proper, that was built later, was designed in Baroque.

Being located in the back of the plot, the church and the belfry form an impressive architectural ensemble linked to Ligovsky Prospekt by means of the chapels. On the same territory the Tikhvinskaya Church has remained, put up in 1764—68 and rebuilt in 1842—44 by the architect V.Morgan.

The Church of the Holy Cross (No 290)

291
THEOLOGICAL ACADEMY BUILDING
Obvodny Canal Embankment, 7
1817—21. Architect L.Rusca

292
THE BARRACKS OF THE LIFE GUARDS COSSACK REGIMENT
Obvodny Canal Embankment, 23—29
1840. Architect I.Chernik

«EAST» PART
OF THE CITY
Between the Fontanka,
Moskovsky Prospekt and the Neva

293
**THE PEOPLE'S HOUSE OF COUNTESS PANINA
(LIGOVSKY PEOPLES' HOUSE)
Tambovskaya Street, 63/16, Prilukskaya Street, 22**
1899—1904. Architect Ye.Benois
Now the House of Culture for Railway Workers and the
Union Industrial Amalgamation

The Peoples' House used to occupy two buildings. The
main building housed class-rooms, a legal advice office, and
an observatory. Here P.Gaideburov's Public Theater used to
perform as well. In 1907 A.Tairov staged *Hamlet* here, with
Gaideburov playing the lead. The second building
(Prilukskaya, 22) housed the Mobile Museum of Visual
Aids.

294
**A DWELLING HOUSE
Obvodny Canal Embankment, 48—50**
1913. Architect A.Fantalov

This six-story building with a corner turret is characteristic
of Art-Nouveau.

Moskovsky (Moscow) Prospekt

The prospekt is one of the widest and longest in the city,
stretching over 10km and linking Sennaya (Hay) Square
with Pobedy (Victory) Square. It took shape in the early
18th century as a post road. By the late 18th century the
road had gained an importance as it had become a link between Petersburg and Imperial country residences. In the
19th century minor enterprises and dachas began to spring
up along the roadside; since in the second half of the 19th

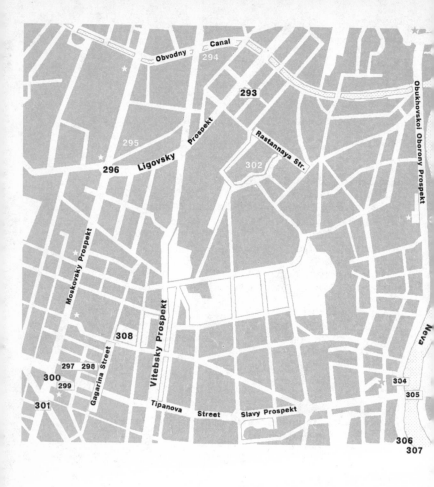

Obvodny Canal
294
293
Ligovsky Prospekt
295
296 Ligovsky
Rastannaya Str.
302
Obukhovskoi Oborony Prospekt
Moskovsky Prospekt
Vitebsky Prospekt
308
Gagarina Street
297 298
300
299
301
Tipanova Street
Slavy Prospekt
Neva
304
305
306
307

century construction of apartment houses had started. The southern part of the prospekt beyond the Obvodny Canal underwent considerable reconstruction works which were continued here in the 1930s. Construction works were continued here in the post-war years as well.

295
THE NOVODEVICHYE CEMETERY
Moskovsky Prospekt, 100

The cemetery was attached to the Resurrection Novodevichiy Convent and laid out in 1845. In the 19th— early 20th century it was one of the most well-tended Petersburg cemeteries. However, in 1929 the cemetery churches were demolished, the Church of Prophet Elijah (1885—88, architect L.Benois) and the Skorbiashchenskaya Church (1855—56, architect E.Giber), erected over A.Karamzin's grave, among them. Many tombstones were destroyed, and the remains of the artist A.Ivanov and composer N.Rimsky-Korsakov were transferred to the Necropolis-museum. However, the cemetery has retained its historical importance. Here are the graves of poets N.Nekrasov, F.Tiutchev, A.Maikov; those of artists A.Golovin, M.Vrubel, composer E.Napravnik, doctor S.Botkin, champion chess-player M.Chigorin and others. Some tombstones in Art-Nouveau style have remained, as well as sculptured monuments.

At the entrance stands the Kazanskaya Church (1906—15, architect V.Kosiakov).

296
THE MOSCOW TRIUMPHAL ARCH
Moskovskiye Vorota Square
1836—38. Architect V.Stasov, sculptor B.Orlovsky

The Arch was erected to commemorate the victory of the Russians over the Turks in 1828—29. They were cast of iron and furnished with wrought copper decorations. This arch in the shape of a Doric portico is of austere outline and was put up between the two forking streets— Moskovskoye Shosse and Ligovsky Canal, thus serving as a piquet as well. On both sides of the road two «cordeguards» buildings were erected for the military men.

The Moscow Triumphal Arch (No 296)

The Moscow Arch glorifying the military triumph, is a sample of Empire style. The sculptural compositions mostly include banners and armor. The triglyphs in the frieze were substituted with thirty sculptures of genii, stamped of sheet copper according to seven different models, this substitution can be considered an architectural innovation. The arch was dismantled in 1936. In 1941, the cast-iron blocks were used for putting up anti-tank obstacles. They were restored in 1958—60 (architects Ye.Petrova and I.Kaptsiug).

The arch is 24m high and 36m wide.

297
THE CESME PALACE
Gastello Street, 15

1774—77. Architect Yu.Velten. Rebuilt in 1831—36, architect A.Staubert

The palace was put up as a temporary residence for the imperial court to take a rest during the trips from Petersburg to Tsarkoye Selo (Tsar's Village). The place had in the 18th century the Finnish name of Kekerekeksinen, which means «the frog swamp», so the palace got the name Kekerekeksinensky Palace. In 1780 it was renamed the Cesme Palace to commemorate the victory of the Russian Fleet in the battle with the Turks in the Cesme Bay in the Aegean Sea (1770). Besides the palace, the architectural ensemble also included outbuildings and a church.

The main building is an equilateral triangle that has a rounded turret at each of the corners and a spacious circular hall in the center. In the façade decoration Velten made use of Gothic devices, that were rarely met in Russian architecture, including toothed parapets over the walls and lancet windows; the walls were left unplastered.

Inside, decoration of some of the halls has remained. In 1831—36 the building was turned into a hospice for the invalid veterans of the Patriotic War of 1812, and partly rebuilt: two wings were attached to the main building, the toothed parapets demolished, and semispherical cupolas erected over the turrets.

The Cesme Church (No 298)

The House of Soviets (No 299)

298
THE CESME CHURCH
Lensoveta Street, 12
1777—80. Architect Yu.Velten. Restored in 1965—68
Now the Cesme Victory Museum, a branch of the Central
Naval Museum

The Cesme Church is one of the few buildings in
Petersburg that have Gothic motifs in their design. The wall
surface decorated with narrow vertical rods and plastic
lancet arches is intersected with high lancet windows. The
walls are topped with a toothed parapet and pinnacle
turrets. Similar turrets with raised decoration ornament the
drum walls of all the five domes. The «tetrafoil»-shaped
composition is quite unusual, each foil representing a
rounded space attached to the main volume. On the church
territory the small Cesme Cemetery is located, where the
Russian army veterans were buried who were staying at the
hospice. During World War II the defenders of Leningrad
were also buried here.

299
THE HOUSE OF SOVIETS
Moskovskaya Square
1936—41. Architect N.Trotsky. Sculptured frieze—
architect N.Tomsky

300
THE MONUMENT TO LENIN
Moskovskaya Square
1970. Sculptor M.Anikushin, architect V.Kamensky

The monument was erected to commemorate Lenin's 100th anniversary. The figure of Lenin giving a speech is cast of bronze and is eight meters high. The pedestal was performed of red polished granite.

301
THE MEMORIAL TO THE HEROIC DEFENDERS OF LENINGRAD
Pobedy (Victory) Square
1974—75. Sculptor M.Anikushin, architects V.Kamensky and S.Speransky

Moskovsky Prospekt ends in Pobedy (Victory) Square, which is perceived as the southern «gates» to the city; it was here that in 1957 foundation was laid to the memorial to the heroic defenders of Leningrad during the Second World War. Construction works started in 1974. Besides specialists in the field, a lot of voluntary workers were involved. The memorial was unveiled on May 9, 1975, the 30th anniversary of the victory in the war.

The Memorial to the Heroic Defenders of Leningrad (No 301)

In the center of the memorial a 48-meter granite obelisk is rising, surrounded by sculptured figures representing defenders of Leningrad standing on bronze pedestals. At the foot of the obelisk there is the sculptured group *The Undefeated*. Several steps near are leading downstairs, into the memorial hall, which has the *Blockade* sculptured group standing in the center. The hall was opened in 1978 and contains original relics of the blockade period.

302

THE VOLKOVSKOYE (VOLKOVO) CEMETERY
Rastannaya Street, 7a
LITERATORSKIYE MOSTKY
Rastannaya Street, 30

The cemetery was laid in 1719 and attached to the Church of the Holy Cross (Ligovsky Prospekt, 128). In the 18th century it was abolished. The present cemetery was founded on the left bank of the Volkovka River in 1756.

On the cemetery territory several wooden and stone churches were built. Only a few have remained, among them the Voskresenskaya (Resurrection) Church (1782—85, architect I.Starov), its belfry and gates were built in 1832—34 (architect P.Votsky); the Church of Spasa Nerukotvornogo (Our Lord the Savior) (1837—42, architects V.Beretti and L.Rusca), as well as the Job the Pious Church (1885—87, architect I.Aristarkhov), that is still active.

The Volkovo Cemetery is one of the largest in Petersburg. The overall length of its pathways is 12km. They were paved with planks because of the damp soil. In the second half of the 19th century north-eastern part of the cemetery became a traditional burial-place for men of letters. This was how the present necropolis came into being, called Literatorskiye Mostki, that has since 1935 been a department of the Museum of the City Sculpture. Here in 1802 A.Radishchev was buried (supposedly in the vicinity of the Resurrection Church), followed by V.Belinsky in 1848, as well as N.Dobroliubov and D.Pisarev buried close by. Among those lying here are poets, writers, composers, artists and actors. Among the authors of tombstones are sculptors M.Anikushin, V.Bogoliubov, I.Ginzburg, A.Sherwood and others.

303
THE NEVSKY PALACE OF CULTURE
Obukhovskoi Oborony Prospekt, 32
1968—72. Architects Ye.Levinson and others

The building of original design fits in very well with the
surrounding parterre public garden, against the Neva
background. The Palace of Culture is quite well-known for
its educational activity. In particular, it was here that the
first avant-guarde artists' exhibition took place in the
1970s.

304
THE LOMONOSOV PORCELAIN WORKS
Obukhovskoi Oborony Prospekt, 151

The first porcelain works were founded in 1744 in the
brickworks building. D.Vinogradov, the inventor of Russian
porcelain, worked here. In 1765 the works got the mane of
the Imperial Porcelain Works. At present it is a world-
famous amalgamation producing high-quality articles. Some
18th-century buildings have remained on the territory of
the works. The main building houses the Museum of
Russian Porcelain.

305
THE VOLODARSKY BRIDGE
over the Neva to Narodnaya Street
1932—36. Engineer G.Peredery. Reconstruction—engineer
N.Tikhomirov, architect Yu.Sinitsa

During the bridge construction many novel solutions were
used that later to be applied in Russian bridge-building.
Recently reconstruction works have been carried out on a
new principle. Ferroconcrete beams have been replaced
with solid steel ones, that are thrown both over the river
and over the bank strip, provided with motorway
intersections. The two-wing draw-span has been replaced
with a one-wing span. The spans themselves have been
raised 4m higher.

The Holy Trinity Church (No 306)

306
THE HOLY TRINITY CHURCH (*Kulich i Paskha***)**
Obukhovskoi Oborony Prospekt, 235
1785. Architect N.Lvov

The Holy Trinity Church was built in the country estate of
A.Viazemsky, in Akexandrovskoye Settlement. It got its
name because of the shape of the buildings, resembling
traditional Russian Easter cakes: *kulich* and *paskha*. The
church represents a rotunda, while the belfry is pyramid-
shaped. The building is located in the open space. The
decoration of the domed rotunda—columns, capitals
ornamented with garlands, oval-shaped windows in the
second tier—is typical of early Classicism. The original
belfry is a good example of non-traditional use of the
pyramid-shape design. The interior is decorated with
pilasters; over the altar apse the sculptured soaring angels
have remained. The carved iconostasis was transferred here
from the Annunciation Church in Vasilyevsky Island. In
1858 a vestry and vestibule were attached to the rotunda
which to some extent interfered with the original design of
the famous Russian architect.

307
THE NEVSKY STEARIN-AND-SOAP WORKS
Obukhovskoi Oborony Prospekt, 80

1850s. Architect L.Bonigert
Now the Nevsky Cosmetics Factory

The building is typical of the 19th-century industrial design in Petersburg. It has been considerably enlarged.

308
THE SPORTS AND CONCERT COMPLEX
Gagarin Prospekt, 8

1980. Architects I.Chaiko, N.Baranov and F.Yakovlev. Construction designers: A.Morozov, Yu.Yeliseyev and O.Kurbatov

This is one of the largest multi-purpose buildings in the country. The hall can be transformed, depending on the nature of the performance. The facades accentuate the constructive design of the building. The ramp is decorated with sculptured groups *Art*, *Sports* and bronze reliefs (sculptors V.Rybalko, G.Bagramian, N.Gordiyevsky).

The Sports and Concert Complex (No 308)

«WEST» PART
OF THE CITY
Between Moskovsky Prospekt and Gulf of Finland

309
THE INSTITUTE OF THE RAILWAY TRANSPORT ENGINEERS
Moskovsky Prospekt, 9-11
1823. Architect A.Gotman. Moskovsky Prospekt, 11. 1893—95. Architect I.Kitner

The institute was founded on the initiative of an outstanding engineer A.Betancour in 1809. It was the only educational establishment in Russia that trained specialists in railroad construction. Up to 1864 it had been a closed institution; later it changed from military to civil purposes.

At the institute the Museum of Railway Transport was established (Sadovaya Street, 50). The modern building was put up by the architect L.Krupinsky in 1902, to be enlarged in 1910 to a design of E.Baumgarten. First exhibits appeared here in 1813, and the museum opened in 1862.

The Technological Institute (No 310)

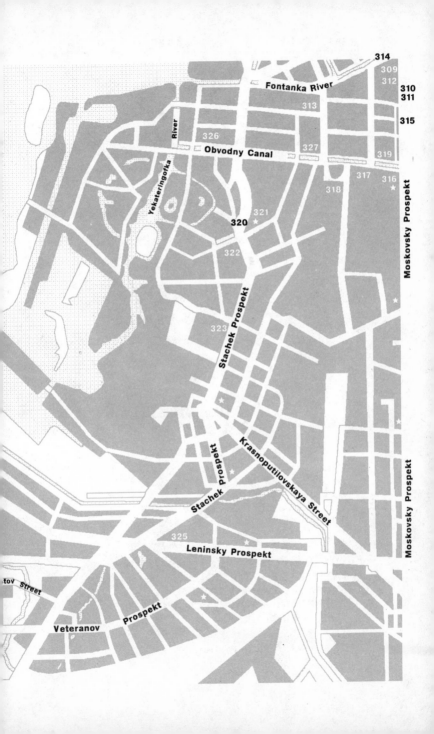

310
THE TECHNOLOGICAL INSTITUTE
Moskovsky Prospekt, 26
1829—31. Architects A.Postnikov and E.Apert

In 1898 and 1913 the main building was raised and new buildings put up after a design by the architects A.Maksimov and L.Shipka. The building in the Moskovsky Prospekt side was added in 1930 (architects A.Gegello and D.Krichevsky).

The Holy Trinity Cathedral
(No 313)

311
THE MONUMENT TO G.PLEKHANOV
1925. Sculptors I.Ginzburg and M.Kharlamov

312
THE COMPLEX OF THE MENDELEYEV RESEARCH INSTITUTE FOR METROLOGY
Moskovsky Prospekt, 19, 21
THE BUILDING WITH A CLOCK-TOWER
1902, architect S.Kozlov
THE «RED HOUSE»
1896—97. Architect A.Gogin

Izmailovsky Prospekt

It came into being in 1762. In that year a road was laid through the Izmailovsky Regiment settlement that had taken shape here in the 1730s—1740s. The road got the name of Voznesenskaya; it was direct continuation of Voznesensky Prospekt.

In the early 19th century this part of it was given the name of Izmailovsky Prospekt. This is a straight, wide, green thoroughfare connecting .Fontanka and Obvodny Canal embankment.

313
THE HOLY TRINITY (IZMAILOVSKY) CATHEDRAL
Izmailovsky Prospekt, 7
1828—35. Architect V.Stasov

The first wooden cathedral was built in the Izmailovsky Regiment settlement in 1753—56. The present stone cathedral reproduces the original design, which is not characteristic of Russian architecture, the five domes placed over the branches of an equi-pointed cross.

The monumental five-dome cathedral is designed in classical forms and has a highly expressive silhouette.

Its grand facades are decorated with porticoes and sculptured friezes. The figures of angels installed in the niches (sculptor S.Galberg) add to the facade ornamentality. Notable, during the dome construction wooden trusses were replaced with metal ones. However, even before the works were completed the big dome was torn down by the wind; when it was being restored the metal trusses were, in their turn, replaced with a framework of radial wooden girders. In the interior decoration Stasov made wide use of white columns of artificial marble.

During the World War II the cathedral-was badly damaged. It was being restored during the 1950s and 1960s.

In 1969 the bust of V.Stasov was put up in the courtyard of the Holy Trinity Cathedral (sculptor M.Litovchenko, architect Zh.Verzhbitsky).

314

DERZHAVIN'S HOUSE
Fontanka Embankment, 118
After 1791. Architect N.Lvov. 1846—48: rebuilt, architect A.Gornostayev

Having in 1791 bought a large land lot with a stone house on the Fontanka bank, G.Derzhavin, the great Russian poet and stateman, commissioned his friend, architect N.Lvov, to reconstruct the house. The main building set at the back of the lot was enlarged considerably; two wings were attached, overlooking the embankment. Behind the house a landscape garden was laid out with artificial ponds, canals, bridges and pavilions, as well as open galleries. In the big hall of the house sittings of the Discussions of Fanciers of the Russian Word Society were taking place beginning from 1811; this was a literary society founded by Derzhavin. Eminent writers were its members, I.Krylov, D.Khvostov and S.Aksakov and others among them.

After the estate was in 1846 acquired by the Roman Catholic Theological Board, the house underwent considerable reconstruction. In one of the flats that have remained, which used to accommodate Derzhavin's study, a memorial museum is soon to be opened.

315

THE FREE ECONOMIC SOCIETY
Moskovsky Prospekt, 33
1806—10. Rebuilt in 1840s

The Free Economic Society is one of the oldest scientific societies in Russia; founded in 1765, it was engaged in the studies of the country's economy. In 1844 the society bought a new house, which in its present shape represents an ensemble of buildings put up at different times. The central building has been many times reconstructed. Of big artistic value is the interior decoration dating back to the 1830s and performed in classical style. In some rooms the ceiling paintings have remained as well as stucco moulding and parquet of different wood species.

In 1923 part of the building came to be called the Plekhanov's House. A separate courtyard outbuilding houses Plekhanov's archives and library, brought into Russia from Switzerland and Italy on Lenin's initiative.

316
THE CITY SLAUGHTER-HOUSE
Moskovsky Prospekt, 65
1821—25. Architect L.Charlemagne
Now a Dairy Complex

A typical sample of classical industrial design.

317
THE VARSHAVSKY (WARSAW) RAILWAY STATION
Obvodny Canal Embankment, 118
1856. Rebuilt in 1857—60. Architect P.Salmanovich

The station is linking Petersburg with many West European countries.

318
THE BALTIYSKY RAILWAY STATION
Obvodny Canal Embankment, 120
1855—57. Architect A.Krakau

319
DYLEV'S HOUSE
Obvodny Canal Embankment, 155
1849. Architect H.Monighetti

The house is designed in neo-Baroque style. It used to belong to a well-known moulder of the time T.Dylev. The lavish façade decoration may have been performed by himself.

320
THE NARVA TRIUMPHAL ARCH
Stachek Square
1827—34. Architect V.Stasov

The arch was put up to commemorate the victory over Napoleon in the Patriotic War of 1812. After the war ended, a wooden triumphal arch was put up in the Narvskoye Road to a design by Quarenghi for the ceremonial meeting of the returning troops. In the 1820s V.Stasov developed a new design, that retained the general features of the previous one. He suggested using brick as the construction material, supplemented with copper sheet facing. This was an innovation in Russian and West European constriction practice.

The Narva
Triumphal Arch
(No 320)

The Narva Arch created by Stasov is an imitation of the Old Roman triumphal arches. It is topped with the Chariot of Glory (the horses performed by P.Klodt, the figure of Glory—by S.Pimenov). At the foot of the gates there stand four statues of Old Russian warriors (sculptors S.Pimenov and V.Demuth-Malinovsky). Over the columns there are four allegorical figures (sculptors M.Krylov and N.Tokarev). The decoration also includes dedicating inscriptions, list of battles, names of the Guards regiments, which took part in them.

Inside the gates there is a room that V.Stasov was planning to use as an exhibition hall devoted to the history of the Narva Arch construction.

In 1941—45 the monument was badly damaged by

shelling. In 1951 the overall restoration works were carried out. In 1987 an exposition concerned with the history of the Great Patriotic War of 1812 was opened in the upper room of the Narva Gates.

The overall height of the arch is more than 30m; it is 28 m wide.

321
THE GORKY PALACE OF CULTURE
Stachek Prospekt, 4
1925—27. Architects A.Gegello and D.Krichevsky

This was the first Palace of Culture to be built in the country. The building was designed in Constructivist style, with clear and functionally loaded spacing. The main part is taken up by the theater hall; the foyers are outwardly accentuated by large stained-glass panels; five-story wings are attached to the projecting staircase towers.

322
SCHOOL No 384
Stachek Prospekt, 11
1925—27. Architect A.Nikolsky

The building is of interest as a sample of Constructivist style of the 1920s. In plan it resembles the hammer and sycle, symbols of socialism.

323
THE KIRYANOVO ESTATE OF YE.DASHKOVA
Stachek Prospekt, 45
1783—84. Architect G.Quarenghi (?)
Now the Wedding Palace

The estate house was put up for Duchess Yekaterina Romanovna Dashkova, President of the Russian Academy and Director of the Academy of Arts. Originally the estate was called Kir and Ioannovo (to commemorate the day of the 1762 coup that brought Catherine II to the throne; Dashkova had taken active part in it); later the two words merged to form Kiryanovo. The structure includes the main building with a four-column portico linked to the side wings by one-story galleries. Later Kiryanovo house used to be leased to the Petersburg Literary Club.

School No 384 (No 322)

324
THE NOVOZNAMENKA ESTATE
Chekistov Street, 13
1755—60. Architect A.Rinaldi

In the early 18th century the estate used to belong to Apraksins brothers. In the middle of the century it was taken over by M.Vorontsov. A mansion with a belvedere was erected for him there. In the 1830s, when the estate belonged to the Miatlev family, the so-called Gothic house was put up there.

The Novoznamenka buildings, that had been badly damaged during World War II, have been restored.

325
CHERNYSHEV'S DACHA
Stachek Prospekt, 162
1770s. Architect Vallin de la Mothe (?)

The house was put up for Count I.Chernyshev. It is designed according to classical canons, the façade center accentuated with a four-column portico, the dome resting upon an octahedral drum, and the side galleries, wings and wide semicircular windows all being present.

Having been badly damaged during World War II, the dacha was restored in 1960 (architect M.Plotnikov).

326
THE RUSSIAN COTTON MILL
Obvodny Canal Embankment, 23—25
Founded in 1835. Architect unknown. The works were supervised by the architect N.Anisimov
Now the Vereteno (Spindle) Mill

The entrance-gate is designed in classical style. It is topped with a rotunda having a statue of Mercury under the cupola. Classical forms were often used in the 19th-century industrial design in Russia.

327
THE HOUSE OF EDUCATIONAL INSTITUTIONS
Obvodny Canal, 181
1911—12. Architect N.Dmitriyev
Now the Tsuriupa House of Culture

This is a sample of a new type of public building dating back to the early 20th century. It accommodated class-rooms, a museum, shops, a theater, etc. The façade is decorated with light-colored tiles, which is typical of Art-Nouveau architecture.

VASILYEVSKY ISLAND

The Spit of Vasilyevsky Island

The Spit is a cape in the island's eastern part. In the late 17th century there used to be a village there. The idea of creating an architectural ensemble originated in the early 1710s. According to D.Trezzini's project (1716) a square was to be laid out there, with dwelling houses running along the bank. However, foundation of the *Kunstkammer* (Chamber of Curiosities) marked the site out as the future city center. In 1803—4 the architect A.Zakharov developed a building project for the spit, that has basically been preserved in the layout. The emphasis was laid on an artistic effect produced by the contrast between the powerful horizontal embankment line and the domineering volume of the Stock Exchange, with its majestic colonnade. The vertical Rostral Columns emphasize the central space of the whole ensemble, taken up by the Stock Exchange.

328
THE STOCK EXCHANGE
Birzhevaya Square, 4
1805—10. Architect Thomas de Thomon

The building of the Stock Exchange is the compositional center of the spit ensemble. It was put up as the main port

The Spit of Vasilyevsky Island

The Stock Exchange (No 328)

The Spit of Vasilyevsky Island

1. The Stock Exchange (No 328);
2,3. Rostral Columns (No 329);
4. The Nord Packhaus;
5. The South Packhaus;
6. The Kunstkammer (No 331);
7. The Main Building of the Academy of Sciences (No 332);
8. The Museum Wing of the Academy of Sciences (No 333);
9. The Twelve Collegia Building (No 336);
10. The Novobirzhevoi Gostiny Dvor (No 334);
11. The Customs-house (No 330)

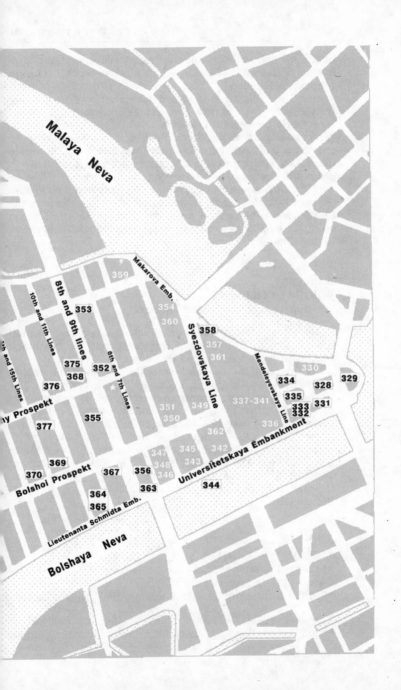

Malaya Neva

10th and 11th Lines

8th and 9th Lines

359

Makarova Emb.

354

360

353

6th and 7th Lines

375
368

352

376

Syezdovskaya Line

358

357

361

Mendeleyevskaya Line

330

334

328

329

335

333
332

331

ny Prospekt

355

351
350

349

337–341

336

377

362

369

347
348
346

345
343

342

Universitetskaya Embankment

370

Bolshoi Prospekt

367

356

363

344

364
365

Lieutenanta Schmidta Emb.

Bolshaya Neva

building, the center of financial and trade operations. The opening ceremony of the new building (the Stock Exchange proper was founded by Peter I as early as 1703) took place in 1806. The building is designed in the style of an antique temple; it is mounted on a high granite socle and surrounded by a Doric colonnade. The socle used to house store-rooms; the central part of the Stock Exchange is taken up by an enormous hall spanned with a caissoned cove vault. In façade decoration sculpture plays the major part, which is placed in attics and made of Pudost limestone by S.Sukhanov (*Neptune with Two Rivers* and *Navigation with Mercury and Two Rivers*). Since 1940 the Stock Exchange building has housed the Central Naval Museum—one of the oldest in Russia; it began as early as 1709 as a store-room for ship models, earlier kept in the Admiralty.

329
ROSTRAL COLUMNS
1810. Architect Thomas de Thomon

In the square before the Stock Exchange two monumental Rostral Columns are rising; they were part of the Stock Exchange project developed by Thomas de Thomon.

Besides serving as lighthouses they stressed the central part played by the Stock Exchange in the ensemble. The pedestals performed of gray granite as well as the columns proper of Pudost limestone are ornamented with metal representations of rostrums, the Latin for ship prows (hence the name). The colossal figures at the foot of the columns personify great Russian rivers—the Volga, Dnieper, Neva and Volkhov. The columns are topped with metal tripods supporting bowl-shaped gas-lamps; they are lighted during national celebrations. There are winding staircases inside the columns.

330
THE CUSTOMS-HOUSE
Makarov Embankment, 4
1829—32. Architect I.Luchini
Now the Institute of Russian Literature (Pushkin House)

The customs-house was to become the last link in the formation of the spit ensemble. It was designed in late classical forms and topped with a dome on a high drum, which made it correspond to the *Kunstkammer* also topped with a tall tower. The main façade facing the Malaya Nevka River is decorated with an eight-column portico raised to the first floor level. In the pediment topping the portico the statues of Mercury, Neptune and Ceres are installed, cast of copper.

Rostral Columns (No 329)

After the building was in 1927 transferred to the possession of the Institute of Russian Literature, the exposition of the Museum of Russian Literature was displayed in the reception halls, based on the private library and manuscripts of A.Pushkin.

331
THE *KUNSTKAMMER* (CHAMBER OF CURIOSITIES)
Universitetskaya (University) Embankment, 3
1718—34. Architects M.Zemtsov, G.Mattarnovi, N.Herbel
G.Chiaveri; rebuilt in 1754—58, architect S.Chevakinsky

The building was designed for the library and the oldest
Russian museum founded by Peter I in 1714 and based on
his private collections brought back from his European
travels. Originally the museum had been housed in Kikin's

The Kunstkammer and the Academy of Sciences (Nos 331, 332)

Chambers; later the *Kunstkammer* moved into a building
especially designed to house it. The story of the
construction was rather complicated. It involved many
outstanding architects of the 18th century. The building
consists of two three-story wings designed in Baroque and
joined into a single whole by the central volume that is
topped with a multi-tier tower. Owing to its size and the tall

tower the *Kunstkammer* building used to play a major part in the ensemble of the city center. One of the wings housed a library, the other one held the museum collections; in the central part there was an anatomical theater, while the tower accommodated the first Russian observatory, the so-called «Hottorp Globe».

After the fire of 1747 the building was restored by the architect Chevakinsky, who introduced some changes into the exterior. To commemorate the 50th anniversary of the Academy of Sciences the *Kunstkammer*'s interiors were decorated with sculptural allegorical groups, busts and medallions representing prominent scientists (of those, two bas-reliefs and a sculptured portrait by M.Pavlov have remained). In the 1830s, due to the growth of its collections, the *Kunstkammer* was divided into several museums: the museums of Zoology, Ethnography, Botany and Mineralogy. The *Kunstkammer* has played a major part in promoting natural sciences in Russia. Many Russian scholars have once worked here. The building now houses the Academy of Sciences Museum of Anthropology and Ethnography, Lomonosov's Memorial Museum, and the Academy of Sciences Institute of Ethnology and Ethnic Anthropology.

332
THE MAIN BUILDING OF THE ACADEMY OF SCIENCES
Universitetskaya (University) Embankment, 5
1783—85. Architect G.Quarenghi

The Academy of Sciences, founded to a project by Peter I in 1724, was originally located in another (Petersburg) district; later, in 1726, it was transferred to Vasilyevsky Island. In 1783 construction of a new, stone building was started, that was designed to house academic shops, a bookshop and apartments for the Academy officials. The building belongs to the best samples of classical architecture; its grand forms make it stand out among the surrounding buildings designed in the Baroque of Peter's period. The central part of the building stretching parallel to the Neva is marked with an eight-column portico. The socle story is faced with granite. Two flights of stairs are leading to the main entrance, raised to the first floor level. The clear-cut composition, plain walls, absence of lintels as well as yellow-and-white coloring are all typical of early classical architecture. The main staircase is decorated with a famous mosaic picture by M.Lomonosov *The Battle of Poltava* (transferred here in 1926); in the conference-hall the 18th—19th century decoration has remained.

The Russian Academy of Sciences resided here till 1934, when it was transferred to Moscow. At present the building houses the Petersburg Branch of the Academy.

333
THE MUSEUM WING OF THE ACADEMY OF SCIENCES
Mendeleyevskaya Liniya, 1
1836—37. Architect I.Lukonin

Behind the building of the Academy of Sciences the Museum Wing was put up, to house the Academic printing works and the museum collections. The two-story building, in the shape of the Russian letter П, is bounding the spacious courtyard of the main academic building. The Museum Wing has circular halls at both corners, spanned with low cupolas. The façades were designed in the style similar to that of the Novobirzhevoi Gostiny Dvor, that had been put up before. The semicircular ground-floor windows correspond to Gostiny Dvor open arcade.

The Novobirzhevoi Gostiny Dvor (No 334)

334
THE NOVOBIRZHEVOI GOSTINY DVOR
Mendeleyevskaya Liniya, 5
Early 19th century. Architect G.Quarenghi
Now one of the University Building

The building was to outline the northern boundary of the spacious square that had taken shape in front of the Twelve Collegia building. The Gostiny Dvor is rectangular in plan, has a spacious inner courtyard and is outwardly a typical sample of the 18th—early 19th century trading stalls. An open arcade runs along the ground floor; the walls are rusticated and complete with a cornice. Later, in the 1930s, the third story was added.

335
THE CLINICAL OBSTETRICS INSTITUTE
Mendeleyevskaya Liniya, 3
1899—1904. Architect L.Benois
Now the Ott Institute of Obstetrics and Gynaecology

336
THE TWELVE COLLEGIA BUILDING
Universitetskaya Embankment, 7/9
1722—42. Architect D.Trezzini; from 1734—with the participation of D.Trezzini, T.Schwertferger and M.Zemtsov
Now the Petersburg University (main building)

This is one of the earliest 18th-century structures, a rarest example of a public building of the period. It was designed to accommodate the highest bodies of state power in Russia — the Senate and the Collegia (Ministries) instituted by Peter the Great. In 1724, after the construction had been started, a competition for the best design was announced for the first time in Russian history. The building consists of twelve separate parts (by the number of ministries), joined into a single whole. The main façade of enormous length (approx. 400m) faces east, while its flanking part overlooks the Neva. According to the original project a navigable canal was to be laid along the main façade, on the site of the present Mendeleyevskaya Liniya. An open arcade was running all along the façade. The building is spanned with

The University (No 336)

a four-stooped roof that makes it look taller and adds to its monumentality. The decorative elements—flat blades, figured lintels and attics, as well as the two-color wall—are all typical of the Baroque of Peter's period. The sculptural decorations of the ceiling and walls that have remained in the Peter Hall, the ceiling painting and painted panels were performed in 1736 (master Ignacio Rossi).

Later the building was partly (in 1819), and, further, wholly (in 1835) transferred to the possession of the Petersburg University. Consequently, in 1834—38, it was partly rebuilt (architect A.Shchedrin). The open arcade was glazed; a garden was laid out along the façade fenced with a cast-iron railing; a grand staircase and a white-columned assembly hall were erected in the central part of the building.

Since its very beginning the University has been one of the major educational institutions in Russia. The names of prominent Russian scientists and men of culture have been associated with it, including D.Mendeleyev, A.Popov, I.Sechenov. I.Mechnikov, I.Pavlov, A.Blok, and others.

On the ground floor, Mendeleyevskaya Liniya, Mendeleyev's memorial museum was opened in 1911 in the flat where the great scientist used to live.

337
THE RECTOR HOUSE OF THE UNIVERSITY
Universitetskaya Embankment, 9
1834—35. Architect A.Shchedrin

The house had been put up before the Twelve Collegia building was taken over by the University. In its outward decoration the architect had followed the main building's architectural forms. It is placed at the back of the plot, its side façade overlooking the Neva fits very well into the ensemble of buildings located in the same part of the embankment.

338
THE PALACE OF PETER II
Universitetskaya Embankment, 11
Now one of the University building

The Palace of Peter II is part of the Neva embankment ensemble, which got its start in the 18th century. The foundation of the building was laid in 1727 on the Menshikov's estate territory. With the death of Peter II the

The Menshikov Palace (No 340)

construction works came to a halt, to be completed as late as 1759—61, when the plot was transferred into possession of the First Cadet Corps. Architecturally it is close to the Menshikov Palace, which is a sample of the Baroque of Peter' period. Later it underwent several reconstructions.

339
THE FIRST CADET CORPS MANÈGE
Universitetskaya Embankment, 13
1756—59. Architect I.Barchard. Sculptural façade decor by I.Just

Typical sample of late Baroque.

340
THE MENSHIKOV PALACE
Universitetskaya Embankment, 15
1710—14. Architect D.Fontana, rebuilt by G.Schadel
Now a Branch of the Hermitage

The Palace of Peter's associate A.Menshikov is not only the oldest, but also one of the largest stone buildings in Petersburg. Originally the palace comprised the main building facing the embankment and two wings bounding a small courtyard. On the large territory attached to the palace a regular park was laid out with fountains, sculptures and a grotto in it; a pier was arranged on the Neva side. The three-story palace was characteristically designed in the style of Peter's period (it has high fractured roof, pilasters arranged story-wise provided with carved stone capitels, blank lintels, two-colored walls, etc.) and stood out for the lavishness of interior decoration; it was here that famous Peter's «assemblies» took place. Russian military victories were celebrated there, as well as foreign embassadors and overseas guests were received there too. Later, throughout the 18th century, the palace underwent several reconstructions. Recently, following continuous restoration works, the building has assumed its original early 18th-century appearance. At present an exposition is open there dealing with Russian culture of the 1700—1730s.

341
THE FIRST CADET CORPS BUILDING
Syezdovskaya Liniya, 1—3
1730s—1740s, 1770s

In 1732 Menshikov's Palace that was confiscated from its owner (he was exiled to Siberia), was given into the possession of the Land Shliakhetsky (Gentry) Cadet Corps. This privileged educational establishment trained future Russian army officers. To suit the Corps' needs a new building was attached to the western palace wing, that was in the 1770s extended considerably along Syezdovskaya Liniya and redesigned in classical style.

342
THE RUMIANTSEV OBELISK
1799. Architect V.Brenna

This is a memorial to Field Marshal P.Rumiantsev. It had been originally put up in the Field of Mars. According to C.Rossi's project it was later transferred to a site in the vicinity of the First Cadet Corps where Rumiantsev had received his military training. In the 1860s a garden was laid out around it, with two fountains and a cast-iron railing. The obelisk made of gray Serdobol granite is a typical sample of this type of memorials.

343
THE ACADEMY OF ARTS
Universitetskaya Embankment, 17
1764—88. Architects A.Kokorinov, J.-B.Vallin de la Mothe
Now the Repin Institute of Painting, Sculpture and Architecture. The Academy of Arts Museum

The last building in the University Embankment is the grand Academy of Arts, which is one of the most outstanding samples of Russian 18th-century architecture. The best view of the Academy, its grand and austere forms stretching along the embankment, as well as the granite landing-stage with the figures of sphinxes at the entrance, is opening from the opposite Neva bank.
    The building is of an original design; into the center of

the rectangular structure another ring-shaped building is inscribed with an inner courtyard, as well as four smaller rectangular courtyards. The interior rooms of different shapes and sizes are laid out deliberately. The main façade facing the Neva is decorated with a portico of paired columns that have copies of antique sculptures (Heracles and Flora) installed between them. The rusticated lower story is treated as a massive socle; the two upper stories are joined into a single whole by Doric columns. The circular courtyard (approx. 40m in diameter) had originally been linked with the embankment by means of a through

The Academy of Arts (No 343)

passage, that was later turned into a vestibule. The upper vestibule comprises a colonnade supporting the gallery. Next to the vestibule in 1817—20 a cast-iron staircase was erected (architect A.Mikhailov the 2nd). The walls are painted to the designs by A.Yegorov, A.Ivanov, V.Shebuyev and decorated with bas-reliefs by V.Demuth-Malinovsky, S.Pimenov, I.Martos and I.Prokofyev. Artistically of most interest is the first floor suite comprising the so-called Raphael and Titian halls (1834—40, architect K.Thon), as well as the Conference Hall (rebuilt in 1864 by the architect A.Rezanov and retaining Shebuyev's mural painting) and the house church (architect K.Thon).

The names of many outstanding Russian artists are associated with the Academy of Arts, that was established in 1754 as «the Academy of the three prominent Arts». Here such architects as V.Bazhenov, V.Starov, A.Voronikhin, A.Zakharov used to study, as well as such famous sculptors as M.Kozlovsky, F.Shubin, S.Pimenov, and such outstanding painters as D.Levitsky, O.Kiprensky, F.Bruni, C.Briullov, I.Repin.

The Landing-stage with Sphinxes (No 344)

344
THE LANDING-STAGE WITH SPHINXES
(in front of the Academy of Arts)
1832—34. Architect K.Thon

The landing-stage with sphinxes is one of the finest sights in Petersburg. It was designed by K.Thon in 1832—34 and erected of massive red granite blocks placed on a foundation of piles. On both sides of the wide staircase leading down to the Neva the figures of sphinxes are installed on granite pedestals; the figures were carved out of syenite in the 13th century B.C. They were discovered during the excavation works at Thebes in the 1820s. Their heads bear portrait likeness to Pharaoh Amenhotep III. They were bought by the Russian government and delivered to Petersburg in 1832. The composition also includes granite benches and bronze lamps imitating antique samples.

345
THE ACADEMICIANS HOUSE
Lieutenant Schmidt Embankment, 1
1808—9. Architect A.Bezhanov, to a design by A.Zakharov

This is a typical sample of the early 19th-century block of flats. The façade is decorated with a monumental portico supporting the enteblature and the balcony over it. For more than 100 years this house, that used to belong to the Academy of Sciences, had been the place of residence for many prominent Russian scholars. Their names are indicated on the 26 memorial plaques placed on the walls. Among them are V.Vernadsky, P.Chebyshev, B.Jakobi and others. The flat where I.Pavlov used to live now houses his memorial museum.

346
THE ACADEMY OF ARTS COMPLEX

Behind the Academy of Arts building there is a small garden; in the center of it the column «To the Three Prominent Arts» is rising, that was put up in 1847 to a design by A.Briullov. The granite column is topped with a bronze capital comprising decorative garlands and three bronze figures—personifications of painting, sculpture and architecture.

In the northern part of the garden, on the same axis with the main building the garden outbuilding is located that houses drawing classrooms; it was erected in 1819—21 by the architect A.Mikhailov the 2nd. The two-storied rectangular structure stands out for its grandeur; it is decorated with a six-column Doric portico ornamented with flutes.

In 1846—69 two-storied dwelling houses were put up

on both sides of the garden outbuilding for the teachers of the Academy, the so-called Professors Houses (architect A.Briullov). They are linked to the central building by means of passages. The third story was added to them, and the Academy garden was fenced with a cast-iron railing.

The building overlooking the 3d Liniya (No 2a) was erected in 1862—64 to a design by F.Eppinger to house the department of mosaics of the Academy of Arts.

347
THE ANDREYEVSKY MARKET
6th Liniya, 9
1789—90. Architect unknown

The market building is a typical sample of the 18th-century trading stalls. The ground floor is girdled by an open arcade. The shops represent similar rooms that are isolated from each other and have individual exits into the inner courtyard, as well as staircases leading on to the first floor; they were also connected with the outer gallery.

348
TROYEKUROV'S HOUSE
6th Liniya, 13
1700—1730s

This is one of the few stone buildings designed in the Baroque of Peter's period. It was erected for A.Troyekurov, high official at the court of Peter I.

349
THE LUTHERAN CHURCH OF ST.CATHERINE
Bolshoi Prospekt, 1
1768—71. Architect Yu.Velten

The church stands at the corner of Bolshoi Prospekt and the 1st Liniya (Line). The architecture is typical of early Classicism. It is rectangular in plan and comprises a vestibule, auxiliary rooms and a large hall divided into there naves by columns. The two-tier building is topped with a small dome on a low drum. The main façade is decorated with a four-column portico and sculptured figures of Apostles Peter and Paul installed in the niches on both sides of it.

350
ST.ANDREW'S CATHEDRAL
6th Liniya, 11
1764—80. Architect A.Viest

The cathedral is designed in a style transitional from Baroque to Classicism and stands out for an intricate plan composition. The semicircular shape of the apse is repeated

Troyekurov's house (No 348)

The Lutheran Church of St. Catherine (No 349)

in the southern and northern façades. A two-tier belfry is attached to the refectory, that is topped with a spire. The main volume is topped with five elongated domes on high polyhedral drums. In 1848—1850s the cathedral had the side chapels attached to it, that changed the original composition (architect N.Grebionka). Inside, the carved wooden iconostasis has remained.

351
THE CHURCH OF THE THREE SAINTS
6th Liniya, 11
1740—60. Architect D.Trezzini (?)

The church design is very simple: it is a rectangular
building with a trihedral apse. This simplicity goes very well
with the typical 18th-century façade decoration (flat
pilasters supporting the cornice, lintels of various shapes,
gable roof). The church is topped with a small cupola on an
octohedral drum.

St. Andrew's Cathedral (No 350)

352
THE UCHILISHCHNY HOUSE
Sredny (Middle) Prospekt, 31
1896—97. Architect A.Gershwend

This building used to house twelve primary municipal
schools. It was the first building of this type in Russia.

353
THE BLAGOVESHCHENSKAYA (ANNUNCIATION) CHURCH
8th Liniya, 67b
1750—65. Architect unknown

The church was built in the Moscow 17th-century
architectural tradition, strange to the 18th-century

*The Church of
the Three Saints (No 351)*

*The Annunciation Church
(No 353)*

Petersburg style. The three-story building, cross-shaped in
plan, is topped with five bulbous domes. The open galleries
that used to run around the church were walled in 1789.
During the same period a multi-tier belfry was put up, that
fit in very well with the overall church composition.

354
THE MARY MAGDALENE HOSPITAL
1st Liniya, 58
Late 18th century. Rebuilt in 1828, architect D.Quadri

In the late 18th century the spacious two-story building,
rectangular in plane, belonged to the merchant I.Kusov.

The main façade facing the Makarov Embankment is decorated with six Corinthian columns uniting two stories. In 1828 Kusov's house was turned into a hospital; consequently, the interiors underwent considerable reconstruction.

A dwelling house (No 355)   *A dwelling house (No 356)*

355
A DWELLING HOUSE
9th Liniya, 30
1907. Architect S.Banige

356
A DWELLING HOUSE
7th Liniya, 16—18
1907—10. Architects Z.Levi, R.Niman; mosaics by V.Frolov

The façade is faced with light-colored ceramic tiles—the decoration typical of Art-Nouveau in Petersburg. In 1983, after restoration works had been completed, a kind of a museum was set up here devoted to Russian pharmaceutics.

357
DWELLING HOUSES
Makarov Embankment, 14—16
1823—24. Architect A.Melnikov

The houses have retained their classical design.

St. Catherine Church (No 358)

358
ST.CATHERINE CHURCH
Syesdovskaya Liniya, 27—29
1811—23. Architect A.Mikhailov the 2nd

The monumental church building is of Greek cross shape in plan. The main volume is topped with a large cupola on a high drum surrounded with columns. The main façade was decorated with a portico demolished in 1863 due to the construction of the stone belfry (architect A.Bolotov). At the same time the refectory, chapel, lodge and fence were put up.

359
DWELLING HOUSES
Maly Prospekt, 5,7
1900. Architect V.Demianovsky

A dwelling house (No 359)

360
THE RUSSIAN ACADEMY
1st Liniya, 52
1802—4. Architect A.Mikhailov the 2nd. 1811—14, architect V.Stasov. 1840s, architect Ch.Meyer

In 1800 a plot in the 1st Line that had since the mid-18th century belonged to the Moscow bishopric, was transferred into possession of the Russian Academy, with a building put up in it especially for Academy's purposes. The main façade is singled out with pilasters that unite the two upper stories, as well as statues on both sides of the pediment. On the ground floor the Secretary of the Academy used to live; on the upper floor there were a large sitting hall, a library and a reception room. The two-story wings linked to the main building by the gates were put up later to a V.Stasov's design. In the 1840s, when the Russian Academy was merged with the Academy of Sciences, the building was taken over by another establishment and considerably renovated.

The Russian Academy, that was concerned with linguistic and literary issues was founded in Petersburg in 1783. Its first president was Duchess Ye.Dashkova (1783—96). Prominent writers, scholars and men of culture were members of the Academy, including G.Derzhavin, D.Fonvizin, I.Krylov, N.Karamzin, A.Pushkin and others. In 1841 the Russian Academy became part of the Academy of Sciences.

361
A.BRIULLOV'S HOUSE
Syezdovskaya Liniya, 21

The house used to belong to the architect A.Briullov, who redesigned it in late classical style in 1845. Later it was owned by the architect P.Suzor. It also housed the collection of the Old Petersburg Museum, of which P.Suzor was one of the initiators.

362
SCHUBERT'S HOUSE
1st Liniya, 12
First quarter of the 18th century. Architect unknown

The house has remained practically unchanged and is a typical example of an average-sized dwelling house of the 18th—early 19th centuries.

363
UMNOVA'S HOUSE
Lieutenant Schmidt Embankment, 5
Late 18th—early 19th century

The Leutenant Schmidt Embankment, which continues Universitetskaya (University) Embankment, differs from the latter by the type of the buildings found here; they are mostly not public buildings, but dwelling houses. It is here that beginning from 1716 the «continuous façade» construction was started in the island to a project by the architects J.-B.Leblond and D.Trezzini. Many houses have reached us with only slight alterations. Typical of the embankment is the «stepped» construction, when houses do not stand in a single line but form projections, following the curving bank line.

Umnova's house is a nice sample of a dwelling house for the nobility of the late 18th—early 19th centuries. The central part of the main façade facing the embankment was accentuated with a triple Venetian window opening on the balcony and a low attic with a large semicircular window—a motif popular in contemporary architecture. The interiors have retained the early 19th-century decoration.

364
THE NAVAL CADET CORPS
Lieutenant Schmidt Embankment, 17
1796—98. Architect A.Volkov. Now Frunze Higher Naval School

365
STATUE OF ADMIRAL I.KRUSENSTERN
(in front of the Corps building)
1873. Sculptor I.Schroeder, architect I.Monighetti

366
THE MINING INSTITUTE
Lieutenant Schmidt Embankment, 45
1806—8. Architect A.Voronikhin

The Mining Institute that was founded in 1773 as a Mining School is the first higher technical educational establishment to be set up in Russia, as well as one of the first in the world. The institute building takes up a large territory and completes the embankment vista. When constructing the building Voronikhin united five existing houses into a single whole. The building is designed in grand and laconic Empire forms and stands out for its perfect compositional

design. The main façade overlooking the Neva is marked
with a grand portico of twelve fluted Doric columns
supporting the pediment. The plain wall surfaces are
ornamented with bas-reliefs on mythological subjects
(sculptor V.Demuth-Malinovsky). At the top of the wide
staircase leading to the main entrance two sculptural
groups are installed on low pedestals, called *Pluto Carrying
Off Proserpine and Heracles and Anteus*, of Pudost limestone to a design by sculptors S.Pimenov and V.Demuth-
Malinovsky. They form an organic part of the overall
composition. Inside, the front staircase has been preserved.
The decoration of the Column Hall and Caryatid Hall was
performed in the 1820s (architect A.Postnikov, ceiling

*Statue
of Admiral I.Krusenstern
(No 365)*

painting by D.Scotti). In the same period several new
buildings were erected on the institute territory to a design
by the architect A.Postnikov, including the laboratory
building decorated with two cast-iron sphinxes placed at
the entrance.

The Institute also holds the unique collection of the
Mining Museum, which was founded in 1773 and is one of
the largest in the world.

367
THE PRINTING-HOUSE OF THE ACADEMY OF SCIENCES
Bolshoi Prospekt, 28
1808—10. Architect A.Mikhailov the 2nd (?)
Now the Nauka printing-house

This is a typical classical mansion erected for the Portuguese consul Pedro Lopez, that was in 1825 handed over to the printing works. Of interest is the stone fence on the 9th Line side. The monumental gates are designed in the shape of an arch supported by two Doric columns.

The Mining Institute (No 366)

368
A DWELLING HOUSE
Sredny Prospekt, 45
1915. Architect A.Baranovsky

369
THE ALEXANDROVSKY WOMEN' SHELTER
Bolshoi Prospekt, 49—51
1897—99. Architect K.Schmidt. Now a maternity hospital

This is a sample of so-called «brick» style in the late 19th-century architecture.

370
A DWELLING HOUSE
Bolshoi Prospekt, 57
1913—14. Architect L.Benois

The building is typical of the Petersburg Art-Nouveau style. The façade is decorated with numerous bay-windows and classical elements of fine design.

371
THE HOSPITAL OF THE FINLAND REGIMENT
Bolshoi Prospekt, 65
1817—20. Architect A.Staubert
Now the House of Culture

This is a sample of emphatically austere version of classical style.

372
THE KIROV PALACE OF CULTURE
Bolshoi Prospekt, 83
1931—37. Architect N.Trotsky, S.Kozak

The building was designed in Constructivist style.

373
A DWELLING HOUSE
Bolshoi Prospekt, 93
1904—5. Architect F.Lidval

The house is of interest as a sample of Art-Nouveau.

374
THE CHURCH OF MOTHER OF GOD THE MERCIFUL
Bolshoi Prospekt, 100
1889—98. Architect V.Kosiakov, D.Prussak

375
THE BUILDING OF THE BESTUZHEV HIGHER WOMEN'S COURSES
Sredny Prospekt, 41—43
Architect V.Tsiedler
Now one of the University buildings

The building is of interest as a sample of the so-called «northern Art-Nouveau». The courses that were housed there were widely known all over Russia. They were supervised by the historian K.Bestuzhev-Riumin.

376
A DWELLING HOUSE
Sredny Prospekt, 53
1912. Architect I.Pretro

The lavishly decorated façade designed in Neo-Baroque style is characteristic of the Petersburg architecture of the time.

377
K.MAI'S GYMNASIA
14th Liniya, 39
1909. Architect G.Grimm
Now the Computing Center

The oldest private boys' school was founded in 1856 by professor K.Mai. It came to be housed in this building in 1910. Among the students there were many people who were to become famous—A.Benois, N.Roerich, K.Somov, M.Dobuzhinsky, the artists; J.Frenkel, N.Kachalov, D.Likhachiov, and others.

378
THE BUILDING OF THE OLGINSKY ORPHAN-ASYLYM
Sredny Prospekt, 80
1897—1900. Architects M.Geieler and B.Guslitsky

This is an original structure with a tall spire in the façade center and colored majolica insets over the entrance.

379
THE OCTAVIAN HOTEL
Sredny Prospekt, 88
1980. Architect M.Chernov

In this building the unusual «toothed» façade is noteworthy. Inside the hall and the restaurant are decorated with compositions of glass and ceramics.

The Smolenskoye Orthodox Cemetery (No 381)

380
FORMER THEODORITI'S HOTEL
Maly Prospekt, 38—40
1903—6. Architect I.Volodikhin

This is a good example of Art-Nouveau style.

381
THE SMOLENSKOYE ORTHODOX CEMETERY
Kamskaya Street, 24

The cemetery had been active since 1756. It owes its name to the former inhabitants of the Smolensk province who were resettled to Petersburg during its construction and later buried here. According to the historic tradition the Smolenskoye Cemetery had been the burial-place for the scholars of the Academy of Sciences, Petersburg University,

The Chapel of Blessed Xenia of Petersburg (No 382)

Mining Institute, as well as for the men of art from the Academy of Arts, all the institutions located in Vasilyevsky Island. The cemetery gates were erected in the 1800s by the architect L.Rusca; the Resurrection Church was put up in 1901—4 (architect V.Demenovsky).

382
THE CHAPEL OF BLESSED XENIYA OF PETERSBURG
(supposedly over her burial-place)
1901—2. Architect A.Vseslavin

Worshiping of Blessed Kseniya began in the 1820s. She was canonized by the Orthodox church in 1988.

Dekabristov (Decemberists) Island
(separated from Vasilyevsky Island
by the Smolenka River)

Until 1925 the island used to be called Golodai, that came from the transformed name of the English physician T.Holliday, who used to own land there. The island was renamed in order to commemorate the members of the Decemberists' uprising executed in 1825. Over their supposed graves an obelisk of black granite was put up in 1939 to a design by the architect A.Bobrov. The obelisk is 3m high. Beginning from the mid-19th century Golodai had been increasingly turning into an industrial district. The oldest enterprises are the paper-mill, dye-works, weaving-mill, and the Kalinin Plant.

383
THE SMOLENSKOYE LUTHERAN CEMETERY
Smolenka Embankment, 9

The cemetery was founded in 1747 and is one of the oldest belonging non-Orthodox church in the city. It is attached to the Lutheran St.Catherine's Church.

Gavan (Harbor)

It includes the western part of Vasilyevsky Island. Cultivation of the territory started immediately after foundation of Petersburg. It became the city territory in 1808, but had remained its outskirts for a long time.

384
THE GUARD-HOUSE
Shkipersky Protok (Skipper's Channel) Street, 21
1820s

385
THE GALERNAYA (GALLEY) HARBOR
1721. Works supervised by D.Trezzini

This is a fine sample of engineering design of the first quarter of the 18th century. It represents a rectangular pool

The Harbor Workers' Town (No 388)

that was dug for military row-ships (galleys) and linked with the Gulf of Finland. Along the gulf shore a rampart was put up supported with piles and laid with stones, to protect the territory from floods. In the 1740s the Galley Shipyard and Galley Port were built, and the harbor reconstructed. The works were supervised by S.Chevakinsky. In the early 19th century the shipyard was abolished. Beginning from the mid-19th century the harbor and the port were used for testing naval equipment.

The Pribaltiyskaya Hotel (No 389)

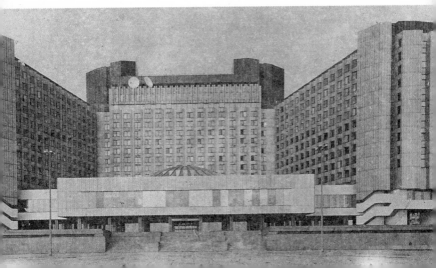

386
THE GALERNAYA HARBOR KRONSPIETZES

The two low towers topped with high flagstaffs were built in wood in the 1720s (architect D.Trezzini) as navigation signs designating the harbor entrance. In 1754 they were reconstructed in stone (architect M.Bashmakov).

387
THE PORT ARRIVAL AND DEPARTURE BUILDING
Morskoi Slavy (Naval Glory) Square, 1
1977—82. The project supervised by V.Sokhin

The building is interesting for its façades faced with solid metal panels resembling sails filled with wind. The station is topped with a 78-meter spire made of titan.

388
THE HARBOR WORKERS' TOWN
Maly Prospekt, 71/47
1904—7. Architects N.Dmitriyev and V.Fiodorov

This is the first successful experience of a complex building up of a whole block (after the revolution of 1917 it was in wide use when constructing housing developments for workers on the city outskirts). The «town» comprised five-story houses, as well as a club with a dining room and a school. The construction of such type was initiated by B.Dril, Chairman of the Association for Better Housing Conditions Philanthropic Society.

389
THE PRIBALTIYSKAYA HOTEL
Korablestroitelei (Shipbuilders) Street, 14
1976—78. Architects N.Baranov, S.Yevdokimov and V.Kovaliov

The building is H-shaped in plan. The side wings overlook both the city and the sea. The interiors are comfortable and stand out for the masterful decor. Ornamental compositions of glass and ceramics, as well as tapestry decorate the Pribaltiysky, Neva, Petrovsky and Daugava restaurants situated in the hotel.

In front of the main entrance there stands the *Taming of the Baltic* sculptural group (1982, sculptor E.Agaian).

PETROGRADSKAYA SIDE

390
THE TROITSKY (TRINITY) BRIDGE
over the Neva to Kamennoostrovsky Prospekt
1897—1903

The first pontoon bridge was built some distance up-stream in 1803. Beginning from the 1880s the projects for a permanent bridge were being developed. In 1892 and 1896 two international competitions for the best project were held. The two first awards were won by the projects by A.Eifel and the French Batignol firm, that was in fact carried into effect. The project envisaged the most rational and economical construction design.

Moreover, the metal, cantilever construction added to the graceful proportionality of the bridge outline. The Troitsky Bridge can be considered the best example of metal bridges in Petersburg, which has especially brought forth the expressive possibilities of steel constructions. The bridge was erected by Russian workers of Russian-made materials. The works were supervised by a special commission including 25 engineers and 11 architects, among them the engineers L.Nikolai and A.Pshenitsky, the architects L.Benois and R.Herdlike; a lot of alterations were

Petrogradskaya Side

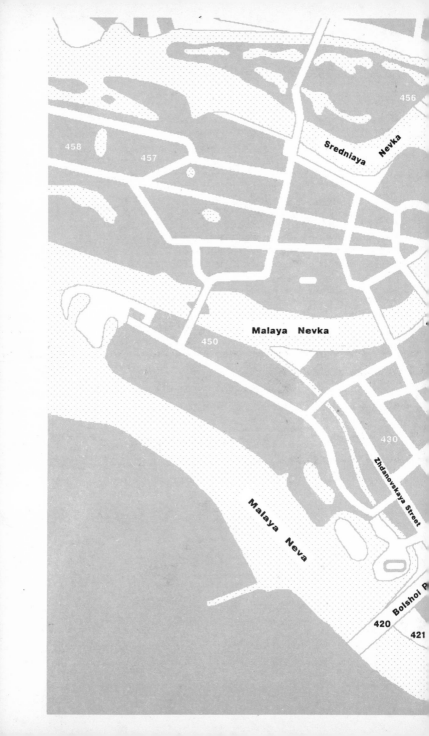

The Troitsky Bridge (No 390)

introduced into the original project by the French architects V.Chambrol and R.Patuliard. In 1900—8 a three-span granite arcade was erected on the Neva left bank, at the approach to the bridge (engineer G.Krivoshein). The entrance to the bridge is marked by two obelisks decorated with rostrums, that are supporting globe-shaped lamps. The obelisks are topped with two-headed eagles. The bridge railings and lanterns are designed in Art-Nouveau style, however, they lack the refinement characteristic of the style.

The bridge is 578.3m long and 23.6m wide.

391
THE PETER AND PAUL FORTRESS

The Peter and Paul Fortress is both the architectural and historical center of Petersburg. It was around it that one of the finest cities in the world had taken shape within a few decades. The fortress was designed to protect the Neva lands that were won from the Swedes during the Northern War (1700—21). Its powerful stone walls, that look as if they were rising out of the water, and the cathedral spire soaring into the skies, make up a unique view opening from afar and constituting an integral part of the wide Neva panorama. One of the islands was chosen as a construction site located at the point where the river branches devided into three arms: the Bolshaya (Big) Nevka, Neva, and Malaya (Small) Nevka. The island was called Zayachy (Hare) or Vesioly (Cheerful); its location was unique from the military point of view. The wide, deep Neva served to protect the fortress, while the latter, in its turn, was covering the entrance to the Neva from the Gulf of Finland. From the fortress walls a large territory could be shelled. The small size of the island made it possible to build up the whole of it, without leaving any land for the enemy to land his troops on. On May 16 (May 27, New Style), 1703, the foundation of the fortress was laid, that was to be named Saint-Petersburg. This day is considered to be the day when the city got its start. The name of the fortress was soon

The Peter and Paul Fortress

1. St.Peter's Gate (No 392);
2. Engineering House (No 394);
3. The Officer's Guard-house;
4. The Neva Gate (No 397);
5. Commandant's House (No 394);
6. The Peter and Paul Cathedral (No 393);
7. The Boathouse (No 395);
8. The Mint (No 396);
9. The Anna Ioannovna Cavaliere;
10. The Kronwerk (No 398).

transferred to the whole city, while the fortress acquired the name of Peter and Paul (after the name of the cathedral built there).

Construction of the first earthen and wooden fortifications was carried on at an accelerated rate and was completed as early as the autumn of 1703. In developing the fortress design Peter I took an active part. The outlines of the fortress depended on the shape of the island proper; it was designed in the shape of an elongated hexagon with six projecting bastions. Construction works were supervised by Peter's associates, including A.Menshikov, G.Golovkin, N.Zotov, Yu.Trubetskoi, K.Naryshkin. Five bastions bear their names, while the sixth one got the name of Gosudarev bastion in honor of Peter I. The bastions are connected with walls—curtains, which are also six in number.

In 1706 they started to rebuild the wooden fortress in stone; the reconstruction lasted till 1740. The fortress was rebuilt section after section, for it not to lose its fighting capacity. This work, forts and foremost in importance, was entrusted to D.Trezzini, the forts fortifier and architect of the new capital. The fortress was being put up as a forts-class military structure of the 18th century. The bastions and curtains built of brick and stone were 10—12m high and up to 20m wide. They consist of two walls; the space between them is filled with sand, broken brick and earth. Inside the curtains, rooms were arranged for ammunition storage, as well as barracks for the garrison soldiers. In the north the fortress was also protected by the strait and

The Peter and Paul Fortress (No 391)

additional installations—earthen fortifications, that were crown-shaped in plan (hence the name of Kronwerk). In 1731—33 construction of stone ravelins was started (these were additional structures protecting the fortress gates and curtains from shelling). On the eastern side the Ioannovsky (St.John's) Ravelin was put up, and on the western side— Alekseyevsky (St.Alexei) Ravelin. They were separated from the rest of the territory by moats that were filled up with earth in the late 19th century. In the late 18th century the brick walls facing the Neva were clad with granite. During the 18th—19th centuries several buildings were put up inside the fortress, among them the Peter and Paul Cathedral, the Commandant's and Engineering houses, the Boathouse and the Mint that constitute the majestic ensemble of the fortress. The Peter and Paul Fortress was put up for fortification purposes; however, it had never been used as such. Beginning from 1718 it was turned into a prison for political convicts. In the Trubetskoi Bastion Peter I used to interrogate his son Alexei and his associates; it was there that Alexei died in 1718. Since the late 18th century the fortress has been the confinement place for Russian revolutionaries. One of the first to be imprisoned there was A.Radishchev who was arrested in 1790 for his book *A Journey from St.Petersburg to Moscow*. The fortress casemates saw the participants of the Decemberists' uprising of 1825. In 1826 five of their leaders were executed on the Kronwerk rampart. Imprisoned here were also members of the Petrashevsky Circle, revolutionary democrats, Narodniks, members of the People's Will and many others. Since 1924 Peter and Paul Fortress has been a museum.

392

ST.PETER'S GATE
1707—8—wooden gate, 1718—stone gate. Architect D.Trezzini

St.Peter's Gate is an imitation of a triumphal arch and overlooks Troitskaya (Trinity) Square. This is the only triumphal edifice put up in Peter's times that has reached our time. Originally it had been made of wood and ornamented with bas-reliefs *The Defeat of Simon the Fortune-Teller* (by C.Osner), *Our Lord in the Skies*, amour, as well as the statue of St.Peter. The stone gate was an exact replica of the wooden one. The carved bas-reliefs and

decorations were transferred on to the new gate. In the
1720s a two-headed eagle was fixed over the gate cast of
gilt lead—the coat-of-arms of the tsarist Russia. In the gate
niches statues of Belonna and Minerva were installed, that
were to personify the wisdom of Peter I as a statesman and
his military talents. The overall gate decoration was to
glorify Russia's victory over Sweden. The St.Peter's Gate is
rusticated and end in a smooth curve of volutes and a
semicircular pediment; it is oriented to the Sts. Peter and
Paul Cathedral. The eastern façade of the latter, that
repeats the gate's composition is accurately inscribed into
the gate arch.

Later, when the St.John's Ravelin was erected in the
1730s, St.John's Gate became the main entrance to the
fortress. The date carved over the arch—1740—marks the
end of the construction works.

393
THE PETER AND PAUL CATHEDRAL
1712—33. Architect D.Trezzini

The Peter and Paul Cathedral is a unique sample of Russian
18th-century architecture that has reached us. Its grand
multi-tier belfry with a gilt spire is an architectural
dominant of the city, an integral part of its silhouette.

Foundation of the first, wooden, church in the name of
Apostles Peter and Paul was laid in 1703 at the same time
when the earthen fortress. Since 1712 Petersburg had
become the capital of the Russian state. Consequently,
construction of a stone cathedral was started on the site of
the wooden church. The cathedral took 21 years to build.
The construction was carried on to a design by D.Trezzini;
the first to be built was the multi-tier belfry with a wooden
spire covered with gilt copper sheets. The spire was topped
with a weather-vane representing a figure of a flying angel
holding a cross. The works had been completed by late
1724; at the same time the chimes were installed in the
belfry, brought to Russia by Peter I. The construction and
decoration of the cathedral were finished only as late as
1732. It was consecrated on June 29, 1733. During the
fire of 1756 the wooden spire was burned down together
with the chimes; the walls were badly damaged as well. In
1766 it was decided to restore the belfry in its original
shape. The works went on for 10 years. As for the

cathedral, its restoration was completed a year after the fire. In 1776 the new chimes were installed in the belfry, performed by O.Crass in Holland, that have remained till nowadays. In 1857—58 the wooden spire construction was replaced by a metal one, to a design by engineer D.Zhuravsky.

St. Peter's Gate (No 392)

The Peter and Paul Cathedral (No 393)

The Peter and Paul Cathedral marked a new stage in Russian architecture. The building is not of a traditional Russian design; it is built in the new, early Baroque style, which combines simple layout with rather modest façade decoration.

The cathedral is an elongated rectangular building. The façades are ornamented with pilasters and Cherubs' heads on the lintels. The belfry tiers, reaching upwards, are connected by volutes that create a smooth transition from the main volume to the tall spire. The cathedral is the tallest building in old Petersburg. It is 122.5m high, height of the spire being 40m.

The cathedral interior is divided by powerful pylons into three naves. It is not designed in the Russian tradition, either, resembling a palace hall with tall windows and chandeliers made of crystal and gilt bronze.

The walls are light colored, while the pylons and pilasters are painted in imitation of pink and green marble; over the windows pictures by best 18th-century artists are placed, including A.Matveyev, G.Gzel, I.Betskoi and others.

The iconostasis performed by the Moscow architect I.Zarudny is a real masterpiece of Russian and world art. More than forty skilful carvers, carpenters and gilders were working on it from 1722 up to 1727. It is designed as a triumphal arch to commemorate the victory of Russia in the Northern War; by the original composition, lavish decoration and skilful performance it can successfully compete with famous world masterpieces of carved wood. The icons for the iconostasis were also painted by moscovites headed by A.Merkuryev.

The Peter and Paul Cathedral had for almost two centuries served as a burial-place for Russian emperors. This was done at the order of Peter I, who is himself buried at the southern wall of the cathedral. All Russian emperors (Alexander III being the last) and many Grand Dukes of the Romanov family were buried here.

All tombstones were made of white marble to a design by A.Poirot and A.Huhn. Two tombstones—those of Emperor Alexander II and his wife—were made of grayish-green jasper and pink rhodonite by the masters of Peterhoff lapidary works (1890—1906, architect A.Huhn).

For a long time the cathedral had performed the functions of the museum of Russian military glory, where enemy banners, keys of the cities and fortresses captured by Russian troops were kept. In the early 20th century all the trophies were transferred to museums. The cathedral now holds replicas of captured Swedish and Turkish banners.

In 1896—1908 a burial-place for Grand Dukes was built next to the cathedral to a design by D.Grimm, with the participation of A.Timoshenko and L.Benois. The building, topped with a dome and a bulbous cupola is perceived as an integral part of the cathedral. In front of the entrance a fence was put up (1904—8, architect L.Benois), designed on the model of the Summer Gardens railing.

394
COMMANDANT'S HOUSE
1743—46. Original design by the engineer de Marin, later—engineer I.de Colong
ENGINEERING HOUSE
1748—49

Commandant's House located opposite the cathedral is a typical sample of the early 18th-century architecture. The spacious two-story building constituting a closed rectangle with an inner courtyard has almost entirely retained its original shape and decoration. Besides the commandant's flat it used to house the rooms where imprisoners were interrogated and court held.

The Engineering House that was put up at the same time has also retained its original appearance. Its façades are similar to the Commandant's House decorated with rusticated blades and lintels semicircular in their upper part.

395
THE BOATHOUSE (BOTNY DOMIK)
1761—65. Architect A.Viest

There is a small pavilion in the square before the cathedral, that was built to house the yawl which Peter I had used in his youth for going on voyages along the Yauza River and Pereyaslavl Lake. In 1722 the yawl that Peter I had called «the Grandfather of the Russian fleet» was at his order with utmost care brought from Moscow to Petersburg, so that it could take part in the naval parade devoted to the celebrations of the Nistadt Peace Treaty. A special shed was put up to protect the yawl, that was later replaced by a stone building decorated with two four-column porticoes. The high roof is topped with an allegorical figure depicting Navigation (1891, sculptor D.Jensen). At present the yawl is kept in the Central Naval Museum.

396
THE MINT
1798—1806. Architect A.Porto

This is the oldest sample of industrial architecture in Petersburg and the only building of the kind on the fortress territory. The Mint was at Peter's decree transferred here from Moscow in 1724; until the present building was put up it had been housed inside the bastions. The grand Mint building anchors the vista of the main alley, approaching it from St.Peter's Gate. Gold and silver coins, as well as medals were produced there.

397
THE NEVA GATE
1731—46. 1784—87. Architect N.Lvov

From the Neva side the Neva Gate stands out distinctly against the granite fortress walls. It is the architectural dominant of this part of the fortress and is meant to be viewed from afar. The order to erect «a gate with architectural decorations on the riverside» was given in 1731. The gate façade overlooking the inner territory had retained its original appearance; the façade facing the Neva, was redecorated, when the fortress walls were being clad with granite. In the gate composition Lvov used the four-column portico motif topped with a pediment. Paired columns are placed on both sides of the arch, while at the bottom they are joined into a single whole by bulky rustic-work. The commandant's pier at the gate built of granite projects far into the river and has a three-span granite bridge connecting it with the bank.

The Neva Gate got the name of the «gate of death»; it was through it that the convicts sentenced to death were taken to the pier and, further, to the place of execution.

398
THE KRONWERK
Lenin Park, 7
1706. 1750s. 1850—60, architect A.Tamansky
Now the Military and Historical Museum of Artillery, Engineer and Communication Troops

Soon after the construction of the earthen fortress, additional fortifications were put up to the north of it, that got the name of Kronwerk. In 1706 a deep moat was dug here and a high rampart built. The new, stone Kronwerk building (1860) came to be used as an ammunition store. Since 1869 old Russian and foreign ordnance, banners, etc. had been accommodated in its eastern part; in 1872 this collection got the name of the Artillery Museum.

The Kronwerk building resembles a horseshoe in plan and is designed in imitation of a Middle Ages fortress. The walls are built of limestone and faced with brick. A water-filled moat and an earthen rampart have remained around the Kronwerk. On the rampart in 1975, on the day of the 150th anniversary of the Decemberists' uprising, a 9-meter granite obelisk was put up on the site where the Decemberists had been executed. The front side of the obelisk carries a bas-relief with the profiles of the five executed Decemberists (sculptors A.Ignatov and A.Dema, architects V.Petrov and A.Leliakov).

399
THE MOSQUE
Maxim Gorky Prospekt, 7
1910—14. Architect N.Vasilyev, with participation of S.Krichinsky, A.Gogen and craftsmen from Central Asia

The Mosque is stylized in imitation of traditional Central Asian architecture. The main prototype is the Gur-Emir Mausoleum in Samarkand. The majolica decoration of the portals and cupola was performed under the supervision of the ceramist P.Vaulin. The interior is decorated in the Moslem architectural tradition.

Kamennoostrovsky Prospekt

This is one of the finest thoroughfares in the city. It was laid in the late 19th century to connect the Kronwerk esplanade with Kamenny (Stone) Island (hence the name). In 1903 the prospekt was extended as far as Troitskaya Square; it is now intesecting two islands (Petrogradsky and Aptekarsky) from south to north. In the late 19th—early 20th centuries the prospekt was mostly built up with apartment houses in Art-Nouveau style. Square situated at the intersections, as well as public gardens enliven the prospekt otherwise solidly built-up.

Lidval's house (No 400)

400
LIDVAL'S HOUSE
Kamennoostrovsky Prospekt, 1—3
1899—1904. Architect F.Lidval

This is one of the first samples of the so-called «Northern Art-Nouveau», representing a new type of a block of flats with an open courtyard decorated with trees and shrubs (*cour d'honeur*). The asymmetrical buildings of different height with various bays, balconies and loosely arranged windows create a picturesque view. The facing includes natural stone, textured plaster and metal. The bas-reliefs represent birds, animals and vegetative motifs.

401
THE FLOWERS HOUSE
Kamennoostrovsky Prospekt, 7
1976—82. Architects Zh.Verzhbitsky, V.Meshcherin, I.Zhuravliova

The building stands at the corner of Kamennoostrovsky Prospekt and Bratyev Vasilyevykh Street. The façade is of a dynamic design; dolomite pylons alternate with stained-glass bay-windows; all stepped elements are topped with glass turrets having open-work spires. The interior is no less expressive; the decoration mostly consists of original luminous structures made of anodized aluminum (artist G.Shilo).

402
THE LENFILM STUDIOS
Kamennoostrovsky Prospekt, 10, 12
1906. Architect Kryzhanovsky

In the late 19th century the Aquarium amusement park was set up here, including a theater, palace of ice, hot-houses, etc. In 1896 the first cinema show in Russia took place there.

403
A DWELLING HOUSE
Kamennoostrovsky Prospekt, 9
1911—12. Architect M.Lialevich

This is a typical sample of the Petersburg Art-Nouveau style. The rounded house corner with triple arches and numerous reliefs can be clearly seen, in the prospect vista.

The Flowers House (No 401)

404
DWELLING HOUSES
Kamennoostrovsky Prospekt, 13, 16, 20
1901—8. Architect V.Schaub

At the intersection of Kamennoostrovsky Prospekt and Mira (Peace) Street there is an octagonal square surrounded by houses with figured balcony railings, turrets, spires, windows of various designs and portals, plastic reliefs. This is an original ensemble in Art-Nouveau style.

A dwelling house (No 404)

405
A DWELLING HOUSE
Kamennoostrovsky Prospekt, 24
1896—97. Architect L.Benois. Raised in the early 20th century, architect V.Androsov

The façades of asymmetrical composition are ornamented with elements of majolica and terra-cotta.

406

ALEXANDER'S ORPHANAGE (ALEXANDER'S LYCEUM)
Kamennoostrovsky Prospekt, 21

1831—34. Architect L.Charlemagne. Raised in 1878

Alexander's Lyceum was transferred here from Tsarskoye Selo in 1844. The long four-story building with a discreet, austere facade was designed in late classical style. The socle story is rusticated; the risalits are topped with pediments.

407

THE FIRST RUSSIAN INSURANCE COMPANY BUILDING
Kamennoostrovsky Prospekt, 26—28

1911—12. Architects L.and Yu.Benois

In 1913—14 a new building was put up on a plot adjacent to the old one; its courtyard overlooks No 29, Kronwerkskaya Street. The two houses connected by inner courtyards made up a single dwelling complex. The facades are faced with light-gray limestone, that does not absorb moisture, and ornamented with plastic details, sculpture and low colonnade.

Leo Tolstoy Square.

Before 1918—Arkhiyereiskaya Square

The square was formed in 1831. However, architecturally it took shape in the early 20th century when intensive construction of apartment houses was started there. At present the ensemble comprises several buildings that are mostly designed in Art-Nouveau style, with some variations.

408

A DWELLING HOUSE
Kamennoostrovsky Prospekt, 38

1911. Architect V.Van der Huht

The domed building with large bays constitutes an integral part of the ensemble.

The Insurance Company (No 407)

«The House with Towers» (No 409)

The Bukhara Emir House (No 412)

A dwelling house (No 416)

A dwelling house (No 417)

409
«THE HOUSE WITH TOWERS»
Bolshoi Prospekt, 75
1912—15. Architect A.Belogrud

This is the main link in the square ensemble. It is also called Rosenstein's house. K.Rosinstein, the civil engineer, took part in designing many houses, including the one concerned. However, construction was completed by the architect Belogrud, who introduced new features into the design thus giving shape to the major city function at the intersection of Kamennoostrovsky and Bolshoi prospekts. Belogrud took an English castle of the Middle Ages for an architectural prototype. He devoted much attention to detailed elaboration of the façade, especially to the finely designed window lintels. The windows themselves are of various shapes: rectangular, semicircular lancet-shaped, etc. The sand-colored walls combined with the brown of the ornamental details make the façade still more picturesque. Two powerful sexangle towers topped with balustrades serve to enhance a romantic impression.

410
THE LENSOVET PALACE OF CULTURE
Kamennoostrovsky Prospekt, 42
1934. Architects Ye.Levinson and V.Munts

In 1910 a ferroconcrete building of a skating-rink was put up on the site by the architect A.Belogrud; it was later used in part during the construction of the Palace of Culture.

411
THE FASHION HOUSE
Kamennoostrovsky Prospekt, 37
1964—68. Architects Ye.Levinson, A.Andreyeva and Ya.Moskalenko

412
THE BUKHARA EMIR HOUSE
Kamennoostrovsky Prospekt, 44b
1913. Architect S.Krichinsky

A sample of strictly Neoclassical style.

Troitskaya (Trinity) Square

Troitskaya Square that extends as far as the Neva in the early 18th century used to be the city center; later, when the center moved first to Vasilyevsky Island, and then to the Admiralty district the square started to lose its importance, and the first city building put up there gradually disappeared. It took its present shape in the 1930s—1950s. In 1948 a parterre public garden was set up there. In 1933 a commune-house was put up at the Petrovskaya Embankment corner (Troitskaya Square, 1, architects G.Simonov, P.Abrosimov and A.Khriakov), designed in Constructivist style. This austere building with a rounded corner and an open terrace fits in very well with its surroundings.

The neighboring building, with its large-scale, monumental forms and a colonnade is a typical sample of the architecture of Stalin's period (1956, architects O.Guryev, Ya.Lukin and A.Shcherbenok—Triotskaya Square, 3/5).

Bolshoi Prospekt, Petrogradskaya Side

The prospekt was laid out in the 1730s. By the early 19th century it had only reached Kamennoostrovsky Prospekt. The plot between Kamennoostrovsky Prospekt and the Karpovka River used to belong to Baroness V.K.Felkel. In 1908 K.Rosenstein, the civil engineer, applied to the State Duma for permission to lay a new street through K.Felkel's private estate. The permission was granted. Thus «private street» came into being, that started to build up quickly. The designers were often house owners at the same time (K.Rosenstein, A.Dalberg, V.Kochenderfer).

413
ROSENSTEIN'S HOUSE
Bolshoi Prospekt, 77
1913—14. Architect A.Belogrud

The house used to belong to K.Rosenstein. It is a vivid illustration of the way the Petersburg dwelling house had changed within the 1910s. Plaster was replaced by glazed brick facing, facade decoration had become more sophisticated, order elements had been renewed: columns, pilasters, cornice, decorative sculpture.

The facade design is founded on Palladian motifs; the two lower stories are faced with granite, the third to fifth have Corinthian columns, the sixth story windows are placed in an architrave, while the seventh story represents an arcade, its pylons being topped with statues (sculptor V.Razumovsky).

414
GONTSKEVICH'S HOUSE
Bolshoi Prospekt, 102
1912—15. Architect A.Belogrud

The house design was developed by the owner, architect Ye.Gontskevich. Retaining the general concept, A.Belogrud redesigned the facade. He introduced rustic-work in the first story and semicircular bay-windows; a modillioned cornice separates the sixth story from the rest of the building, giving it an attic appearance. The facade is due for its spectacular effect to the proportionality between the details and the whole. This is a sample of Russian classical tradition put to good use.

415
THE VVEDENSKAYA GYMNASIA BUILDING
Bolshoi Prospekt, 37
Rebuilt in 1883—84 to a design by the architect A.Akkerman

A. Blok used to study here in 1891—98.

416
A DWELLING HOUSE
Pionerskaya Street, 31
1912—13. Architect I.Pretro

417
A DWELLING HOUSE
Bolshoi Prospekt, 44
1906—7. Architect I.Pretro

Windows of various shapes and sizes, high gables, a powerful lancet portal, combination of granite facing with textured plaster are all typical of the «Northern Art-Nouveau» architecture.

418
A DWELLING HOUSE
Bolshoi Prospekt, 9
1840. Architect G.-R.Zollikoffer

A sample of late Classicism in Petersburg.

419
SYEZZHY DOM (HOUSE)
Bolshoi Prospect, 11
Architect unknown

The oldest building in the prospekt.

420
THE TUCHKOV BRIDGE
over Malaya Neva to Vasilyevsky Island, 1st Line
1962—65. Engineers V.Demchenko and B.Levin, architects A.Areshev and L.Noskova

The first wooden bridge was erected in 1833—35. The present three-span ferroconcrete one is based on the frame-cantilever system, the lower cantilever belt running in a smooth curving line.

The bridge is remarkable for its graceful silhouette. The fine proportions create a classical outline, while the construction work emphasizes modern design. You can approach the water by granite staircases fenced off with a metal railing (architect A.Areshev).

421
THE TUCHKOV BUYAN (PIER)
Bolshoi Prospekt, 1a
1760—70. Architect A.Rinaldi

The building of the former hemp stores on the Tuchkov Pier is typical of the mid-18th century Petersburg architecture; this utility structure combines simple layout with façade decoration in the «palace style». The warehouse complex consisted of the central two-story building for weighing hemp and two symmetrical wings on both sides of it. The walls of the lower stories are rusticated, while the upper ones have blades decorating them. The main building is ornamented with a fine wrought-iron balcony railing. Formerly the pier had stood on one of the small islands that merged with Petrograd Island after the canals has been filled up in the early 20th century. The name comes from the wooden bridge across the Malaya Nevka erected in 1759 by A.Tuchkov, as a contractor.

422
THE YUBILEINY SPORTS PALACE
Dobroliubov Prospekt, 18
1967. Architect G.Morozov. Engineers A.Morozov and others

This is one of the largest world class sports complexes in the city. It includes three buildings: the Cetral Hall (round-shaped) and two rectangular buildings—the Big and the Minor. The engineering and architectural designs were a novelty for this country. The shrouded roofing of the Central building is 93m in diameter and resembles a gigantic bicycle wheel. The Central Hall can hold from 6.5 to 10 thousand people, depending on its configuration. The arena can be turned into a sports ground with artificial ice floor, a sports field or a stage.

423
THE CATHEDRAL OF PRINCE VLADIMIR
Blokhina Street, 26
1741—47, architect D.Trezzini, to a design by M.Zemtsov.
1766—72, architect A.Rinaldi, 1783—89, architect I.Starov

The cathedral that was originally named Uspenskaya (Assumption) Church, was to be one-domed according to the original design. In 1747, after it had been completed in the rough, an order was passed to «add cupolas so that they make five in number, according to the old Russian custom». Almost all prominent Petersburg architects of the mid-18th century took part in the design development.

The Prince
Vladimir Cathedral
(No 423)

After A.Rinaldi's design had been approved and construction started, a fire broke out in 1772, that caused considerable damages to the building. Later the works were resumed under I.Starov's supervision. In 1789 the cathedral was completed and consecrated. It is a sample of the transitional style from Baroque to Classicism. While the façade decoration is classically discreet, some Baroque features have been retained, among them semicircular pediments and cornice, oval windows elongated horizontally, etc. Interior decoration is also remarkable for its austerity.

424

**THE ALEXANDROVSKY PARK (LENIN PARK)
AND THE MONUMENT TO THE HEROIC SAILORS
OF THE DESTROYER** *STEREGUSHCHY*
1909—11. Sculptor K.Isenberg, architect A.Gogen, caster
V.Gavrilov

For a long time the space around the Kronwerk—the
esplanade—had remained vacant, in order not to black out
the view and access to the fortress. It was only 150 years
later, in 1844—45 that the Alexandrovsky public park was
laid out here (engineer Sobolev, architect A.Kutsi). The
park is located between the Kronwerk Canal and
Kronwerksky Prospekt (now Maxim Gorky Prospekt). The
prospekt, 2km long, is built up on one side only, with a
landscape park running along the other as far as Troitskaya
Square. It is near the square that the most picturesque park
site is located, with bridges and a grotto erected in 1904.

Not far from the grotto, a monument was put up,
devoted to the feat done by the *Steregushchy* destroyer
crew. The boat was damaged in a battle during the Russian-
Japanese War of 1904—5 and was surrounded by enemy
ships. The two sailors who had stayed alive chose to sink
the ship rather than let the enemy capture it. The
monument stands on a low hill and has lanterns imitating
lighthouses on both sides of it. The monument resembles a
cross in shape, in the center of which two sailors who
remained still alive opened the cocks and went down with
their ship are depicted.

425

THE ORTHOPEDIC INSTITUTE
Lenin Park, 5
1902—6. Architect K.Metzer

This is one of the best samples of the «rationalist» Art-
Nouveau. The façade carries a majolica composition by
K.Petrov-Vodkin.

426

THE NARODNY DOM (PEOPLE'S HOUSE) COMPLEX
Lenin Park, 4

Its first section was put up in 1900 by the architect
G.Liutsedarsky. In 1911 the Opera House building was

erected there to his project. Later the building came to house the Opera Theater of the Narodny House, the Music Hall, Musical Comedy Theater, Velikan cinema-house, etc.

427
PRINCE LEICHTENBERG'S HOUSE
Zelenina Street, 28
Architect F.Postels. Mosaic work performed to the designs by the artist S.Shelkovy in V.Frolov's workshop

428
THE CITY OFFICES' HOUSE
Maxim Gorky Prospekt, 49
1912—13. Architect M.Peretiatkovich
Now the Institute of Precision Mechanics and Optics

429
THE SYTNY MARKET
Sytninskaya Square, 3/5
1711. Traiding building, 1912—13. Architect M.Lialevich

This is the first marketplace in Petersburg. It was originally named Obzhorny (Glutton Market) and located in Troitskaya Square. The market was transferred to the present site in 1711. Until the 1840s it had occupied a large territory including part of the Kronwerk esplanade. Since the 18th century the marketplace had several times served as a place of execution. It was here that in 1740 A.Volynsky and his associates, P.Yeropkin and A.Khrushchev, who organized the struggle against Biron, were put to death there. In 1861 the «civil execution» of a revolutionary writer M.Mikhailov took place here.

430
THE BUILDINGS OF THE SECOND CADET CORPS
Zhdanovka Embankment, 11—13

The site had in the early 18th century belonged to Count B.Mienich, later to be transferred into possession of the main artillery office. In 1733 the Engineering School came to be housed here (established in 1712), that served as a basis for the Artillery and Engineering Cadets Corps; these were, in their turn, transformed into the Second Cadet Corps. The school buildings are samples of classical architecture. The main building (architect F.Demertsov), facing the Zhdanovka River, was put up in 1797 and several times rebuilt in the course of the 19th century. The three other buildings, forming a closed square together with the first one, were erected in 1800—3. The main building stands out for its marked discreetness. The *Exerzierhaus* (Manège) building is more spectacular, with its powerful portico of Doric columns. Students of this largest Russian military school were M.Kutuzov, many heroes of the Patriotic War of 1812, the Decemberists, as well as poets V.Benediktov, S.Nadson and others.

431
THE HOUSE OF PETER I
Petrovskaya Embankment, 6
1703
Now the Peter I Memorial museum

The House of Peter I is one of the oldest structures in Petersburg and a unique historical monument. It was put up on May 24—26, 1703; two days later Peter I moves into

The house of Peter the Great (No 431)

his new place of residence, accompanied by ceremonial gunfire. Similar to traditional Russian wooden huts the house was built of pine beams and consisted of two rooms with a passage between them.

The tsar's «palace» could be seen from afar—not only from the Neva, that had in the early 18th century already turned into the city's main thoroughfare, but from the opposite river bank as well. Even in Peter's times some measures had been taken to protect the house from destruction; a shed had been arranged over it, that was in 1784 replaced by a stone case. In 1844 the case was reconstructed by the architect R.Kuzmin. In 1872 the plot was fenced off with a cast-iron railing, while in 1875 a bronze bust of Peter I was installed in front of the house (sculptor P.Zabello). In the 1970s overall works were carried out that restored the building in its original shape.

The Petrovskaya Embankment where the house stands was the first embankment to take shape in Petersburg. Already in the early 18th century houses were built here for the most prominent officials, including A.Menshikov, P.Shafirov, N.Zotov, M.Gagarin, G.Golovkin. Since the late 18th century hemp and flax stores had been located between Peter's house and the Bolshaya Nevka, called Gagarin Buyan (Pier).

Petrovskaya Embankment was clad with granite in 1901—3 (architect L.Novikov, engineer F.Zbrozhek). As a result the bank-line was moved 30m forward, The embankment became part of the city center ensemble. The wide staircase going down to the water is of special interest; in 1907 ancient granite figures of Shi-Tsa (half-lions, half-frogs) were installed on the platforms here, brought from Manchuria.

432
KSHESINSKAYA'S MANSION
Kuibyshev Street, 2—4
1904—6. Architect A.Gogen, with participation of A.Dmitriyev and A.Samoilov

The mansion was put up for dancer M.Kshesinskaya. The building is an excellent sample of Art-Nouveau style; it has asymmetrical composition, is faced with colored ceramic tiles, and decorated in the most picturesque way; the interiors are lavishly decorated too.

Kshesinskaya's mansion
(No 432)

A dwelling house
(No 433)

Kshesinskaya's mansion saw the revolutionary events of 1917. It was occupied by the Bolsheviks, frequented by V.Lenin, it also used to house various communist party establishments. During the recent years the building has housed the Museum of Russian Political History.

433
A DWELLING HOUSE
Kuibyshev Street, 21
1912. Architect K.Baldi

434
BELOZERSKY'S HOUSE
Kuibyshev Street, 25
1913—14. Archritect A.Ol
Now a children's clinic

In the 1870s a stone mansion was put up on this site to a design by A.Parland, that imitated the traditional Russian *terem* structure. A.Ol reconstructed it for G.Belozersky, a physician, adding some elements, typical of Neo-Classicism;

pilasters with Corinthian capitels, a pediment with a semicircular window, a low cupola and a balustrade mark the façade center. The interiors have retained a superb two-tier marble vestibule of oval shape.

435
THE PETER THE GREAT CITY SCHOOL
Petrovskaya Embankment, 2/4
1910—12. Architect A.Dmitriev
Now the Nakhimov Naval School

The site for a school building was chosen on the Neva bank, in the «old city», where construction had started long ago; this accounted for the architectural style, which is an imitation of Peter's Baroque. The image of the building, with its needle-like spire, high «broken» roof, lattice-type windows, stucco moulding and plastic lintels, as well as the combination of blue and white colors, harmonized very well with the spirit of Peter's epoch. The bust of Peter I, Atlantes' figures and the cartouche in the pediment were done by the sculptor V.Kuznetsov to the designs by the artist A.Benois. Some interiors are designed in the style of Peter's epoch as well, including the conference hall decorated with panels of painted tiles and figured

The Peter the Great City School (No 435)

fireplaces. The Naval School building is located at the spit of the Petrogradskaya Side and commands a beautiful view of the opposite bank, thus playing an important part in the Neva panorama.

Aptekarsky Island

Between the Malaya Nevka,

Bolshaya Nevka and the Karpovka Rivers

436
THE BOTANICAL GARDEN
1823
THE MAIN BUILDING OF THE BOTANICAL INSTITUTE
Aptekarsky Prospekt, 1
1911—15. Architect A.Dietrich

437
THE BUILDINGS OF THE ELECROTECHNICAL INSTITUTE
Professor Popov Street, 5
1899—1903. Architect A.Vekshsinsky. The new brick buildings—1970s, architect N.Matusevich

438
THE INSTITUTE OF CHEMISTRY AND PHARMACEUTICS
Professor Popov Street, 4
1911—12. Architect A.Ol

439
MIKHNEVICH'S HOUSE
Professor Popov Street, 10
Mid-19th century. Rebuilt in 1894. Architect Ye.Veinberg

The house was rebuilt for a well-known journalist V.Mikhnevich, author of *Petersburg Spread Before Your Eyes*.

440
THE BUILDINGS OF IOANNOVSKY (ST.JOHN'S) MONASTERY
Professor Popov Street, 36
1900s. Architect N.Nikonov. Designed in so-called «Byzantine style»

441
A DWELLING HOUSE
Professor Popov Street, 41
1914—15. Architect F.Lidval

The Ioannovsky Monastery (No 440)

442
A DWELLING HOUSE
Professor Popov Street, 43
1930s. Architect Ye.Levinson

443
THE PALACE OF YOUTH
Professor Popov Street, 47
1967—79. Architects P.Prokhorov, V.Tropinin, A.Izoitko

Built on the site of the la Valle family estate.

444
THE BUILDINGS OF THE GRENADIER REGIMENT
Karpovka Embankment, 2
1805—7. Architect L.Rusca

Designed in strictly classical style.

445
DWELLING HOUSES WITH CORNER TURRETS
Kamennoostrovsky Prospekt, 53 and 54
Architects S.Ginger and D.Kryzhanovsky

The TV Center (No 446)

446
THE TV CENTER
Chapygin Street, 6
1960—63. Architect S.Speransky, V.Vasilkovsky and
A.Kats

447
A DWELLING HOUSE
Kamennoostrovsky Prospekt, 61
1906—7. Architect F.Lidval

448
A DWELLING HOUSE FOR THE EMPLOYES OF THE INSTITUTE FOR EXPERIMENTAL MEDICINE
Kamennoostrovsky Prospekt, 67—71
1935—36. Architect N.Lanseray

449
GLUKHOVSKOI'S HOUSE
Admiral Lazarev Embankment, 10
Early 20th century. Architect unknown

The building was designed in the house with a mezzanine style. This is the only house of the type remaining in Petersburg.

450
THE HOUSE OF THE THEATRE VETERANS
Petrovsky Prospekt, 13
Rebuilt and enlarged in 1946—58 to a design by V.Taleporovsky and F.Miliukov

Kamenny (Stone) Island

451
THE KAMENNOOSTROVSKY PALACE
Malaya Nevka Embankment, 1
1776—78. Architect unknown; construction works supervised by Yu.Velten

This is a vivid sample of classical architecture. The interiors have retained the late 18th—early 19th century decoration. At present it houses a sanatorium.

452
THE CHURCH OF THE NATIVITY OF ST.JOHN THE BAPTIST
Kamennoostrovsky Prospekt, 7
1776—78. Architect Yu.Velten

The church is designed in neo-Gothic style; it has lancet windows, a tall tent-like belfry and combines red brick with white stone ornamentation.

The Kamennoostrovsky Palace (No 451)

453
DOLGORUKOV'S DACHA
Malaya Nevka Embankment, 11
1831—32. Architect S.Shustov

It is a monument of wooden architecture in Classicism style. Its interior decor was re-designed in the late 1830s by the architect A.Stakenschneider when it came into the possession of Prince Oldenburg.

454
KAMENNOOSTROVSKY THEATER
Krestovka Embankment, 10
1827. Architect S.Shustov

This is a sample of a wooden building in classical style. In 1844 the building was dismantled to be rebuilt by the architect A.Kavos, who introduced some alterations into the facade decoration and the theater hall layout. Further changes were made in 1932 by the architect Ye.Katonin.

Polovtsov's dacha (No 455)

After the reconstruction of 1966—67 (architect I.Benois) the building has been housing the television theater.

455
POLOVTSOV'S DACHA
Bolshaya Nevka Embankment, 22
1911—16. Architect I.Fomin, with Baron Stieglitz's included

The building is designed as an estate residence house in Russian classical style. The gobelin hall, dining hall and

bedroom are decorated with mural paintings by the artist
I.Badininsky, reliefs on the facades are made by the
sculptor V.Kuznetsov. At present the building houses a
sanatorium.

Yelaghin Island

456
THE YELAGHIN PALACE
1785. Architect G.Quarenghi (?). 1818—22. Architect
C.Rossi
Now the Museum of Russian Applied Arts and Interior of
the 18th—20th Century

The palace-and-park ensemble in Yelaghin Island took
shape in the second half of the 18th century—early 19th
century. The focus of the ensemble is the Yelaghin Palace
(the first palace has originally been built for I.Yelaghin in
1785). The two-story stone palace, that stands on an
elevated terrace provided with a roundabout platform and
monumental staircases, is topped with a low dome and
decorated with a graceful semi-rotunda. This is the first
important work by C.Rossi performed in Petersburg. The
side risalits and the western palace façade are accentuated
with porticoes, while the wide staircase has cast-iron lion
figures standing on its both sides.
    The interiors are remarkable for their lavish decoration
(sculptors V.Demuth-Malinovsky and S.Pimenov, artists
D. B. and P.Scotti, A.Vighi, B.Medici).
    Simultaneously with the palace construction large works
were underway to lay out a landscape park in the island
(1812—26, G.Bush), provided with artificial ponds of
«natural» outline, alleys, and a lawn. This unique ensemble
also includes outbuildings and pavilions—the Kitchen and
Stable outbuildings, the Guard-House, Musical Pavilion, as
well as stone hot-houses. Their classical forms correspond
to those of the palace and natural surroundings.

Krestovsky Island

The largest among the group of islands used to be a
popular place of recreation in the mid-19th century. Since

1846 it had been the home of the Petersburg River Yachting Club; a monument to Peter I was installed here in 1872, sculptor A.Sokolov. In 1804 the island was bought by Prince A.Beloselsky-Belozersky; since the second half of the 19th century his lands had been leased and built up intensively. Dachas and mansions, as well as apartment houses were springing up here. In the 1920s—1930s buildings were constructed here of the newly developed material called «thermo-concrete»; construction of stadiums and sports-grounds was started.

457
PRIMORSKY PARK POBEDY (VICTORY PARK)
1945
Laid out to commemorate the victory in the Great Patriotic War (1941—45). Has the Kirov Stadium on its territory

The Kirov Stadium (No 458)

458
THE KIROV STADIUM
Morskoi Prospekt, 1
1932—50. Architect A.Nikolsky, K.Kashin and N.Stepanov. Reconstructed in 1980, architect S.Odnovalov, A.Pribulsky and M.Tsimbal, engineer V.Arsenov and A.Chugunov

THE RIGHT BANK OF THE NEVA
AND BOLSHAYA NEVKA

*The Liteiny Bridge
(No 459)*

*Detail of the railing
of the Liteiny Bridge (No 459)*

459
**THE LITEINY BRIDGE (THE BRIDGE OF ALEXANDER II)
over the Neva, connects Liteiny Prospekt with
Academician Lebedev Street**
1875—79. Engineer A.Struve. 1966—67, reconstructed,
engineers L.Wildgruve, N.Shipov and K.Klochkov; architect
Yu.Sinitsa

This was the second permanent bridge to be erected across
the Neva, the first one to be illuminated with electric
lanterns. It comprised six steel spans, one of them being
drawn. The new building material made it possible to make
the bridge spans 1.5 times longer than the cast-iron arches
of the St.Nicholas Bridge. The draw-span could revolve
horizontally, round the vertical axis, on the first wide and
bulky pier. The cast-iron railing was performed to a design

by the architect A.Rachau. Each section depicts a mermaid holding a cartouche with the coat-of-arms of Petersburg. The pillars between the sections carry images of fantastic sea creatures that are compositionally similar to the vegetative ornament decorating the sections.

During the reconstruction the piers were raised, the spans provided with new steel-ferroconcrete beams, and the revolving span replaced with a drawn one. The bridge became 10m wider, and, what is more important, traffic intersections were arranged at two levels.

The bridge is 396m long and 34m wide.

The Finland Railway Station (No 460)

460
THE FINLAND RAILWAY STATION
Lenin Square, 5
1870. Architect P.Kupinsky. 1955—60, architects P.Ashastin, N.Baranov and Ya.Lukin; engineer I.Rybin

The laconic station building, elongated horizontally, is topped with a rectangular clock-tower ending in a spire. The façade is decorated with vertical niches that have sculptural bas-reliefs in their upper part, depicting the revolutionary events of 1917. There is a locomotive standing in a glass pavilion on the platform, that had brought Lenin from Finland into Russia in October 1917.

In the square before the station a monument to Lenin was put up in 1926 (sculptor S.Yevseyev, architects V.Shchuko and V.Gelfreich).

The central projection of the old station was incorporated into one of the new buildings.

461

A DWELLING HOUSE
Botkinskaya Street, 1
1907—8. Architects F.Miriti and I.Gerasimov

This type of houses is characteristic of Art-Nouveau. The fire-proof wall carries a mosaic composition *Man and Space* (1960, artist V.Anopova).

462

A DWELLING HOUSE
Komsomol Street, 35
1882—87. Architect A.Geschwend

463

AN ADMINISTRATION BUILDING
Komsomol Street, 4/41
1935—40. Architects Ya.Rubanchik, A.Balkiv and N.Ioffe. Reconstructed in the 1950s

The massive building with paired half-columns is designed in modernized classical forms.

464

THE BUILDING OF THE MIKHAILOVSKAYA ARTILLERY ACADEMY
Lenin Square, 2
First structures date from the early 19th century. Several times rebuilt. Architects A.Staubert, A.Farafontyev and others. Reconstructed in 1952, architect M.Rusakov

465

THE MAIN BUILDING OF THE MILITARY MEDICAL ACADEMY
Academician Lebedev Street, 6
1798—1803. Architect A.Porto

This building, decorated with a six-column portico, is a typical sample of classical architecture.

466

THE CLINICAL MILITARY HOSPITAL
Vyborgskaya Embankment, 3
Rebuilt in 1863—69, engineer G.Voinitsky

This is the oldest building of the Military Medical Academy complex (established in 1798). During the reign of Peter I the Naval and Land Forces hospitals were put up on the site to a design by D.Trezzini. After the 19th-century reconstruction the building of the Institute of Natural Sciences was erected next to them (Vyborgskaya Embankment, 1). All these structures stretching along the embankment constitute a single ensemble at present.

467

THE ST.PETERSBURG HOTEL
Vyborgskaya Embankment, 5
1967—70. Architects S.Speransky, V.Struzman and N.Kamensky, engineer Y.Izrailev

A restaurant and a concert hall are attached to the multi-storied hotel on both sides of it. Construction works are still underway.

468

A DWELLING HOUSE
Sampsoniyevsky Prospekt, 14
1933. Architect A.Barutchev
THE VOLKHOVSKAYA SUBSTATION
Sampsoniyevsky Prospekt, 16
1926—27. Architects V.Shchuko and V.Gelfreich

The St. Petersburg Hotel (No 467)

469
THE YA.VILLYE CLINIC
Sampsoniyevsky Prospekt, 5
1865—73. Architect K.Sokolov
Now the P.M.Kupriyanov Surgical Clinic

In the garden behind the main façade stands a monument to the President of Medico-Surgical Academy, Phisician-in-Ordinary Ya.Villye (1859, sculptor D.Iensen, architect A.Stakenschneider), who financed the clinic construction.

470
THE MONUMENT TO S.BOTKIN
(in front of the Clinic building)
1908. Sculptor V.Beklemishev

S.Botkin was a prominent physician and public figure; he worked at the Academy from 1861 until 1889.

471
THE VYBORGSKY PALACE OF CULTURE
Smirnov Street, 15
1927. Architects A.Gegello and D.Krichevsky

472
THE BUILDINGS
OF THE LUDWIG NOBEL COMPANY
Sampsoniyevsky Prospekt, 26—30
Now the Russian Diesel Plant

In 1842 E.Nobel founded a factory producing floating mines here. Twenty years later L.Nobel set up iron production. In 1908 the plant started making internal-combustion engines.

Industrial structures were erected by K.Andersen, R.Meltser and F.Lidval. L.Nobel's property extended from the Bolshaya Nevka up to the Finland railway line. In this block a few houses have remained that used to belong to the plant's housing development. Buildings 1,2 in Sampsoniyevsky Prospekt, 27, date from 1906, architect R.Meltser, Buildings 3—6 were put up in 1893—95 by the architect V.Schreter.

473
E.NOBEL'S APARTMENT HOUSE
Lesnoi Prospekt, 20
1910—12. Architect F.Lidval

This building combines some Art-Nouveau traits with Neo-Renaissance motifs.

474
E.NOBEL'S MANSION
Lesnoi Prospekt, 21
1910. Architect F.Lidval

A sample of Art-Nouveau style.

475
E.NOBEL'S PEOPLE'S READING HOUSE
Lesnoi Prospekt, 19
1897—1900. Architect R.Meltser

476
ST.SAMPSONY'S CATHEDRAL
Sampsoniyevsky Prospekt, 41
1728-40. Architect unknown

This is one of the oldest Petersburg buildings put up on the site of the wooden church laid by Peter I to commemorate the victory at Poltava in 1709 (on the day of St.Sampsony). The design involves some old Russian architectural motifs,

St. Sampsony's
Cathedral
(No 476)

which are rarely met in Petersburg architecture, the multi-tier tent-like belfry, refectory and the main volume being united into a single whole. The cathedral is spanned with a high roof which is topped with one large and four minor drums, ending in small cupolas. The southern and northern facades represent galleries with arcades. Of big artistic value is the carved five-tier iconostasis with painted icons in it, as well as the carved altar and canopy.

On the adjoining territory stands the monument to A.Volynsky, P.Yeropkin and A.Khrushchev, who were in opposition to Biron and his associates and were executed in 1740 (1885, sculptor A.Opekushin, architect M.Shurupov).

477
A DWELLING HOUSE
Sampsoniyevsky Prospekt, 43
1882. Architect P.Suzor. 1896. Architect N.Nikonov

Designed in neo-Russian style. Used to belong to St.Sampsony's Cathedral.

478
L.ERIKSON'S PLANT BUILDINGS
Sampsoniyevsky Prospekt, 60
1899, 1910—13. Architect K.Schmidt
Now the Krasnaya Zarya Amalgamation

A sample of «brick style» in the 19th—20th-century industrial architecture.

479
BATENINSKY HOUSING DEVELOPMENT
Lesnoi Prospekt, 37, 39
1930—33. Architects T.Katzenelenbogen, G.Simonov, B.Rubanenko, A.Solomonov and others

This is a sample of Constructivist architecture and one of the largest housing developments in Leningrad before the 1940s. Developments of this type include «the textile workers' town» (Lesnoi Prospekt, 59. Architect N.Rybin), the so-called «House of Specialists» (Lesnoi Prospekt, 61. 1934—37. Architects G.Simonov, B.Rubanenko and others), the Polytechnical Institute students' «town» (Lesnoi Prospekt, 65. 1929—32. Architects M.Felger, S.Brovtsev and A.Petrov).

480
THE NEW LESSNER PLANT
Lesnoi Prospekt, 66
1898
Now the Karl Marx Amalgamation

This is a sample of the 19th-century «brick» style architecture and one of the largest machine-building enterprises in Russia.

481
MERCHANT BASHKIROV'S SHOP AND TEA-HOUSE
Lesnoi Prospekt, 83, 85
1905

Both are built in Art-Nouveau style.

482
NOVOSILTSEVA'S ALMS-HOUSE
Engels Prospekt, 1—5
1834—38. Architect I.Charlemagne

483
THE FORESTRY ACADEMY
Institutsky Prospekt, 5
1826—33. Architect A.Nellinger

In the late 18th century the lands used to belong to an English firm. In 1811 the Forestry School was transferred here from Tsarskoye Selo. Later the Academy was established. The building is designed in austere forms of orderless classical style.

The Polytechnical Institute (No 484)

484
THE POLYTECHNICAL INSTITUTE
Politekhnicheskaya Street, 29
1902. Architect E.Werrich
Now the Technical University

This is a sample of a well-designed complex of buildings for educational purposes. It is one of the largest higher educational establishments and research centers in the country.

The Piskariovskoye Memorial Cemetery (No 485)

485
THE PISKARIOVSKOYE MEMORIAL CEMETERY
Nepokorennykh Prospekt

This is the main burial-place of Leningraders who perished during the blockade of 1941—44. The architectural ensemble took shape in 1956—1960s (architects A.Vasilyev and Ye.Levinson). In the center stands an allegorical bronze statue of the Motherland (sculptors V.Isayeva, M.Kharlamova). At the entrance there are two pavilions holding exposition of the materials concerned with the blockade period.

486
THE PETER THE GREAT HOSPITAL
Piskariovsky Prospekt, 47
1907—14. Architects A.Ilyin and A.Klein. 1930s,
architects N.Lebedev, A.Sibiryakov and A.Yunger
Now the Mechnikov Hospital

The buildings are designed in the Baroque of Peter's
period. The brick walls are ornamented with white figured
pediments, lintels and pilasters.

487
THE GIGANT CINEMA-HOUSE
Kondratyevsky Prospekt, 44
1933—35. Architects A.Gegello and D.Krichevsky

The monumental building decorated with a multi-column
portico is one of few samples of Constructivist style in
Petersburg. In the 1930s it used to be the largest cinema-
house in Petersburg.

488
THE NEW ARSENAL
Komsomol Street, 1—3; Arsenal Street, 2—4
1844—51

The Arsenal was set up on the site of the former State Civil
Shipyards. Production was transferred here from the
Arsenal put up on the left Neva bank by the architect
Demertsev, rebuilt in the 1870s by the architect
R.Heinrichsen (Liteiny Prospekt, 1—3).

489
DURNOVO'S DACHA
Sverdlovskaya Embankment, 22
1785—86. Architect N.Lvov (?)

This is an architectural monument in classical style. The
ten-column portico was added in 1813—14 (architect
A.Mikhailov). The interiors have retained stucco moulding
and mural painting dating from the 1820s.

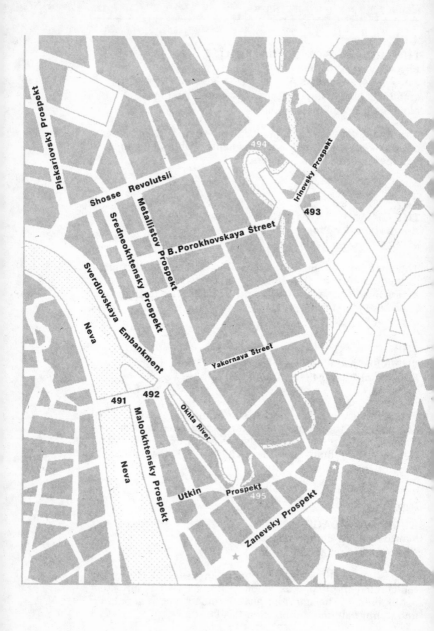

Bezborodko's dacha (No 490)

490

BEZBORODKO'S DACHA (KUSHELEVA DACHA)
Sverdlovskaya Embankment, 40
1773—77. Architect V.Bazhenov (?). 1783—84. Architect G.Quarenghi

The central building with two round turrets was put up to a design by V.Bazhenov. The arch-shaped galleries connecting the building with the side wings were erected by G.Quarenghi, who had also redesigned the main façade. The whole structure has an original fence running around it, where pillars are replaced with cast-iron lion figures holding chains. To the north of the house there used to be a large landscape park. In the mid-19th century it was a popular place for outings. The descent to the Neva with a granite pier and stone sphinxes was restored in 1959—60.

491

THE PETER THE GREAT BRIDGE (BOLSHEOKHTINSKY)
over the Neva to Bolshaya Okhta
1908—11. Engineer G.Krivoshein, architect V.Anyshkov

In 1901 a world-wide competition was announced for a best bridge project. Engineers from the USA, Germany,

France, Austria, Spain and the Netherlands took part in it. The competition was won by the project of the engineer G.Krivoshein and the architect V.Anyshkov, under the motto «Free Navigation». This was the main point. Krivoshein placed the draw-section in the middle of the river (the competition conditions required it to be next to the bank); he conceived it as consisting of two wings drawn upwards. The rest of the river was to be spanned with two girders, each 136m long. These are the longest girders in Petersburg. Only two piers were to be installed in the river-bed, so navigation enjoyed maximum freedom, indeed.

The girders are connected with each other by arched trusses, that have the motorway suspended below. The interlining supports are clad with granite and topped with beacon lanterns.

492
PETROZAVOD (PETER'S PLANT)
Krasnogvardeiskaya Square, 2

Established in 1721 at the confluence of the Okhta and Neva rivers, on the site of the Swedish Nyenskantz Fortress, as St. Petersburg shipyard. At present the plant produces shipbuilding equipment.

The Peter Great (Bolsheokhtinsky) Bridge (No 491)

493
ZHERNOVKA, THE BEZOBRAZOV'S FAMILY DACHA
Irinovsky Prospekt, 9
Late 18th century. Architect G.Quarenghi

This is a monument of classical architecture, a sample of a small country estate house. The central part is accentuated with a four-column portico, the one-story side galleries end in side wings. The central part houses a two-story hall with large Venetian windows. The house had a landscape park attached to it.

494
THE CHURCH OF THE PROPHET ELIJAH AT THE POWDER-MILL
Shosse Revolutsii, 76
1781—85. Architect unknown. In 1804 the refectory, three-tier belfry and altar apse were added (architect F.Demertsev). The belfry was rebuilt in the late 19th century

This is a sample of classical architecture. A small rotunda-shape church building with loggia on the northern and southern façades is topped with a semispherical dome. The dome has retained the painting depicting Elijah in the chariot.

495
UTKINA'S DACHA
Utkin Prospekt, 2
1790s. Architect N.Lvov (?)

The house was designed in classical style and built for A.Poltoratskaya; since 1829 it had belonged to Duchess Z.Shakhovskaya, or Utkina by her second marrige. The house stands at the confluence of the Okhta and Okkervil rivers, which accounts for its «angular» composition. In the angle vertex a rotunda-hall is placed, topped with a cupola and opening on to a loggia with a Doric colonnade. The column bases and capitals as well as the balcony railings are cast of iron. The round hall has retained the plastic cornice with medallions and the mural paintings. The arch-shaped courtyard outbuilding ends in the symmetrical pavilions on both sides of it.

496
GOLOVIN'S DACHA
Vyborgskaya Embankment, 53
1823—24. Architect L.Charlemagne.
1803 — auxiliary outbuildings. Architect A.Voronikhin
Now a Children's Dermatological Hospital

A wooden house in classical style.

497
AN APARTMENT HOUSE
Chiornaya (Black) River Embankment, 51a
1902. Architect M.Rozyenson

498
THE GRECHKO NAVAL ACADEMY
Vyborgskaya Embankment, 73/1
Architects A.Vasilyev and A.Romanovsky

The Academy buildings were erected on the site of the
estate that had belonged to the President of the Academy
of Arts, Count S.Stroganov. In the back of the lot the
remains of the park have been preserved where Stroganov's
dacha used to stand, built by A.Voronikhin in 1759.

499
THE OBELISK ON THE SITE OF PUSHKIN'S DUEL
Kolomyazhskoye Shosse
1937. Sculptor M.Manizer, architect A.Lapirov

500
THE SERAFIMOVSKOYE (ST.SERAPHIM'S) CEMETERY
Serebriakov Lane, 1
1905

In 1906—7 a wooden Church of St.Seraphim Sarovsky was
erected here (architect N.Nikonov). During the Leningrad
blockade this cemetery became the second burial-place
(after the Piskariovskoye Cemetery) of the victims of the

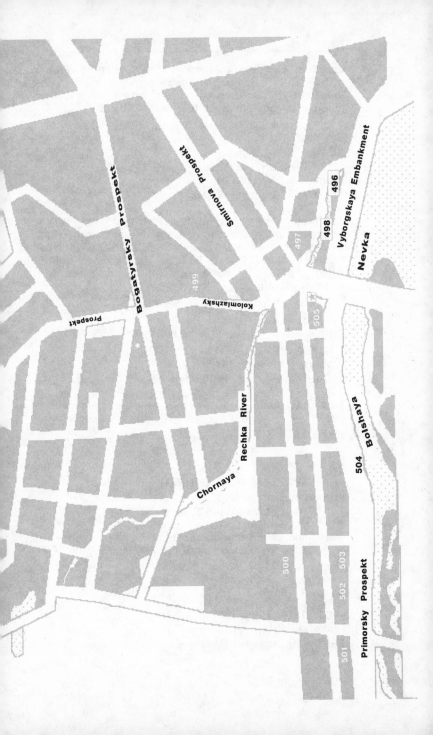

blockade and the soldiers of the Leningrad Front. In
1957—65 a memorial ensemble was put up, that has a
four-span granite portico in the center of it with five
monumental sculptures (author of the project Ya.Lukin).

501
THE BUDDHIST TEMPLE
Primorsky Prospekt, 91
1909—15. Architect G.Baranovsky

The Temple was put up on the initiative of Dalai-Lama, with
prominent orientalists as consultants (including V.Radlov,
S.Oldenburg. N.Roerich and others). In its design Tibetian
architectural motifs and Buddhist symbols were used. In
1990 the temple was returned into possession of the
Buddhist community.

502
SHISHMAREV'S DACHA
Primorsky Prospekt, 87
1824—25. Architect A.Melnikov

This is a sample of an estate house with a mezzonine and
one of few remaining wooden buildings in classical style.

503
THE ANNUNCIATION CHURCH
Primorsky Prospekt, 79
1805—9. Architect V.Mochulsky

The round church building reminds of the rotunda-shaped
churches of the second half of the 18th century.

504
A DWELLING HOUSE
Primorsky Prospekt, 14
1908—10. Architect F.Lidval

505
SALTYKOVA'S DACHA
Academician Krylov Street
1837—47. Architects N.Sadovnikov and G.Bosse

The two-story mansion with stone gates shows some Gothic architectural motifs.

HOTELS

The Astoria Hotel ****
Bolshaya Morskaya Street, 39
Tel. 311-2453, 210-5045

A very elegant hotel in an Old European tradition. In the heart of Saint Petersburg

The Angleterre Bar, the Angleterre Restaurant, the Christopher Columbus Restaurant, the Astoria Restaurant, the Winter Garden Restaurant, the Astoria Night Bar

InNis Car Rentals, Fitness Center, Sauna & Pool, Business Center, the elegant Astoria Shop, the Astoria International Shop

Hairdresser's, currency exchange, clothing & shoe repair, train & plane tickets desk, theater tickets desk, excursions bureau

Right in Isaakiyevskaya Square

The Chaika Hotel (for foreign specialists)
Serebristy Boulevard, 38
Tel. 301-7575
Fax 301-5622

The Commodore Hotel ****
Morskoi Slavy Square, 1
Tel. 210-1383, 119-6666
Fax ·119-6667
Restaurant, bars, night clubs

The Europe Grand Hotel *****
Mikhailovskaya Street, 1/7
Tel. 119-6000, 113-8075
Fax 119-6001
Telex 121-073 GHE SU

The Europe Restaurant, The Brasserie, La Trattoria, Sadko's Mezzanine Atrium Cafe, Lobby Bar, night club, Fitness Center, 24 Hour Room Services

Beautifully restored to its Old World elegance. On the corner of Nevsky Prospekt and Mikhailovskaya Street in the historical center of Saint Petersburg

The Kareliya Hotel
Tukhachevskogo Street, 27/2
Tel. 226-3519, 226-3534
Fax 226-3511

Restaurants, discotheque, sauna, currency exchange, The Beriozka shop, train & plane tickets desk, clothing & shoe repairs, florist's

The Morskaya Hotel
Morskoi Slavy Square, 1
At the head of the Harbor
Tel. 355-1417

Sauna, hairdresser's, massage & make-up rooms, clothing & shoe repair, dry-cleaning, currency exchange, The Beriozka shop, theater tickets desk, excursion bureau, train & plane tickets desk

The Moskva Hotel***
Alexandra Nevskogo Square, 2
Tel. 274-3001
Fax 274-2130
Telex 121669 INTER SU

Sauna, currency exchange, duty-free shop, clothing & shoe repairs, hairdresser's, dry-cleaning, car rental, train & plane tickets desk, theater tickets desk, excursion bureau
    Metro: Ploshchad Alexandra Nevskogo

The Nevskiy Palace Hotel *****
Nevsky Prospekt, 57
Tel. 275-2001
Fax 113-1470
Telex 121279 HERMS SU

Perfectly located in the heart of St.Petersburg in its main thoroughfare the Nevskiy Palace Hotel provides comfortable accomodation in its 287 rooms exquisitely renovated in a modern style and offers its guests an extensive range of services including secure parking under the hotel, business facilities, conference rooms, fitness center; a number of restaurants with international and Russian cuisine
    Managed by the Marco Polo Hotels & Resorts, Vienna, Austria

The Octavian Hotel
Sredny Prospekt, 88
Tel. 356-8516
Fax 355-6714

The Octavian Restaurant, a night bar, The Variag Art Shop,
Business Center, translators, Meeting Room, sauna,
chauffeured cars, hairdresser's, clothing repair, dry-cleaning
    A Russian-English Management Firm
    Convenient to the Sea Port & exhibition halls

The Okhtinskaya Hotel
An international *** hotel
Bolsheokhtinsky Prospekt, 4
Tel. 227-4438
Fax 227-2618
Telex 121128 TUR SU

Double & de luxe suites with telephones, cable-satelite TV,
air-conditioned. This new mid-sized hotel, is liked by
businessmen for its friendly staff. The Okhtinskaya
Restaurant offers excellent Russian-European cuisine. Two
bars, sauna, Conference Hall, meeting rooms, Business Center, International Communications, kiosks & shops, service
desk and a mini-bus
    A comfortable, modern 1991 hotel, beautifully located
on the bank of the Neva, right opposite the Smolny
Cathedral. Just 8 minutes to Palace Square
    The Victoria Russian-French Firm

The Oktiabrskaya Hotel
Ligovsky Prospekt, 10
Tel. 277-6330

Restaurant, bar, dry-cleaning, laundry, camera, clothing &
shoe repairs, currency shop, telegraph
    Metro: Ploshchad Vosstaniya

The Olympia Hotel-ship
Morskoi Slavy Square
Tel. 119-6800
Fax 119-6805

The Repinskaya Hotel
Repino (near Petersburg)
Primorskoye Shosse, 428
Tel. 231-6637

A small quiet hotel at Repino in a beautifull pine forest right on the shore of the Gulf of Finland. You can enjoy the beach, swim, bicycle in summer, X-skiing & ice-fishing on the Gulf in winter. Restaurant, bar, service bureau, private showers, balconies and telephones. Less than an hour from St.Petersburg by train or car along the St.Petersburg—Vyborg Highway

The Pribaltiyskaya Hotel **
Korablestroitelei Street, 14
Tel. 356-0263
Fax (international-direct) 356-0094
Fax 356-0372

Most pleasant, elegant decor
Beautifully located on the Gulf of Finland. First-class, de luxe and suites. The Neva, Leningrad, Daugava (with a grill-bar), Panorama Restaurants. The Heineken, Stella Artois Beer Bars, Night Club, Casino. Sauna, mini-swimming pool, bowling. The Baltic Star International Shop. Satellite TV with CNN & Cable TV. Direct International Dialling. Business Service Center. Saluta Pharmacy & Drug Store. The Inpress Kiosk—foreign publications. Post, telegraph, Bank, photo service. Ford Cars with Drivers 24 hrs/day. High-secutity parking
Beauty parlor, massage room, clothing & shoe repairs, bureau de change, dry-cleaning, florist's, train & plane tickets desk, excursion desk, theater tickets desk
Metro: Primorskaya

The Pulkovskaya Hotel **
Pobedy Square, 1
Tel. 264-5122
Telex 121477 PULKA SU

The Meridian and Turku Restaurants and the Bar. Cafeteria, sauna, hairdresser's, duty-free shop, bureau de change, clothing & shoe repairs, dry-cleaning, florist's, fax facilities, photocopying, car rental, train & plane tickets desk, excursion desk, theater tickets desk
Metro: Moskovskaya

Rechnaya
Obukhovskoi Oborony Prospekt, 195
Tel. 267-3196
Metro: Proletarskaya

The Rossiya Hotel
Chernyshevskogo Square, 11
(Moskovsky Prospekt)
Tel. 296-7649, 296-7349

Restaurant, café, hairdresser's, clothing & shoe repairs, train
& plane tickets desk, theater tickets desk, excursion desk.
    Metro: Park Pobedy

Peterhof Hotel-ship
Makarova Embankment (near the Tuchkov Bridge)
Tel. 213-6321
Fax 213-3158
    Metro: Vasileostrovskaya

The St.Petersburg Hotel **
Vyborgskaya Embankment, 5/2
Tel. 542-9411
Fax 542-9042

Restaurants (Petrovsky & Zerkalny). Three night clubs, two
pools, sporthalls, bars, the hard-currency Beriozka shop,
sauna, chauffeur-driven car for hire, bureau de change,
duty-free shop, train & plane tickets desk, florist's, clothing
& shoe repairs, dry-cleaning, theater tickets desk, concert
hall, two conference halls
    Just across the Neva from the Summer Gardens
    Metro: Ploshchad Lenina

The Sovetskaya Hotel
Lermontovsky Prospekt, 43/1
Tel. 114-5409
Fax 251-8890
Telex 121705 XOTS SU
·   Metro: Baltiyskaya

The Sputnik Hotel
Morisa Toreza Prospekt, 34
Tel. 552-8330
Fax 552-8084
Telex 121702 SAP SU

A small, cozy, well-kept hotel in the NW quiet green zone.
All rooms with bath, telephone, satellite TV. Restaurant,
bar, Finnish sauna, Small Conference Hall, Business Center.
Single, double & de luxe
    Metro: Ploshchad Muzhestva

The Vyborgskaya Hotel
Torzhkovskaya Street, 3
Tel. 246-2319

Restaurants, bar, clothing & shoe repair, hairdresser's,
bureau de change, train & plane tickets desk, theater
tickets desk, car rental
    Metro: Chiornaya Rechka

THEATERS

The Akimov St.Peterburg Academic Comedy Theater
Nevsky Prospekt, 56
314-25-01

Baltiysky Dom
Park Lenina, 4
233-09-32

The Briantsev Youth Spectators Theater
Pionerskaya Square, 1
164-06-79

The Demmeni Puppet Theater
Nevsky Prospekt, 52
311-35-57

Drama Theater
Liteiny Prospekt, 19
275-41-92

ETNO Folklore Theater
Mokhovaya Street, 3
275-42-26

Khoreograficheskiye Miniatiury (The Academec Ballet Theater)
Mayakovskogo Street, 15
275-53-12

Krivoye Zerkalo
Bolshaya   Koniushennaya
Street, 27
312-45-44

The Komissarzhevskaya St.Petersburg Drama Theater
Italianskaya Street, 19
315-53-55

The Polunin's Litsedei Theater
Karavannaya Street, 12
311-52-83

Molodiozhny Theater on the Fontanka
Fontanka Embankment, 114
251-80-15

Malevannaya's Municipal Drama Theater
Sredny Prospekt, 55
218-13-13

Maly Drama Theater
Troitskaya Street, 18
113-23-83

Mariinsky Opera and Ballet Theater
Teatralnaya Square, 1
114-44-41

Miniatures Theater
Mokhovaya Street, 15
272-00-15

Music Hall
Park Lenina, 4
232-94-66

Musical Comedy Theater
Italianskaya Street, 13
277-47-60

**Musical Theater
(Conservatory)**
Teatralnaya Square, 3
311-81-65

**The Musorgsky Ballet
and Opera Theater**
Iskysstv Square, 1
219-19-88

**Na Liteinom Drama
Theater**
Liteiny Prospekt, 51
273-44-58

Otkryty Theater
Vladimirsky Prospekt, 12
113-21-91

**The Pushkin Drama
Theater**
Ostrovskogo Square, 2
315-44-64

Satire Theater
Sredny Prospekt, 48
213-00-12

**The St.Petersburg
Children Ballet Theater**
Stachek Square, 4
143-56-60

**The Tovstonogov Bolshoi
Drama Theater**
Fontanka Embankment, 65
310-04-01

CONCERT HALLS

Concert Center
Nevsky Prospekt, 41
315-52-36

**The Glinka Academic
Kapella**
Moika Embankment, 20
314-11-53

**The Glinka Kapella
Chamber Music Hall**
4th Liniya, 15
213-34-88

Jazz-Philarmonic Hall
Zagorodny Prospekt, 27
164-85-65

Oktiabrsky
Grechesky Prospekt, 4
275-16-06

Stiers-St.Petersburg
Stachek Square, 4
186-95-22

**The Shostakovich
Philarmonic Society,
Bolshoi Concert Hall**
Mikhailovskaya Street, 2
311-73-33

**The Glinka Philarmonic
Society,**
Maly Concert Hall
Nevsky Prospekt, 30
311-83-33

**The St.Petersburg Concert
Hall**
Lenina Square, 1
542-37-32

**St.Petersberg Sport and
Concert**
Center (SKK)
Gagarina Street, 8
298-21-64

ART MUSEUMS

The Brodsky Apartment Museum
Iskusstv Square, 3
314-36-58

Circus Museum
Fontanka Embankment, 3
210-44-13

Isaakiyevsky Sobor (St.Isaac's Cathedral)
Isaakiyevskaya Square, 1
315-97-32

Mikhailovsky Zamok (St.Michael Castle) (The Russian Museum Branch)
Sadovaya Street, 2
210-42-01

Mramorny Dvorets (Marble Palace)
Millionnaya Street, 5/1
312-17-88

Mariinsky Theater Museum
Teatralnaya Square, 1
114-33-17

Menshikov Palace (The Hermitage Branch)
Universitetskaya Embankment, 15
213-11-12

Museum of Applied and Monumental Arts
Solianoi Lane, 13
273-32-58

Musical Instruments Museum
Isaakiyevskaya Square, 5
314-53-45

Penaty (Repin Museum)
Repino,   Primorskoye Shosse, 411
231-68-34

Peter III Palace
Town   of   Lomonosov, Verkhni Park
422-37-56

The Peter the Great Anthropology and Ethnography Museum
Universitetskaya Embankment, 3
218-14-12

Peter the Great House
Petrovskaya Embankment, 6
314-03-74

Russian Ethnography Museum
Inzhenernaya Street, 4/1
219-17-10

Russian Museum
Inzhenernaya Street, 4
315-64-36

**The Sheremetev Palace
(Theater and Music
Museum Branch)**
Fontanka Embankment, 34
272-38-98

**Spas na Krovi
(Resurrection Cathedral)**
Canal Griboyedova
Embankment, 2-6
314-40-53

Summer Palace of Peter I
Summer Gardens
312-77-15

City Sculpture Museum
Nevsky Prospekt, 179/2A
274-26-35

The Hermitage
Dvortsovaya Embankment, 34
311-95-45

**Theater and Music
Museum**
Ostrovskogo Square, 6
315-52-43

Yusupov's Palace
Moika Embankment
314-98-92

The Yelaghin Palace
Yelaghin Ostrov, 1
239-11-30

Санкт-Петербург

Архитектурный путеводитель

Составители
Елена Василевская и Нина Василевская
Перевод с русского Е.Казей
Макет Н.Лакатош
Редактор В.Волкова
Редактор
английского текста И.Стукалина
Набор О.Панайотти

●

ЛР № 063132 от 17.11.93.
Подписано в печать 25.03.94. Бумага офсетная.
Формат 84х108 1/32. Гарнитура «Таймс».
Печать офсетная. Печ.л. 11,00
Усл.печ.л. 18,5. Уч.-изд.л. 19,00.
Заказ 458.
ТОО «Издательство Библиополис»,
198147, С.-Петербург, Бронницкая, 15
АООТ «Иван Федоров»
Комитета Российской Федерации по печати.
191126, С.-Петербург, Звенигородская, 11.

KREDIT
PETERBURG
Commercial Bank

Full Banking Service

1, Dumskaya Street
St. Petersburg, 191011
Russia

Tel. (812) 110-47-56
Fax (812) 110-44-32

Praise for *The Girls are Good*

'Chilling, disturbing and utterly compelling. I couldn't put it down.'

Sarah Morgan, *Sunday Times* bestselling author of *The Christmas Escape*

'A tight, frightening story of friendship, rivalry and obsession, told in sparse and beautiful prose. Tense as the space between the uneven bars.'

Abigail Dean, author of *Girl A*

'What a book! A stunning and revealing look the world of elite gymnastics. An unforgettable debut.'

Jo Jakeman, author of *Sticks and Stones*

'Brilliant, immersive, page-turning.'

Gillian Stern, judge of The Lucy Cavendish College Fiction Prize

'Brutal and brilliant – I read it in one sitting.'

Harriet Tyce, author of *Blood Orange*

'Dark, disturbing, desperately sad – I was totally gripped. What an incredible setting for a novel – a glimpse into a wonderfully dangerous, screwed up world. I couldn't put it down.' **Cesca Major, author of *The Other Girl***

'Dark and memorably uncomfortable.'

Sofia Zinovieff, author of *Putney*

THE GIRLS ARE GOOD

Ilaria Bernardini is a writer and screenwriter. She is the author of nine novels, a graphic novel and two collections of short stories. Her novels *Faremo Foresta* and *The Portrait* were longlisted for Italy's prestigious Strega Prize. She has created TV shows, including *Ginnaste* and *Ballerini* (MTV) and has written for *Rolling Stone*, *Vogue*, *Vanity Fair* and *GQ*. *The Girls are Good* is based on her novel *Corpo Libero* which subsequently morphed into a cult reality show. The story is inspired by Bernardini's exclusive exposure to the world of gymnastics over the past decade. The book has been adapted into a six-part TV series by Indigo Film and was co-developed with the support of All 3Media International and the Creative Europe Media programme of the European Union.

THE GIRLS
ARE GOOD

Ilaria Bernardini

HarperCollins*Publishers*

HarperCollins*Publishers*
1 London Bridge StreetLondon,
SE1 9GF

www.harpercollins.co.uk

HarperCollins*Publishers*
1st Floor, Watermarque Building, Ringsend Road
Dublin 4, Ireland

First published in the United States by HarperCollins*Publishers* 2023
1

First published in the United Kingdom by HarperCollins*Publishers* 2022

A catalogue record for this book is available
from the British Library

ISBN (PB): 9780008581091

Set in Sabon by Palimpsest Book Production Ltd,
Falkirk, Stirlingshire

Printed and bound in the UK using 100% renewable electricity
at CPI Group (UK) Ltd

MIX
Paper | Supporting
responsible forestry
FSC™ C007454

This book is produced from independently certified FSC™ paper
to ensure responsible forest management.

For more information visit: www.harpercollins.co.uk/green

How long can music
override the pain?
She reaches for the playlist.

Diane di Prima

MONDAY

In seven days there will be a dead gymnast, yet this morning, as I open my eyes, everything looks the same. Then again, my life is a loop and everything always looks the same. My first alarm wakes me at five past six, the second one at ten past. I like the first one because there is the second, these five minutes are mine only. I think of nothing, I am nothing. They are the longest five minutes of my day. At ten past six I wake up properly, click my neck and stretch my arms, my hands, each finger. I get up and feel the carpet under my feet. It prickles, as usual. It isn't one of those soft carpets, like they have at Anna's house. Ours is cheap and beige, the cheapest colour with the exception of school grey. Dad says being poor is OK because we love each other and, as long as we have our love, nothing else matters. I always make sure to nod in agreement, otherwise he and Mum get even sadder and I'd feel both poor and mean.

1

I wash my way-too-red hair, check my way-too-many freckles in the mirror, get dressed, close my bag. I walk twice around the chair, zip up the fleece of my team tracksuit and check my way-too-many freckles again. I open the door, tap the knob twice, go down to the living room. Which is also the dining room, the TV room, the kitchen and my parents' room. I eat my cereal, drink my juice.

Mum gives me a kiss and says, 'We'll miss you' and 'Don't forget your passport.'

From the sofa bed, Dad says, 'See you in a week' and 'Break a leg, little mouse!'

We really do love each other. Even though Mum's eyes slant downwards and even though Dad looks more depressed than ever. I won't miss them. I never do, I never did, I never will. But I want to win for them, or at least qualify for the individual finals at this tournament so that maybe – thanks to me and my road to the Olympics – one day they can have their own bedroom. Or kitchen, at least. Then I could stop feeling guilty that sometimes when they come to watch me compete, I pretend I don't know them.

I'm now 15, I was only 4 when I started doing gymnastics. Back then, no one knew if I'd be good at it, or if I'd grow to be tall or short. I also had no idea that from the age of 10, it would mean I'd find myself training at seven o'clock in the morning before school. Then again from three to seven p.m., and that I'd have to be doing my homework during dinner, sleep, then get up the next morning, six days a week, to train again at seven and so on. I didn't know Sundays would forever be for competitions and that my days would be so repetitive. I didn't know that I'd end up liking how things repeat themselves.

At least, most of them. Even though training sessions and exercises don't really ever repeat themselves because even in repetition there's always change. And in a gymnast's life there's always change. Like today we're flying to Romania to compete. This is new.

And new is both scary and great.

I open the front door and our team's minibus is coming up the road. I cross the yard, feel the freezing cold pressing on my cheeks, my eyes tearing up in the wind. The sky is lower than usual. Just like my hair today feels redder than usual. Fire red. Or maybe more strawberry red. I wrap myself up in my scarf, then do it twice more, before getting on with life and all the movements it requires. Walking, sure. Being with other people. Breathing, smiling.

Praying I won't die.

Inside the bus, it's silent. None of my teammates look at me. Anna and Benedetta are asleep, Nadia and Carla just don't bother. Rachele, our coach, is smiling at me, though she always tries too hard. When smiling. When talking. When all things. I give her a little wave, then nod to the physiotherapist, Alex. Even from here I can smell his last drink. And just like every day over the last five years I can smell his cigarettes, then the smell of his cigarettes on my skin. The smell of him on my skin. And that's another thing I learned when I was 10.

'Slept well last night?' he says.

'Yes,' I say.

I imagine him with his wife, sleeping well despite the horror he is capable of. Maybe she hates his smell too. Maybe she too tries to rinse it off with water, alcohol, or by scratching her skin with her nails. Will he really only touch us while we look like kids, as Carla says? Or is this too a lie? It could mean that when I'm 16, or max

3

17, he'll stop, and that will be the only good thing about being older.

That, and being able to eat more.

The only empty seat is next to Nadia and Carla, so I sit there and we all say 'Hey.' It's a one-hour drive to the airport, then a three-hour flight from Italy to Romania, and I feel claustrophobic already. I tap the window twice, zip and unzip my fleece, count to a hundred. The others are streaming music through their phones, but I still use an old iPod that was handed down to me from the hairdresser my mum cleans for. I have to switch it on and off a few times before it works. Nadia and Carla look at my dinosaur contraption, then they shut their eyes, at the same exact time. It's like I'm watching them in slow motion, a choreography they've rehearsed. There's also a sound for the movement of their super long eyelashes and that sound has an echo too.

Whatever Nadia and Carla do, even breathing, they always seem to do it together. Maybe even their heart-beats are synchronized. Maybe their names, both five letters, are part of a larger picture. Carla wears more make-up and skirts and Nadia is all tracksuit bottoms. One is blonde, the other one dark. But these differences were probably decided at planning stage, so they'd be a better pair.

The first time I met them, they were 8 years old. Before that I'd only seen them at the training camp but they never mixed with anyone else. They'd come to visit Rachele's club where I was training. Carla was already a prodigy. And famous for being in a TV advert in which she said to a boy the same age as her 'Look what I can do!' and launched herself into three roundoffs and a double back somersault. She landed, smiled, and sat down

4

at the table to wolf down a cereal bar that was supposed
to give her the energy to do that routine. The boy moved
away, dejected, but Carla ran after him to give him a bar
of his own and they were both happy.

I know she'll have spat out that cereal bar as soon as
they'd cut the scene.

I remember thinking that I wanted to be her and how
was it possible she could smile for the cameras so naturally
after a double backflip with twist. Then I realized I was
always trying to smile for the juries and for the coaches.
And for Mum and Dad too.

We all looked fine, from the outside. We still do. Some
of us are just better at faking it.

I select the playlist of my floor routine and put it on
quietly, because I hate it when music hurts my ears. I
follow the notes and visualize a move for each one of
them – the front pike, the aerial cartwheel – then I imagine
the tune without the singing. I visualize being full of grace
in a double tucked back somersault and a front one, a
tick-tock bending my back to make an upside-down V
shape, before doing the split leap. If my mind helps me,
if my body helps me, this week I'll add a triple twist,
which I've been able to do quite well for a few months
now. I imagine crying a single tear of satisfaction after it,
and smiling to the jury.

Then, to the world.

I curl up on the seat, my back to Carla, and go to
sleep. I can sleep anywhere – my mum taught me. Even
as a small child, I could fall asleep under a desk while
she cleaned offices, at the hairdresser's while she cleaned
salons, and on overnight buses when we were coming
back from one of her faraway jobs, no problem. I sleep
immediately and deeply. I dream of nothing. I am nothing.

When I wake up, we are at the airport and Nadia and Carla are laughing at Rachele's bum, which they say is looking bigger and fatter and flabbier.

'I can see the cellulite holes from here,' Carla says.

'I can see them through her tracksuit,' Nadia confirms.

'I can see the plates of pasta and greasy sauce she ate. I can see it on her face too, her skin is as glossy as cheese. Can you smell the mozzarella?'

Nadia laughs. She always laughs when Carla's being mean. Or when Carla is being anything, really. She laughs and she adores her.

I follow them, making it look like I am not following them – they hate me when I'm too close, and I hate myself when I'm too close. So I walk almost alongside them but a step and a half behind. Carla is swaying her hips and her designer handbag, which is printed with large letters. Now she's going on about flirting with her teacher during a history test in school last week. She asked him if it really was important to know what diseases were around in the Middle Ages. 'Should we not,' she apparently said, 'worry about other things?' Then she tells Nadia that she blinked in a *very* explicit way.

I've been listening to Carla and Nadia for years now. I've heard them analyse the growth – or non-growth – of their boobs, my boobs, and scan every boy, every girl. I've heard them, one by one, go through their families' obsessions, anecdotes, and secrets. For years too I've seen Nadia staring at Carla in the shower, admiring her back handspring in the gym. Praising her. Loving her.

I know she loves her. We all know.

I also know that they pray a lot at Carla's house. They read the Bible at dinner and in bed, before going to sleep, then they read more Bible with their morning coffee. If they have lunch together, well then, more Bible will go with that lunch. It's because they read the Bible together with their morning coffee, or with their chicken at meals, that her parents decided to stop Carla from being in adverts. It was OK to be famous before God got into their lives. It was permitted. Now it is no longer the right way to Give Thanks for the Precious Talent and Gift Carla has been Given by Him.

'You are God's gymnastic angel,' they tell her.

And even if Carla mocks them, I wonder if some of that sentence has stuck with her. She does seem to believe in being one. This faith, together with being able to fly, must help her with not falling at the vault. At the bars. Or ever.

Nadia's mum is very different from all the other mums. She had her when she was our age and absolutely hadn't wanted to. She's only 29 now and she'd be cool with Nadia having a boy sleep over at her house. Nadia isn't interested in having a boy stay over but tells us so we can see what her mother is like, that she and Nadia deal with fun stuff, like love, affairs, sex, and how to end things with boyfriends without hurting them or yourself. She tells us so we can see that they talk. That she exists.

'Just don't make my mistake, girls,' her mum told us one of the few times we spent any time with her. 'No pregnancies before you are twenty. Or thirty, even. Having kids is a terrible idea.'

I looked at Nadia and wondered what she felt at the idea of being often mentioned in a warning that was about mistakes and terrible ideas.

At the airport, we are the shortest people in the queue for the low-cost flight, and Anna and Benedetta are the shortest of the shortest, here and maybe in the universe.

7

That's only partly the reason we hardly ever notice them. The other one is because they are so scared of everything they have chosen silence as a way of pretending not be here. Or to be alive. Or in danger. Carla has nicknamed Anna and Benedetta the Useless Ones. We used to only see them when we trained to get into the national team because they came from faraway clubs, and Carla always reminded us that theirs were poor people's clubs. For poor people's gymnasts. But then Rachele invited them to join our club, so here they are. Here they uselessly are. Carla also repeats that both the Useless Ones and the entire team of the boys at our club are a disgrace. The boys never even make it to the tournaments, and she says they should become waiters, carpenters, or disappear, disintegrate. Maybe die.

Rachele always defends both the boys and the Useless Ones.

'They are your valued teammates,' she tells Carla. 'You know very well that when they win, you win too.'

But as much as Rachele reminds us of this, Carla never lets it go. And, to be fair, they never win.

'Let's not overdo it, Coach,' Carla told Rachele last time. 'Benedetta, in spite of her spectacular anorexia, is an elephant on the balance beam. Anna's scared of the vault and when she does a floor exercise she looks at her feet. They're *so* pathetic! Why do you even let them compete with us?'

In the queue for our plane, like everywhere in the outside world, people stare. I guess we look weird, little people with over-muscular legs and very coiffed hair all trapped in our identical tracksuit tops. In the gym, I like our bodies, I cherish them, but here I feel misshapen. I'd like to have it written on my forehead: We are gymnasts.

In this sport, it's a great advantage to have short bodies like ours and grow super muscular legs! We don't want breasts! We don't want periods! It's OK to develop osteoporosis at 13 years old, we don't care about growing tall! The important thing is to win and for this body to be strong and not look pretty when we are queuing!

But these would be way too many words to fit on my forehead.

Rachele always says thank God we are built like this, thank God we are short with no boobs, and thank God very few of us have periods and we really must thank God for our bodies, so tiny yet so strong. Otherwise, we could not excel at this sport and be champions and carry gymnastics high like a flag of the nation's power and strength. That's why she-who-puts-on-weight is done for. She-who-grows-tall is done for. She-who-grows-boobs, done for, unless she can endure very tight wrapping. Our body is our most precious possession. That's also why we live and travel with a physio. And that's why we have daily sessions with him. In theory, the sessions are there to protect our most precious possession.

In reality, it's in there that it all gets broken.

'The girls are good,' Rachele will say when someone asks if we might want to eat a bit more, train a bit less, or if we're happy about this life of being called dogs or elephants or losers as we work and sweat and hurt through our routines.

'We are good,' we confirm. And we nod. And we smile.

In our country there are almost four thousand gymnasts at competitive level. Barely a dozen are as strong as us. Physically and mentally as strong as Carla? I think there are none. Maybe that's why she's able to never talk about Alex. And maybe that's why she is so combative. Our discipline consists of floor exercises set to music, the balance beam, vault, and asymmetric bars. We do all the exercises individually but we are scored as individuals and as a team. It's an Olympic sport and it's the national team and the Olympics that we are aiming for. That is why Carla and Nadia moved to the North with their families and took up training at my gym. That is why Anna and Benedetta are trying to fit in too. Rachele is known as the best. She's also the toughest, OK, and we now know she's also a liar and covers things up, OK, but in her hands you get your closest shot at the Olympics. She has produced more gold medals than any other coach in this country. How many of them wanted to die, that we will never know.

'Be your best self,' she always says. 'Ask yourself if you want to be a prisoner of the past or a pioneer of the future.'

I wonder if she saw the sentence on a T-shirt. Or a meme online. I wonder if when she mentions the past, she thinks about the horrible past she knows we share. The horrible present she knows we share. And if that changes what kind of pioneers we could turn out to be in our future. I wonder if she thinks that as pioneers we will come back for vengeance. Or if she knows that we will be completely broken by then.

You do nothing for years but improve, jump higher, become more precise, more elegant. But as you get closer to turning 18, they tell us, you do nothing but get worse, weigh more. That moment is an ugly one, except it will mean getting rid of Alex and his fingers inside us and his smell on our skin. It's not even that far off. More or less three years to go until our decline. It's a bit like knowing when you'll die and that's a strange thing to know when you haven't even really lived yet. It might be useful, OK, because you have to make choices, like deciding how to spend the last days of your life, what to leave behind, what to be remembered for. And you have to take into account that although you think you can decide what you'll be remembered for, in the end, in gymnastics, or in life, it's not really your choice.

You might fall before. You might die before.

The tall girls for instance, even the great ones who get to competitive level, at some point they all disappear and for most of them it's a tragedy. What did those surplus centimetres have to do with them? They never asked for extra height, never wished to be taller. And yet their shin bones got longer, their shoulders more suited to swimming or weight-lifting. Their backs grew twice as wide as ours and, from behind, their backs were saying goodbye.

At least that's what they were saying to me, but I could never tell anyone because it would be weird, to explain about backs that are saying goodbye.

And then there's always Khorkina, the Russian who – despite sometimes insulting other gymnasts for being weak or moaners or bringing the power of God's punishments to quite a few sentences – gives all tall gymnasts hope. She is 1.65 metres, and is a constant reminder that, after being squeezed into bandages for years and after having been hungry for years, anything is possible. Even being tall and a supreme champion. Even being named *The Flamingo of Belgorod*. Even being beaten but thankful for it. If you want to achieve something, of course, as she says. If you want to be a pioneer.

At her last Olympics she had a black leotard, all made of Swarovski crystals. She named it her wedding leotard.

But there's one Khorkina every ten, twenty years and

in this ten, twenty years she's been the one, with exercises created especially for her, modified to fit her, so that even doing a twist with 1.65 metres to spin around can look elegant. Now those moves are part of the repertoire and are named after her, forever and ever. And when your name is repeated forever and ever in gyms across the world, somewhere inside you'll hear it and you'll feel it for sure. You'll feel someone is saying 'Khorkina' in China, or in a small gym in Spain, or maybe in Japan. Someone, while flying through the air in Canada, is mumbling, 'Now, I'm going to try the *Markelov-Khorkina* combination,' and that must be so beautiful.

Rachele is going over the away rules: mobile phones switched off in the gym, good manners when travelling and at the hotel. Responsibility and respect for our own bodies because each of our bodies is everyone's body. We must take care of our teammates and of our host country too. We must be polite. Smile. Say thank you.

Be good girls.

Looking at us from the outside, you wouldn't think that us teammates are also in competition with one another. Individually, each one of us has the potential to win her own event, to beat a teammate who's become an enemy. Nadia against Anna on the balance beam for example or Benedetta and I trying to better each other at the vault all the time. But there's no competing with Carla and you wouldn't even think of measuring yourself against her. And Nadia, who is second best, seems happy as she is. She seems, in general, happy for Carla to get what she wants.

'Don't even think of practising any romantic routines,' says Rachele, trying to be funny.

We don't find her funny. We find her gross. Carla mocks

her and makes the shape of Rachele's fringe with her hands, so stiff it could be made out of plaster. Once, after training, I saw Rachele blow-drying it with tons of hairspray. She was also lining her eyes with kohl and painting her mouth with a brown lip pencil to make an outline, filling it in with this thick paste. She was making herself look pretty but her eyes were teary. It might have been the black eyeliner or maybe it was because she knew that even if she put lipstick on, she was still lonely. And anyway, she knows way too many things that have happened to us, and to her, to ever be happy or pretty again. She is guilty. There's no amount of black eyeliner and orange lipstick to cover that up.

'She'll be sure to practise,' Carla whispers to Nadia, loud enough to make sure we can all hear. 'She'll do weird shit with some weird man she'll find in some weird Romanian bar.'

Carla starts making up her own rules.

'Rule number one thousand three hundred and six, respect the poor Romanians who are poor,' she says. 'Rule number one hundred thousand and seven, do not touch other girls' tits. Rule number two million three hundred, do not touch the boy gymnasts' dicks or, let's see, noses!'

We all laugh. At least we all do that sound that comes across as a laugh.

Rachele never gets too cross with Carla. She's our champion and this is why she gets away with everything. She gets away with a lot of things that we – who are good, but not champions – are forbidden to do. Be loud. Hurt others. Lie. We don't get cross with Carla either. At most we roll our eyes when she can't see us. Or we clench our jaws and grind our teeth.

We'd be nothing without her.

A downpour splatters the immense airport windows and a storm sets in. We all put our earphones back in – I choose a soundtrack for the storm – and wait for the time to pass, and the lightning to subside. Nadia's afraid of flying and she's turning pale. She has so many fears that we've lost count: falling off the asymmetric bars, being in the dark, being in lifts or locked in rooms of any kind, including public toilets. Loud noises and even very swift noises, like when someone whispers.

'They freak me out,' she says, 'like they'd bring bad luck.'

Carla always says that Nadia's half-poor but not really 'dog-poor like Martina'. And Nadia's always reminding us that if anyone knows anyone that needs a babysitter, she's free Saturday nights. Her house is very small – it's more like a room – and her dad's been gone right from the start. Her very young mum looks after very old people but only some of the time. She's trying to get a degree so she can earn more money.

'I need to repair my mistake,' she says.

Carla, on the other hand, is, according to her, 'half-rich' – which to me means very rich. Her family has a car, a scooter, two jobs, three bicycles and enough bedrooms for each one of them. They also eat meat at least three times a week. Or so we're told. They go on holiday to Sharm-el-Sheik or Djerba every two years, and in the summer they go to the seaside. If Carla wants, she can buy new skirts and T-shirts and doesn't have to wear her cousin's castoffs like me. Carla has an adopted brother, Ali, and she calls him 'my half Black half-brother'. To prove a point, because their parents are so religious, she says she doesn't believe in God at all at all at all, but we know she prays before going to sleep. And she always brings the Bible when we travel. We also know she loves Ali because when he comes to the competitions she hugs him a hundred times, saying, 'I love you, my half Black half-brother.'

'During thunderstorms it's possible for the fuselage to funnel the airstream so it hits the plane, usually without anything bad happening,' Nadia says.

'Did you really say *fuselage*? I'll never use the word fuselage in my whole life,' Carla says. 'You also said *funnel*. You're scaring me so be quiet, OK?'

When we're let on the plane we are the only ones on board who are sitting comfortably. The seats are so close together that people of regular height nearly have their knees in their mouths. I'm sitting next to a man who stinks of something like rotten fruit or rotten something and is reading the paper. He's stuck on the weather forecast page for the whole take-off, and spends at least twenty-seven minutes on the football page.

Maybe he too, by forecasting his life through the daily temperatures, is trying to be the pioneer of his future.

Nobody reads newspapers in my house. Mum likes the gossip mags she finds lying around the salon, but because she only works in the salon if someone is off sick, she very rarely gets any. Sometimes we go through them together and we laugh or comment on the love stories or the scoops on people we've never heard of. They get married. They have babies. They cheat. Get fat. Skinny. They shout and they cry. They die. Dad sometimes reads stuff about horses, the winners and the losers, and racing magazines so deadly boring the articles are about things like what's the best hay to feed your horse and the answer is always good-quality hay. He also gets puzzle magazines from his friend Nino's bar, usually already half done by someone else. I wouldn't be able to explain why our money situation is so bad or why we need to use things half used by someone else, T-shirts or puzzles. There must be a reason, but I don't know what it is. Once, I asked, and the answer I got was another question: 'You want something you don't have?' I could have answered with a list. I could have answered with a few drawings. But I said 'No' because that also felt true.

I didn't want anything I didn't have.

I turn off the used-by-someone-else iPod and look at the clouds outside. On the wings there's a shimmery dust, but maybe it's just in my eyes. The blue is bright and from here the sky looks like a safe place. Falling does not seem possible, and the thunderstorm is very far down below us. If I could, I'd stand on a wing, take a bow to the universe exactly like I bow to the judges, and launch myself into a never-ending succession of *Yurchenkos*. I'd love to land in some uncharted forest or island or river, with a perfect smile, my feet firm on the ground.

'I am Martina,' I would say. 'I am good, see?'

In the seat behind, Carla is reading a magazine questionnaire out loud. 'Are you the jealous type?' she asks Nadia. 'You're in a bar and a good-looking guy is watching you even though he's with another girl. What do you do? a) You look down. b) You look back at him. c) You go over to his girlfriend and tell her the boyfriend is a cheat.'

Nadia doesn't even get the time to answer before Carla is arguing with the questionnaire.

'How would you fucking know who he's sitting with?' she says. 'In the movies it's always his stupid dumb sister, put there on purpose to make you *think* she's his girlfriend. I'd definitely do this with my tongue.'

I can't see what Carla is doing with her tongue, but I can guess. Repetition. Loop.

Nadia laughs and says 'Gross' and 'Take your tongue off the window or you'll catch hepatitis, Ebola, malaria.'

'Rubbish!' Carla says and then adds, 'Anyway, talking about tongues, I kissed my next-door neighbour. The stoner. I wanted to give him a hand-job but got bored halfway through it.'

When I hear 'hand-job' I almost swallow my chewing-gum.

Carla pops up from behind the seat and shouts, 'Have you been listening properly, Martina? Are you spying on us, you snitch?' Nadia pops up too and smiles and doesn't say anything. 'Martina's getting horny!' Carla bursts out, and I go all red and worry that going red will really make it look like I am horny.

Which maybe I also am.

Meanwhile the rotten fruit man beside me is still poring over the pages of his newspaper, stuff about finance now, which he must find very interesting, at least as interesting as the temperature in Tokyo. After another hour or so, we start going down. I stick my earphones back into my ears and the first thing I see in this new world is the snow falling. I watch it turn the universe white, turn the land into a simpler map, all made out of black dots to be joined from one to ninety-nine to see what comes out at the end. Maybe a prize? And maybe my prize could be not to have to hear or speak to anyone anymore. I could stop talking completely, and everything would be easier. I'd become the girl who never speaks and in this new, easy role, I might even achieve some fame.

'How did it all begin?' they'll ask in the interviews.

'With the silence,' I'll answer.

The first thing I hear after the captain announces we've landed in Sibiu, Romania, and that the temperature outside is minus three, is Nadia laughing with relief. Carla starts with her evil parent-fed, TV-fed, shitty-people-fed theories again. According to her, Romania is sickeningly dirt-poor and Romania looks disgusting even through the window and even at the airport. If there's one place we could die on a plane, it's Romania. In Romania they eat dogs, they eat each other, they eat raw mouldy black potatoes thinking they're a delicacy. The Romanian gymnast Angelika has to die and we could stuff her mouth with tiny twigs, so she'd choke forever.

'I saw on YouTube that she's getting fat,' she says. 'She's a fat desperate ugly pisser of a gymnast. I'd like to spit in her eyes until she's blind.'

Nadia sometimes says that when Carla says these things, she really sees them happening, as if they were true. She looks at Carla to show her she is visualizing her words. She smiles, as if being able to visualize the ghosts of other people's words was a gift. But I don't think it's a gift and I don't think Nadia really likes to see the things Carla is talking about, as they are mostly disgusting and cruel enough to make you want to throw up or cry. I too have just seen the image of Angelika with spit dripping out of eyeless sockets, tiny twigs stuffed inside her mouth. I too have just seen her dead.

And now I don't know how to unsee it.

Once off the plane, we go through passport control. We collect our luggage and our first breath in this new white world is a mouthful of ice. In the time it takes us to wrap up in our hats and scarves, we're at the minibus. Waiting to share the ride with us is a gang from the national team's selectors who must have been on another flight or maybe they've walked all the way here and they started their hike months ago. We all say 'Hi.' Alex and Rachele get all formal, fake, and friendly, and we all cringe, just like when you see your parents trying to be funny or cool. Just like when you know that at home your parents shout and kick you and hate you but when someone shows up, they go all cuddly and lovable and that's even more painful than when they hit you on the head and in the stomach.

At least that is straightforward. At least you know what to do with that pain.

I zip my team jacket up and down again a few times, trying to make some order and sense of this day, of this new land. Carla takes a packet of Gummy Bears out of her pocket and shares them with Nadia who shoves a handful in her mouth. They check to see if anyone is looking and then chew and swallow. Maybe Nadia is treating herself for surviving the flight. Or for surviving Carla's words. I count to a hundred to stop craving those Gummy Bears and try instead to listen as Rachele goes through the roll-call of the athletes we need to watch out for, as well as our duties when we arrive at the hotel, and the timetable of our training sessions and competitions.

'Well, sort of hotel, more like a wartime vacation resort,' Carla says, having checked on Google.

'It's a classic one-week schedule,' Rachele continues, 'with training tomorrow and team qualifications the next day.'

The worst teams will leave then. Individual qualifications will be on Thursday and team finals after that. The event finals are on Saturday and, for those who make it, on Sunday there will be the individual All Around – where any qualifying gymnast will compete against all the others, on all the apparatuses. Only the best of us will make it to the All Around. We all want to get there, of course, but most of all we must want Carla to be on that podium.

One body, one heart.

The last thing Rachele says as we're going up the mountain roads, and just before getting to the wartime hotel, is: 'Carla, sit properly, we can see your knickers,' at which Carla blushes for about one second, during which I imagine Alex imagining those knickers. And ours.

But Carla has chosen to be Popeye.

'Seeing my knickers isn't a bad thing,' she replies. 'They have the days of the week on. Anna, do you want to check I'm wearing Monday? As you are already staring, you might want to make the most of your good eyesight.'

Anna wasn't staring so she doesn't keep on staring.

At the hotel, on the borders of the Cozia Forest, the rooms are already assigned and it turns out I have to share a triple with Carla and Nadia. Anna and Benedetta will think it's an undeserved treat, as sleeping in the same room as the champion is meant to be a privilege. But I feel nauseous just thinking that I'll have to be with them for six long days.

I'm used to being by myself and I like being by myself. I have never even asked my parents for a brother or a sister – not that we could feed anyone else. I've always thought it's better to be an only child. I even almost like our dinners for three, Mum, Dad and I, when we have nothing left to say and there's a silence, which I'm sure would seem sad from the outside. But I'd say it's a comfortable sort of silence, easy to curl up in. If we're silent when we're out in public though, having a picnic in the park or queuing for something and someone looks at us, then we immediately start talking, because we'd be ashamed if anyone thought we might be an unhappy family. And we smile. And I guess in some way we also bow.

In our rooms we unpack and pick beds. Well, I don't. I'm assigned mine, when Nadia and Carla push theirs together into a big double.

'I wish your mum was here to clean this shitty room,' Carla tells me even though the room is not dirty or messy at all.

'Your mum is adorable,' Nadia giggles. 'Like a soft, stuffed teddy bear. Adorable.'

'She is,' I say.

Or maybe I don't because I can't quite hear the sound of my own voice. I lie down on my back to check out how I feel, in this room of our new white universe, of our short-term brand-new life. I like short term and I like brand new. There are lots of beds in all the hotels, hostels, and bed and breakfasts of the world. I want to try them all and if I concentrate hard enough, even here, near this forest, I can see rain instead of snow outside this window, a tropical landscape instead of this white land. I can imagine lying down on a bed in Bangkok, and seeing Bangkok through the window. I do the same with Rio de Janeiro. Paris. I climb Kilimanjaro. I bow from there too.

'Don't drink the tap water,' Carla says. 'You can get a number of fatal diseases from it.'

We don't drink the tap water; we shower, watch TV, and put on clean clothes. Nadia checks her bruises and with a biro draws a circle around two she has on her thighs from last week's training. Rachele's been pushing her a lot and Nadia says she's grateful for that. We stare at her bruises. Then I stare at mine, comparing them, trying to feel grateful for the bruises too.

21

'These are record bruises,' Nadia says. 'They're sort of cute.'

We study the bruises some more and they're nothing we haven't seen before, and the longer we stare, the worse they look and something unspoken shifts between us, so we change the subject and chew one more Gummy Bear each. Mine tastes like watermelon. Or maybe peach.

Carla reminds us that in order not to put on weight, we should eat carbs only and exclusively before midday. Also, she says, as we are now 15 this is the ideal age to start having proper sex. She tells us she's discovered that to get our nipples to point out under our leotards all we have to do is stick a piece of Sellotape on them, then pull it off like a waxing strip.

She does it and shows us her nipples. They are in fact red and pointy. She also bets us that before the week is up, Rachele will make out with at least two rival coaches from different parts of the world, who the morning after will creep out of her room, shamefaced. And maybe Alex will bang her too.

'Vomit,' says Nadia.

'No shit,' says Carla.

We turn up the TV, I guess all trying to get rid of the image of Alex. I get distracted thanks to the Romanian music blaring out at top volume and I tune out until I hear Nadia ask Carla if she's seen the gymnastics accident on YouTube, the one where the girl falls on her head and doesn't move anymore.

'It says in the comments she died a month later,' she reads. 'But it also says she just retired.'

'So what?' Carla asks.

'Makes me cry,' Nadia says. But she is not crying at all.

'That's Romina Laudescu,' Carla says. 'She's alive and getting better. She's stopped competing and you should stop watching those things. Concentrate on yourself.'

'What's the point? I won't make it to the Olympics.'

'Don't talk crap. Of course you will.'

The truth is they will both make it to the Olympics, while I won't.

'Let's make a bet,' Carla says. 'If one of the ten first places at the All Around is yours, Nadia, I want to see you stark naked in the middle of the gym.'

'What?' Nadia laughs. 'OK!'

'Promise?'

'I promise.'

Later that night, as we queue for the buffet, I remember Carla's rule about carbs. It's way past midday so I get grilled chicken, white beans and a small bottle of water. At the end of the queue, Rachele examines my tray.

'Put those beans back, Marti,' she hisses. 'You'll end up with a bloated tummy.'

Like a good girl, I do as I'm told. I put back the beans and consider bowing but I don't.

As I sit down, Angelika makes her entrance. Since the last time we saw her at the Europeans, she's become even more striking. Angelika Ladeci, now 15 years old, with bright blonde hair, super tiny and with a perfect body, is joining her team, at the far end of this neonic room. The big bum Carla said she saw on YouTube is a total lie. She's half our size and we're already half the size of a normal person. She's stunning, obviously a champion, a multiple prize winner and ever so light. When she walks it's like there's music playing just for her. Her eyes are the perfect blue and her nose is as small as a baby's.

23

I hear Carla ask Nadia, 'You think she's beautiful, don't you? Well then, picture her having to eat dog food because she's a bitch among dogs. She's actually more revolting than the most revolting dogs. Then picture her sleeping on the floor because she doesn't even have a bed, not even a blanket, not even a mattress. She has to make her leotards out of tablecloths or curtains.'

Thinking of these things makes Angelika seem even more special to me, like Cinderella or Snow White. I even think about 'The Little Match Girl' and the other million stories in which very pretty, but above all, very unfortunate girls, manage to bring about nuclear change to their tragic destiny. I turn around and see Nadia's eyes have gone weird, like when she's seeing things. She is probably visualizing Angelika on all fours eating out of a bowl. Maybe she's imagining her covered in fur, with a smelly damp muzzle.

That's what I'm doing, anyway.

Later that night, my body aching from the absence of exercise, I get into bed so full of other people's words, I feel like I've been poisoned. Carla still has stuff to talk out and Nadia is laughing happily, listening to an explanation of how to give boys the kind of massage they like.

'Would you do it to Karl?' Carla asks.

'If you teach me,' Nadia answers. 'And if you want me to.'

I put my pillow over my head but the sound of their voices comes through, and with them the image of little Karl, the Polish athlete who has become the sex symbol of junior competitive gymnastics. I'm not in the mood to imagine Karl and massages so I ask them if they can keep it down and Carla says, 'You are so boring, Martina!' but then she switches to whispering, and with the pillow over my head I can barely hear anything anymore as I finally feel myself drift off.

In the middle of the night, I get up and tiptoe to the loo to pee.

I open the door, tap the knob twice with my fingers, then I tap it twice again to close it behind me. When I return to the room, I look at Carla and Nadia sleeping in each other's arms. On Carla's bedside table I see the Bible, and her painkillers.

Watching the girls breathe quietly, I have another flash of Alex, his bloodless knuckles, holding my ankle with one hand and touching me inside with his other hand. His breath. My breath. I wish I could find comfort in Carla and Nadia's arms too. Or should I try Carla's Bible? Maybe the painkillers. I go back to my bed and choose the usual method. I start counting to a hundred then to another hundred. I make it to a million.

'Help me,' I say. But nobody can hear me.

TUESDAY

'You bitch!'

I open my eyes and see Carla leaning out of the window, then hear water, and an image comes to me of Nadia under the shower, still charting her bruises. I pop the usual painkiller and stretch, feeling the stiffness and aches in my muscles. Today they are worse because I didn't train yesterday.

I say, 'I'm starving' and Carla turns around, startled.

'Oh, hi,' she says, 'I forgot you were here too. That bitch of an Angelika was training just under our window. What the fuck? You think she does it on purpose?'

I'm wounded she'd forgotten I was here, so invisible and irrelevant to her. At the same time the thought strikes me that I'm not at home, so can't eat double breakfast portions and instead will have to endure Rachele watching what I choose, weighing my cereal with her eyes.

I touch my nose twice, count to a hundred while I blink in repetitions of ten, pause, then do another five repetitions of ten.

'Get a grip,' says Carla. 'Stop doing that shit.'

'Leave her alone,' Nadia says. 'At least in here, when Rachele isn't watching.'

Rachele has been my coach for eight years, and for six years she's been on my case. Like when she insists on making me repeat every exercise twenty times even when I say my arms are so tired I can't hold them straight and she tells me I'm just lazy. When my arms give in and I end up bumping my chin or my shoulder on the mat, she sighs, like I'm worth nothing. Once I hit my nose so hard it bled.

A few years ago, we had a teammate, Caterina, whose mother was more in tune with what was going on at the gym than any of ours. True, Caterina suffered more fractures than the rest of us but then I think about the falls I have taken, my constant feeling of being about to snap in half, and I guess someone could have saved me too. All of us have suffered stress fractures but nobody has ever come to take us away.

Besides, I wouldn't have left. Nor would Carla or Nadia.

'Good girls,' Rachele always says when we don't complain and instead of crying we push ourselves so much we cut our palms, injure and bruise our bodies until we are layers of hurt. And we smile. We nod. And we bow.

I wait for Nadia to come out, then I get dressed in the bathroom. I don't want her or Carla to see me naked. Especially Carla. I can put up with being naked in the changing rooms, where I blend in with the others, but in the bedroom I'd be too visible.

Carla always has something to say about other people's bodies and she fixes her eyes on you without a trace of embarrassment and checks out disgusting stuff like pubic hair or cellulite or bulging veins. Once I even saw her sniff Anna and Benedetta's armpits, right up close to their skin.

'Dogs,' she whispered.

And Nadia had mimicked a dog, on all fours, barking.

When I come out of the bathroom, Carla and Nadia are sitting on the bed, fully dressed, their pulled-back hair buns almost identical, busy lacing up their trainers. They are picture perfect, so pretty you love them or hate them straightaway. Carla with her blonde hair, full lips slick with gloss, plump cheeks, and bright blue eyes. And Nadia, with her delicate hands despite her callouses, her long slim fingers, her slender neck.

Her hair, so curly and so dark.

'Do you remember that time you said you wanted to see wolves?' Carla says to her. 'We were at your house and we saw that film about the little girl who lived with them.'

'They protected her and killed for her. I loved those wolves.'

'Well, look out there.'

We press our noses to the window. I see the ground covered in snow and Angelika sprinting round in circles, near the low gate that separates the war-like hotel from the nothingness beyond. She looks so carefree, as if she doesn't have a worry in the world. But then again, it could be the distance.

Or it could be her being a good girl too.

It would be such fun to go and shake the trees and stand under the falling snow and stick my tongue out, I think. The cold down on our backs would make us laugh

29

and we'd forget everything – all of our pain, all of our life – for a few seconds at least. But there are no wolves to be seen, and anyway we wouldn't be allowed to go out there and play.

'Where's the wolf?' Nadia asks.

'It vanished into the forest,' Carla says. 'Didn't you see it?'

'No,' says Nadia. 'Was it really there?'

I tap the window twice and they look at me.

'Sorry,' I say.

I wish I could stop doing things in sequences. And I wish I didn't make so many mistakes on the uneven bars. Or in life. I must have got it from Mum. Sometimes when she talks she makes stupid mistakes with her words. Or with the clothes she wears. She used to be pretty but now she hardly ever washes her hair. She usually does it on Sundays but by Tuesday she has to tie it back because it's already gone greasy. I haven't seen her naked for years now, but I remember she used to look great in her swim-suit. And perfect in her knickers and bras. And why doesn't Dad go out every morning to look for a job? He wants to be with us, he says, but I go to school, then gymnastics, and Mum works every day. He only smokes, goes to Nino's, does half-finished crosswords, and reads that stuff about horses. Who knows why they fell in love and how they managed to make me. Had it been down to them alone they wouldn't even have had the energy to complete my feet or DNA.

Stepping away from the window, I have to touch my hair twice and take two steps with my left foot and two with the right, before I can sit on the bed.

'That idiot goes running when it's zero degrees outside,' Carla says. 'She's going round and round in the snow.

Earlier, I saw her disappear into the forest wearing just a leotard and tracksuit bottoms. What a pathetic show-off!'

'She's been doing it every morning and every night forever,' says Nadia. 'I read it online. Her first coach taught her. That gross man Florin, who dropped dead of a heart attack when some of the girls accused him of hitting them.'

Their Florin, our Alex. Their man. Our man.

'She might get eaten by wolves,' Carla says. 'Or maybe because of the cold she'll get diarrhoea. Just when she's doing a floor routine, a proper bout!'

Carla starts to do an impression of Angelika getting a bout of diarrhoea during a handspring. She pretends to be Angelika greeting the jury, on the beam, sitting in a corner, having belly cramps. Angelika with diarrhoea and belly cramps has screwed-up eyes and her mouth is wide open. 'Ouch, ouch,' she moans. 'It hurts, it hurts!' Then, she puts a hand on her bum to hide the mess she's made.

'A bit like you, Martina, when Rachele gave you laxatives,' Carla says.

'You promised never to repeat that,' I say. 'You *promised*!'

They are both smiling.

'Just having a laugh!' Carla says. 'We love you so much, Marti.'

I try to take it as a joke, glad that Carla is smiling at me. To do so I press my nails into my palms. Then, in the thighs. As we leave the room, I tell myself, *Be happy. They love you. They love you so much. You too can love them so much.*

As the door slams behind us, we see Anna and Benedetta

31

coming out of their room. They are jolly and tidy. I envy their peace. I envy their room with no Carla inside.

'Morning, Useless Ones,' Carla says.

'We love you, girls,' Nadia adds. 'We love you *so* much.'

'We love you too,' they answer.

When the lift arrives, we find that a wall of Chinese girl gymnasts are inside it. We are so tiny we can all fit in, but coming across the Chinese team is always very scary. They scare us because they are strong and because they remind us that we aren't free, even if we pretend to be. So we roll our eyes and make a face. We don't want to meet their eyes as we think theirs are the eyes of loyal vassals, faithfully pleasing their own enemy. Just like ours, but more obvious. Carla says that Chinese gymnasts are like beaten dogs, or beaten poor dogs or beaten stunted dogs. What she doesn't mention – but we all know – is that we belong to the same pack. Carla uses the word dog at least one hundred times a day. And if she uses it ninety-eight times, Nadia will add the missing two to make it to a hundred. Or she will make the usual impression while barking on all fours.

Once we watched a documentary on YouTube about Chinese gymnasts and it made us cry. There were 5-year-old kids dangling by their arms, and their tiny bodies were crushed by the coaches, feet bound and hands shattered, to make it clear who was the boss and to what extent their life didn't matter. We watched it feeling gross and complicit, like when you watch porn, but this was way worse because we were in that movie too. It was also like watching real-life footage of nursery teachers slapping 10-month-old babies, and being those babies and feeling those same slaps.

We've also hated doing the splits, taking ice baths for

our muscles, and those coaches and physios who went way too far and tried to make our arms longer by pulling them over and over again. We hated them for calling us pigs and losers. Or dogs. We hated them when we tried to smile anyway. To be good anyway. And this is why we are afraid of the Chinese more than any other team. Looking at them is looking at what we cannot rebel against either. It's like looking at the most honest mirror.

When we reach the ground floor and the lift doors open, we exhale.

'Fucking robots,' Carla hisses.

'Weak animals,' Nadia adds.

We raise our chins towards the ceiling, adopt the gait of the confident team we know we are, winners at seven o'clock on this Tuesday morning in Romania, and walk into the hotel's canteen. The neon lights above us flicker in sync with our steps. A high-paced soundtrack would really work well now. We are a team – one body, one heart – and even if sometimes we forget, we have the ability to become it in an instant. Even though we have not chosen each other and we may not even like each other, we protect and look out for each other. We are the guardians of our collective memories and secrets. Of our childhoods and of our present. We know if we'll ever succeed in doing a *Yurchenko 2.5* at the vault or a double dismount on the balance beam, and how much we can endure before bursting into tears. We know what makes us angry or terrified. If we have our periods. If during a routine we are in the middle of a panic attack or in the middle of what we call the *twisties* – a mental block that makes us lose spatial awareness during a routine – which will eventually crush us. We know that when one of us scores a point, the whole team scores

33

a point. And that Carla is the strongest part of our body. She knows it and we know it and this is why she's more precious than us and we take better care of her than of anyone else. We ache when she does, we have a temperature when she is feverish, and her weak left knee scares us as much as it scares her. When Alex touches Carla under her leotard, he is touching us under our leotards too. We can sense when it happens to her and I am sure she can sense when it happens to me. To Nadia. This is also why I can sense that the Useless Ones have been, for whatever reason, spared Alex's attentions. We also know that Carla has decided never to tell or say anything about any of it – 'Nothing would change,' she said – but she knows the exact words Nadia and I used when we told Rachele what Alex was doing to us. And nothing has in fact changed.

There's something icy about the canteen; the sub-zero temperature outside makes everything white and blue, electric blue and bright white. The light coming through the window slows down our hearts.

'Even Transylvania looks better covered in snow,' Carla says.

From what I have seen, Transylvania is beautiful. The forest, the emptiness, the maybe-wolves and the maybe-bears living out there. I could stay here forever, never go back to Mum and Dad. I could be a warrior in this other new Romanian life of strength and freedom. I could be a winner.

We pour ourselves some orange juice, drink our coffee, bite into one plain cardboard biscuit. Better it tastes grim, as it makes it less desirable.

'The towels here are so scratchy, what the heck?' Carla says to the Useless Ones. 'Have you noticed?'

They nod. We all do.

'They practically scraped my skin off,' Nadia adds.

'We should recommend them to the Polish girl with the yellow acne,' says Carla. 'If she rubs them on her face, the pus will come off.'

I suddenly realize I'm incredibly hungry, so hungry it's like being the whole world's hunger. I want to say it out loud: 'The whole world's hunger, that's me!' But over the years I've already come up with too many nonsense phrases. Like the time I said, 'When I'm on the uneven bars I feel like I'm between two galaxies.' Everyone went silent and at first I thought I was special and clever, that my friendless phase was over. I could open myself up to the world and everyone would admire me. And love my cute ideas on life. But they'd all laughed hard and inside I'd died of shame. What kind of dumb idea was that about galaxies, anyway? And what did it actually mean to be between one galaxy and another?

I keep silent while Carla comments on the Portuguese coach's bum, on the German athlete's boobs, and the French champion's eczema. Then she moves on to the Hairless Anorexic with Stinky French Breath of Stinky French Garlic.

'But the French are rich,' Carla adds. 'They can stink, as far as I'm concerned. You can't smell their breath in the huge frescoed rooms of their palaces.'

We all nod and say we only know Versailles from the TV, if that. None of us have ever been to France or seen a frescoed palace. And we've never tasted any French food either and the garlic thing is only something we heard – Carla included – about a million times from the cleaning lady who works at our gym.

'They're free to eat garlic, or rats even,' Carla continues. 'They will always have Paris. And the French *R*. And the money.'

Carla and Nadia are getting on my nerves and it feels as if my head is creaking with pain. I watch them while trying to hold my eyelids very still. I want them to understand how sorry I feel for them. But they never look at me, so I give up. The second Karl, the Polish champion, comes into the canteen, all the girls look up, or down, straightaway.

He really is handsome.

Hair slicked back with gel, square jaw and hooded top with the zip open. He queues with his little teammates then sits with them. We've watched Karl grow up and now all of a sudden he's turned into an Adonis. Does he have wings, too? To fly maybe with me to Bangkok? I wish our boys had made it to the tournament. They would at least have got us closer to the demigod.

All the girls, including us, resume chewing when Karl starts chewing. He is looking at Angelika, of course. Then at Carla, of course. Carla raises one eyebrow only and Nadia studies him without changing expression, sort of hypnotized.

'Beautiful,' she whispers.

'Well,' says Carla. 'He'd be perfect for an underwear advert.'

'He's grown at least twenty centimetres taller.'

'He's still a record-breaking dwarf though,' says Carla. '*Guinness Book of Records* stuff. Now can we please stop staring at him or do we want to look like total losers?'

We stop staring at him and looking like total losers. We walk to the gym in the snow and I study the trees, the colours, the temperature and try to come up with new details for my life here. I'll be a warrior and I'll have escaped all of my present and all of my past. I will choose a new name. Build a cabin. I will be able to hunt for food. And I will stop doing things twice.

'Move that arse,' Carla says to me.

I move my arse, we cross a bridge over a highway, walk further in the snow, and arrive at a vast building. Rachele lets us know that for the warm-up we are sharing the gym with the French, the English, and the Romanian squads. The other group will be turning with the Chinese, the Germans, and the Spanish. Tomorrow we will have the team qualifications, so now, she tells us, we'd better familiarize ourselves with the space, adjust to the apparatus and the atmosphere.

'We're sharing with the boys!' Nadia says. 'Karl forever!'

It's a proper, uber, mega gym. The floor and walls are painted in blue. It smells good, a mixture of lemon-scented detergent, clean air, and discipline. I like discipline and I like things to be tidy. And predictable. I suddenly feel so good I say, 'Karl forever!' But I say it so quietly I manage to make it sound like a cough.

Rachele shows us the section of gym we've been assigned. I can't wait for the warm-up, and all of today's training. My muscles feel like they're made of wood. We haven't used our bodies for at least forty hours and now we have to move them to bring them to life again. To make them happy again, and ours again, by warming them up. I'm always afraid that if I don't train I'll be punished and find myself incapacitated by a divine astral cosmic spell, as if I've been dreaming all this time and my efforts, the medals, and the days of gymnastics were never there.

'Please be back,' I whisper to my body. 'We're in Romania. We need to adjust. But you know all the same things you knew back home, OK?'

Alex rubs my muscles with some heated cream. I look at his hands, making sure he doesn't move upwards. His are hairy hands. With brown age spots. One of the spots looks like a star.

'Feeling ready, Martina?' he says.

I nod, imagine pulverizing the star, look away. I count to three hundred and he's on Anna's legs. He looks so focused. He looks so nice.

'Feeling ready, Anna?' he says.

I look at his hands, making sure he doesn't move them upwards on Anna either. Then I stand up, go near the uneven bars. Carla and Nadia say very quickly, 'Red red yellow blue – Coca-Cola Fanta glue – teeth straight feet straight – me me but it's you – blue pooh Fanta glue – I protect and so do you.'

They do it before every training session and before every competition. Back home the boys parrot the good luck rhyme to make fun of them, but with swearwords or only the part about blue pooh over and over. Nobody knows where their mantra comes from. Blue pooh. What's blue pooh, anyway?

We all start with a run. We go on to stretching, floor exercises, walkovers, handsprings. Kick walks, walks sideways, handstands. Rachele watches us move to the vault, then to the uneven bars. So does Alex.

'Creep,' Carla says, looking at him.

'Pig,' Nadia says.

'Good work!' he shouts from his corner.

I wonder if the other girls – just like me – are imagining him dead.

To feel our bodies breathe again, move, to welcome sweat on our chests and backs, is the best. Our movements get easier with every second, our legs more flexible with every step. Not training gives us backache and two weeks is long enough to see muscles turn into fat. We have watched an endless series of ex-gymnasts get chubby. It's one of our top three fears. Together with paralysis and never winning anything in our whole lives.

As we bend, jump, and land, we peek at the other teams. The Japanese club, the American one, the Hungarians. The French, the English, and the Romanian. Not all clubs will qualify today, and some will disappear tomorrow and have to leave Romania. We spy on their routines, scope out their weaknesses. We hate the pretty girls and admire the Romanian coach, Tania, who is much thinner and more stylish than our curvy Rachele.

'She's thin because she doesn't eat,' Carla explains. 'They no have money for food.'

'Their leotards are better than ours. And they are also allowed to wear shorts to train like the Germans. I hate spreading my legs without them on,' Anna says.

'Not wearing your shorts keeps you elegant and in shape,' says Carla. 'Don't moan.'

Sometimes I think Rachele and Carla have secret meetings to decide how to make us all obsessed with things like not wearing shorts during training or staying thin to not get our periods.

During another round of abs, Nadia starts talking about calamities like falling and fracturing our vertebrae. While we are stretching our legs, she tells us about that Chinese girl who died and the French one who was left paralysed and the Swede who is currently disappearing in hospital with anorexia.

We are used to hearing Nadia make lists, recounting accidents and updating the quadriplegic roll-call in gymnastics. She goes on about stuff like this because she's convinced that it's statistically impossible to end up paralysed if you talk out loud about the possibility of ending up paralysed.

I kind of trust her. Or again, the repetition has turned her superstition into a solid theory.

A couple of years ago, Nadia went as far as making charts and tables. She would sit with a notebook and pen, cataloguing the month's known accidents in order of seriousness, categorizing them by age, school, and region. It was so scary Rachele had to officially stop her. Nadia tried to make light of it.

'It's maths,' she protested. 'What's so bad about maths?'

Rachele's sanction was non-negotiable and the rest of us heaved a sigh of relief because it was impossible not to go through that notebook and fall into the same manic computation. But I think that it's surely worse seeing Rachele make the sign of the cross on her chest before we do our jumps or turns. Or hearing Carla and Nadia repeat their idiotic rhyme and having to wonder about blue pooh forever or seeing the boys touch their dicks eleven times before every jump at the vault. Then again, maybe we're all a bit obsessive. I have to do things twice, and sometimes even ten times in a row, and in the end we usually all turn a blind eye to each other's monsters and manias and we'll pretty much take any spell that we think will make us win and not die.

After an hour of warm-ups, when our bodies and our minds are strong and ours again, we start practising our competition routines. Floor routine first. Then beam. While we are working at the bars – our hands covered in chalk that will maybe one day leak right into our blood through cracks in our skin – other teams work on the rest of the apparatus. We rotate around the gym in shifts of thirty minutes. I am unsure and weak in every single section, the beam being the worst.

Also, my rhythm sucks.

We are close to the Romanian team and every time I look up, I catch Angelika's smile. I see her bend her back like she has no skeleton and is made of liquid matter, so perfect and so light. She seems to be doing it on purpose, a master class in effortless grace and control, because it isn't normal to be so smiley during training. Or maybe she's playing to a hidden camera, the prodigy, always on top of her game, always strong and sure of herself. Protected from pain and from breaking. And maybe that's true, for her. Bodies have gifts, it's how you're born: some can sing and some have the best brain for maths and can explain x and y factors as if they were nothing. In our case it's not only about training. Champions are champions right from the start. There are no miracles, there never will be. Anna, Benedetta, and I, for example, we are diligent, we work hard and have managed to become decent gymnasts. But none of us will ever be a star. We are good enough to be useful to the team, to help our stars and to pass the ball to those whose names will be remembered. I am proud of this too but it's clearly not enough. And seeing Angelika's inbuilt genius, wanting to be her and wanting to beat her, it's clearly not enough to be able to get to the individual apparatus finals or to the All Around on Sunday.

Let alone to the Olympics.

On the uneven bars, Carla lights up the whole hall with a *Nabieva*. I watch her shadow on the wall, like that of a superhero, the lines of her body showing the world she can fly and that even in this universe, magic exists and sometimes it is so visible and so near. Her outline is perfect, the neatness of her sequence is extraordinary. She's fast. She has control. Her gymnastics is a poem about love. As soon as she lands, with the full twisting double tuck she has been doing so well for a year that she is almost bored with it, she winks at Nadia and makes a rude gesture towards Angelika, who isn't even looking.

'Now you're afraid, aren't you, doggie?' she hisses.

A hand clutching at her chest, she also pretends to be Coach Florin, Angelika's hero, having his ultra-famous heart attack.

Rachele's eyes are darting from side to side, checking out if the other coaches are staring at her little prodigy. During the competition she's not allowed to look at the jury's reaction, but today she can enjoy the moment. Have they seen what Carla can do at the bars? I don't think they have and I feel sorry for Rachele because maybe they will all stare now, when it's my turn and they'll see me struggle. They'll see I am made of hard wood and fragile clay. Of fear and pain.

I jump, grab the lower bar, and hear Rachele shouting out my usual mistakes, calling me lazy, while my body loses confidence, then precision. I'm not doing well and we all know it, but for every one of her words, I do even worse. More than that, I fulfil her prophecy. I become lazy. The loser. My gymnastics is a bad song that hurts your ears and annoys you. When I dismount, trying to keep my chest up, Alex says, 'OK,' and nobody adds anything. Rachele's silence is worse than her insults.

I tie my hair bun twice and wait for my heart to slow down. I've been waiting for years now.

When it's Nadia's turn, everything stops. Her eyes, her feet, Rachele's breathing. The million snowflakes in the huge sky above the Cozia Forest take a break too, hanging in mid-air.

'What's the matter?' Carla asks her.

'Nothing.'

But we all know what the matter is. Nadia is seeing things. Once I heard her explain that she saw things as if they'd been filmed at low resolution. As if instead of coming to life through her eyes, they come through a very old cell phone.

'Or downloaded from a very slow internet connection,' she'd told us.

This makes it even scarier for her. She doesn't recognize the images as her own or chosen by her. Like if someone is sending them to her. But from where? And why?

I start counting to a hundred. The Polish boys start sniggering. Karl is looking. And some of the other coaches are looking at us at last.

'Nadia, go on, it's your turn.'

'One second.'

'Nadia, you're scaring everybody,' Rachele says. 'Get a grip.'

I can sense Nadia's jaw clenching so hard it could break her teeth.

'OK, OK. I'm right here.'

But Nadia isn't right here. She is somewhere there, and she can't go anywhere and she can't do anything. When she gets stuck like this, Carla will often go up to her and call her an idiot or tell her to 'Move, for fuck's sake. Now!' Sometimes she pinches Nadia's bottom, to try and make her understand she should deal with it as if it were a joke. A pinch on the bottom. Just one of those things in life that you take, like Alex's fingers moving up and down and left and right inside you from the age of 10 onwards, or the Bible to be read ten times a day by the voice of your godly mother.

No need to turn it into a big drama or be too precious about it.

So this time Carla goes up to her and we watch the usual sequence of her cold looks and her encouraging whispers. But Nadia does not react and all I can think is that she is pretty even when she's crazy and even when she's paralysed. Her hair catches the light and looks so shiny, so beautiful. She is as still as a picture I'd stare at for hours if it were on my bedside table. I'd look closely at it to understand how hips can be so delicate and how it's possible that a girl's skin can glow as if it were made of tiny pink lights.

'Listen, little snail. Move,' Carla says.

But Nadia remains frozen.

'Do you want me to bite you?' Carla says. 'What is it you can see inside that weird head of yours? Tragedies and broken necks? Are you dreaming that pathetic Angelika over there will do us a favour and shatter a foot? Die?'

Nadia doesn't even look at her. Carla seems to be doubting her abracadabra will work and even though she keeps giving Nadia orders, you can see by the way her neck is tilted and her hands are moving that something isn't right. Then, as though her freeze-up had never happened, Nadia smiles.

'Here I am.'

And here she is and here she goes. She arches her back a couple of times, runs to the bars, begins her routine, gets the *Maloney* wrong halfway through, starts again and does it beautifully. Her wall shadow is shorter than

Carla's. And lacks definition. She'll never manage to perform a straight full twist followed by a *Derwael-Fenton*, but she's still our second best. And she is still a very strong gymnast. She does well in spite of the error and, as usual, in spite of her fears, which are very often also our fears. And so we breathe out – jolly, relieved – and we smile at Nadia's swerve from danger, at our swerve from danger. We hope it won't happen during the competition, but hey.

Here she is. Here we are.

Not one of us is here against her will. Our families don't force us. It's not as if we're footballers and they're getting rich exploiting us. And it's not as if our parents can really look after us – or protect us – when we spend so much time away from them. Except for Caterina, of course. Her mother did rescue her. But, as Nadia says, statistically, there's already been one: a mum has taken her daughter away and the fractures that have been healed have already been hers.

We are here to stay.

When we were 7 or 9 years old, we complained. To the young assistant coaches, who seemed nice enough. And to our parents. We tried again at 10. 11. We sometimes told them what was going on, the pills to block our pain or to calm our panic. We repeated the names we were called day in day out. Those who managed to at 13 said something about Alex. We said, 'I don't like it, Mum.' Or 'Is that OK, Coach?' Or 'Can you stop him?' But, when nothing changed, we started complaining less, until we were silent.

Until we smiled again. And again we bowed.

Now, when we talk of other gymnasts, of our rivals, we use the same names that hurt us so much. Now these

45

are our words and when we say them we feel nothing. They mean nothing. Gymnastics is all of our lives. This team is all of our lives. Each one of us has her own secret plan, a reason to stay.

I like to think that if I'm good enough and make it to the Olympics, I'll gain money. With money, I'll be able to get a bigger house for my family and one day buy a gym where I will teach and host local and regional championships which will bring in even more money. We will work together at the gym, the three of us. Me, Mum, and Dad. Maybe I'll marry someone nice – not a gymnast, a coach or an athlete, for sure – and I might have a couple of kids who won't be as poor as I am. This alone will make me a better person and make my life better too. My gym will be painted in shades of purple. Or blue. Yes, blue. There will be a sauna and huge windows facing out onto a garden. And when I'm done with this life, the one I have now, I will not put on weight. I'll jog and swim. I'll laugh. And talk.

'Time to go and eat,' says Rachele.

'To go and fast!' hisses Carla.

Nadia grabs Carla's hand and leads her towards the exit. We follow, glancing back as Angelika executes a spectacular floor exercise. Double layout full, *Mukhina. Silivas.* The sequence of her elements, of her routine, is the most difficult I've ever seen in this arena. Or maybe ever. Her gymnastics is beauty itself. And magic itself. Then, as if we haven't just witnessed her supernatural powers, we busy ourselves and Carla imitates the way ducks, lions, and cats walk, going up on her tiptoes, trying to make the whole team laugh. And we do laugh when she pretends she's a snake on the floor. Bums sticking up and tongues hissing, we copy her, bent double, trying to rid ourselves of Angelika's existence, sequence, and beauty. Nadia also waves at Karl from the floor and Carla says, 'Stop it, you idiot.' But she's laughing and anyway Karl hasn't seen us: his eyes are still on Angelika, her perfect body, her perfect routine and maybe he too, just like me, is thinking *At night Angelika is a cat*.

And maybe, at night, Angelika is safe.

It quickly turns to evening, like in the movies when the sky and the clouds change colour in five seconds and life goes into fast forward and suddenly we are in front of Rachele's bathroom for our post-exercise ice bath. No matter how much I know it's good for me, it's hard to get into the tub. At first it really hurts and I only want to run away. But after exactly sixty seconds, one minute to count down through gritted teeth, the pleasure floods in. I feel it in my throat at first, then the warmth spreads everywhere, to my bum, my eyes, to the root of each hair. I shout out in ecstasy and I don't care if Rachele or anyone hears me. My skin tingles, and twitches, my muscles shiver and quiver and I can feel them thanking me.

'Thank you, Martina,' they say. 'Thank you for having the courage to immerse yourself today, for feeling your heart stop and then beat again. You truly are a warrior.'

We warriors then all go and have our physio session with Alex and we are almost allowed to relax during it – let our muscles get the best out of his practice – as he never touches us under our leotards when we are away for a championship.

'He might be scared of the police in foreign countries,' Carla sometimes says, brushing us off. 'Or he might become a different monster in different time zones. Maybe here he eats people.'

And she might laugh too.

But I can never bring myself to join in with her laughter. I don't even think it's laughter, it just sounds like it. I just think Carla has chosen not to care. But she does care. She pretends she is not hurt but she is hurt. Just like Nadia, who in order to survive, has chosen to move the fear from Alex to that of everything. I guess I have chosen to repeat things in sequence. And stay as silent as I can.

During today's session I stay as silent as I can too. He does not touch me inside and I count until I zone out. Until I see my body as still as a corpse. Then as stone. I try to breathe in the smell of the massage bed – the plastic, the soap to clean it. I try not to get infected with the smell of his body. I try to imagine the supermarket where the soap was purchased. Paid for. Here are the four euros, thank you, have a lovely day.

'Send Carla in,' he says.

And I send Carla in.

Back in our room, wrapped in my bathrobe, I lie on my bed, my skin red with ice and heat, and I call home. Not that I want to, but I made a promise and it's better to keep that promise when the other two are still out. As the phone rings, I picture the girls eyeing up Karl and the other good-looking boys, all the Spanish ones, or the French one they admire for his 'juicy French butt'. I picture Carla and Nadia, identical but with different colour hair, like twins in a horror movie. I also picture them playing some kind of trick on Angelika, like cutting through her leotard or staining it with ketchup or something disgusting like spit or cat pee. I hate myself for spending so much time thinking about them. I'd really like to be able to stop doing it.

But then again, it's just another one to add to the list of things I'd like to be able to stop doing.

When Dad answers the phone, he immediately tells me that according to a celebrity monk's almanac of prophecies, tomorrow and Sunday are my lucky days.

'It's most likely you'll qualify and it's more likely than not that I will find a new job. Very soon, maybe even as soon as tomorrow,' he says. 'Next week if I have to stretch it.'

'Awesome,' I say.

'Maybe the factory is reopening as we speak and everyone will be taken back on. Your luck is also my luck!' His voice is a slur and I can hear the drink in it. 'You will win and you will fall and you will win again. In love, in life, in everything,' he continues. 'My mousy mouse, you must be happy!'

'Where's Mum?'

'She went to clean the salon. To pick up hair,' he says. 'She dreams of finding it in her mouth and wakes up trying to pull it out from between her teeth. Cute. And weird. I suppose this is one of the reasons we, the Family of Mice, love her, isn't it?'

He starts laughing and I say, 'Yes, we do love her.'

I say it even though saying 'love' or any phrase with the word love in it makes me feel sad. I mimic a couple of kissing noises and put the phone down. As soon as I hear the click, I start crying.

At least this time he didn't sing 'That's Amore'.

I look out of the window, to see if the wolves are there in the whitest white. Instead, I see Nadia and Carla, and a few Romanian girls, some Chinese gymnasts and some

I don't know where from. They look like they're friends, sharing jokes and laughs, but are probably saying mean things to each other in their own languages. I open the window and the cold air hits me, together with the sound of the girls' voices.

From here it's like hearing howls.

During tournaments, when we aren't training, we often challenge each other, to see who can hold a handstand the longest or somersault through the air. Tonight, close to the dark forest, they are competing for who can stand the longest with their hands in the snow. From up in my room, I feel their pain, freezing fingers, blood becoming ice. It's almost cool to watch these Olympic hopefuls challenging each other out there, ten degrees below zero as I stand in the warm, my blood pumping after the ice bath and the heating full on.

I've never taken part in these kinds of competitions, but later, at home, I always try out whatever the challenge was, timing myself, just to see how I would do if the opportunity to compete came up.

I'd do good.

Now, as they endure freezing handstands in the snow, I watch their upside-down backs exposed, the snow still falling and Nadia winning against Angelika and Carla. When she finally comes down, everyone applauds her. I clap too, and wonder if the other two – the champions, the strongest of us all – lost on purpose. Whether Carla and Angelika are both way too clever to risk hurting themselves just before the team qualification. And whether they are both way too clever not to know that they are both using Nadia, while also making her weaker.

WEDNESDAY

'This is the first time I've fancied someone so much,' Nadia is saying, as I wake up.

I'm cold. It's still dark. I think I am still me but I need to check the red hair and all.

'Even if he's short?' Carla laughs. 'Even if he's not me?'

I can count my heartbeats without needing to hold a finger to my wrist. All I have to do is listen to what's going on inside. My body is an empty room in which the beating of my heart is loud, making space for itself in the gaps between my flesh, my organs, the blood. My heart is the size of a fist, then if I want it gets bigger, like a ball, the sun. I can see my blood go in and out of the ventricles of this sun, round my veins, my capillaries. I'd love to say it out loud, to tell Carla and Nadia, 'Can you see how my blood gives colour to my lips? Can you see that if I concentrate I can warm up my hands and make my heart the size of the sun?'

But because I am still me even in Romania, I am still the silent one even in Romania. So it's Nadia who speaks instead.

'I bumped into him in the downstairs loo last night,' she says. 'I was jumping up and down to feel the soda bubbles in my tummy. He came in and he laughed.'

'When did you go there?' asks Carla. 'What was I doing?'

'You were talking to Anna and Benedetta,' says Nadia. 'Obsessing about the imaginary fat girl.'

'Anna has such greasy hair. I don't understand it. With all that money, why doesn't she buy herself the most expensive conditioner? And shampoo. And hairdresser.'

Blah blah blah. How many times have I heard her say things about Anna's hair or Anna's money? My sun-heart skips a beat. It would be best to make it small again, from the size of a whole hot plasma mega star, to that of a fist.

'He smiled at me,' says Nadia. 'Then we said *hi* at the same time.'

'How romantic,' says Carla, her voice like glass.

'He did a cartwheel in the corridor and I copied him. I also did a backflip and he copied me. We carried on with different moves until we found ourselves face to face, my tummy against his tummy, my handstand resting against his—'

'His penis?'

'His handstand!'

I can feel the sensation Nadia had in her back in that moment. How her ponytail jolted when she was in the bridge position and what the world looked like from there. Upside down, of course. And wonky, like from inside a

52

pool. To feel this way is the special magic of the bridge position, like the special magic of a double somersault is to hold your breath and turn into a flying fish. But I say nothing about blood and red lips, pools and flying fishes.

'We touched noses, too. We rubbed them upside down,' Nadia continues.

'Gross!' says Carla. 'Not sexy at all.'

'It was so nice,' says Nadia, and starts laughing. 'I think noses can be very sexy.'

Carla climbs on top of her and forces her to rub their noses together and I force myself not to look and start my counting. I get to seven hundred, then fall asleep.

The next thing I hear is Carla.

'I hate that bitch,' she is saying, and I know she's talking about Angelika.

I hear their duvet moving, then footsteps on the carpet. I open my eyes and Nadia and Carla are looking through the window. Nadia is completely naked and all Carla has on is a fluorescent bandage around her left knee which glows in the moonlight, like those little star stickers on bedroom walls. Those same star stickers that eventually stop glowing and leave black glue on the walls forever.

Seen from behind they look like little boys, their bottoms round and firm, their legs short, their backs arched. Two little boys of maybe 5 or 7 years old, with long hair and bruises and scratches all over their skin. This too would be a lovely picture, the whiteness outside and the blonde and the brunette staring outside, lit only by the sky, their hands grabbing each other, confirming their eternal pact of togetherness, as they curse Angelika. Angelika the mad, Angelika the enemy, Angelika the dog that needs to die.

'But why are you still running? Florin is dead, you idiot!' Carla shouts out of the open window.

'You can stop now!' Nadia yells. 'We got the sense of it, you are a show-off!'

They hold on tighter to each other, shaking their heads, and they hop on the spot before rushing back under the duvet. They are still giggling at the cold as I shut my eyes again. I can feel the ice on their skin and as I cross back into my dreams I can see Carla and Nadia's naked bodies, mixed up with the hair in my mum's mouth and Angelika on all fours like a dog and I can hear the rhythm of Nadia Comaneci's most famous sequence on the uneven bars. It's a solfeggio I know by heart. I wonder if I can force my heartbeat to copy that rhythm too.

I'm still dreaming when the second alarm goes off. I stretch, pop a painkiller, then get in the bathroom so I can rinse off my dreams and check the level of redness of my hair. I like being underwater. I can hold my breath under the jet for a very long time. If I hadn't chosen gymnastics, swimming would have suited me well and maybe once I'm finished with hand holds, it still could be an option. Maybe I'll swim to the competitions.

I'll cross all oceans and all of the immense seas.

Back in the bedroom, we are focused and tense. We pull on our blue leotards for the team qualifications, covering our bodies from the crotch to the shoulders. We spray some glue to stick the fabric to our bums so it won't move. We can get deductions if we fix our leotards during a routine or if any of our underwear is showing. These leotards are not as fancy as the one I'll wear on Sunday if I get through, and that's why I prefer them. I always like those for the qualifications better – they're simple, only one colour and not too flashy. The ones for the All

Around finals are bright pink and covered in way too many sequins.

I don't like pink and I don't like sequins. I am not even sure I like finals.

Nadia and Carla fix each other's nail polish, smooth each other's hair buns, and check how they look from behind. They look amazing, they agree. They turn me around to check how I look. My thighs. My butt. *Your body is not yours, it's the team's*, I hear Rachele say.

'Aren't you worried you'll get cellulite?' Carla asks me. I'm guessing I don't look amazing from behind.

'Did you know redheads get cellulite early? Are you scared?' Nadia says.

'No,' I say. Even though the real answer is yes. Now I *am* scared of cellulite. I hate cellulite and cellulite has to stay away from me. Just like carbs, Rachele's squeaky voice, Alex's fast breathing, and the wolves out there.

Nadia pulls the elastic wraps on Carla's knee as tight as they will go and sticks on the knee support. Carla sighs.

'Does it hurt?' Nadia asks.

'What do you think? Two lots of surgery, it'll hurt forever,' Carla replies.

'Yes, but today, how badly?'

'Stop bugging me and pull tighter.'

'I'm pulling, but you've got to tell Alex and Rachele if it hurts.'

'Listen, headcase, do I have to kick you in the butt or something? The knee is fine. I can do pain no problem. What I can't do is your voice.'

I slip on my wartime iPod, choose shuffle mode, and carry on getting ready while I secretly watch them. Have we taken enough care of that left knee? I am starting to feel the pain it might cause each one of us. It's the same with guilt or responsibility, we share it. And because we share it, we will all be weak on Sunday too, when we need Carla to be strong and to win her medals. One body, one heart. One knee.

In the canteen all the teams are quiet and orderly, each at their own table, each with their coach and physios at the head of the table, everyone wearing their club's track-suit. I am sure many of them have an Alex. Quiet and kind from the outside, all formal and sleazy when needed, but capable of the worst behind closed doors. Have the other gymnasts asked for help and nobody's heard them either? And did they feel that saying it out loud was so painful it seemed their teeth could fall out and their heart would break? Did their coach, just like Rachele, promise them they were now safe?

Are we all counting to a thousand then to a million, at night?

The girls have too much make-up on and the boys have too much gel in their hair. Today eight of the sixteen teams will be eliminated. We shouldn't worry and we kind of know already who will be gone – that Irish team, the Greek one for sure, and so on. Yet we do worry, also because not being worried means not being humble. Or good. And it's also bad luck.

We drink our coffee, eat our cardboard half biscuits, and listen to Rachele. This morning we pay more attention mostly because we're frightened of what lies ahead. We even manage to listen to Alex without hatred spilling out of us, or feeling faint, as he tells us to warm up properly and how to take care of our injuries. Nadia is beginning to go pale, Anna looks panicky, Benedetta is shaking, Carla is being louder than usual as she psychs herself up at Rachele's dos and don'ts.

'And don't eat too much,' Rachele finishes, looking at our plates.

'As if,' Carla says.

I immediately decide to leave half of the half biscuit.

'When we get to the gym, as Alex just said, we do our warm-ups. The qualifiers start at eleven,' Rachele says. 'Carla, please stop giggling. And, Nadia, please, don't encourage her. Respect, elegance, honesty. I don't want to hear any comments on the opposing teams. Be strong, because you are strong. Be brave, because you are brave. That's why you are here and all the other girls that started gymnastics with you have disappeared.'

She looks at us. Is she secretly selecting who will soon disappear from this club too? Me?

'Benedetta,' she snaps. 'Redo your hair. We are one heart. One body. And with hair like that our body sucks. Right. Let's get to work. Be good, girls.'

Work, work, work. Rachele says it so often, just listening to her repeating the word work is work. The same way she's always repeating, 'Be strong because you are strong' and that we have to be good girls. We know her catchphrases by heart but before a competition we need to hear them again and again and again. Because what she says is always important in terms of spells and superstition and repetition and because she's been the most constant presence in our lives so – despite everything – we have to stick to her and to what we imagine is also a nuance of love. It's not like we have a choice anyway. We have spent more hours with Rachele than with our mothers. She knows about the holes in our teeth, our braces, our blood tests. She knows our past, our present. She probably knows our future too, what we will become and who will really get into the national team. She knows who has not fulfilled their promise and in spite of all efforts, is getting worse. She probably also knows whether or not I'll qualify in the first fifteen on Sunday. And who, sooner or later, will surrender to the horror. She knows, for sure, every single detail of what Alex has done to me. And to us.

'Leave it with me,' she said. 'You're safe now, Marti.'

It had taken all my courage from this and all the other universes, to put one word after the other. To say them out loud. It had taken me nights of crying and vomiting to be able to look her in the eye and to tell her that during most physio sessions Alex would stick his fingers inside me. That sometimes, I wasn't even sure I had breasts when he began doing it, he reached for them and gave me massages. And that I could often hear him panting while he was working on me, touching me, caressing me. Is it rape, Coach? Can you make him stop, please?

'Don't worry,' she said. 'Let me look into that. And thank you for trusting me.'

She hugged me.

For about two and a half hours I believed her. I believed the strength of her hug. I thought that by summoning up all my courage, I had been the pioneer I am supposed to be, and I had fixed it. I could see myself watching Alex being dragged away by the police, never seeing him again and finding out on the news that he was in prison. I imagined writing to the wife. Then erasing the words on the card. Then writing them again.

But when the time of my next physio session came, all was the same as ever. In the room there was Alex. No Rachele. And for sure no police. He was in a good mood. His voice was gentle.

'Now, Marti,' he said, 'what you have been saying to Rachele sounds terrifying. And I am so sorry you had to be afraid for no reason. You've completely mistaken my practice and yes, perhaps I'm the one to blame for that. I am sure I am: who's the adult here, right? Point is, I didn't give you the key information for you to understand that all I do is for a medical reason. Watch this.'

He showed me a low-fi video of a chiropractor doing something to someone's hips. As I was watching the clip, I zoned out and started counting, so I didn't pass out. When the clip was finished, I lay down on my belly as he began working my hips. I had reached number 1,007 when his medical finger was medically back inside me. And half an hour later, having reached number 4,023, I was back in the gym.

It was two years ago.

Floor exercise is my speciality. The beam is my weak spot. I can't say if I'm strong enough to make it on Sunday or ever, because it's not easy to be able to see and understand yourself from the inside. It's not easy to understand if you are good when they tell you that you are good. Or if you are safe when they tell you that you are safe. So today all I know is that I'm a redhead, and redheads get cellulite earlier. I know it's better to eat less and to work harder. To smile and to fight for the team. I also know that when Carla prays at night, when she recites the *Our Father*, she's trying to figure everything out too, and that when Nadia spits her food out into a napkin she's doing just the same. I know that's why Benedetta cuts herself near her pelvis, where the leotard will cover her, and that sometimes she manages to do it with her nails but she mostly uses a razor. Looking around at the other tables

I know many of these coaches or assistant coaches insult or assault the girls and the boys in their teams. That's also why loud shuffle music is better than words, being strong is better than being weak, surviving seems better than dying.

Half of half a biscuit will forever be better than nothing.

Carla nudges Nadia and they start watching Karl. Even Karl seems more serious this morning; so much is expected of him and who knows if he's had a good night's sleep. Karl peeks at Nadia and Carla winks at him.

'Stop it, you idiot,' Nadia says. 'Why would you wink at him? He's mine.'

I can see the anger in Nadia's eyes. In the tension of her whole body.

'You're such a pain. And *you* are mine only. I'm going to speak to him by tongue,' Carla says.

I turn round and Carla is licking her lips. Her lips get shiny with saliva while she hides her mouth from the coach behind her hand. But she really wants the rest of us to see her, as well as Karl's whole team. And of course, we all do see her.

'Do it like me,' Carla tells Nadia. 'Let's make him go crazy.'

Nadia is about to copy her but instead stares at Carla's tongue as if she's studying her glossy and luminous saliva.

'I hate you,' she says to Carla.

'You love me.'

She loves her.

On the other side of the canteen, Angelika is looking deadly serious, not even blinking while listening to her coach. In my opinion, to be able to keep yourself from blinking is a sign of utter dedication. I'd like to be Romanian, I think, right here and now. Because the Romanian gymnasts are really beautiful and not at all unhappy and hunched like care workers, who are the only Romanians that get mentioned on TV or by Carla. Not only are they more beautiful, they are also usually better at gymnastics.

My dad is always going on about how in this messed-up world no one can look after their own children. Nannies leave their own kids behind and move to another country to look after the children of slightly better-off mothers, who don't look after their own kids so they can go to work. This, he says, turns into an absurd vicious circle. This, he says, is a sick world.

'Especially if you consider that the super-rich, like famous actresses,' he adds, 'adopt dirt-poor children, who themselves are other parents' children and mothers, and this too must say something about our idea of love, right?'

And usually he then goes on to say that it might be a good thing, a thing that works in some way, and in hundreds, thousands, millions of years we'll have created a system with a fluidity of its own, mega families of very faraway mothers that mother other mothers' children because it might even be better.

'It might even be better not to just mingle with your own blood. It might be a stepup in terms of civilization, and bring in peace. Like giraffes having long necks and some people not being scared of blood so they can be doctors while others can't. Maybe our way of developing a long neck is not taking care of our own kids anymore: imagine what would happen if that was the world system, imagine how racism would vanish? The idea of owning a land, a country? Wars would end!' he says, and at that point he always adds, 'But for now, mousy, we're still here, and it mostly has to do with money, so we've been really lucky in this respect too, because we couldn't even afford help, so we brought you up ourselves one hundred per cent. Of course, with the help of Gymnastics.'

Of course with the help of Gymnastics.

I slept in the offices that had to be cleaned, and I was never apart from my parents. But when I took up gymnastics, order took over too, other adults began watching over me, helped bring me up. There were the coaches. The doctors. And even if some of them were like Alex, others really cared about me. There was the team now, and my life outside our home and our family. There was the opportunity to better my life, whatever that really means, and to make a home out of a gym.

I have always liked the idea that in taking up gymnastics, I relieved Mum and Dad of myself. The club pays for all my travelling and food when I'm away at competitions or anywhere with them, plus they sometimes help if I need a new leotard or something we can't afford but really need. The club pays for my school books, my physiotherapy, my pills, and a part of me is so proud of this it makes it a secret driving force for not stopping.

I want to be good, so I am good.

Another plus is that when I'm away, my parents sleep in my bedroom, so they have a room to themselves and don't have to crash on the couch. Sometimes I wonder what they say to each other when I'm not around. Maybe they make plans. Or lists of the dreams that might seem more reachable when I'm not there.

That's why they probably didn't listen to me about Alex either.

We leave the canteen, in a line of well-behaved girls. We really are very small, very short, and I notice it even more when I walk past the waiters or I am near some other hotel guests who must think we look like aliens. It's humiliating to see the world from down here, the level of most people's bellybuttons. It's humiliating yet fascinating, just like many other things in life. Starving so you can be called beautiful. Staying silent so you can be called strong. Lowering your eyes so you can be called humble and grateful and graceful.

We are finally free when we cross the white field and it's us alone. Us, the gymnasts. Us, the good girls. No one is commanding us. No one is calling us names. And now we really are striking, and now we really are an army. We cross the bridge intoxicated with the cold, as we leave the forest and the wolves behind. As we leave all of our thoughts behind.

We just walk, and run. We laugh.

The arena is all lit up. The audience is here, the seats almost full. We acknowledge them but try not to get distracted by them. I feel their gaze. I hear their sounds, their shoes on the floor, the spatters of applause, the rumble of their chatter. I feel their excitement, which becomes my excitement. Angelika's name shouted out. That of Carla. I hear their heartbeats. Then, mine.

I synchronize them all.

To try to gather more strength and focus, I keep some distance from my teammates while they take off their tracksuits. They remain in their leotards while I am still zipped up, like I'm inside a cage. I can see Carla and Nadia repeating their stupid rhyme and I lip-read the words about the blue pooh. The jury is assembling and the scoreboards are lighting up. I concentrate on the brown outline drawn with lip pencil around Rachele's mouth and on the orangey lipstick she has filled it with. She's used too much again and the result is doughy, like Plasticine. She'll have lipstick stains on one or two of her teeth and when I see them I know I will lose some more trust in her, for failing to be careful enough to check her teeth. So I stop looking, because I'd rather not know. Same reason I will never tell her about Alex again. I'd rather not hear her lies again. And never crumble again in the silence that would follow.

'I need you to keep an eye on Carla and Nadia,' Rachele whispers to me. 'Those two make each other strong but they can also make each other very weak and you are well aware of how we must look out for each other and we all must especially look out for Carla. Right?'

'Right,' I say.

Or maybe I don't. We both don't care if I did.

'Please,' she continues, 'if there's anything wrong, come and tell me. If you see them do something, I don't know, dangerous, or that looks dangerous to you, come and tell me.'

'Dangerous? Like what?'

Like flying backwards three times in the air trying not to die? Like being left alone with Alex since you were 10? Like not eating or bingeing on pills? Like what?

'I'm not asking you to be a snitch,' Rachele says. 'I'm asking you to help me keep an eye on their, let's say, peace of mind. Because *their* peace of mind is what?'

'*My* peace of mind?'

'Exactly! And now back to you, Marti. Take care of the *Tsukahara*. With hard work you can achieve anything, my love. Remember to smile, especially when an exercise goes well. You can be pretty too, you know? Be the pioneer of your future.'

I want to throw up. *My love*? *You can be pretty too*? I feel beyond doubt the ugliest girl in the team. Or in this hemisphere. On top of that I am also the invisible one, the best behaved one, made to share with the two prettiest and strongest girls in the team just so I can snitch on them. If this was a movie, I'd have braces and glasses and spots on my skin.

I clench my jaw and feel it creaking all the way to my eyes. I clench more and try to feel it in the skull too. Why talk to me now, right before the competition? Rachele ought to get a different job and get as far away as possible. I feel exhausted, lost, until I get my breath back and it's in that second that there is a thud and then one vast whispered murmuring.

The stillness that follows is the stillness of disaster. We know something bad has happened even before checking with our eyes. We've been raised by these very loud and terrible thuds followed by stillness.

It's our soundtrack.

As the world starts moving again, I watch the doctors run towards the mat and paramedics running with a stretcher. I bend down to see who is lying on it, on the mat under the bars, because a thud is always the sound a body makes when slamming on the floor, and a murmur is always the crowd's murmur when a body remains motionless. All I can see are a pair of small legs and feet, completely still. Feet pointing straight up to the ceiling without moving, not trembling, nothing. Seeing unmoving feet, not even trembling and without being able to see a face, is worse than seeing the whole body not moving in one go. My teammates have their hands in front of their mouths. Some are terrified, others look like they are almost laughing. It must be the nerves.

Rachele tells us to sit down and be still and quiet and so we do. Toy soldiers, good girls, we sit still and quiet.

'What a disaster,' Nadia says.

'You don't know what happened,' Carla replies. 'Maybe

it's Angelika. Let me see if the dragonfly got herself squashed.'

'Don't joke.'

'Don't you want me to be happy, Nadia?'

Nadia looks at Carla. I think she is picturing Angelika lifeless on the mat, or out of action, maybe paralysed. We've seen that happen already, it wouldn't be the first time and won't be the last either. Maybe Nadia is already seeing this sequence uploaded onto YouTube. Clicked on a thousand times, commented on and voted for. Thumbs up. Thumbs down.

Nadia starts breathing so heavily I think she'll faint.

Carla takes Nadia's hand and strokes it. She strokes the back of her hand then turns it over and strokes the palm too. I guess she wants her to feel two different sorts of caresses. Then she pouts and rests her head on Nadia's shoulder, and looks so sweet as she whispers how a dead or damaged Angelika would be an option not to be scoffed at. Carla's hair is tied up in a bun as yellow as honey. She has blue eyeshadow on her eyelids, and her tiny, manicured hands are still stroking Nadia while she repeats the words 'coma' and 'paralysis' and says, 'Out of the games, out of my life.'

Nadia is pale. Like an actress in a costume drama, the protagonist of a romantic tale set in the eighteenth century or perhaps the seventeenth, who coughs all the way through the second half, precisely to let us know that she's going to die. Which of course she does at the end, of TB or consumption.

'You're shaking,' says Carla.

'I'm not,' she replies. 'I'm fine.'

'Let's talk about Karl,' says Carla. 'How we'll kiss him to make him forget he's so short.'

'Please,' hisses Nadia. 'Leave me alone.'

The crowd moves away, the stretcher is carried out and on it, like a limp rag, is a tiny Polish gymnast. I don't remember seeing her before. Now I will see her in my dreams forever.

The adults are still talking to each other as they move away and the girl is carried out in a neck brace. No one will tell us anything, at least until the end of the day. So I take off my tracksuit and I start warming up. I know it's what we are supposed to do. Work. And deep inside, we are all actually relieved, because as Nadia has taught us, the statistics of potential disaster are now on our side. One of the girls has got hurt already, a stretcher has been carried through the gym and this has immediately made us safer.

But with this relief, comes guilt.

'Sad, but nothing we can do about it,' Rachele says. 'Let's get to work.'

'Don't worry, girls,' Alex says. And the 's' of girls in my mind becomes a slippery slimy snake. I kill it with a stick. Cook it. Eat it.

The jury takes its position. Rachele tells us the usual million things and gives us the running order of competition. I almost check out her teeth, the lipstick smear, but I manage not to look. Nadia is the first in line and we say, 'Break a leg,' and saying it I think about our broken legs, and suddenly the wolves in the forest appear again in my mind. Could I learn how to live with them out there? Would they protect me and kill for me? I imagine the cave I'd keep warm in, a bonfire, sleeping peacefully near the animals. I know they are good with game hunting as a team and I can do game hunting as a team too.

'Be a good girl,' Rachele says to Nadia. 'Be strong.'

'I want you naked in the middle of the arena, if you make it to the first ten at the All Around,' Carla whispers.

'Shut up, you idiot.'

But I know Carla helps her when she does this, because Nadia gets distracted and she can rest her mind from her demons and monsters. And in fact from that moment on, we become the army and the game hunters that we can be.

Carla's words work better than Rachele's. So does her talent.

When she runs towards any jump, it's like we were running with her. We follow her beauty and fast pace on the uneven bars and we celebrate her perfection on the balance beam. By the time we move to the floor exercise, thanks to her energy that becomes our energy, we are all doing great. We are focused. We are a team. Despite Benedetta's general weakness and Anna's average performance, we are getting near a 160 score that will put us in the first ten teams. I do OK on the beam, Carla is a star throughout, and Nadia is strong and confident when she begins her last routine on the floor. After her wolf turn double, the twisting split leap and a beautiful front tuck, she salutes the jury, proud of all the beauty and the precision she's capable of. Her back bends as she waves, her humble smile lights the entire arena. The audience responds with a booming applause. Carla nods in acknowledgement.

'I love you,' she tells Nadia.

'I love you too,' Nadia replies.

It's my turn on the floor and I have to touch my nose several times before my routine, but no one notices. As the music begins, the memory of the muscles reacts before that of the mind. I start with an acrobatic sequence and I'm quick in the jumps, in the runs, and my shape is tight. I squeeze my bum, tuck my tummy in. I land perfectly on my third diagonal. My rebound is clean, and so are my combination passes, as I continue with a double layout followed by a tuck landing.

Maybe Romania has really turned me into a winner, I think.

On my last diagonal I also dare to think about the team's reaction as they witness my effortless grace and that's exactly the moment in which I lose control, and all of my elegance. I go for the front flip, a shaky roundoff then a triple twist, before losing my body shape. After I punch, and twist once more, I land with my feet apart and make two extra steps.

I salute the jury and quickly meet Rachele's eyes. Her smile is not quite there. I don't check to see whether Alex is smiling or not.

We move to the vault and Carla is on first. During her magical ninety seconds that last an hour, or maybe an entire lifetime, I am forgotten. They don't need me. And when Carla hypnotizes the arena, time and space expand in her honour and all is forgotten and everyone is forgotten. As she finishes her routine and salutes all the known and unknown universes, I'm sure I see glitter coming from the ceiling.

Trying to grab and welcome some of Carla's magical glitter, I run to the vault, but lose my body shape once again. Maybe her mum is right. Maybe there is a God and Carla is a chosen one.

Nadia, Benedetta, and Anna do their acceptable vaults, then we wait for the sum of our last scores near our bench, drinking water, loosening up our shoulders and legs. Zipping my fleece up and down, I scan in my mind all my mistakes, and start to deduct tenths and hundredths of points from the team's success.

'Fuck, Martina, you were about to ruin us,' Carla says. 'Thank God we didn't need you.'

'Stop,' Nadia tells her. 'We don't do that.'

'Good job, girls,' Rachele says as Carla scores 15.66, Nadia gets a 14.77, and I receive a 13.66. The Useless Ones receive 14, but overall – despite me – the team has done really well and we bring home a solid 168.40. We are in, for sure.

So we smile. And we hug.

We study the scores of the teams that made it to the next phase, and we see the Greeks and the Portuguese girls crying. We've been those girls. We take in the success of the Romanians and the Chinese, and try to digest it. We've been those girls too. We acknowledge the average scores of the Spanish club and move on with life.

'Tonight you can eat carbs,' Rachele tells us. 'You deserve it.'

'You did great,' Alex says.

As usual we try to cancel his voice from the spectrum of the sounds of the world, like those of bombs or cars when crashing, while he goes on and on, commenting on every single second of today's qualifications.

'Why doesn't he shut up?' I hear Nadia say. 'Like forever.'

I turn around and look at her. It's the first time I've heard her say something out loud about Alex in front of the team. It's scarier than I thought.

When we leave the gym at seven, the snow has fallen in mountains around the war-hotel car park. I look at the sky and the snowflakes fill my eyes. They become icy-cold tears, crystals instead of drops, so when no one is looking I stretch my tongue out, waiting for the tickling and the minuscule, magical cold.

Thank God we didn't need you, I hear in my head again.

They all run, shouting out loud, feeling the snow crumble as their boots sink into the white. But I am about to cry and they all notice.

'One body, one heart, Martina!' Carla says. 'You'll be great tomorrow, sorry about earlier. I love you girls.'

And when she says it we know we all need to hug. It's the rule. If Carla makes peace, you make peace. So we do it, we hug and become one body again, squeezed, cheeks against cheeks, arms holding arms, near the vast dark forest.

'Say it.'

'Tomorrow I'll be great,' I say. And I jam my nails hard into my palms.

Tomorrow I'll be great, and tonight we are allowed not only to eat carbs but also to leave the hotel as a treat, to see a world without carpeted halls or scoreboards, to think less of falls and broken legs – of how the Polish girl's life might change forever today – and more of what girls our age usually think. I'm not entirely sure what that would be, but it seems to involve being at a shopping mall. It's the best night out we've been offered in months. I would actually say in years, if it didn't sound too pathetic.

We wash, dress up, and plaster too much make-up on. We sit in the minibus and drive to the village. We leave behind the mountains, the river, a closed aqua park, the sound of the wind when it hits the woods. The city centre is clean and I think medieval kind of old. Or maybe some other era, I don't know. Trams pass close by and make the same noise as the ones we have at home. Some of the streets in the outskirts are really wide, the constructions bleak and repetitive, I love this repetition and I love pressing my forehead against the cold bus glass, loud music in my ears, the other girls shut out of my mind. I measure the buildings, study each one of them and compare the colour of the Romanian streetlights with the ones I see after training when I get on the bus back home.

I look at their stars. Their moon.

When I grow up, I could travel and do nothing else. I'd need to work out how to earn money and maybe this idea is better than the gym one. I don't really want children or a husband. Or to work with Mum. I'd far rather hold my forehead against cold car windows in cities I don't know. Study their buildings. Their stars. Their moon. Hear foreign languages, turn them into familiar ones, foreign street corners into familiar ones. I'd rather get lost, disappear, vanish, than always having to be me. And if I have to keep on being me, I'd rather change the backdrop anyway.

'Where are you, my mouse, my love?' Mum would ask on the phone, sounding very far away. And from very far away her squeaks would hurt less.

'I've just arrived in Africa,' I'd say.

'Weren't you in Alaska?'

'I was. Now I'm in Senegal.'

'The snow makes Romania look less revolting,' Carla says, so I cancel her voice more, by turning up the volume more. Also because Romania is in fact striking. Poor, but with music, in striking Romania, I tell myself, is OK. Poor, with no music, back home, is against the law.

Earlier today Carla was interviewed for the *Federation* magazine and posed for the photos, flexing her arm muscles in an imitation of Popeye, like she always does. We stood behind her and smiled. Nadia kissed her and told her that her posture was like a queen's.

'Queen of the dogs, you mean?' Carla said.

'I've had enough of your dogs,' Nadia replied.

'What's with the hair bun?'

'What about it?'

'It's messy. Sweaty. And dirty. Try to be better.'

Nadia had immediately fixed her not-at-all-messy hair and pulled it really tight, trying to be better. While she was pulling it, she had stuck her bottom out, as if by yanking from the top of her head her pelvis got pushed out.

'There, that's more like it. Now you're beautiful as only you can be,' Carla said. 'And anyway, the photographer was a dirty dog. I saw the way he was looking at me. I bet he won't even be able to download the photos because of his sweaty excitement and because he'll be punished, by God, for staring at me like a paedo pig. Did you know that because we are so short, paedos find us more attractive?'

We had looked at her, unable to add anything. She had chosen this way to try to be brave. To try to make it not hurt, and make it a joke. But we know it hurts anyway.

We park in front of the mall and it's exactly like ours. Same brands, same food ads, same neon lights. Same smell of fried chips and frozen vanilla yogurt. I feel at home and, when I realize it, I also feel sad. Rachele tells us we are allowed to split up any way we want, go wherever we want, as long as we met up again 'In precisely one hour and a half under this big M, OK?' We can't help looking up at the big M. Does it remind us all of the word mother? I leave the others, send Mum the Mother a text saying that the first day of competition has gone super well and we are now out for a meal. I write that it's very cold here but I like it, and that I love her.

She calls after one and a half seconds.

'My mousy love, how are you?' she gushes. 'Not too tired? How are you feeling? Are you cold? Don't catch a cold. Are you wearing your hat?'

'I'm good. But I got a 13.10,' I say.

I'm not in the mood to talk to her. I just texted her *I love you*, which I'd never say out loud. And now she is asking me questions, forcing me to hear her voice and her confused words. I let her talk on, worried I'll get snappy like I do at home. Or worse, that she may burst into tears for some minuscule reason, at something I say or don't say. Then I'd feel guilty and we'd be back to square one. I'd be scared of her sadness, which is my sadness too. I'd be aware of my guilt, which again would feed her sadness. Her and Dad's sadness will then eat up all of us, especially me, even though we keep saying we are happy.

It's Wednesday and her hair will already be greasy.

'Who are you sharing a room with, what's the food like, is it cold in the hotel?' she asks, as though she can't stop questioning me.

I don't know which one to answer so I tell her, 'It's all nice.'

She switches to instructions.

'Take care, don't tire yourself out, think of me, don't miss me too much, be happy you are far away from us.'

'I'll see you soon,' I say.

I inhale as much stinky fried-chips air as I can, thinking of when I told them about Alex and they weren't able to save me either. I guess they didn't want to cross the club. And I guess Rachele and Alex's words were more convincing than mine. They might honestly have believed all that medical low-fi crap video. Or maybe they were too weak, just like me. But it's still good that they do get that bed when I'm gone. And that from that bed she can give me instructions on not tiring myself when I'm away.

'OK, I won't tire myself,' I say. 'OK, I'll wear a hat.'

I inhale more, hoping an electromagnetic storm between our house and the Sibiu district will cause the line to die. While I'm counting down the seconds to the end of my patience, I catch a glimpse of Nadia and Carla going into a lingerie shop. I move a few steps closer and spy on them through the windows, while my mum goes on about life and how it is happy but also unhappy, about Dad who still can't find a job but having him home is 'also nice'. Then she rants about the hair on the hairdresser's floor but as usual she adds she shouldn't complain because even if we're not exactly fortunate it's not as if we have to go without shoes.

'We're lucky even when we're unlucky,' I say, repeating another one of their favourite quotes.

'Bravo! Because we love each other.'

'I have to go now, Mum, this is expensive, isn't it? To talk long distance.'

'OK. We're going to have pizza now.'

'Me too, maybe.'

'So we can feel closer,' she says.

It's the saddest sentence ever. All my hunger – which usually is the entire world's hunger so it's really huge – disappears. The remaining little joy that had bubbled up at the idea of being at the mall dissolves. I feel sorry for me. I feel sorry for my parents. Nobody in this world thinks about them, no one needs them. Replaceable in any of their jobs, in all the things they say or do, as humans and as a mother and father. Weak, alone. Deaf.

'So when you are munching on your pizza, make sure you think of us!' she says and I can hear her smile. 'Think about us here in the cosy mousy mouse home.'

Nadia pulls back the dressing room curtain and through the shop window I see her wearing a bra with strawberries on it. She doesn't have any boobs so the cup is empty, like a pocket. She could keep things in that empty space. Stones? Money? Maybe a very small gun. Carla is standing in front of her, chatting and stuffing something into her handbag; she is probably stealing a pair of knickers. It's something blue anyway and seeing her steal is nothing out of the ordinary. Nothing I haven't already seen her do in shops and changing rooms over the last seven years. Once she stole a lamp the size of a watermelon from a gym.

'I threw it in a bin,' she said the day after. That day too she had a gold medal round her neck.

I remember a birthday party at Nadia's house, maybe it was two years ago, when they tried on Nadia's mum's dresses and came out of the bedroom to be admired by us, wearing lace bras and knickers, necklaces, red lipstick smeared on their faces. Carla explained that Nadia's mum had lots of boyfriends and Nadia had laughed and said, 'I met another one of them yesterday.' At the time she had said it in such a funny way that I felt envious of how free and wild her mother was.

'Doesn't it bother you?' Anna had asked.

'Zero bother. I want her to be happy.'

I move away from the shop window and the strawberries on Nadia's bra. I see Benedetta and Anna getting into the pharmacy, then into the make-up shop. I go up all the escalators I can find, take the lift to the eighth floor and again down to the fourth and then the third. I do it ten times. Then, another ten. All I can think is how much I sucked today. And the thud of the Polish girl on the mat.

I don't go into any shops, or into any of the cafés. I let the time pass while forcing myself not to look at clothes, at food or people or anything. I make it my punishment, and my bet. I won't eat, I won't buy, I won't talk. I won't want anything. If I resist, this too will make me stronger. If I resist, I'll do great at the individual qualifications tomorrow. And I'll make it to the All Around on Sunday. If I resist I'll survive all of this pain and I'll be the pioneer of my future.

After two hours of going up and down as the pioneer of my future I'm exhausted and join the team again. They've all bought something, and are holding bubble tea cups. Their mood is great. Or so they are able to show.

'I had a pizza,' I say. Not that anyone asked. But so I am able to show.

On the way back to the parking lot, I listen to Rachele praising us, her good girls, and how today she's so proud. She also says that we are beautiful. By contrast, we are not proud of Rachele, and she is not beautiful, so we don't say anything. Alex, walking near her, looks wasted. We are not too proud of him either.

'All happy, girls?' he asks.

I wonder why his questions have to be so disgusting and pointless. Or exist at all. He's already the silent type, why doesn't he stick to that and decide to completely shut up? A silent monster would be less nauseating than a monster who makes small talk in a Romanian parking lot.

I remember telling him to please stop. I remember his face when he said, 'Give me just one more second.' He didn't shut up back then either. He wanted one more second, and he wanted me to hear him breathe, and was ready to let me know that the pace of his breathing had changed.

'All happy?' he repeats.

'Not while you're alive,' Nadia murmurs.

I look at her again. She smiles back, shrugging.

'So happy,' Carla responds with sarcasm.

They laugh, hold hands. I see the strawberries of Nadia's bra rot. They smell of the man sitting next to me on the plane here.

'Why don't we go and find Karl's room later?' Nadia whispers. 'Can't be that hard.'

'Deal. We'll go when everyone's asleep,' Carla says.

I ask myself if I should tell Rachele, protect their body, which is my body too. Protect their sleep, which I'm guessing is my sleep too. I look at Carla and Nadia, their hands held so tight, then turn away and look up at the sky.

'Tonight is our night,' Carla repeats.

I breathe in all of the darkness, and all of this cold. Is tonight our night? I stare into the void, the moon, and the million snowflakes, feeling hungry as a wolf. I wish I'd had that pizza. I walk faster so as not to think about it. Then to the bus. And to try to be alone again.

'You can't run away forever, Marti,' Nadia says, laughing. 'There's nowhere to go, anyway.'

THURSDAY

I hear a muffled scream. I try to bury myself in sleep but the noise doesn't stop. I open my eyes. Outside the moon is so bright it throws its light into the room. I can see Carla holding Nadia face down onto the mattress, her hands pushing into her neck. She is struggling for air and just about manages to free herself.

'I'll fucking kill you,' Nadia wheezes. 'Stop it.'

'You're the one who's got to stop,' says Carla. 'You hurt me, I hurt you.'

'Stop what?'

'Stop wanting *him*.'

So this is about Karl. I shut my eyes, try to zone out. They'll be laughing soon enough. Inside my head, I say my name twice, I touch the tip of my nose twice, hold my breath and count to thirty. Sixty. A hundred. Why the hell did Rachele give me the penance of sharing a room with them? I quietly do my movements – touching the linen, my forehead, then the linen followed by my nose – times two, then times two and another two. The repetition works, slowing down my heartbeat.

Just as I'm drifting off, I hear Nadia gasping for air again. I sit up. I need to remind myself that I exist and I need to remind them too. That I can hear everything – *everything*, always – and counting isn't enough and won't make me disappear. If I had that power, I would have disappeared already, right? From Alex. Rachele. And probably from my entire life. But guess what, I'm still here.

'What's happening?' I say. 'Nadia, are you OK?'

'Mind your own fucking business,' Carla says. 'How *dare* you speak to us.'

My heart is about to explode, my hands are sweating. My head is full of things and words and noises, thuds and whispers I don't want, or need, or understand.

'Yeah, *Martina*,' says Nadia. 'Fuck off back to sleep.'

No, I think. No and no twice. No and no forever.

'You both fuck off,' I hear myself say. 'You stop. You shut up.'

A silence fills the room like a canyon, so deep, so gigantic, we could fall into it. Even the moon seems less bright. Maybe my anger is making everything darker, everywhere. Maybe when I'm in Romania, Romania goes dark too.

'Fuck off,' I repeat, louder this time.

They'll probably kill me, I think. I'll be dead and done for. I'll die in my stupid pyjamas, and someone will find my body with its absurd red hair, while I have achieved nothing in my life. I will not own a gym in shades of purple. I won't ever have been to America, India, or Africa.

I will never wake up under a torrential monsoon in Bangkok. Or nail a *Yurchenko 2.5*. I'll die as uselessly as I have lived while still sucking at the balance beam.

'Wow,' Carla whispers.

'Unreal,' says Nadia.

I realize that something worse than death could happen to me. The girls could decide to break my arm or my knee, and sew up my mouth to stop me talking. I get a flashback to the day Carla and Nadia grabbed Anna in the middle of the changing room and pushed her in the communal showers. Carla had accused Anna of badmouthing her to the rest of the team. To be fair, Anna had said that Carla was a bully. She was right and had just tried to be brave, to speak out. Carla *is* a bully. But in a team you shouldn't speak out, you should resist, get stronger, forget. Stay silent. And that day too, we learned the lesson.

'Did you really think I wouldn't find out?' Carla asked her. 'Or that anyone would believe you rather than me? You need to behave.'

I'd looked at Carla's mouth, and heard Alex's voice instead. Were those the same words he had used with her? She did behave accordingly.

'You need to be a good girl,' Carla said. 'Not go around destroying me and our team.'

Naked under the jet of ice-cold water, Anna begged for forgiveness as Carla sprayed shampoo into her mouth, squirting it out like it was sauce, right down her throat.

When I said, 'Stop it, Carla,' I did it quietly, because I was scared.

Carla took no notice anyway, shampooing Anna's hair, rubbing it in harshly, the water still freezing cold, and telling her how revolting her hair was and how come she wasn't ashamed to walk around with it being so filthy, her face being so embarrassing, her soul being so disloyal. But then her voice had switched and her anger seemed at once fierce and lovable. It was the sweetest voice I had ever heard.

'I'm going to take care of it and make you presentable, OK?'

'OK,' Anna said. 'Thank you for your help.'

'It's my duty. And my pleasure.'

I cried because I couldn't stop Carla. I cried because Anna was grateful for her punishment. And because Nadia didn't show any discomfort watching Anna's pain and fear.

'I am so sorry your mother doesn't love you because you're ugly,' Carla said. 'And I am so sorry that she prefers her poodles to you because their fur is softer than your hair. It's not your fault, OK?'

'Yes,' said Anna. 'You're right.'

'I'll help with that absence of love too,' said Carla, her tone even gentler. 'I love you. We love you. If you want, I'll kill her dogs for you.'

'Thank you but no,' Anna said. 'They can live.'

'Well, let me know if you change your mind,' Carla said, kindness now dripping from her mouth.

Carla took Anna's hand and led her back into the changing room, where she dried her body and hair like a caring mother, a caring friend, a caring teammate. They hugged.

That day, I went back home and again I asked if I could leave the team and train with another coach and in another club. But my parents, tired and weak, repeated their mantra of the tired and of the weak, and said that it was too complicated, pointless, and unexpected and was it a mega problem if I were to stay? Their faces were those of people who knew nothing. I couldn't stand looking at them. I nodded, and zipped up my tracksuit twice.

It wasn't a mega problem.

Today, in Romania, I guess I'm nodding again. And again I'm doing my ponytail twice.

'Fuck off,' I say, louder this time. 'Just fuck off!'

Romania freezes, the wolves are all staring at this side of the forest, in awe of my courage. The whole world is staring at this side of the forest in awe of my courage. From their king-size bed, the girls stare at me too. And after the emptiest and longest silence, I hear Nadia and Carla laugh. Belly-laughing, as if I have just been really funny. With the sound of their laughter, Romania starts breathing and moving again, and the wolves get back to their own business, dealing with their hunger and with their team games. Eating other animals. Trying not to be eaten by other animals.

'Well done, Martina,' Carla says. 'Impressive. You might want to put that energy into vaulting.'

'Yes,' says Nadia. 'Use it for your *Tsukahara*. We like you, warrior.'

'Now, though,' says Carla sharply, 'go back to sleep and leave us the fuck alone.'

I lie down feeling proud. But also sad for being proud because of a 'fuck off'. I try to slow my heartbeat and get rid of the adrenalin clogging my muscles. It's toxic – the room, Carla, Nadia, the need to spit out poison in order to save myself. I count five, six minutes, second by second, and my breathing gets fuller, taking me away, millions of light years from here. I can still hear Carla and Nadia whispering, I can still hear the duvet rustling, then I hear them kissing. In my haze I imagine their tongues being really long and their boyish bodies naked in the snow. I nestle into that kiss. And in that nestle I sleep.

When I open my eyes again it's still night and their bed is empty. I get up and feel their duvet to check they aren't still under it. I look in the bathroom, in the closet. In my head I hear Rachele's voice asking for my help. Then I hear my voice asking for her help. One body, one heart.

Putting on my tracksuit and puffer jacket, I open the door and peer into the corridor. It's empty and in the empty corridor I see my future implode. Even this one second spent here, and the interruption of my sleep, is putting my performance in jeopardy. My concentration for the individuals will be fucked, my future in a national team will be fucked too. I have worked for years to be here and I'm not getting the sleep I need, and I'm not thinking of the things I need to be thinking about. I am walking around a hotel in the middle of the night, on the top of a mountain, because of a pair of evil and selfish idiots. I keep repeating to myself that I'm doing it for Rachele, for the team. For myself. That it's my duty to look after Carla and Nadia so we can all be on the path to glory. So we can all be safe.

I step out into the corridor. It is so silent and still, I can hear the lift humming. As I go down the service stairs, I'm filled with dread at the thought of bumping into Rachele and some lover of hers. Maybe Carla is right, and Rachele does get up to porn things at night. I don't see anyone and when I reach reception, I open the door facing the forest. Have they gone out into the night? For one of Carla's bets? Outside it's dark and freezing, at least minus one million degrees. I see their footsteps in the snow. My feet sink into them, one after the other, and my heart feels like it's about to explode.

I hear howling and I pray it's the wind and not a wolf.

'I know I said I wanted to live with you guys,' I say towards the forest, 'but maybe not tonight?'

The bridge to the gym looks a lot further away than it did this morning. I start running but I keep sinking in the snow, and I can feel my hands, my face, and my toes turning to ice. From here, the sports centre looks like a sci-fi town where the rules of life are different, harder. And secret. I keep on walking and see myself falling off the vault tomorrow morning, then slipping on the beam because my hands have been damaged by the cold and by my wrong decisions. I have never felt as far from the Olympics as tonight. I see myself dead near the uneven bars. Then dead in this darkness.

I run more and I know I should turn around and go back to the hotel, and my duvet. Instead, I keep running until I get to the sports centre and slip through the open door where the heat welcomes me and the roof seems to protect me. I hear distant sounds coming from inside the arena. I tiptoe forward, trying to breathe quietly like a spy. I push open a door, pressing half an eye and half my nose into the tiny crack. But it's all switched off in here, the uneven bars are empty, and the rings are hanging still. For a moment, I think about slipping in and practising my routine, the turning headstand, the grips. I could go through all the movements singing or shouting, with no one's eyes on me, no judgement, no scores. Remember my dream. The reason I'm here.

I hear a noise and I turn my head towards it. I see that Nadia and Carla are in the furthest corner lying on the balance beam, one on top of the other. It seems like there's no gravity over there, and they are weightless, and free. They really are one body and their body seems to be strong and indestructible. Then I spot Karl.

The three of them are now laughing as I watch him move onto the mat. He starts tumbling, imitating Nadia's floor routine first, then goes straight into Carla's. I can't believe his accuracy, how he nearly knows their choreography by heart. Nadia laughs and claps at Karl's almost-perfect technique, then stops when Carla moves away from her and gets on the mat. There, she gets into the bridge position and climbs onto Karl. He touches her arms, her shoulders. Both of the girls go and hang from the uneven bars, side by side, thighs touching. Karl gets up from the floor and goes over to them. Their eyes close as Karl strokes their legs, his hands as far up as their leotards. First he does it with his hands, then with his mouth. Carla is doing all she can to become the centre of attention. She passes her tongue across her lips. She calls him back anytime he goes to Nadia. She kisses him. Then she quickly kisses Nadia. I hold my thighs really close together to try to feel what they are feeling. Nadia tilts her head back and her mouth falls open. I think I hear her go 'Ah' in one exhalation, so I try to do the same.

'Ah,' I whisper.

When she lifts her head back up I realize she is looking at me. She doesn't say anything, the expression on her face hardly changes, but I'm scared and I flee. Outside it is darker, colder, it is now at least minus ten million degrees, and the distance between the gym and the hotel seems ten million times longer, my legs ten million times shorter.

'You can't run away forever, Martina,' I say to myself as I run in the snow. I fall and I run more.

Back at the hotel I run straight into the lift. My cheeks are stinging and I feel feverish. I get to the fifth floor and as I stand in front of Rachele's room, ready to knock,

I don't know what to do. Or say. I press my ear to her door and try to make out any noises coming from inside. But no noises are coming from inside. I knock so lightly that nobody answers. I did what I was asked and I wasn't heard. Story of my life, I guess. Story of her life too, I guess. And because it seems that the truth is that I can in fact run away forever, I run away once more.

I go back to my room, pull off my clothes, get under the duvet, and lie there shaking, counting how many seconds I can go without breathing and how many seconds it will take to get my feet to warm up again. I try to think of something else, anything but Nadia and Carla's bodies, Karl's hands, the wolves invading my brain. Is this what is happening to Nadia's brain when she sees things? To distract me I try to visualize the layout of each class I've been in, nursery, primary, and middle school. I place each one of my classmates in their own seat, each classroom on its own floor, in its own building and street. I try to place myself in those classrooms. In the world, and in this story.

I even try to smile for a picture no one is taking.

Maybe soon after or maybe much later, Nadia comes back. I wake up at once as she slams the door. She's crying, gasping for air, and goes straight over to the window. As she opens it icy-cold air comes in and I think I will never be warm again, until I leave this country. Or maybe this life. Then I see that Nadia is naked.

'Aren't you cold?' I ask.

She doesn't answer but she shuts the window. She gets into her bed, still crying and shaking. Did Karl rape her? Did Carla and Karl rape her, one after the other? Why am I even thinking about rape? You see a lot about rape on TV and maybe it has actually happened to her. Or maybe it's just me being obsessed, not able to leave words like rape or thoughts of Alex behind.

I rub my feet against each other twice. I blink twice, then twice again.

'Is Carla still at the gym?' I ask.

I'm still deciding which words to use with Rachele tomorrow, when Carla steps in. I check the time. It's half past five.

'Thanks for leaving me behind,' she says. 'What the fuck?'

Nadia doesn't move. I stay still too, pretending to sleep.

'I'm talking to you,' Carla says, undressing.

But Nadia doesn't reply and Carla appears to fall asleep the moment her head hits the pillow.

When, at seven thirty the next morning, we are putting on our leotards and pulling up our ponytails and fixing our hair buns, Nadia is still not speaking to her. Did they have a fight at the gym? Was it Karl's fault? These thoughts are making me lose all of my focus on the day of the individual qualifications. I cannot afford this distraction. I put my earphones in, and put the music up as loud as possible.

We have our mini breakfast, spit the food we secretly have to spit, and pop the pills we secretly have to pop, then we go to the gym. During the warm-up Nadia sits next to me, without uttering a word. Her movements are so soundless it's like she's floating, hovering half a centimetre above the floor, the chair, and above us all. We stretch and together we do our ab crunches. Then, mouths shut, we do our squats and burpees. Maybe from today we both will be the silent gymnasts and maybe we could be a new duo.

Carla sits by herself, her face crumpled with sleepiness, fresh red blotches on her cheeks. Rachele keeps asking her if she is feeling well. If she is feeling feverish. Sick in any way?

'Have you eaten something that's disagreed with you, Carla?' she asks.

'I'm fine thanks. What about you, Coach? How are you feeling?'

'I'm fine,' says Rachele, irritation and concern in her expression.

'You look a bit fatter, you know? I don't mean to be rude. But your bottom really looks bigger nowadays.'

Rachele pulls up her tracksuit as if suddenly remembering that she has a backside. I wish I could tell her I too have become aware of my cellulite since Carla has said the word cellulite and Nadia has been seeing images of Angelika being tortured and killed in every possible way for three days now, just because Carla has said the word torture. So we really are one body and one heart but we have to always remember that we are one mind too. And anyway Rachele still has a nice figure, very feminine, and the tracksuit actually sort of suits her. Maybe she could just stop having pasta at dinner, for a month or so.

'Benedetta,' says Carla. 'Help me stretch.'

Benedetta blushes as she sits on Carla's back. Only Nadia has ever been allowed to sit on Carla's back. This, I notice, scares Rachele more than anything she has seen up until now. We pretend this doesn't terrify us too. We take off our tracksuits and are about to start our individual qualifications, when Carla comes over to Nadia. I stare straight ahead, trying to look invisible, and as though I don't have ears.

'Why did you run away last night?' Carla asks Nadia. 'What the fuck is wrong with you?'

Nadia doesn't look at her and doesn't answer.

'Are you *stupid*? What's with the silence and the attitude?' Carla asks. 'We searched everywhere for you.'

Carla isn't getting anything from Nadia, so she starts with their 'Red red yellow blue – Coca-Cola Fanta glue – teeth straight feet straight – me me but it's you – blue pooh Fanta glue – I protect and so do you.'

Still nothing happens.

She tries two, three times more, hoping Nadia will join in. Then she looks at Nadia, challenging her with a death stare. The rest of us are spellbound. Rachele is covering her mouth with her hand, as if something really tragic has just happened. As if one of us has fallen off the bars and is being taken away on a stretcher. Or as if a physiotherapist has been sticking his fingers into our vaginas since we were 10, 11, 12, 13 and it was considered just fine.

Nadia does not break the stare.

'You're dead to me,' Carla says. And walks away.

Once – when they were 11 – Nadia had refused to wear a skirt to a gymnastics Federation party. Carla wanted her to wear one just like hers, telling Nadia it was a matter of principle because she had nice legs, even if they were 'a little short'.

'I don't want to wear a skirt,' said Nadia. 'Your wanting me to is becoming an obsession.'

'So come in your tracksuit,' Carla replied. 'You'll look great.'

'I don't want to come in my tracksuit. I want to wear trousers.'

Nadia won the battle; they didn't speak for half a day or so, but through their mantra and a few other stupid jokes they made up. Another time they had a row because

Carla had given Nadia a shove to wake her up during one of her stuck moments. Nadia had reacted badly when Carla called her *demented* and *loser* – but that was that. I can remember only silly things like these, which would be forgiven straightaway. And it was Carla who would always say or do something silly to make Nadia laugh. Rachele would laugh, we would laugh too. Carla was our Popeye. She was strong, had huge biceps, and always won.

But today it's different. Today Nadia doesn't say 'red red yellow blue', and this is such a serious snub that I almost feel like reciting the rhyme in her place. How can Nadia leave Carla in this state? How can she do this to us, to the team? After all her theories about statistics and superstitions! We hate the rhyme, we hate the sodding blue pooh, but reciting their mantra now, during this competition, during *any* competition, is compulsory.

Carla swallows the humiliation, then flexes her back a couple of times. She goes to the bars, breathes in, smiles, and jumps to grab the lower bar. Nadia keeps looking down at her feet, her lip trembling, her chest going quickly up and down. She only tilts her face once, to look at Karl, who has stepped into the arena, so she doesn't see that when doing the *Bardwaj* Carla loses her grip. And falls. She doesn't see when Carla stands up, touches her left knee, and gives Rachele a long look as if to say that something is wrong. I feel the pain in Carla's left knee and grit my teeth.

'Up,' Rachele mutters.

'Up,' we all mutter.

Carla jumps up again and Rachele watches her best athlete hesitate during her routine at the bars then again at the beam. Her movements and her scores today are average, her rhythm and elegance a pale reminder of the girl everyone saw yesterday. Today she's not God's angel. Angelika is beating her on everything. All the Chinese girls and Nadia are beating her too. I, incredibly enough, do better than her both on the beam and on the floor routine.

Rachele marches towards me. She too must be thinking about blue pooh and that after years of work, all is going to shit. I zip and unzip, and I have to do it ten times before being able to breathe properly again, while the other coaches fix their eyes on us and gloat. Or so it seems to me. Rachele drags along that enormous backside of hers. It probably now weighs around one hundred thousand kilos. Skipping pasta at dinner might not be enough. Or maybe she could just embrace this new body, eat more and more pasta and more of everything, always, become titanic and powerful and strong. Being as vast as, let's say, the stratosphere, she could shout more, crush us better, be more scary. It would be very straightforward. It would be honest. We would recognize the monster better. And we'd know better who we need to kill.

After her loose vault, we all see Carla's success at Sunday's All Around vanish.

'Martina, what's happening?' the monster hisses.

'I don't know, Rachele,' I say, my heart hammering, my legs shaking.

'What happened last night?'

'I slept.'

I look at Nadia then at Carla. I go through the speech I have prepared for our coach – their disappearance, Karl, the fight, Nadia's pain – and decide to forget it. I didn't ask to be put in Nadia and Carla's room. It's not my place to sort them out. I've done OK at the beam, I got a 14.20. I can't complain. She can't complain. I actually feel like telling Rachele to fuck off too. What if that was to be my abracadabra for all things in life?

'Martina, we must get to the Olympics. Right?'

'Right.'

'And we also know that Carla must get up there on the podium at the All Around. And Nadia must be in the first ten too.'

'I don't know what to say, Coach.'

I see the last tiny bit of love Rachele has for me evaporate. To make it easier to hate her back, I picture her thighs full of cellulite, fat holes, like Carla said. I imagine her getting older, weaker, and looking at me with that fake smile of hers. I add a stinky fag to her decrepit face, to her lifeless lips. In my thoughts she is 80 or maybe 1,000 years old.

'I'll take care of it, Marti,' she had told me. 'Just don't tell anyone else. For the club's sake, OK?'

I waited. Hopeful.

'She told me not to tell anyone else, for the club's sake,' Nadia said to me.

So we both waited. Hopeful. It was for the club's sake.

I walk towards Nadia. She's crying even though she's just done more than OK at the floor routine. She is fourth. Carla is behind her.

'Do you want some water?' I ask.

She nods, so I give her my bottle. She cries more so I worry more.

I never worry when it's me who cries. I know that even if I'm crying, I can deal. Be a pioneer of my pain. But when I see other people cry, I feel they must be really desperate and that they're so unhappy they might kill themselves. When my mum cries for example, I'm so scared I could pass out. Once, when we were doing the cleaning in an advertising agency at five in the morning, I caught her crying while she was dusting and it was the most unhappy hour of my life. Outside it was freezing and the streets were empty. I had climbed up on a desk and was watching the traffic lights flash amber. In terms of sad nights, we'd seen much worse. We'd cleaned old people's homes. And hospitals. But in that office, seeing her cry made it the saddest hour and turned the night into the saddest ever. I had looked at the street below and the city doing its best to go dark. I did it so as not to embarrass her, and tried distracting myself by thinking of the houses where people slept while we were working, searching for a way to make her happy, even here, with the window cleaning spray in one hand and the duster in the other. I looked for a way for us to save ourselves. But she was crying too hard, so eventually I did look at her and she explained she wasn't sad, only tired. It was like she had to justify herself to me. Had I not been there, had I been invisible, she could have cried without feeling embarrassed or guilty.

'Why can't I sleep at home and stay with Dad?' I'd heard myself say. I wanted to be sweet but I could only be bitter.

'Dad starts his shift at four in the morning.'

'I hate you,' I said. 'I hate both of you.'

But it wasn't true. I could have said 'I love you' and I don't know why I said 'I hate you'. On the bus back home, she fell asleep with her forehead against the window.

'It's not true that I hate you,' I said.

'I know,' she mumbled. Her mouth was dry, her skin so grey.

I snuggled under her armpit and slept, thinking of a way to save her. Then me. To this day my plan remains the same blurry one that involves gymnastics and glitter on the eyelids and sometimes in my hair.

Nadia and I watch Carla talking to Rachele, her head bowed.

Even when she's crying Nadia is prettier than me, no contest. I stare at her lips. At her tears, which make her cheeks pinker. We watch Alex approach Carla and Rachele. He seems genuinely concerned. I have to admit he might love this sport. And I bet he has a blurry plan for the future just as I do. The home-made video of some chiropractor working a girl's spine somewhere in Nevada must be part of it.

'What is it, the knee?' he asks Carla.

She nods and sits on the floor, to let him work on her leg and spray her with the dry ice.

'Better?' he asks.

'Worse,' she says. 'You've touched it.'

When she comes back towards us, Carla sits down next to Anna. Benedetta makes room for her and a Carla-place is instantly created on the bench.

'Did Karl rape you?' I ask Nadia.

She stares at me for a few seconds, disgusted, her forehead shining with sweat.

'Or are you sad because Carla wants to steal Karl away from you?'

She looks at me with hatred now, then probably finds it tiring, gets up, and goes to sit further away. Full of her hate and my hate for myself, I go to the vault and nail two perfect jumps. While I fly and twist, I think *Fuck off, Carla. Fuck off, Nadia. Fuck off, Alex and Rachele.* I think it with utter conviction and the more I think it, the cleaner my moves become. I do a round-off on the springboard, pre-flight, first flight. I nail a

Yurchenko full and a half. I land. I salute. I fuck them all off once more in my head and suddenly see myself making it to the first ten at the All Around. I even dare to see myself at the Olympics.

I smile, while outside it starts snowing again and I decide there and then, that fuck off will be my favourite mantra forever. The more I look at the snow, the more I also think I need to go north to countries like Finland, Sweden, and Norway. And Iceland: where there are no trees but volcanoes so powerful they can ground planes and hot water with geysers and natural milky-blue pools. I'll go there when I can drive and like Goldilocks I will try them all and choose one that will be the perfect one. I will build a wooden cabin next to it. I will have a fire-place in the bedroom. All the wolves of Iceland will be my friends too.

I put my earphones in and lie down on the bench, watching the beautiful Romanian girls in their beautiful leotards do routines that are more beautiful than ours. I see Angelika being a million times better than Carla. And anyone. I spy Karl with his gelled hair who is looking over at Carla while also eyeing up a Polish gymnast with decent-sized boobs. I see Benedetta failing one movement after the other.

'I suck,' she says. No one dares contradict her.

Nadia is still crying and Carla is plaiting Anna's hair. It kills me that Anna is looking so grateful, her bright pink cheeks on fire with happiness. I want to go over and remind her of the times Carla has hit her or humiliated her. The time she told her that her father was always away because her mother was a dog.

'Like mother, like daughter,' she said.

But I pull my zip down and up to stop myself from

spoiling her party. Even though I know that later Carla will wash her hands to rid them of the feel of Anna's hair.

'It was like touching vomit,' she'll say. Or maybe she'll say 'like touching crap'. Or shit. Or saliva.

We close with our floor routines. We are all clean and precise, even if Carla is uninspiring and even if we are all downhearted. We pray for the other girls – especially the Romanians, the Chinese, and the Russians – to do badly, just to make us look better. And we pray so hard that apart from Benedetta, we all qualify for the All Around individual finals. For the others it was sort of obvious, for me it's a mega win. I will be competing among the best gymnasts at this tournament. And despite the pain for today's darkness, my heart is about to explode. I am instantly so happy that I want to scream. The idea that Nadia and Carla are weaker than usual, thanks to the fact that they are angry and distracted, suddenly seems appealing too.

That evening in our room, Nadia moves her bed away from Carla's, and she begs me to swap with her. Carla is still having her physio session with Alex, then she'll be in Rachele's room for the ice bath.

'I want to be near the window,' Nadia says.

'But what if Carla gets cross?'

'Shut up, OK? I don't care what she wants.'

We strip the beds and swap sheets. I lie down and stay still, as if I'm dead, as invisible as possible. I shut up. A corpse. A stone. When Carla returns she's ice-cold and silent. Maybe the ice bath froze her heart too. Maybe we will all be silent eventually.

I spend the evening with them on either side of me. Nadia watches videos on YouTube with her earphones in. Carla is restless. She puts on make-up. She takes it off. Then applies it again. I pick up my history textbook and read stuff about the Iron Age, the Golden Age, and whatever comes next. I'll never remember any of it and the teachers will never really test me on any of it. The schools we go to are so easy, we attend them just because it's the law. We need to train, that's our duty, and the teachers know it. They don't really care about me knowing anything. I am reading just to keep my eyes moving, my head occupied, my soul elsewhere.

Carla waxes her legs, then applies a face mask.

'I'm going out tonight, I need to have some sort of good time,' she says. 'When it's covered with snow, the village looks like Paris.'

She tears off a strip at the edge of her groin. Another one, on the other side. She cannot go out. And cannot have some sort of a good time.

'Please don't,' I say. 'You need to rest.'

'Do you want me to show you how to wax?' she says.

I've always shaved with a razor, in the shower, because this is how my mum taught me. Besides, she always says, it's cheaper. Once she also said something awful about how the wax makes your skin saggy in the bikini area. But Carla's mum is a beautician, so she must know and waxing must be better. I don't trust my mum: she always says we are happy and then she cries. Why should she be reliable on groins? Thanks to the beauty salon, sometimes after a shower Carla spreads mud over her body to prevent cellulite, wrapping herself in cling film. She smells of rosemary and mud. It's all stuff her mum has nicked, like the hairclips she and Nadia have in their hair, the paper knickers and nail varnish in all sorts of colours she has in her make-up bag. I wonder if Carla's mum, who is so religious, does penance for being a thief. I imagine the words she uses at night to talk to God, about anti-cellulite mud and her desire to own nail varnish in every shade.

'Karl is going to show me around,' Carla is saying to me.

I try not to add anything. I just know I have to stop looking at Carla and Nadia as if they are characters in a movie, a mystery to be solved, the grammar of a foreign language I'll eventually learn. I concentrate on the wallpaper, on the history book and all its ages and stages. I flip from page forty-two to page forty-three. Then forty-four.

'Are you listening to me, Martina?' says Carla. 'Look at me.'

I look at her. She is pushing her leg behind her ear, tearing off hair from a spot on the back of her thighs. I didn't even know there were follicles there.

'You can't go,' I tell her again. 'It's the finals tomorrow. The Romanians are ahead. So are the Chinese. We need you at your best. Angelika was perfect today and you weren't.'

'I'll fucking destroy her,' she says. 'I'll add a *Khorkina* and a *Kim*, no worries.'

'You haven't tried the *Kim* enough. Don't.'

'Shut up.'

'Nadia saw Karl before you,' I blurt out.

Carla bursts out laughing. But her eyes aren't laughing. Nadia still has her earphones in and I wonder if she really is oblivious to what we're talking about. She's never looked so small.

'Do you have chairs and meat and a TV at home?' asks Carla. 'Or can you not afford them?'

'We can't afford them. So what? Nadia liked Karl first,' I repeat. 'Also, she's clearly not well.'

'I like him too and there are things you don't know. And you don't know them, because who'd tell you anything?'

'You. You're talking to me. Now.'

'Your voice is weird,' says Carla. 'And if you ever tell me to fuck off again, I'll kill you.'

All dolled up with blue eyeshadow and pink nail varnish, she leaves the room. Nadia puts her face in her pillow. I go to watch Carla from the window as she crosses the snow-covered yard. I don't think she really is as cruel as she'd like me to think. I don't think she's kind either but as I watch her stumble and rub her eyes, I feel sad for her. In the snow, near the forest, I see Angelika doing her solo night training. Then I see Karl run and catch up with Carla. I have to retie my ponytail twice before I can move away from the window and convince myself that my voice is not weird. And that I don't have to go and tell Rachele that she's gone. I go and sit near Nadia. Her bed seems the loneliest spot in the Milky Way. Like it's floating, alone, in nothingness.

'Are you OK?' I ask her.

'Yes,' she says.

And she hugs me. She can't be OK if she's hugging me. Also, her body is shaking.

'Shall I switch off the lights?'

She nods, grateful, and turns her back to me. I put my earphones in and hope not to hear any other sound until morning. But when in the middle of the night I open my eyes, I catch a glimpse of Nadia through the bathroom door as she is inserting a tampon. So she's started her periods and already knows how to use a tampon. Maybe she's watched her mother. I wouldn't know how to use one and I hope I don't have to for months. Years, possibly. I'll just have to cut out more food to make sure.

Nadia wipes a tiny spot of blood off the bathroom floor and drops the stained toilet paper in the loo. As I am watching I already know this is one of those moments that will stay in my memory forever. There's nothing I can do about it, it will be right there, along with a couple of fights with my mum, the sound of Alex when he comes, and learning the colour of a dead girl's skin. All the details will be mixed up, forever, together with some fears I had when I was 3 or 4 and the sound of that time I fell off the beam and banged my head so hard I passed out.

FRIDAY

I get out of the shower and dry myself with the stiff towels that could help the Polish girl with the yellow acne. When I step into the bedroom, Nadia is not there anymore. I didn't hear Carla come back last night but here she is now, half leaning out of the window, spitting and most probably aiming for Angelika's head. She turns around, wraps herself in the curtains, and smiles at me, a thread of saliva on her chin. She wipes it off with her wrist then spits again in my honour, louder, like smokers do in the street. I'd love to be able to hawk like that.

Her phone rings.

'Hi, Mum,' she says. 'Yes, I'm doing great. Loving it here.'

She rolls her eyes. As far as I can see she isn't doing great at all. She also looks tired.

'What?' she says. 'I'm fine. I don't know what Rachele told you, but I'm fine. I promise. Yes, Mum. I love you too.'

103

She winks at me. Pretends to vomit.

'Yes, Mum. I'm the best. The Lord, yes. We love him forever and ever.'

She ends the call, zips up her tracksuit. I do the same. Then I zip it down and back up again.

'Aren't you gonna ask me if I had fun last night?' she says. 'If I had sex?'

'Did you have fun last night? Did you have sex?'

She nods and brushes her hair. I am not sure if nodding counts as an actual yes, so I am not sure she really had sex. With Karl or with anyone else, ever. I focus on her hair, which is so long and blonde that if the Lord hadn't come into her life she'd be great for a shampoo ad.

'We went to the city centre and had a kebab. We also went to a bar to get a Coke. I think I saw Alex getting wasted.'

'I hope he dies.'

'Oh, Martina,' she laughs. 'Pretend he's just a nightmare. Then you'll wake up.'

'We'll never wake up. Not if we don't get rid of him.'

'We will. Eventually,' she says. She changes tack. 'When I got back you were snoring big time. Like a fat fifty-year-old man. I'm going to record you.'

'Did you speak to Nadia? She's not well.'

'Big news. Anyway, she left when I was sleeping. Not that she would have spoken to me anyway.'

'What's going on?'

'She's obsessed with me. You know it. I know it.'

'Thought it was about you stealing Karl from her?'

'I wish it was that simple,' she laughs. 'Shall we?'

We leave the room, Carla by my side. The way she is talking to me, you'd think we were friends. The way she smiles, you'd think we really are happy. But, as she says, nothing is that simple. I hope Nadia doesn't see us because she might think I'm on Carla's side. And if I had to choose, I'd still bet on Carla being guilty. But even guilt is not that simple.

'Fix your hair,' Carla tells me. 'You could be so pretty if you only put in the effort.'

So I fix my hair, and put in the effort.

In the reception area, some of the boys are lounging about on the sofas. They're ugly, all of them – spotty, short, or greasy-haired. And they smell. They smell more when they bathe themselves in cologne than when they sweat. We sit down without even saying 'hi'.

'The Polish girl is not dead,' one of them says.

I'd forgotten about the Polish girl. Am I so cruel that I haven't given more thought to the motionless body of a girl like me, being taken away on a stretcher, her neck in a brace, her feet stiff? If she had died and nobody had talked about her ever again, I would have probably been OK with it.

'Not even paralysed?' says Carla.

'Only injured,' another boy answers.

Only injured. And one less competitor.

We don't have anything to add. So we don't say anything and we just stay there, waiting for Benedetta, Nadia, Anna, and Rachele. Outside the glass doors, we watch two men shovel the never-ending snow from the hotel entrance. They pour salt on it, then they shovel some more, puffs of steam coming out of their mouths. They say something, then laugh. One of them is older than the other; maybe they are father and son. Their cheeks are red and their shoulders so wide, they look like bears in coats. I would like to say it out loud – *see those bears in coats?* – and for people to whisper 'what a cute sentence that was, Martina. What a cute soul you have, hon.' I would like to go there and help them. Instead, I retie my ponytail twice.

When she arrives, Nadia sits far away from us. Her forehead is damp with sweat. She is wearing sunglasses and has her earphones in. As Benedetta and Anna approach, I can see how they take in the enormity of Carla and Nadia's separation, while we all pretend it's nothing. Like when your parents fight and you know you can't ask, 'What happened?' It's their business and anyway the embarrassment shuts your mouth, scares you to death, and gives you a parent-fight type of tummy ache. I have different kinds of tummy aches. One for competitions, one for Alex, another one for when Nadia looks so ill. So today I go for this specific one and welcome its specific pain.

'Hi,' the Useless Ones say. And I am the only one who responds with a 'Hi' back.

Carla doesn't look at them nor at Nadia. Nadia doesn't look at Carla either. I look at both of them but once again I prefer the snow out there, the shovels and the laughter of the bears in coats. I wish there was no one fighting around me as making up can be really difficult and the sweat on other people's foreheads really troubles me.

'Did you go running in the forest?' Carla asks Nadia quietly. 'Did you see Angelika?'

Nadia doesn't answer. She rubs her hands and stares straight ahead.

My parents split up once. My mum said to my dad, 'You're a horrid human being.' Every time she walked into a room and he was in it, she shooed him away. He cried and said, 'I'm leaving because you hate me.' I looked at them through one eye, while the other eye stayed fixed on the TV. He moved out, onto Nino's couch. He came to my school once to hug me and he cried. At some point, weeks later, they made up and she was kind to him again. I'm not sure what happened in between, maybe just the passing of time, but something on Dad's neck looked bruised. Had he tried hanging himself? Had my mum tried to choke him? These were the first things that came to mind: suicide and homicide. No one spoke of it again. If they ever feel they should tell me why they got back together, it will be when I'm a grown-up, and I'll care even less and the back-drop to my life will be that of Los Angeles.

I'll be smiling, somewhere near the canyons.

Rachele comes into the lobby, her fringe the biggest, puffiest giant fringe in Europe. If she ends up in prison, I think there and then, she should do fringe tutorials online as a job. Three-minute videos, hairdryer extrava-ganza and all. Thumbs up. Thumbs down. She could nail it. She could go on with her theories on beauty and girls and bodies. People would comment, ask questions about the products she uses: *And the orange lipstick you always wear, what brand is it?* But today, after we have whispered nasty things about her mega-big bleached hair, we don't ask anything. We just fall silent again. She beckons us and we follow her to the usual physio check-up with Alex.

I go in first. I am the pioneer of the check-up.

'Forty-four kilos, one metre forty-eight, a hundred beats per minute,' says Alex.

Please let me go, I think. *Please die*, I also think.

'Heart's a bit fast. And you're getting taller. Anything else you want to tell me?'

'I'm fine,' I say. I am not. *I hate you.* And getting tall sucks.

'Nervous about the championship?'

'I'm fine.'

'Hang in there and be brave.'

'I'm being brave now, here, with you,' I manage to say.

I count to five. Then to ten. I try not to meet his eyes while he checks my blood pressure, then my bruises. He quickly manipulates my left ankle. I move my left ankle away. I stand up.

'If I say "Martina", what do you say?'

He wants to sound normal but his voice is cracking. He is trying to follow his script. I hate his script. I hate his script, I hate his hands, his mouth, his penis, which I have seen get hard in his pants tens of times. I hate his smell, his voice, his hair. His name.

'I say winner?' I mutter.

I manage to look him in the eyes. He lowers his. Piece of shit.

'OK, Martina. You're a winner. You can go now.'

I am a winner. I can go. So I go.

Alex gives us a physio session daily, and a check-up every week. If we are travelling, the check-up can last less than six minutes. If you're quick at taking off your clothes and putting them back on, stepping onto the scales, standing up straight, and pretending to cough, it may last five minutes and that's it. I still haven't worked out what triggers him to touch us in the other way. The sick, disgusting, other way. I often wonder what drives him more. Is it our happiness or our sadness? His strength and our weakness? Or our strength and his weakness? Should I cry or smile when I'm with him to be safer?

'I know it can be uncomfortable,' he now sometimes says, after I complained to Rachele.

Somehow, speaking about it must feel more medical to him. More professional. He does the same with Nadia and Carla.

'I'm almost done,' he might add. 'Your hip needs fixing so that's where you have to work when you work on the hip.'

And he touches me, again, where – now I know – my hip that was never weak, or never broken, needs constant fixing. Nadia's problem seems to be the lower back. Carla's the knee and the shoulders. Somehow the nerve to work all of these broken bits of us is inside our vagina.

'Nothing is wrong with my lower back,' Nadia had told Rachele.

'Guys, he's the best,' she'd replied to her. 'He walked me through all of it. All is fine.'

I cannot 100 per cent say that she didn't believe him, or that with a tiny part of ourselves we didn't believe him either. We believed them. We desperately wanted to.

I leave the door open behind me and I sit outside. I can hear my team members being weighed and Alex's questions. I can hear how often he repeats 'Now you must eat a bit more. If you don't eat anything, you can't compete.' All of us are told the same in Alex's room, but less than half an hour later Rachele will tell us to cut our portions, our carbs, the sugars. Do they have an agreement on that too?

'You won't like how you look in your leotard,' she'll whisper. 'Trust me. No movement looks good if you have a chubby belly.'

Nadia goes in last. She walks in with her earphones still in, dragging the dirty heels of her trainers, taking her beautiful tormented face into the medical room. Even when she's furious, or ill, I always see her beauty first. But today, looking at Nadia's soaked shoes, I also see her having the same gaze as the crazy old lady in my neighbourhood who walks around with a doll in her arms.

Nadia looks as lost and lonely as her. As sweet and kind as her.

'Stop doing that,' Carla says, pointing at my teeth.

'Doing what?'

'Stop grinding them. And stop shaking or whatever the fuck you're doing.'

Nadia disappears inside. I wish I could go in with her.

'Nadia, you're making a mess on the floor,' I hear Alex tell her. 'How come your shoes are so filthy and wet? Have you been in the forest?'

'I needed a breath of fresh air,' she says, and her voice is dry. 'And to be alone.'

'You're not allowed. Always go with someone else.'

The door shuts behind her.

'Martina, control yourself,' Rachele says. 'Please.'

So I try to control myself and to stop shaking or whatever the fuck I'm doing. The walls are so shit-thin that from where I am sitting, I can still hear bits of Nadia's check-up. I hear her say she has started her period and tell Alex that no, it doesn't hurt. I am pleased she doesn't have period pains. She says she thinks her wrists feel weaker than usual. Here they come, I think, more stress fractures. We all know they will break us, eventually. Then, I hear a loud noise, like metal crashing to the floor, glass shattering.

Carla turns round to face Rachele.

'Why do you leave us alone with him?' she asks. 'You're just as bad as he is.'

Rachele stares at her, horrified. She goes into the room and closes the door. Carla gets up, but when she realizes I'm watching her, and the others are watching her too, she shrugs and sits back down. I try giving her a grateful look but she doesn't meet my eyes. She is pale. We are all pale. If one of us goes pale we all do. If one of us is in there with Alex, we all are.

Has Nadia killed him? Has she killed herself?

We are always afraid of suicides. As if they're a kind of flu we could catch if we're unlucky, and because we are between 14 and 16 years old. If we trust Nadia's loathsome statistics and those on TV, they seem to happen all the time. The figures are terrifying and always accompanied by descriptions of the scene. Belts hanging, pills on the floor, an uncle's gun that has gone *bang* with brains splattered on bathroom tiles. The number of uncles' guns that are around, Jesus! To these figures and to the belts hanging from showers, you have to add the anorexia deaths, which in a way are suicides too. Anorexics who don't die from vomiting or weighing under 26 kilos or from a heart attack, are more likely to kill themselves than the non-anorexics, and this too is another statistic I learned thanks to Nadia. It goes without saying that we, for the same reasons and for all the other reasons that Carla wants to pretend are nightmares from which we can wake up, are more prone to suicide.

Last year, a Chinese gymnast and a French gymnast killed themselves. Different months, different methods, but we studied both cases with great attention. The Chinese girl was found hanging in the boarding school where she lived. She was 13 and she used the bandages we wrap around our hands for the uneven bars. She tied them to the shower, climbed onto the towel rack, slipped her head through them, and let herself fall. When the news became public, it had already been two months since her death. Their team made a brief statement but we couldn't find any interviews on the internet. Not a coach, not a teammate saying anything out loud. Rachele explained that the Chinese are very reserved. I guess she could relate with the approach, the nuance one can give to the word reserved.

'They are lying,' Carla had said, 'like hell they're reserved.'

'They don't want anyone to know because otherwise the world would find out about the stuff that goes on over there,' Nadia added.

'They say athletes are sixteen when they are in fact twelve. They kill them and pretend nothing's happened. They die and nothing is said. Dogs!'

Rachele had waited for us to stop repeating the words 'dogs' and 'death', then got us to do a relaxation exercise she had learned at yoga. She explained we would repeat this exercise regularly; it was good for concentration and for relaxation.

'It helps when you're scared,' she told us. 'You learn to breathe more slowly, when your body wants you to breathe faster. In a nutshell, it helps *you* to be in charge, and not your fear.'

That week we did yoga, but soon Rachele forgot about it or thought that too many of us had fallen asleep, so we went back to traditional stretches. I still use bits of the exercise she taught us to survive some physio sessions.

Alex's door remains shut for a few minutes. When it opens Rachele comes out. We look at her. She tries to smile to reassure us, and I have to say her smile does, weirdly, make me feel calmer. Despite everything, I do love her and I know she loves us. I guess it's the same for kids whose mums beat them. They still love them, don't they? They'll still enjoy that one hug. They still only have that one mum. I watch her smile again, before she starts talking in the most serene tone of voice she can master.

'She fainted. Nothing to worry about.'

'Why did she faint?' Anna asks. 'Is she ill?'

'Low blood pressure. She's fine now.'

'But why did she have low blood pressure?' I ask.

'It just happens,' Rachele says. 'Nothing to worry about.'

Carla has tears in her eyes and when I notice she puts on her sunglasses. She looks like a celebrity. Or a mourner at a funeral. Or a celebrity mourning at a funeral. She walks towards the windows, Rachele follows her, and I look at them from the back, Carla with her shoulders slumping towards the ground and Rachele's moving up and down as she talks too fast, using way too many words. I want to shout, 'If you just shut up, Rachele, maybe Carla will talk to you. If you take a break, maybe she will tell you something. Stop going on about the Olympics. Stop going on about your plans! You and Alex should use fewer words, fewer looks, less of *everything*.' But of course I remain silent. I zip up my fucking fleece. I zip down my fucking fleece.

Alex comes out and says Nadia needs a couple more minutes. She is feeling better, but low blood pressure can do this. After fainting, you need to get up very slowly.

'If you've already had your check-up,' he tells us, 'you can go to the gym.'

Low blood pressure? She's never had that before. Did Nadia push Alex away as he touched her? Did he push her back? Has she found the strength to do what we've all yearned to do?

I go to the gym and concentrate as best as I can, despite replaying images of Nadia fainting, the saliva on Carla's chin, her real or fake hand-jobs on Karl, the tampons, the blood, the tears. I can't make sense of any of it. Nor put order to any of it. So I start repeating things twice, saying 'help' twice, 'Carla' twice, 'Nadia' twice and doing abs crunches, and stretching my legs on autopilot. By the time Nadia and Carla start warming up, I feel better.

The other teams arrive. The arena fills up. The competition needs to begin. The finals need to begin. So, despite never being less of a team, or never having felt less focused myself, I try my best, I do my best to be a pioneer and to be here now. When it's my turn I also manage to get a high score at the bars. I thank my anger for it but have to hate my anger soon after, when I fall off the balance beam for it. I hurt my ankle. I hurt my wrist. I hope the ankle isn't linked to the same nerve as my hips and that Alex won't need to fix it in the same way.

Benedetta is our weakest spot and confirms it today too. Carla, on the other hand, is being a diligent, talented gymnast, no doubt about it, but that's about it. No sparkle. No magic. Again she doesn't seem to be God's angel today. She doesn't seem to be a Popeye either. She's just one of the good girls.

'Be your best self,' Rachele tells her. 'Please.'

Her voice comes out more like a lamentation. She's losing her sparkle and magic too. Anna tries to help us with her average, diligent consistency, but we are all lacking strength, precision, and beauty. Nadia is still so fragile we cannot count on her, she shouldn't even be competing, and when I land badly at the vault I cry.

'Girls,' Rachele says. 'Be the winners that you are. This is a shit show.'

Once at a competition in Sydney, the athletes kept on making mistakes at the vault and at some point – when many of the girls had already landed on their knees – they realized it was the vault that was off by a few centimetres. Maybe there is something wrong with these Romanian beams too. I am also getting taller and this is horrible. Nadia is getting her periods and this too is horrible. Then again, what about Khorkina's height, she who we always thought was absolutely perfect? At least before she started calling other gymnasts who spoke out about abuse 'liars in search of fame'. But we all heard Khorkina had started training with a coach who used to beat her and who would sometimes not let her eat for a whole week. Despite the beating, and the hunger – or maybe because of them – she won nine golds, eight silvers, and three bronzes. So, she probably thinks it has all been worth it. Or at least, we guess that that is the lesson she wants us to learn from her. And today, when we all seem to be failing badly, I am not sure anymore of what we need either. More beating? More care? I watch Angelika's flawless jumps and twists at the other end of the gym. Her smile. Does her perfection come from love or hate?

I watch the Chinese team pile up points. The Russians too. I envy them and feel sorry for them, at the same time.

By noon we make it to fifth place and none of us beat Angelika on any of the apparatuses and throughout the entire competition. We don't make it to the podium. We don't make it to anywhere decent. We still have the individual finals and the All Around, but as a team we are crushed.

By the evening, on top of our club being placed fifth overall, Nadia and Carla still haven't spoken. The atmosphere between them is tense. The atmosphere of the entire universe is tense.

Back in our room Carla and I discuss calculations for the All Around on Sunday. Discuss is a big word; Carla is talking and I'm listening. She is determined she wants to try the *Produnova* vault. It's called the 'vault of death' for a reason, as it's nearly impossible to control the forward momentum of a handspring into a triple front flip before a completely blind landing.

'Better paralysed than a loser. I've got this,' she laughs. 'Martina, you've got this too.'

Every so often Nadia rolls over on her bed and snorts. She is still pale, she has barely spoken, and I haven't seen her eat.

'What happened in the room with Alex?' I ask Nadia.

'Nothing,' she mutters. 'I fainted.'

'You're obsessed with Alex,' Carla says to me. 'Stop it.'

'But look at us. We're a mess.'

'We're not,' Carla says. 'Just focus on how impressive you can make your floor exercise. You need points.'

'It's their fault,' I say. 'All of this. They are making us crazy.'

Nadia turns to me and by the way she looks at me, I feel it's the first time she seems to have heard me. My voice has made it to her brain. But her cry for help, the horror I can see appear on her face, is so vast and so dark, I can't look at her anymore. I turn to the window. I walk towards it and look out there, where things might be easier. I see the bears with the coats and I hope they are taking care of everything. At least better than us up here.

'If Angelika gets fucking lost and a few Chinese super robots get fucking lost, we can still make it,' Carla continues. 'Then I'll get myself a nice spread in *Playboy* just like Khorkina.'

'How old do you have to be to be in *Playboy*?' I ask, thinking what a lame question this is but trying hard to bring us back to something jolly. To us being girls who joke. Who care about joking.

And that is why, Nadia and I, dark circles under our

eyes, stare at Carla doing a *Playboy* pose, rolling her T-shirt up over her tiny tits so they are showing better. She then lies down and poses with her back arched like a siren. Her arms are muscular and her skin is covered with bruises. She lets herself be watched so brazenly, I feel embarrassed.

'I'm going for a walk,' I say. 'Just to the vending machine and back.'

'You love me bad,' Carla says nastily to Nadia. Nadia shoves her face back against the mattress. 'Get me a Coke,' Carla adds. 'And get yourself some stronger moves for the beam!'

I think about Nadia loving Carla bad. She'd just lifted her face off the mattress and now we've lost her again. Carla is an idiot and I have a feeling she knows it.

'Did you know that if you douche with Coca-Cola you don't get pregnant?' Carla tells me.

'Could you be pregnant?'

'What the fuck are you talking about, Martina? Get me a Coke, will you?'

As I open the door she changes pose. I see her pulling her T-shirt back down and lying there, pretending to be bored. Then getting on all fours. As I shut the door behind me I hear her call Nadia twice.

I go to the vending machines and get Cokes for us and a Fanta for Nadia. She hasn't eaten anything so some sugar will do her good. I send Dad a text and write, Keep concentrating on Sunday! It's still our lucky day, isn't it?

I get his answer in two seconds. Sunday Revolution and Wonder. The cards are favourable. Luck! Ps: kisses from Mousy Mum.

As I walk back I hear noises coming from Anna and Benedetta's room. Music and laughter. The Useless Ones, the girls in the shadow, have their moments of happiness and have a soundtrack for it. It must be way more relaxing in there than with Nadia and Carla. Maybe it's because in there they are still safe. I walk further and get to Rachele's room. The door is half open so I stick my head through and I see her make-up and a few thin white cigarettes on a shelf. I can also see her reflection in the mirror. She's sitting in front of the TV, eating a chocolate bar, and she's crying. Then I see Alex, a towel around his waist, a little bottle from the minibar in his hands. He walks towards the door as I run away.

Back in the room, the first revolution has happened. I am tempted to call my dad and confirm his shamanic powers. Carla is now on Nadia's bed. Nadia's face is still buried against the mattress but Carla is embracing her from behind like one of those rucksacks in the shape of a cuddly toy that were fashionable when we were small.

Back then, I would have loved a panda backpack but there wasn't enough money. My dad had a go at making one out of those fluffy prize toys you get at a fairground shooting range, disembowelling it by pulling out the stuffing in its belly. He had made straps with a pair of old braces and the result was so sad I threw it in our outside wheelie bin at the first opportunity and pretended it had been stolen from the gym. A few months later I found it back in our flat, hidden in a bag of old things.

'You mustn't be sad,' Carla is telling Nadia. 'If you're sad I can't breathe or think straight. I can't jump or eat or sleep or anything.'

The list of things Carla can't do if Nadia is sad turns out to be so long I get pins and needles in my foot. I put the fizzy drinks on their bedside table and sit on my bed.

'I saw Rachele and Alex having sex,' I say.

'You didn't,' Carla says.

I realize I didn't.

'I saw Alex with no clothes on in Rachele's room.'

'Was he completely naked? Was his cock hard?'

I feel like fainting. I need some air.

'He had a towel round his waist.'

'So you didn't *see* them having sex. *Nor* was he naked.'

'What difference does it make? We should call the police!'

'Because maybe they fuck?'

'Because of what they do to us! Why would you ever protect them anyway?'

'I'm protecting the team, the medals. I'm protecting you!'

I look at Nadia, searching for a bond I don't find. She's under Carla's spell again. And she will be forever. I count to a hundred, two hundred. Nothing happens. Just the pins and the needles getting worse in my foot, then making their way up to my waist, my lungs. The tongue. My eyes.

'Come back, my love,' Carla is saying to Nadia. 'Can't you see without you I fail?'

During the pause that follows I switch off my bedside lamp, decide to forget them forever, and try to sleep. If they want to stay up tonight too, fine. I sure don't. If they don't want to call the police and become completely mad, fine. And if they don't believe me or don't ever want to speak about Alex, I don't care either. Maybe I can revise my mat routine in my head or think about some school stuff. Yes, some school stuff. English for instance. I am. You are. We are.

'Come back, my love,' Carla says again.

'Karl,' Nadia mumbles. 'He needs to go.'

'All right. Who gives a shit about Karl, anyway?'

Nadia turns her face, streaked with tears, and looks at

119

her best friend. Her love. My bed is in the dark while Nadia's is lit like a stage. I am the only spectator and I can't even clap.

'I will be really cold, a piece of ice,' Carla tells Nadia, her voice a bit elated. 'I won't even say hi to him. It was about you always.'

'I like that.' Nadia giggles. 'It was always about you for me too.'

'I'll cover my eyes with my hands every time he goes past. I'll run away every time he comes near me, like he's a bad smell. And I won't ever say any word starting with the letter K. I'll never say Karl again. Or king, Kraków . . . Kukaku!'

'Kukaku doesn't mean anything,' Nadia laughs. 'Kukaku doesn't exist!

'Kukaku is dead!' Carla shouts as she starts jumping on the bed.

'He is dead. The K is dead,' Nadia whispers.

They huddle together under the duvet, hugging and not talking any more, or maybe it's me falling asleep at last, with all the 'We are' and 'You are' I've been repeating to myself. Carla is never going to be able to say Khorkina again, if she means what she's promised.

But I decide not to point this out.

SATURDAY

They are both spitting out of the window, so I know things are better. And I know Angelika is down there running. Nadia is hugging Carla who seems to be back to her usual self. Their saliva is hanging down from their chins – like slugs' trails, shiny and white – and that counts as being back to their usual selves too. The sun is huge, phosphorescent yellow, and my heart weighs at least 100 kilos.

'Do you know what the only name more stupid than Angelika Ladeci is?' says Carla. 'Actually, it's so stupid I can't think of anything worse.'

'It's an old woman's name. And it's got a K in it, careful!'

'Right, that letter is dead. Why the fuck did I use it?'

I don't dare say Angelika Ladeci sounds like the name of a gymnast that will resound through the centuries. A name that's been around forever and will last forever.

Angelika Ladeci. Ladeci, Angelika: I can imagine her Wikipedia page with the list of the trophies she has won. Then all of the movements invented by her. I repeat her name and surname in my head until they lose meaning.

I get dressed and find a text from Dad. Mum and I are counting the hours till the All Around! To your competition and to your return. We are good here in the Mousy Mouse Land. I picture the sun in our suburb, also called the Mousy Mouse Land, hidden behind a static yellow mist. I picture them lost in that yellow mist, all mice and rats and litter around them. I try to hug them but even if it's an invented hug, I can't get myself to hold tight and I have to look up at the imaginary sky instead.

Before I started travelling, I used to think the sky was naturally faded blue, the sun always far away, just like at home. But then on our travels I began to see the sun for what it was and for what it could be, and my world back home became bleaker. Even here, in freezing Romania, the sun comes up cleaner, and larger, and it's so big it feels as if it's about to fall on you. It's so colossal it's easy to understand how much heat it can generate, and why it keeps us alive. Or sort of alive.

I brush my hair and it's so red it hurts. It's a fire and I can feel the heat. I zip up twice, down twice, drink two sips of water and try to forget about my hair and the heat on my skull and my forever untidy bun. I put on a smile and turn towards them.

'Shall we go and have our breakfast?'

'You're so common, Martina,' says Carla. 'Sophisticated people say *petit dejeuner*. That's what they'd call it at Anna's house.'

'Not that Anna would invite you,' says Nadia. 'Or us. Carla, could you give me a quick neck massage?'

When we were younger, we used to be invited to Anna's house a lot. Then the invitations stopped. I think it was after Carla tried on all her mother's shoes and left them scattered everywhere for the maid to pick up. Or maybe it was after Nadia and Carla got drunk on the liqueurs in the living room, and practised the routine from one of our old competitions, between the stairs and the basement, smashing a few vases along the way.

'Sorry, my love,' Carla said. 'Tell me if we owe you something.'

At Anna's house I discovered what real carpets were like and that there was a dryer that wasn't a washing machine. I learned of the existence of rooms that don't belong to anyone and stay empty, in which the beds are tidy and the sheets are clean and not one person sleeps in them. I imagined jolly ghosts, lying under the printed quilts, tapestries, and over them the softest blankets. It must be strange to change sheets that haven't been used, from beds that haven't been slept in. When do you do it? And why? Even if there was room for all her family, and spare people, it always felt empty. Her mother would come and go so fast it was like she was one of those cloaks magicians wear, with empty space underneath. We never saw her father but we heard words like 'diplomat', and 'girlfriends'. The kind of words that when put together explained why we never saw him and why Anna hated him.

The maid would come and tell us our snacks were ready, that they had put mats out in the garden for us to practise on, or that it was time for our bath and the bubbles were making it foamy. Anna was fond of the maid but Carla positively hated her. Even back then any maid would make me think of my mum, but Carla, bold and rude, just ordered her to bring her this and that. Or she would complain she was too cold. Then too hot.

'Maid!' she'd shout. 'What are you making for Princess Anna's dinner?'

And Anna would end up crying. But it was not like she had parents or someone that heard her.

In the canteen we sit with the rest of the team. Rachele starts smiling the moment she sees that Carla and Nadia are friends again. She's happy for Carla, our star, who now has her Nadia back, but more than anything she's happy for herself. So she starts talking as if she's never going to stop. Every so often, while she is going on and on, she winks at Carla. Or she says, 'Do you agree, Nadia?' And Nadia has to say, 'Yes, Rachele. I do.'

Turn it down a bit, I want to tell her as usual. *Turn it down, Coach, they're all looking at us, you are loud, you are bad*, but the blah blah has started; the tsunami of words cascading from her lipsticked mouth is in full swing. There is no way of stopping it.

Last night I saw you lying in front of the TV eating chocolate, crying, I'd like to say. *I saw you with Alex, he was naked – so despite all your words and this laughter, I don't trust you.*

But I remain silent. I redo my hair instead.

'I've been told that last night, there were three or four wolves in front of the lobby,' she is now telling us, 'so look after your little legs, girls!'

'Romania is full of stray dogs,' Benedetta murmurs. 'They say there are two or three hundred thousand. They must be dogs, not wolves.'

'Romania is the main European stronghold of wolves and bears,' Anna says. 'The presence of wolves is reported over an area of fifty-seven thousand square kilometres, and that of bears on fifty-two thousand square kilometres. The areas of distribution of the species cover twenty-five per cent of Romanian territory and are located especially in hilly and mountainous areas.'

We look at Anna like you would at some crazy person or a green alien. One, how does she know? Two, she has never said so many words in one go, let alone the word 'stronghold'. Three, so there really are wolves. Our mouths drop open, one by one.

'I looked it up on Wikipedia,' she whispers, and goes all red.

'You looked it up *and* memorized it,' says Carla. '*The areas of distribution of the species*? Who talks like that?'

'It also says they tear at their prey, starting from the belly. Because it's fattier,' Anna adds.

At the word 'tear', we all close our mouths, maybe because it's the opposite of what a wolf would do to a dead body. His mouth would open. He'd grab a hand. The arm. The face. Rachele tries to change the subject and starts explaining how the centralized system of Romanian sport works, and how the athletes live together all year round. She goes on about their dorms and bunk beds and discipline. I guess she'd be ready to list all their shampoos and menus too.

'Real discipline,' she says. 'Do you understand, children?'

She calls us children only once or twice a year. It's a treat. And here it is, the treat is being given to us today.

Some journalists come into the canteen, a clear sign that the most important day of this competition is really close. They take a few pictures, chat with the coaches, sneak a peek at Angelika. Then at Carla. I repeat 'Sunday Revolution and Wonder' and hope tomorrow one of them will need my photo too. I'll be sure to write my name down on a piece of paper, spelling it clearly, so both the Spanish and the Chinese press will be able to use it in the article about the Olympic hopefuls. My name will be on everyone's lips, on billboards, on the radio, and they'll be able to easily copy it from there. The M of Martina will be as big as the one at the mall.

'Martina,' says Carla, 'are you coming with us? Or do you want to keep stuffing yourself?'

I don't want to keep stuffing myself. I suddenly feel really fat, with the redhead's cellulite that can be seen through my tracksuit. My hair turns back to fire so I quickly get up and follow them. Rachele looks at me as if to say, 'Thank you' and I think, *You really are hopeless, Rachele. Stop smiling. Stop everything.* I must be thinking this with some force because she does stop smiling.

'Good girl,' Carla says when I stand up. 'Good and brave.'

Outside, the sunlight is bright on the snow, the sky dazzles, and the air smells incredible. I am good and I am brave. I am Martina with the biggest M in the world. I look back at the hotel and I see the bears with coats shovelling the snow, and they are still laughing. I like them, and their laughter, so I laugh too.

'You really are crazy,' Nadia says. 'But in a cute way.'

'Do you remember when Martina was little and she could only do left cartwheels?' Carla asks her. 'She used to say it was a question of order, whatever the hell that means.'

They have memories of me as a little girl, me and my left cartwheels, so I smile wider. I want to tell them that it didn't mean anything. It just seemed weird and terrible to start from the right. I tried to trick myself into it lots of times. Right cartwheels as a penance, right cartwheels as a challenge. In the end, after a whole year of trying, I managed to do them. Maybe now I'll get stuck again, just because they've mentioned it. I look up and see Karl watching us from a window. He waves, a large, exaggerated wave.

We run faster.

As we cross the bridge, we stop to watch the cars speeding along the A road below. We spit at them, we laugh, and we get to the sports centre in a great mood, despite all of our bruises. Despite all of our lives, hunger, and all of our pain. Outside the building there are birds and a few of the two or three hundred thousand stray dogs eating out of the rubbish bins.

'Gross,' says Carla. 'We should feed them the gymnast that has to die.'

'Aren't birds vegetarian?' I ask. But then I remember a documentary where an eagle was eating fish, snakes, and other birds.

'When I grow up, I want to know loads more things,' Nadia says, grabbing Carla's hand.

'Like what?' Carla looks at Nadia's hand. She smiles.

'How cities work. Or where the light comes from, through what pipes. How walls stay up. I'd like to know how you build bridges. All the things we take for granted. The hidden mechanisms. The mathematics of things.'

'The mathematics of things?' says Carla, laughing. 'Two and two is four. Ten plus ten is twenty.'

'Like what kind of mixture the pavement is made out of? Or our breath?' I say.

'Yes, that,' says Nadia. 'And stars. And water. And our hearts. Love.'

'And you want to know how babies are made, right?' Carla laughs.

'She wants to know how and when the wind changes direction,' I say. 'And what happens to your brain when you scream.'

'How darkness works,' Nadia adds. 'Or the void.'

'All that's on Google,' says Carla. 'Nothing special.'

She lets go of Nadia's hand. Light leaves Nadia's eyes.

'Aw,' says Nadia. 'You've ruined the magic.'

She has ruined the magic.

It's so early that the sports centre looks deserted. We walk down the corridors with their high ceilings and dim lights and we step into the first gym, which is still dark. The rings hang above our heads. Our steps echo in the stillness. As we cross it to get to our station, we hear the Chinese team in the second gym. It's dry. Quick. Terrible.

'Fucking dogs.' Carla clenches her jaw.

I know she's angry because she thinks she's different, but I know I'm angry because we are all the same. Romanians. Chinese. French. Italians. Girls of the world.

We move towards the noise and the shouting. I can also hear someone crying, so I look at Nadia and Carla. It is obvious they hear it too. My feet are made of wood, stone, glue. They are made of all the mistakes that got us here.

'Should we look?' Nadia whispers.

'I don't know,' I say. 'If they see us, they'll kill us.'

'It's more like if you see them, you'll kill yourself,' Carla says. 'They'll give you nightmares for a whole year.'

Carla and I look. I grit my teeth and immediately feel ill.

The shouts are coming from two girls and two boys. The face of their coach, standing before them, is dripping with sweat, thick lines – like cuts – on his forehead. This is what the face of someone who's about to die of a heart attack must look like. The face of that mythical coach Florin must have looked exactly the same. The face of Alex when his penis is hard is quite similar too.

Nadia pushes in between us, so we can all see. I squash myself against them, while the Chinese girls are caned on their backs and the boys are caned on their chests. I feel their pain. One body, one heart. One mega cane on all of our chests. One mega cane on all of our backs. I can feel it in my tummy but also where the cane lands and if the coach's face is that of someone about to die, then please let this be the moment for it to happen.

The coach manipulates them all into bridge positions, and starts kicking their feet and hands so they'll fall. And they do fall. Bridge, kick, fall. Bridge, kick, fall. We hear the sounds of broken breathing and choking, of lungs hitting the floor. I see their beautiful scores on the board during this past week. Then, the cane again.

'Why?' Nadia asks.

'They must have done something bad,' I say.

'Get real,' says Carla. 'This is how they always train. This is them being good athletes.'

The coach turns towards the door. His forehead is dripping and he is still shouting. The expressions on the faces of his gymnasts don't change despite the shouts, the falls, the cane. The coach's brain must be about to explode. He goes even redder while squeezing the arm of one of his athletes.

'This man has to die,' Carla says. 'They all have to die.'

Nadia looks at her and I know she has started seeing things. Now in her head the man is dead.

One of the boys falls to the floor. The coach runs towards him, so fast I think he's going to punch him. He gets him to do a handstand instead, and pushes him down as soon as he's up. Another handstand. Then, down again. He does it about twenty times, thirty maybe.

'How will they compete today?' I say.

'Maybe this is exactly what they think they need before competitions,' Carla says.

The boy looks at us. I close my eyes, hoping to disappear. Hoping to change the backdrop to my life and remove myself from here. But I open them again and the boy, in a handstand now, is still looking at us and I am not in Los Angeles nor in Bangkok. Eyes wide open, his back so very straight, right in front of me. Then he smiles the kind of smile you smile for the jury. Wide, perfect. And he smiles even more, until we run for it.

Gasping for air, we get to the main gym and take our tracksuits off. We stuff them in our bags and hide the bags under the chairs. When I get up, I see Carla kiss Nadia's eyes. She looks at me.

'Were you scared too, Martina? Do you need a kiss?'

I nod, so they hug me. And they kiss my eyes. I disentangle myself as soon as I can and start running around the gym. I can feel my breath bringing oxygen all the way to my knees, leaning into my chest, loosening my shoulders. I speed up, my heart speeds up too, and there is speed to my blood. Soon Carla and Nadia are running near me. We start jumping, stretching, and when Anna and Benedetta arrive, together with Alex and Rachele, we are already in a state of full concentration, right inside our own heads, good girls in their routine. No image of a raging Chinese coach can destroy us. And nothing can really touch us. We have warmed up, our backs are damp with sweat, adrenalin is already pumping. We have already erased all of what is evil from our drive. The lights come on with a loud click, the other teams take up their sections of the gym, and so the day begins.

'I love gymnastics,' Carla says. And we laugh because we really do. It's still our dream.

When Karl comes in, we're at the vault and the audience has already filled the arena for the Individual Finals, where the top gymnasts compete against each other for medals on each apparatus. Despite the busy stands, Carla must sense him coming in, with her shoulder blades maybe, because I'm standing right in front of her and see her face change. Nadia's face changes too but neither of them gives in and looks at him.

I do, because I can. He is sad. He is handsome, short and sad.

I watch him perform on the rings and his execution is faultless. His arms are straight and strong. I look at his hands and think back to him stroking Nadia and Carla's legs. It's very clear to me why you'd want to run off with him at night to see Romania-like-Paris and why it is difficult to stop wanting those hands, those eyes. I look at Carla, warming up at the bars now, fully focused for her day as a champion. She's quiet and Nadia, for the first time in years, seems to be in full control. Now that she has won Carla back, and Carla is no longer allowed to pronounce the letter K, she seems at peace. Her chin is pointing higher, and I'm sure that as of today her heart has a different shape too.

Maybe that of the moon.

Karl is watching them, Carla especially, with every chance he gets. I'm sure he doesn't understand what goes on between her and Nadia. And what exactly has expelled him from the system. How could he? How could he even begin to understand their one body and one heart, the blue pooh and their decision about the letter K? He cannot even begin to know that they have been sharing a bed since they were 4 years old, or about that abracadabra of theirs, which is so important to the whole team. He cannot begin to know that nothing can come between Nadia and Carla without being crushed. And if he doesn't know any of it, how could he possibly understand that Nadia has become the boss overnight? The one that sets the rules. The one to please and whose heart now has the shape of the moon. At any rate, looking carefully, Karl is not quite as handsome when he is sad, which is interesting in itself. His shoulders slump and his eyes slant downwards. I still hate Rachele for telling me 'Smile, Martina, you look prettier', but I understand her now, through the very easy example of the very sad face of the very sad Karl.

Carla is so sure of herself she convinces Rachele to let her add the *Produnova* at the vault. I imagine her ending up paralysed – still better than being a loser, according to her – but we have no time to picture her life in a wheelchair as she's already performing her jump so well it's like she has wings. The arena responds with sighs of wonder and a mega applause. In the crowd, the little girls that want to be us, here with their parents and friends, are all in awe. I was once one of those girls too.

'I love gymnastics,' Carla repeats. And we all repeat it too.

With her 15.6 on the vault, she is second only to Angelika, and conquers the silver podium. I look at them from eighth position, and try to feel proud of myself even here, where no medals are given but smiles are still needed. Eight is great for me, I tell myself. *I love this eight*, I repeat. And I love gymnastics.

Carla is then perfect at the bars, so precise and so fast she gets the third position on the podium. She smiles. She waves. Both her and Nadia perform a fantastic floor exercise. Their D scores are high, their execution is fault- less. But Carla is second again and Nadia is third. Angelika, with her gymnastics that is beauty itself and magic itself, is always on the top step.

'Fuck that bitch,' I hear Carla say, looking at Angelika. 'I need her out of my life.'

She composes herself and goes with Nadia to the balance beam, confident and upbeat, possibly until the end of time, amen. But however well they perform on the beam, they don't beat Angelika. And their anger is so great that even if I do very well at the beam too and there is joy in my feet – and even if my shoulders and my hands are strong and my shape is elegant – nobody notices. There's no time to acknowledge me or any of the mediocrity of life. We quickly digest Benedetta's disappointing scores one after the other, and we try to just be glad that today, at the individuals, her presence doesn't affect the team. Today we compete for ourselves on every single apparatus and we win or we fail for ourselves in every single appar- atus. As Carla holds back her tears on the podium when she receives her bronze medal, I find myself in fifth place at an international tournament for the first time in my life and for the first time since we arrived in Romania, Rachele gives me a genuine smile. I deserve a smile. I am strong. I too can be pretty. I am the pioneer of my present and my future.

After we are all done, we linger at the gym a bit more, to get all the other team's final scores. They appear on the board one after the other, one breath after the other.

'Whore,' Carla says, looking at Angelika winning her three gold medals and a silver. 'Whore, shithead, bitch.'

But we manage to celebrate Carla's two silvers and two bronzes anyway, and we manage to hug Nadia for her bronze at the bars. So as not to obsess about Angelika, we also decide to forever hate a few Chinese girls who stole our places on the podium and for the same reason we despise a Hungarian. I get a hug too, for my good score at the beam and my solid overall performance. The Useless Ones uselessly failed, but weren't as bad as the Spanish girls and that, for today and maybe in life, is just enough.

'I love you girls,' Rachele says. And we all say, 'We love you too.'

After lunch we go for an ice bath. There's no training in the afternoon, so that we won't be too tired tomorrow, for the All Around finals. Nadia and Carla get into the tub together, while I look at myself in the mirror. If today I nearly made it, will I be spectacular tomorrow? Or will I fail and will being fifth forever be the best I can do?

'Can you get into the ice if you have a period?' Nadia asks.

'Of course,' replies Carla. 'Blood might become ice, though!'

They mumble '*Brrr*,' launch a few swearwords in the air and sit down, gritting their teeth.

'China is stronger than ever,' Carla says.

By this stage in the game, all we can talk about is the competition. We evaluate, we estimate. We hate and we curse. We praise and we insult and we count and we wish. The way the scores are calculated has changed so many times that the maths has got complicated. So Nadia and Carla get into that.

'I need to get 14.70 on all the apparatus,' Carla adds. '14.90, for the glory.'

'I've got too much competition at the beam. And I am scared of getting stuck.'

'I need to crush the bitch. I can't fucking shake her off!'

'Khorkina: All Around world champion in 1997, 2001, and 2003. European champion in 1998, 2000, and 2002.' Nadia goes on reciting all of Khorkina's wins and scores as if numbers were a poem. A mantra. A rhyme.

'Why the fuck would you say that? What's with using a K?'

As I look at my face in the mirror, I notice a couple of spots and a few new lines under my eyes. I imagine myself older, making it to a hundred. I bite my lips, because Carla has told us it's an excellent way of plumping them up and making them look juicier. I bite and bite and my lips get juicier, smoother, and redder. It is a good trick. I plait my hair, while they rub ice over their heads and necks. The worst of the chill must have passed, if they're able to play with the cubes; the back is the part of your body that hurts the most in the ice. Then comes the head. Then comes the pleasure.

'What if I cut my hair?' I say.

I have never thought of it before. Or that I could ever cut my hair without my mum.

'Great idea!' exclaims Carla.

In one single second she gets out of the bath, ties a towel around her waist, and takes a pair of scissors from her make-up bag. Her nipples are pointy even without the Sellotape treatment. She sits me down on the toilet and Nadia watches us with a half-smile.

'How do you want it?'

'Short,' I say.

Carla chops off my plaits in one go. She smiles, so I smile too and look at my hair on the floor, still red, but no longer mine. And no longer on fire. It took me years to grow it long and I've decided to get rid of it in less than one minute. The broom my mum uses at the salon would sweep it up off the bathroom floor in a blink.

Carla carries on cutting and at this point there is nothing I can do. Nadia climbs out of the bath and asks if she can cut it too. She hates it when Carla touches someone else, and I can feel it.

'What do you say, Martina?'

'OK by me,' I reply.

'It's like a blood pact,' Nadia says. 'But with hair.'

Nadia grabs the scissors and takes over. Carla finishes putting lotion on her not-there tits, on her bruised legs, and on her bum. She brushes her hair, which now looks really long and precious, and every so often comes over to supervise. Nadia is cutting really slowly. I can feel the scissor tips caressing my skull, then the snip of metal and some very short hair falling on my shoulders.

It's gentle. I like it.

When they've finished they brush the hair from my neck with a make-up brush. They stand a step back to study me, tilting their heads, first to the right then to the left. I stare back at them, hoping to see a smile. But everything goes in slow motion as I watch them blink.

'So?' I ask.

Rachele will kill me, I think. Everyone will see the bald patches Carla and Nadia have left. I'll look like a crazy person and they'll probably upload photos of my crazy person's head online. Whatever I will do in my life, whatever backdrop of Vietnam or Laos I'll have behind me, people will know. They will remember. 'She's the crazy gymnast, see?' they'll say. I touch my nose twice but don't feel it under the tips of my fingers. The third time the nose is back there.

'You're beautiful,' Nadia says.

'Gorgeous,' Carla confirms. 'Like a superstar.'

I look at myself as Nadia runs her fingers through my bristly hair. I shiver as I spot no superstars in the mirror. I've never seen a girl with hair as short as mine and there is probably a reason for it. I touch it and it tickles against the palm of my hand, like the beige carpet at home scratches under my feet. I am not beautiful and my nose looks ten times bigger. I wish it really had disappeared, never mind searching for it with my fingers. I want to tell Mum, right away. I also want to tell her, 'Maybe if you cut all yours off too, you'll stop dreaming you have hair in your mouth.'

My eyes fill up with tears.

'Why are you crying? Have you changed your mind?' Carla asks.

'Not one bit. I love it.'

I hate it.

'And we love you,' says Nadia.

They probably hate me.

'So that's sorted,' confirms Carla. And once again we pretend that because someone says things are sorted, they really are sorted.

At seven we go for our physio session and I'm pleased to realize that my new hair makes me feel safer. Stronger. So I step into the battlefield with a new heartbeat. That of war. And, eventually, that of peace.

'What happened?' says Alex, looking at my shaved cranium.

I lie on my stomach. He gets the cream. My lungs close and the air in the room disappears. He squeezes the cream on his palms. The vastness of my pain is so enormous I can suddenly feel its power. With a scream I could break walls. With my agony I could make this whole hotel disintegrate and crumble. Then I would take care of the entire world.

'You want to talk about it?' Alex says.

'Shut up,' I say.

As I hear him massaging his hands, passing the white liquid from one to the other, I take a deep breath in, and shut down, I guess preparing for apnoea. In two seconds those hands will be on me. One second. I feel pressure building in my skull. My diaphragm clenching.

'Relax,' he says. 'It's all good.'

'Fuck this. Fuck you,' I say.

I stand up. I look at him, facing the monster full on. The room is moving. My head is spinning. I breathe out my terror and his terror, my pain and his horror, without lowering my eyes once.

'Fuck you!' I shout again.

'Martina,' he says.

I won't listen ever again. He can't say my name ever again. I walk away, I shut the door, and I shut my heart, with the certainty that he will never touch me again. If he does, I'll fucking kill him.

I go straight to the scheduled one-to-one meeting with Rachele. When we are staying in a hotel, each one of us is called to her room where she shifts the TV stand to make it look like an office desk. She puts a chair on each side and invites us in, saying, 'Come in. I'm so glad I get to see you alone for a few minutes.' But today, as I enter, she freezes. Her script fails her. Her smile vanishes as she gets up off the chair.

'What have you done to your hair?'

'Trimmed it?'

'Martina, it's *butchered*, not trimmed. Was it Carla?'

'It was me.'

She remains silent for a few seconds. I don't understand if she feels sorry for me or if she's about to get angry and shout at me. Whatever will follow, I can take it. Whatever will follow, my agony will pulverize it, so the doubt doesn't bother me much. I see the Chinese coach's cane, and imagine him giving it to Rachele to beat me. Then me beating her. I focus on her cheesy thighs and hope she's not going to cry. Emotions are the worst.

'I feel better with my hair short,' I say.

As she still isn't saying anything, I repeat myself, louder.

'I feel better with my hair short. And I feel stronger.'

Strong is the right word to use with her. Even though I might have done something stupid, tomorrow I have my most important competition to date, and if shaving my hair off makes me feel stronger, then she has to support me. She can tell me off on Monday. She will also be able to tell me I am stupid and dumb and horrible. But now she has to say that I really do seem stronger and that she believes in me.

She looks at me closely. She gets up and studies the hair at the back of my head.

'It looks terrible from behind. Like someone ate your hair.'

She rummages around in the bathroom then comes back with a pair of nail scissors. I think about her toenails, hard and a little yellowed. I think about her skin when she hugs me, the smell it leaves. She wets my head with water from the tap and tidies up my haircut as best she can.

'It's true you look strong, Martina.'

'I feel it. I also feel safer.'

She pauses. We both know what I mean. But once again she decides not to hear me. Or to say anything out loud. Suddenly I wonder if she had in fact gone to the higher floors, and she had told everything about Alex, and she too was waiting for something to happen. Maybe she even went to the police but the police were for some obscure reason on Alex's side. Reasons like those you find on Twitter, of secret paedo gangs going up to all the places of power and the FBI and the Vatican and the White House being part of it all.

'Strong and safe is good,' she murmurs. 'It's great, actually. You must remember it tomorrow. And remember that you can succeed at anything if you really want it.'

I listen to her and know she will repeat this same sentence to the team until eight o'clock this evening. I know that she too has gone back to her script and wants to help us sleep, compete, be serene. Win. I also know that at the end of the day she will cry and eat too much chocolate and drink too much vodka and, after all, she has never been a champion herself, and she has failed in everything herself, so all these words have not worked for her.

'Have Carla and Nadia been nice to you this week?'

'Of course. So nice.'

'Why did they fall out?'

'I really don't know.'

'Did you see them make up?'

'No.'

'Do you mind talking about it?'

'It's boring.'

Rachele swallows my rebuff as I run my hands over my strong-girl hair.

Tomorrow is Sunday, and Sunday is the first day of Revolution and Wonder. I will be clean and precise in the

140

exercises. I will not fall off the balancing beam or be scared. I will grab the bars with strength and I will execute faultless twists, and holds, and jumps. At the end of my perfect routine, I will smile and shed a single tear while running my hand over my super short hair. Over my super strong skull. The gesture, the caress over my skull, my head leaning back a little and my eyes looking up at the neon lights, will become my new abracadabra. And my signature pose. I've been looking for one for ages.

When we were little, we did competitions on mats arranged lengthwise. In a row, one after the other. The floor exercise didn't include diagonals. We spent our Sundays in our leotards and our plimsolls, snacking on fizzy drinks and crisps. There were always vending machines in the gyms and we liked them a lot, even if back then too we were forbidden from putting on weight. Sometimes my mum came and sometimes she worked or slept instead. When my dad came I didn't look at him like some other girls looked at their dads before a competition. Carla's parents always came and Nadia's parents, actually her one parent, her mum, practically never did. Nadia used to say her mum was happy that competitions were on Sundays because she could have at least one complete day of the week not being a mum. On Sundays she'd have her girlfriends round, or go for a motorbike ride with her gang and do fun stuff, which since she had Nadia the mistake very young, and Nadia was still small, she could hardly ever do. This taught us that it's not necessarily nice being a mum and it is possible to wish to be as away as possible from your children. But it also taught us that some mums have a gang of friends and ride on motorbikes, drink beer, and really laugh.

There was one time when Nadia's mum came to watch us and Nadia didn't perform as well as usual. She was getting over tendonitis of her left foot. In the previous few months we had trained hard and each one of us had reacted to the punishments our bodies took in different ways. Benedetta and Anna, for example, had started taking laxatives to lose weight. Carla had experienced her first twisties – she had lost her bearings while turning in the air – which left us terrified. Caterina had suffered all those fractures and had abandoned the team. I had started doing things twice, and so on.

Nadia's mum had been impressed all the same because it had been ages since she'd watched her daughter do gymnastics. I don't think she actually knew what doing gymnastics meant and involved. She hadn't realized how good Nadia had got and how complicated her skills had become. She came into the changing room while we were showering, congratulated us, and while I worked shampoo into my hair, I saw tears of happiness pouring down Nadia's cheeks. Or maybe it was just the shower.

'You're all so tiny,' her mum said, peering at us under the jets of water. 'And so cute!'

She said it as if she'd just seen some little puppies. Nadia got dressed and smiled because it really was a lovely Sunday and she was so tiny and so cute. She was also good and got lots of compliments. Her tendonitis was getting better and now that her mum had seen her, it'd all been worth it. Carla nestled on Nadia's mum's lap to have her hair brushed and Nadia brushed her own. I felt jealous for her. Her mum was very beautiful and I would have liked to nestle in her arms too. She had been so lovely that I'd hoped for weeks that she would come back. But she never did.

Before dinner we call home. To be precise, three texts are sent from our three beds at the same time to our mums or dads and a few seconds later our phones ring, each with their own ring tone. Mine is embarrassing, the tune of a Mickey Mouse cartoon I used to watch when I was maybe 8 and that I'm now too superstitious to change.

'It's raining here,' Dad says.

'Here it's snowing.'

'How are you?'

'I like Romania. I'm good.'

'Have you been on any other outings since the mall?'

'We've been busy training.'

'We're treating ourselves tonight and going to the cinema.'

I know he is lying but I don't want to ruin the lie for them. I breathe in. And out. He'll have to come up with a fake plot and a fake review for the fake movie.

'Tomorrow,' he says. 'Revolution and Wonder!'

'Do you think I've already been to Romania in a previous life?' I ask him. 'I feel good here.'

'We'll have to check the cards,' he laughs. 'But my gut feeling is yes, big time.'

'I thought so. We'll watch the videos together when I'm back, OK?'

We used to spend entire evenings at home, and some-times entire afternoons at the gym, watching videos of the competitions. Whenever I watch myself, I'm again afraid of falling over, as if I don't already know the outcome. I picture myself crashing down on my neck and being taken away on a stretcher.

'Look at those chubby legs,' Carla would say when she rewatched herself. 'When we're done with gymnastics, let's go straight to get ourselves fixed!'

'Can we be stretched taller?' Nadia would ask.

'And we can have cameras filming us as our height and width are modified. But it's too late to do something about osteoporosis.'

'We'd get that anyway by the time we're fifty. So what's the difference in having it done at fourteen?'

Since the very beginning, when Carla trained or when some exercise didn't come off the way she wanted, she was always the most diligent in the whole gym. She didn't talk, she kept her head down, her jaw clenched. She was able to repeat her routine more times than all of us, like she was not allowed to leave that Tuesday, that Wednesday, without having given her best and without having found a solution to the problem. And the next day, she'd never feel tired, despite the effort she'd made. She started all over again, rested, attentive. Her head bowed down, abs tensed, eyes focused.

'Good girl,' Rachele and all the other coaches always told her. And Carla would nod.

She knew she was a good girl.

Tonight we have such an early dinner, it isn't even dark outside. Rachele gives us a team speech and for a second I am worried she will say 'Amen' at the end of it. She doesn't, thank God, and pours herself a beer. I see her raise a glass to a few other coaches. Some smile back but they all probably think she's pathetic. Alex is telling another physiotherapist something he's read about. 'Overtraining,' I think I hear as I watch the judges sit at a table by themselves. Do some of them exchange our naked pictures? How many of them are good and how many are bad?

'Anna, do you see how beautiful Martina has become?' Carla says.

Anna looks me in the eyes to work out if I've been punished or if I'm happy with my haircut.

'It would be even more dramatic if you did it,' Carla tells her. 'Shear off all that wool!'

'I'll think about it,' Anna mumbles.

While Benedetta is pretending to read Anna's palm and predict her future, Karl comes in and walks towards our table. I look down and watch his legs until he is right next to me. Nadia and Carla are staring at the void near him, making him instantly invisible. A moment ago, he had a body, now he is a ghost. Abracadabra.

'There's a terrible smell,' Carla says. 'Of people from underprivileged countries.'

When she says 'underprivileged' she rolls her eyes, to stress her aversion. Someone should stop her. And fight the evil and the bad she brings in. But we don't. We comply even when we hate it. Even when we know it's wrong and disgusting. That's how most evil things of life work. They slip in without finding any resistance.

'Yes, and of dwarfs,' Nadia adds.

'I can smell poverty, dwarfs, and pimples,' Carla continues.

'I can smell poverty dwarfs, pimples, and losers.'

'And too much wanking,' she finishes under her breath.

I don't know how much Karl can understand. But even if he doesn't speak or understand our language, Nadia and Carla's tone of voice is so cruel that his knees swivel and he moves away. The words keep going round and round in my head too. They are like glue and have such sticky filaments they won't budge from behind my forehead and the back of my eyes. All I can now see is a pimply dwarf in a poor room wanking after losing a competition. Such is the power of Carla's voice.

'Down with the letter K!' Carla says.

'Down with the letter K!' Nadia echoes.

That evening we tidy up our room and throw away the cans of Fanta and Coca-Cola, our notes, the trash. We fold some of our clothes. We check our hair in the bikini area and under our armpits. Nadia rewatches the Chinese training session, which she secretly filmed while Carla gave us a test on phobias. She asks: *Do you believe that if you perform specific actions (like counting, checking, engaging in ritual behaviour to ward off bad luck, etc.) you will be able to change your destiny?* and something inside me dies a little. I do believe that by counting I can change my destiny. It turns out Nadia and I score between seventy-seven and ninety-eight points, which isn't good.

'Too bad.' Nadia smiles.

We hang up our pink competition leotards and worship them as if they are our gods. We kneel in front of them, laughing, and we pray to the snow and to the cold, to Romania, and to our motherland, and we promise our souls to the devil, to Khorkina despite the letter K, to Nadia Comaneci, and whoever the hell may want them, in exchange for a crushing victory.

'To win, to win, to win,' we whisper.

'Come on, come on, come on!' we shout.

Carla goes to the bathroom and Nadia and I go back to the window to see if we can spot a lucky wolf. Or Angelika, which is kind of the same. Down there the bear father and the bear son in their coats are shovelling the snow.

'Thank you, Martina.'

'What for?'

'For not spilling the beans to anyone,' Nadia says. 'For protecting me, Carla, and our secrets.'

'I wouldn't have known what to spill anyway.'

And Nadia, grateful and soft, tells me that she loves Carla and Carla wanted to kiss Karl and they'd all started touching each other and then Carla stopped touching her and couldn't take her hands off Karl. Nadia was so jealous she wanted to die.

'That idiot Karl. I hope he is the one actually dying,' she says.

We really hope way too many people will die, I think.

Nadia explains she's never really fancied him, she just pretended she found him handsome – well, she says he really is handsome but who cares? She did it to provoke Carla. To bring her closer. To bring her only love closer. But things got out of control.

'Now everything is OK.' She turns to me and runs her hand over my head. 'Carla loves only me and there are no wolves and no Karls out there.'

She walks over to the bathroom and goes in to see her only love. I quickly take my clothes off and slip into my T-shirt for the night, taking advantage of the fact that I'm on my own and there's no one staring at my growing cellulite and my dwarf's hips. I lie on the bed and switch off the ceiling light. Through the window I can see at least a million stars and I hope I'll find my only love too. I hope our love will be glorious. And together we will walk all the streets and roads and paths of the world.

'I'm scared,' I hear Carla say in the middle of the night.

I've never heard Carla say she's scared. But I must not obsess over it. If Carla and Nadia can't sleep even the night before our most important competition, fine. But I know my legs will turn to jelly and my hands will go all tingly. I *must* sleep. I *must* do well tomorrow. It's my great chance to be noticed. To do even better than today. To aim for the Olympics.

'Don't be scared,' says Nadia. 'I'll protect you forever.'

'If only that fat dirty revolting girl had died tonight. Then first place would be mine.'

Another one we want dead, see? I've lost count.

'Don't worry,' Nadia says. 'You've got this.'

'Yes, but if she wasn't here everything would be easier. For me and for the team.'

'You'll win anyway.'

'You don't know that.'

'I do. You are a superstar.'

'Remember just one thing,' Carla says. 'If tomorrow you go over 60 you must take your clothes off. In front of everyone.'

They giggle.

'Getting to 60 would be like liquid gold.'

'We'll all see you naked and that will be like liquid gold.'

They start laughing loudly and say silly things about liquid gold and how it must feel to have liquid gold poured over your head and down your back. They repeat it so many times I end up picturing it too. I can feel hot shiny gold wax running down my spine, through my legs, to my feet. It feels great, it feels magic. Most of all, it feels healing. So I fall asleep at peace, ready to greet the Sunday of Revolution and Wonder, all covered in magic and liquid gold and not, as it would turn out, in blood.

SUNDAY

Revolution and Wonder

'Look at her,' says Carla.

I stretch my arms and see the whitest sky. It's like a sheet of paper and I want to reach out and write *Today is the day of Revolution and Wonder* across it.

'Martina, get up and come and look at her.'

Carla presses her face against the window so I do the same. As our noses are squashed against the glass and our eyes are still sleepy, I imagine someone taking our photo from inside the woods. The hotel in the snow, the atmosphere of competition. Our room seen from outside. Our eyes seen from outside. The anticipation they carry. The fear.

'What?'

'Can't you see her?'

When the last bit of this competition is done and the All Around scores are totted up, the best of us, along with very few of the best losers, will get to *book a ticket* to the next country, the next qualifiers, then finally, the Olympics. We always say 'book a ticket' and I hate the expression, it sounds like we've won a prize holiday to somewhere warm that will have a tropical buffet and piña coladas when in fact we are killing ourselves with hard work. With sweat and anger and pain.

'She's been like that for over six minutes,' Carla says.

I expect to see Angelika but I look closer and I see Nadia is doing a handstand at the edge of the forest, risking strain and cold. She knows very well we can see her from here. And she knows very well she shouldn't be out there alone. Her puffer jacket has fallen down over her face but we recognize her feet, her tracksuit and her being Nadia in every bit of her body. She's wet and dirty. There is mud on her.

'Why is she doing that?' Carla says.

I shrug and run a hand over my prickly new hair. Maybe Mum will never dream of hair in her mouth again, because as of today, the Sunday of Revolution and Wonder, certain threads and memories, fingers and horrors, are destined to disappear not only from my head but from her mind too.

'If she gets sick before we crush the other clubs, she really is an idiot,' Carla says. 'She was out all night.'

'Was she?' I ask.

You can see all the way from here that Nadia is shaking. She comes off the handstand, looks at us and smiles, waving her hand. She runs towards the hotel and I lie back on the bed. I feel very tired, as if I haven't slept for a single minute. Or ever in my life. All the words and the wolves in the forest and these two tossing and turning in their beds and leaving in the middle of the night have left me exhausted. I look at Carla and she is shaking too.

'Everything OK?' I ask. 'You look pale.'

'Let's just be silent,' she replies.

It is OK by me, so we stop talking. Nadia comes back, drops her very dirty jacket, goes straight into the bathroom, and turns on the shower. She stays in there forever. When she gets out, she is very quiet and we embrace that quietness, the focus that we need. We do our hair – mine takes zero seconds – and make-up in silence. Carla puts eye shadow on both of us and they add eyeliner. I don't because it makes everything blurry.

'What's wrong?' she asks Nadia.

'All good,' she says.

But she keeps on scratching her hand. Then her arm.

We slip on our way-too-pink-with-way-too-many-sequins leotards. We stick them with the spray glue on our skin, we prepare our bags, drink some water, and brush our teeth. We also wash our feet with great care, especially the soles, which today of all days should not be dirty.

'Off we go,' Carla says.

And off we go.

Rachele is waiting for us in the hotel conference room for what she calls our 'visual training session'. The room is almost dark and in the dark it seems less drab. At 'visual training' we are not even allowed to say 'hi', so we don't say it. We just go in and take our places on the floor.

I sit next to Anna and Benedetta, and together with Carla and Nadia we all cross our legs. Alex looks at us. I wish we could all look at him in the same second and as one body, one heart, judge him so hard his heart will break, then he'll fall to his knees and ask to be forgiven.

We wouldn't forgive him.

We all look down, sitting in this circle of love and trust, and do some slow breathing before Rachele starts her speech. I open and close my fleece twice, while we mimic our intent faces. We know it's what is expected from us and from our faces. Deep focus. So deep focus we deliver. We listen to her as she talks us into a state of relaxation, making us visualize a place that is clean and silent, pure and safe, while we climb the seven steps to concentration, so our minds will lead our bodies. It smells like pee in here, and I wonder if I have actually been smelling it all the time I've been away from home. Or since the very beginning of my life.

'Your body is your mind,' Rachele says. 'Your body is the team's body.'

We stay silent. We are too close to the competition to say stuff that doesn't have anything to do with it and even stuff that does have something to do with it. When I peek at them, Alex and Rachele have their most serious faces on, furrowed and severe. Sometimes I sort of remember that the two of them work for us – and it's not the other way around – and this makes me feel like I have some sort of power. And control. I know I don't, but it's an easy way out of pain.

I count, breathe in and out, and start visualizing the warm-up. I visualize the gym as Rachele is telling me to do, well lit and empty of people.

'The audience doesn't exist,' she whispers. 'Gravity doesn't exist.'

And the audience doesn't exist and gravity doesn't exist. The stands are empty. I feel light, strong, and I am able to perform the exercises faultlessly. I place my feet, hold in my tummy, straighten my legs. I jump, I fly, and I conquer all beauty and all magic. The vault is a trampoline able to make you cover the distance to the other planets. The beam is a line, nothing under it, where it's impossible to fall and get hurt. Then I land. My heart is beating a regular rhythm and the spotlights are shining only for me.

'The warmth you are feeling on your face, on your body, is the light of victory,' Rachele says.

In the light of victory I get distracted, because I see myself with long hair and I have to readjust the image halfway through a handspring. I open one eye and see Carla look at Nadia. She looks at me too, scared, and immediately closes her eyes.

'You are ready, girls,' Rachele finishes. 'And you are the best.'

When we, the best, are done with the visualization we leave the conference room and walk to the canteen. My tummy is relaxed, all my muscles are relaxed, and I feel good. I look over at my teammates and hope they all feel like I do. Good, relaxed, and focused. I hope that Nadia isn't too anxious, and Anna will be sure-footed in the double somersault on the last diagonal. I hope Benedetta isn't too desperate about not being able to compete today or too angry that she had to warm up anyway: it's the rule and you don't discuss the rules. I hope Carla crushes Angelika and that we will all get to fly on more planes, sleep in new places, and win, always. I hope I'll put in a great performance, the best one of my life, and I hope they notice me. I hope I make it to the top sixteen gymnasts of this tournament. Better, to the top ten. And all the coaches and the national team's technical director will come and tell me I'm good.

I also really hope I don't die.

'You are one heart,' Rachele says once more when we get to the canteen, 'and I love your heart.'

Her voice is annoying me now. It gets creepy, especially when she wants us to feel emotional and pretends to love us. It's a bit like when Mum starts explaining to me why people are sad or why people are happy and her tone is a cross between storytelling and fake sweetness. She gives me the shivers, with those eyes of hers when they try to *communicate*. We all know by now that it isn't her biggest strength.

'Even when you compete against each other, you are one body, take care of it,' says Rachele.

'And you are one mind, take care of it,' Alex concludes as we sit down.

With our shared mind, we knock him down. Carla burps, a burp which fills the room, flying over the other tables, our heads, and the whole Sunday. Here comes her body. Here comes her gut. We laugh, forget about the seven steps, the concentration, and we start our breakfast. Rachele drinks her coffee and finally stops talking.

Wrapped up in our puffer jackets, our heads in our hats, we cross the forecourt, then go over the bridge and cross the A road. I turn around and look at the other teams walking in the snow behind us. I see the Russians and spot the Hungarians. I see the Chinese club.

Sometimes I still believe this is not only my life, but also my most-hoped-for dream. Like now, when I'm walking towards the vault, the podium, the mat, the beam. All I have to do is compete and there's nothing I want more. I'm about to perform a floor exercise that has cost me years of deprivation, mornings of training, afternoons of preparation, strict diets, and hand cramps and back pain. Bone pain. Pills. But I am not scared and I am not sad. I feel great, I feel like a warrior, and maybe it really is the Sunday of Revolution and Wonder.

'Karl,' Carla whispers.

The Polish team is at the other end of the bridge. Karl is walking in front of us, alone, and he doesn't turn. Looking at Carla's face, you'd think the word Karl had come out by accident. Like the burp in the canteen. In fact, she doesn't say it again or add anything. I stick my earphones in and crank up my old iPod and picture the same scene with a soundtrack. I replay the same scene with a soundtrack and myself as the romantic lead. I am the girl Karl is thinking about, we are in love, walking in the snow, in a foreign country of mountains and villages with medieval buildings.

We say 'I love you'. We kiss. We know how to fly.

At the arena each club sits under their own flag. The lights are very bright. Too bright. Not exactly like I had visualized in the conference room. The names and countries of the athletes competing at the All Around are announced through the loudspeakers to background tracks of the chosen floor music. The stands are crowded and from down here, the people look like confetti, the noise like a buzz of a giant mosquito about to bite us. The smell is a mixture of floor soap and sweat. Their sweat. My sweat.

We take up our positions on our team bench, not too far from the Chinese and the Spanish. I pull my zip up and down twice and pick up and put down my water bottle twice. The judges are milling about in the jury area, while Rachele is talking to Alex. He is massaging Anna's sore ankle.

'Better?' he is asking her.

And as usual she is only capable of nodding and holding back her tears. I imagine going to the microphone and saying out loud, *How many of you guys are being touched by your physios? What about your coaches? How many of you want to stop being alive and can't breathe at night?* Shall we be the pioneers of that more than anything, the pioneers of our dreams and of our freedom, and still jump and fly between uneven bars – between one galaxy and the other – but without any of the adults making up the rules?

In the far corner of the arena, Nadia is peering at the uneven bars as if they're a mathematical formula she needs to solve. She is so pale it's like the blood has left her body forever. I look at the French girls, I look at the Spanish girls, and I look for a way out. I look for the Romanian girls but they aren't here yet. Anna lies down on her back. She has made it here, despite being a Useless One. She should be proud.

'Are you proud?' I ask her.

'Not really. And I need to relax. I'm not focused yet.'

'I'm not OK yet either,' I say. 'Something is off today.'

She looks as if her eyesight has gone fuzzy, like short sighted people peer in photographs. We are one body, one heart, so I turn away from her blurry eyesight. I don't want to get infected by her virus of blurriness. From where I stand, the Polish girls look like they're going to be today's losers. I can see their anxiety from here and in their grey, terrified faces. I don't know if I should tell Rachele, explain how obvious it is that they are going to lose. Or better yet, say nothing because it might bring bad luck.

Better say nothing.

'Red red yellow blue – Coca-Cola Fanta glue – teeth straight feet straight – me me but it's you – blue pooh Fanta glue – I protect and so do you,' Carla and Nadia are reciting. They then take turns to run their hands over my bristly hair. If the competition goes well today my skull will become a fixed part of the spell. I risk having to carry these caresses with me for years.

'Have you tried abracadabra instead?' I hiss.

'What's up with you?' Nadia asks me. 'Are you angry?'

Her hands are covered in scratches. What's up with *me*?

'Look at how she's working her jaw. She's nervous, that's what,' sneers Carla. 'Marti at the All Around is a big deal!'

They walk away and I touch my jaw. I am not *working* my jaw. What an expression anyway. Why would Carla say that? Immediately, my face feels like a camel's, my mouth moving sideways, my teeth sticking out. Working it. I strip down to my leotard and on cue, Alex comes over and starts rubbing my legs, my arms. He also gives me a hand massage, pulling on each finger, and with a cloth he wipes off the leftover lotion.

'We don't want to slip, do we?' he says. Then, 'Shall we make peace?'

I see myself slipping from the higher bar and I have to chase away the sound of my neck breaking. I then see myself breaking his neck.

'Fuck off,' I tell him.

I stand up. Leave. The Romanian club arrive and the girls are the most beautiful of all of us. I mean, each one of them is prettier than each one of us and than all the other teams in the universe. Even their lactic acid and their muscles are probably better. And their blood. They have glitter in their hair, shiny red leotards, and blue eyeliner tipping upwards on their eyelids. I watch them and in my mind I imagine them performing in slow motion, ponytails swinging and bandaged feet stepping lightly on the lino floor, as flexible as caterpillars. The bandages on their wrists look like precious bracelets, their legs are longer than ours, their hips narrower. I choose a soundtrack to highlight their superiority, classical music will do, it makes everything even more striking. I look for Angelika Ladeci, the star of my own slow-mo movie, but she isn't there.

'Angelika?' comes a murmur from all sides.

'Ladeci?' we hear.

'Ladeci?' we say.

Maybe she wants to make a special entrance and arrive after everyone else, so we'll all watch her, the protagonist. Or maybe she wants us to worry, so we'll love her even more. But the Romanian coach's eyes are panicky, their upward-pointing eyeliner failing to hide their terror.

'Angelika's missing,' Carla whispers. 'What the *fuck*?'

Nadia grabs her arm, ecstatic, as she recites their rhyme again. I look at Rachele, her hand over her mouth, the other in a tight fist. Anna and Benedetta are standing next to her and they all look terrified. We sit close together and watch the Romanian coach approach the jury. Only Carla looks relieved.

'Maybe they trained her too hard and her body has broken,' Anna says.

That has happened before. Something in the body of a gymnast broke suddenly, and she couldn't compete at the last minute. Or ever again. Or maybe Angelika has run away out of despair. Maybe she's had enough of faking her perfect smile. Of winning gold medals that stink of men. She has *booked her ticket* but for out of here.

Lucky her.

Rachele exchanges looks with the other coaches and they walk up to the jury in a group. The LED numbers are blinking quickly, too quickly, so I figure that the scoreboard technician has disappeared too. Maybe he is with Angelika and everyone else who has decided, this Sunday morning, to restart their lives elsewhere. I see them all walking free, feet sinking in the snow, towards an easier place where they won't be constantly watched and constantly judged and yelled at, and where no one is cruel. Maybe this is the Revolution my dad was talking about. Maybe this is the Wonder. Today is the day when we free ourselves from constriction, routine, and the fear of falling and dying with a broken neck. From the claustrophobia we get from push-ups in sets of thirty and another thirty and another thirty and another thirty. From this Sunday onwards, winning in a gym will no longer be important and bowing with a smile will no longer be needed.

At the jury's station, the coaches are getting worked up, moving their hands, frowning. I can't hear them. I think about their lives, which might even be more skewed than ours. Where are their families? Why are they so sick? Am I going to turn into them? We've had several coaches, at our local clubs and then at the national squad. At the beginning we would always look up to them. Love them, even. Slowly we would fight with them and they would made us cry, often just because they wanted to. They intended to upset us. To enslave us. Make us feel weak and useless. By then, we would only fear them and stick to fear as the key sentiment to make us move forward. And better. But now I know from watching Rachele and Alex, from looking at the monster in the eyes, that they cry too and they are lonely too; they are liars, weak, evil, and worst of all, they are failed gymnasts. They have no talent whatsoever. Fear is leaving space for something new, which is only ours. And is our true weapon. Hate.

The first coach we had at the Team Training Camp, Vittorio, used to give us lessons on our possible future path in life, letting us know that staying had a price and a meaning bigger than ourselves. And our happiness. Once, I must have been 7 or 8, he explained that training a gymnast is like holding a sparrow in your hand.

'If you hold too tight, it dies. If you don't hold tight enough, it flies away,' he said.

At home I repeated the sparrow metaphor. I found it poetic and something to be proud of. To be a sparrow in someone else's hands, what delight. Vittorio said it many more times and used to repeat it when he pushed us over our limits. And just like that, 'sparrow' stopped sounding like a lovely word, and being in someone's hands ceased to be something to be happy about.

'In gymnastics you need a pianist's precision of execution and the muscular effort of a weightlifter,' he would say. 'They are opposite skills, which should be trained in different ways. The pianist must practise daily and at length. The weightlifter, by contrast, only occasionally needs to exert maximum effort and needs a lot of rest. But if a pianist makes a mistake nothing happens, while if a gymnast makes a mistake she can die.'

I saw myself and a million sparrows die.

'It's like dissolving salt in water,' Vittorio said, before leaving us and gymnasts forever. 'You are trying to add more and more. At first, it's easy, then it gets more difficult. You need to stir harder, longer. Maybe with water you can make a science of these things. But in training there is no magic formula. It doesn't take much to overdo it. It doesn't take much to get an oversaturated solution.'

'What does oversaturated even mean?' Carla had asked.

It was one of the first times I had seen her train. We

were all kids. And even with no magic formula, no rhymes, and no Bible, she was already magic.

'Whatever it means, it doesn't sound too good,' Nadia had told her.

At some level, all gymnasts are oversaturated solutions and maybe Angelika had become oversaturated. I picture her in a glass full of water and salt, and in that glass there is no air to breathe, nothing to be happy about. We are in there too. So is the Chinese team. Together with all of those who are in this room sporting Lycra leotards and deformed muscles. Oversaturated solutions and bruised bodies floating in glasses of water and salt.

Rachele comes towards us and whispers something in Alex's ear, who in turn whispers something in her ear. It is like a game of Chinese whispers and I know it will fall to me to try to make out the meaningless sentence and say it out loud. Rachele looks over at the other coaches whispering in the other physiotherapists' ears. They are all standing, and it's clear this is an emergency.

She turns to us.

'Angelika Ladeci has gone missing,' she says.

'*Missing*?' I say. 'Since when?'

'Last night. This morning. They don't know.'

'They don't *know*?' Carla asks. 'Has she gone home because she can't stand the threat of me?'

'They saw her go to bed but they don't know if she went missing during the night or this morning.'

'Idiots,' Carla says. 'They make out they're so strict, punching their athletes in the guts, and then they go and lose Angelika.'

'So what happens now?' Anna asks.

'Now the competition happens,' says Rachele. 'Obviously the Romanians want it stopped while they look for her.'

And here she makes a circle above her head to indicate the crowded terraces, the bright lights, the polished apparatuses, the teams who have started warming up. 'But do you think an event like this can be stopped? Plus, we've all got flights back. If they can't look after their champion, why should we all pay the price?'

'What could have happened?' Benedetta asks.

'Broken record. How about moving our well-trained backsides?' Carla suggests. 'Benedetta, next time you decide to speak, warn us, because it's always a shock to be reminded you have a voice.'

Carla gets up, pinches Benedetta's bum cheek, and takes off her tracksuit. She runs her hands through her blonde ponytail and stretches her fingers and her shoulders before rubbing her ankles. She touches the callouses on her hands to check they are all still there. They are. It would be enough for one of them to come off to make the exercises painful.

'She's finally out of here,' Nadia says.

'Maybe she's got diarrhoea and is too embarrassed to say anything,' says Carla.

She winks and bursts out laughing. She puts her index finger in front of her mouth and with her eyes seems to also be saying *don't overdo it, come on*. Nadia strips down to her leotard, fixes it, and thanks to the shiny sequins, and thanks to their smiles, the competition begins. I caress my cropped hair, adjust my pink leotard too, and try to concentrate, with my earphones in. I stretch, rub my hands and feet, peeking every so often at the other teams. I close my eyes, think of my mum and dad. Of their few real smiles. Of their few real hugs. I reopen them and see snow outside the window, flakes like flying saucers. I'd really like to taste them. To catch a few on my tongue and crunch them like crackers. It's my first All Around at such an important competition and I still can't believe it.

'You are the best,' I say to myself. 'You are a warrior and a pioneer.'

The five of us walk in formation to the vault. Benedetta is with us because even if she is not competing, we are still a team and we are still one body. We cannot walk without her two legs. The other competitors are everywhere, behind us and in front of us. The Romanians, who look worried, and the Chinese – whose expressions mirror ours, efficient robots who won't rebel – the French, who can all aspire to be models but currently all suck at gymnastics, and the Polish, who look like they had food poisoning about two hours ago. Each one of us today will compete against one another on all the apparatuses, and at the end of the day there will only be one podium, three rankings on the most coveted one of this competition.

One and only one gold medal.

The soundtracks for the floor routines start by the mats and every so often I hear a tune repeated because a Spanish athlete has chosen the same one as a Russian and an English athlete has the same preference as a French one. I bite my tongue twice, very gently, and twice again a little harder.

'Pioneer,' I repeat.

Even though, I am not sure why, in my mind the word becomes musketeer. Behind us, a French competitor approaches the uneven bars. Her sounds on the bars suddenly remind me of when my mum's hoover bangs against the stairs as she cleans, then the sound of my forehead moving up and down on the physio bed.

'You are a warrior,' I repeat to myself. 'But a nice one that fights for peace. Nothing bad can happen to those who are good.'

'Red red yellow blue – Coca-Cola Fanta glue – teeth straight feet straight – me me but it's you – blue pooh Fanta glue – I protect and so do you,' Nadia and Carla say before moving apart.

And by then all things are in fast forward, the bodies, the thoughts, the words, the jumps, the falls, and I am already running towards the springboard, rotating my hands, bouncing in the air, double twisting – then nailing a *Yurchenko* and landing without problems, without shifting my feet by one single millimetre.

I bow to the jury. I bow to the audience.

I wait for my score, and welcome a good 14.4, as I watch a perfect Chinese gymnast jump after me, then land planting herself on the ground without moving a single muscle, not even an eyebrow. Maybe not even a heartbeat. There comes her 14.8. She is followed by a French, then a Spanish girl I will not see again because she isn't good enough, and because her team isn't as strong as mine, or the Romanians and the Russians, let alone the Chinese.

I move on to the balance beam. I perform my routine as if I'm still in Rachele's guided meditation. All is clear. All is easy. Gravity doesn't exist. Pain doesn't exist. I jump. I land.

I bow to the jury. I bow to the audience.

To the world.

As the morning goes by, Carla – accompanied by the soundtrack of feet landing, of bodies thudding or falling, of numbers spinning on scoreboards, and polite or wild applause from the audience – is carving her name on everyone's mind. After her incredible 15.183 at the vault, and a 14.86 at the beam, she receives a great 14.8 at the bars. When she smiles, her smile is the sweetest ever. When she jumps, she jumps like no one else in the arena and when she dances, her moves are so fluid and so light, she makes it look like dancing this way, while also flying, is very easy. Her clips will go viral online in no time. Thumbs up. Thumbs down. Watching her, it feels as though you could be just like Carla, your foot stretched out and your back arched like a feline. And her smile, how easy would it be for you – for us – to smile like that and to seem happy like her? But then we can't.

The judges nod, Rachele is making a V for victory sign with her fingers, and every time Carla finishes an exercise she says 'Yes!' which is almost sweet. Carla is taking herself to the Olympics. She is *booking her ticket*. She is also making Rachele the best coach here.

I rub my head and smile before launching myself towards the bars. I am focused, lucid. I jump high and clean, but as soon as I get on, I feel a callous come off my hand at the second release move. The bar turns into a knife. My hand is now an open wound that hurts and is distracting me. I let go of the upper bar and in the fraction of a second that passes before grabbing the lower bar, I anticipate the pain I am about to feel. I imagine its intensity, like a whiplash across my face, invading my brain. I imagine it being so terrible that when I feel the actual pain, the one that comes from raw open skin, it is bearable. It's something I can do. So I do it. It's something I can bear, so I bear it.

Maybe it's my new short hair and maybe Dad has been right all along. We are happy, we love each other, and money doesn't matter one bit. Life is doable and it's OK to work nights, it's OK to cry and for our palms to weep, and this Sunday is my Sunday so I focus on my routine's magic, on the form, the technique and composition. I manage to enjoy it. Then, to love it. I embrace the pain and celebrate it. I land in what is a really good landing and I land as if I have just conquered Mars. I have. I raise my arms. I salute and I smile the biggest smile of all the known and unknown galaxies when I suddenly realize I'm smiling with my dad's mouth instead of my own and that I must look really ugly, and desperate.

So instead of enjoying the applause that follows, I rub my lips with my hand and erase it.

We wait for Nadia's score at the bars and for mine. I keep my fingers crossed, and hope my points will bring me up, and that the absence of Angelika will help us all in this too. Nadia gets a good 14.66. I receive another 14.4 and smile with my own smile, not my dad's one, and as nobody greets me, I go back to Rachele. I stand next to her and hope someone will remember I was here too, and that I too was good. That I am Martina with the biggest M in the world, I've been training for a thousand years, I've been falling and failing for a thousand years and I've been crying for a thousand years. I'm nailing it today, at my level, OK, but I am. *Tell me well done*, I think. *Just tell me*.

She doesn't.

Anna pats my shoulder. Maybe I said that I needed a pat out loud? Are we now all so out of control we don't even know if we are thinking or talking?

'You're doing so well,' Anna says. 'You've got this.'

'Thank you,' I say. 'How are you feeling?'

'My ankle hurts. And I won't make it in the first twenty.'

'You are getting better,' I lie.

'Promise?'

'Promise.'

I see Karl in the stands; he still has two hours to go before the boys compete and before we, the girls, are finished. He has come here to watch. Especially to watch her, Carla. Anna looks at him too but immediately lowers her eyes. She has always been this way; she lowers her eyes and maybe she thinks that this is how she is going to live longer.

I am fidgeting with my zip, rubbing my leotard as I try not to look at Karl. But then I do. His eyes won't leave Carla. And Nadia. Again Carla. Why is he here? After a little while Rachele notices his presence, the eyes of her girls moving towards him and his towards them, and she looks flustered. It's a question of superstition too. It's all going quite well and nothing is supposed to change. No new audience needs to come. No new problems need to come. No Karls are allowed. The hours have to go by quickly, Carla has to stay focused, the snow has to keep falling. Rachele has to stick to Alex's side and she has to keep standing because when things are going right and you are standing, then you must not sit down until the end of the competition. If things are going right and you are sitting down, then you don't get up until the end of the competition. But now Karl has come in, and things might change and maybe Karl will bring bad luck and maybe Carla will fall.

'Nadia is in love with Carla,' I say to Anna and Benedetta.

Anna lowers her eyes more. I wonder how low they can go, maybe to the very core of the Earth? In that moment I see her lowering her eyes and crying when she was 10, after getting her hands slapped by Vittorio. I see her getting driven home by her chauffeur, closing her eyes in the back seat, and crying after failing at the beam. Then crying with Carla, after she had pulled her hair so hard she screamed. I try hard to remember her laughing and manage to come up with the time we threw ourselves onto the mats singing cartoon theme tunes. There was another time at a regional championship, when we were 11 or 12, and her mother had come to watch. After, she had taken all of us out for a meal. That evening Anna was laughing and her mum must have thought her little girl was always happy.

'She really loves her a lot,' I say.

Why am I telling Anna and Benedetta? I really don't know, but the fact I have chosen to tell the Useless Ones must mean something. Maybe I'm just a coward. They won't say the wrong thing and they won't tell anyone. Or maybe we are friends?

'And Carla?' Benedetta asks. 'Does she love her back?'

'I don't know,' I say. And I truly don't know if she does.

Anna rubs her ankle. It is swollen and you can see at a glance that there is something wrong with it. I have never loved her as much. I manage to come up with another time she was laughing. It was while we were all dancing, after training, to the tunes of some new popstar's single.

'It's not that I don't want to tell you,' I say. 'I really have no idea.'

'I know,' Anna says. 'It's OK.'

Benedetta isn't a happy sight, shoulders slumping, sad face. She looks like she's making a show of being desperate, about to have a temper tantrum so she can get what she wants from her mum. She isn't competing today and she won't compete elsewhere much longer.

'The beam hates me,' she whines.

'Might do,' Anna says. Then lies, 'But the mat loves you.'

Benedetta is on the verge of tears, but she holds them shimmering inside her eyes. Every tear looks like a small fish in a tank. We have never been thrilled with her performance at the beam. Nor with her performance at the bars. It is now clear there are us four, then her. She is less skilful, less strong, less precise. With tantrums. She is also getting too thin.

'It's OK not to be a gymnast,' I say. And I am not sure if I am saying it to her or to me. 'Might actually be better.'

I drink two sips of water and stand up. I don't want my muscles to think it's over and go to sleep. I move towards the floor mat, where the Spanish doctor is trying to bend the leg of one of their athletes. The poor girl grits her teeth. It's making me feel sick so I look at the snow until they carry her away. Nobody pats her head or gives her a kiss. Three months' rest? One year? Out for good and all this pain was worth what?

'It's OK not to be a gymnast,' I could go and tell her too. Maybe in Spanish. *Esta bien*, then what?

Carla is celebrating her stunning 14.88 at the floor routine. The sum of her scores shows that she's leading the championship big time, and that she's about to become today's star. Even if the battle for gold is not yet over, they are shouting her name from the terraces. Nadia is mouthing, 'I love you' and some of the photographers' cameras are flashing. They light her up and when she realizes, she flexes her arm like Popeye. She really has found a good signature pose, with that arm thing. I smile, even though I see Nadia say 'I love you' again, and she is saying it to no one, because Carla is actually smiling at Karl in the audience. I shiver, then count to ten, to a hundred, and know we will be dogged by bad luck because Carla has not kept her promise to hate the letter K and to never again look at a K.

Where is Angelika with a K?

Nadia's expression doesn't change. I thought she'd get angry, that at the very least she would give them the finger, make a face, but maybe today is OK. Maybe bad luck is just silliness, maybe promises don't last long and the only thing that matters is what we are really able to do. Resist. Jump. Fly. Win.

The Romanian club is keeping up with the pace, without excelling spectacularly, but with a unique cleanliness, and no major errors. They no longer have Angelika but they are still very strong. They are probably thinking of their star all the time as they glance around, expecting her to walk in at any moment, but they're keeping it together. Maybe they are even praying for her, while also being good little soldiers. Good little girls. Their coach Tania is inscrutable, her back straight, a delicate smile on her lips. Her face is a blank sheet of paper on which you can read either good or evil, depending on how you feel. If you were in a good mood you could draw laughter on it.

Nadia comes to stroke my head. Carla copies her. Again.

'Do you remember that dog of a Romanian coach who kicked his gymnast in the belly?' Carla asks, caressing my head too. 'The pisser?'

I nod. First because Carla often adds the word 'pisser' to the word 'Romanian'. Just like the Polish girls always add *mafiosi* to any Italian name. Second, because when I heard about the gymnast that peed herself at the bars, I knew I'd never be able to forget it. When she'd finished her exercise, the coach had intercepted her on her way out and – thinking they were probably hidden enough in the arena's corridor – he had kicked her so hard, she doubled up in pain.

'They are mad,' Carla says. 'And that girl was a pisser. I bet they've tortured Angelika a bit too much and broken her.'

'Picture her with sticks in her mouth.' Nadia giggles, remembering Carla's abracadabra.

And her voice is the same as when she sees things.

Anna's music for her floor routine begins. I watch her acrobatic sequence. Then her backward somersault. She's doing well but I can see how her sore ankle is affecting her performance. I follow the shadow of her body and realize she too has got really thin. She must have not touched food this week. But then again, it may have happened in the last two hours. If we put our minds to it, we are able to lose weight in one day. You just have to stop drinking water.

Knowing she shouldn't give any more attention to Anna – she's a lost cause now – Rachele goes up to Nadia. I can smell Rachele's lipstick from here, her hairspray, her shampoo. Her lies.

'Nadia,' she says. 'What's that face? You look like you've seen a ghost.'

Carla is behind us. She's done with her spectacular competition and she now sits in silence, praying, her eyes fixed on the scoreboard. I am sure she's reminding God she's his angel and her enemies need to disappear from her path to glory.

My back aches, my feet and most of my hand are in pain too, and it's worse where the callous got ripped off. I want to pour disinfectant on it, feel a terrible sharp pain, then nothing. I try to pray some invented prayer then I quit. I lack the alphabet. The gods.

'Nadia, you are OK,' Rachele says. 'I wanted to let you know you are mathematically OK.'

'Why are you telling me that?' she says.

'I'm telling you so you won't be scared. You are OK, you are in the first ten.'

She really can't hack it any longer, our coach. Or maybe she has never been able to and we were just too young to notice. Her words sound wrong, in all sorts of ways. I add the numbers up again and in fact Nadia is not OK at all. Carla is at well over 60 already and *she* is OK. But Nadia still has to do her floor routine, where she needs at least 14.50 to be in the first ten.

Nadia must have done the sums too, because she twists her face towards her shoulder, like a dog when hearing an unfamiliar noise.

'You're lying,' she tells Rachele. 'You are a liar. Stop doing that!'

'You know Rachele's a liar deep down,' Carla sneers.

Rachele knows we could all attack her now. She knows what we are talking about. I can see her guilt. Her worry. Alex is pale too. The whole world is pale and the whole world is guilty. We could push both of them on the podium, defendants of their trial, and accuse them and judge them and destroy them in front of everyone. *There, get your medals*, we would say. And we would throw at them medals that would feel like stones.

'Carla,' Rachele says. 'Let's all calm down.'

Carla doesn't even look at her. She keeps her eyes only on Nadia.

'The only bit of truth, though, Nadia,' Carla says, 'is that if you make it to the first ten, you have to take your clothes off as promised. If you bring home a disgusting 13.50, a beggar's 14 or worse, you can leave the club without looking back. See if the Spanish take you with them.'

'You're a bitch,' Nadia says.

But she smiles. Rachele smiles too. I wish all her teeth would fall out.

'Doing it for you, my love.'

They hug so tightly, I look away, and so do Anna and Benedetta.

'You're right. Promises are promises, a pact is a pact,' Nadia says. 'A lie is a lie, and K is dead and K is not dead.'

'And dogs are dogs and the snow is supposedly still snow. Whatever. Now turn your sexy butt around and show us what you can do,' Carla says. 'Go crush them.'

Rachele must be feeling left out so she says again, 'Show us what you can do, Nadia.'

I stick my nails into my hands and grit my teeth so hard I feel them powder on my tongue. Nadia walks to the floor and her legs look stiffer than usual, moving like doll's legs. The light in here has never seemed as bright. As Nadia walks to the mat, she is showing us her arched little back exactly like I've seen her do a thousand or a million times. I see her past. Her present. If I keep on watching I will probably see her future too, her body in her leotard, putting on weight, growing big.

The music starts and as Nadia starts moving, I close my eyes. When I open them again she is vaulting. A *Tsukahara*. An *Arabian layout*. Carla clenches her fists and Rachele chews harder on her gum. In the stands Karl stands up to see better and I feel sorry for him. Maybe this afternoon I will help him understand.

'There's no place for you here,' I'll tell him. 'Run away from them and from us as fast as you can.'

I see a couple of policemen walk up to Karl. I look

Ilaria Bernardini

again and I see another three near the jury and another one walking towards us.

'Look,' Anna says. 'Police, everywhere.'

Nadia finishes her impressive performance with a lean double full; only a small hesitation then her feet land strongly on the ground. She gives a beautiful wave, a tear falls from her eye, Carla claps her hands.

She was great. I smile too.

Carla goes towards Nadia and Nadia looks at Karl, Carla, the police, the spectators, and at the jury. She looks at the snow outside, so much snow now you can no longer see the sky, the air, the present. She looks at the lights above us, at the cuts on her hands, at Rachele. Alex. She looks back at Carla, her only love, while her 14.70 appears on the scoreboard, so stunning it looks enormous, and so magnificent it gets her to 56.88. I start clapping with the others, until I see Nadia wink at Carla.

Then, I see Nadia pull off one of the sleeves of her pink leotard.

Over the years I have thought of at least twenty different ways of leaving gymnastics. Some nights, before falling asleep, I even prepare the speech I'd give. I choose the tone of voice and the look I want them to remember me by as *my look*. They will say, 'And then, when she started talking, she had *that look*.' I could choose to go in a spectacular way, shouting that they are all blind, we are slaves, adults abuse us, we could die every day to nail a *Tsukahara*. Other times I picture myself calm and very wise. A monk. I explain that even if this was my dream, competitions have nothing to do with me, that I feel a million light years away from them all, and the world is not the size of a gym. It isn't rectangular and the ground is not covered with lino. I ask them how come you can

174

almost never open the windows in gyms? They are sealed shut or too high up or too big for us, so we can't let in the fresh air.

'There's fresh air outside, you know?' I'll whisper.

I'll add that many years ago, I heard Vittorio talking to his replacement, Rachele, and what I'd heard had terrified me. It was a simple anecdote but one I had kept in my mind for years, as I expected it to come in useful at some point in my life.

'Now, when I train the little ones,' he said, 'I pray not to come across real talent. I never want to meet another champion in my life and have to be responsible for leading them to a terrible life.'

'Come on,' Rachele said. 'We love gymnastics.'

'I feel sorry for them. You should feel sorry too.'

To have people feel sorry for you is not that great, I guessed.

And so, I'll say everything and I'll say it well. This is why I compose my speeches in the right order, one perfectly placed passage after the other, one carefully chosen word after the other. A twist in the plot and a tear, a reflection, followed by a fit of anger.

'There's fresh air outside,' I'll repeat. 'There's ultraviolet light.'

At which point they will most likely laugh and blow raspberries at me. Loudly. Nice fat raspberries, one after the other. But I will keep talking, adding I had heard the coach Vittorio say we are *victims* and that we were so short because we never got any direct light, so we were not able to synthetize vitamin D to help us fix the calcium in our bones.

'All in all, it isn't a miracle to be so small. It's more like a scientific experiment,' I'll say. 'We are *sick*.'

I'll then execute seven joyous handsprings and two triple somersaults in a row and maybe someone will cry and will remember me from that day on, forever.

But the next morning I don't want to stop anymore. And deep down I know that competitions have a lot to do with me too. I like being in a gym without ultraviolet light better than anywhere else. To be fair, I even like being afraid. Closed windows are not really a problem, and fresh air and light gets in through the doors anyway. When I do a good floor exercise, or nail a dangerous jump, it all falls back into place, including the words I say to myself on the bus home, in order to love that Tuesday too, and the Wednesday that will follow.

'This is your world, Martina. This is your family,' I say to myself. 'You never really leave your family.'

Staring at Nadia grabbing her pink sequinned sleeve, Carla looks as if she's about to faint. Her face has the kind of colour it gets when your blood pressure drops to fifty, thirty, ten. Her lips are dark, her skin is grey. Nadia, on the other hand, has red cheeks, one of those wide smiles of hers. The smiles she smiles when the stats are on her side, or when Carla gives her a hug or a kiss or anything really. I move next to Anna and Benedetta, who have moved next to Rachele.

'It's a bet,' I explain. 'Something they promised each other.'

They look at me in terror. The fear inside Rachele's pupils is the shape of the wolf we've all been looking for. Nadia pulls off the first sleeve and lets it dangle under her armpit. Her feet are still; her eyes are fixed on Carla's. She pulls off the second sleeve and spins around on herself. The sleeves lift up in the air, like a multi-coloured toy windmill. The other gymnasts at the bars look at her. I see some of the boys turn slowly towards Nadia and stand on their chairs to get a better view. I see phones being opened up on the terraces, video cameras pointing towards her. I see camera flashes. I see her tears. Rachele's.

Carla takes another step closer to Nadia. Maybe she wants to show her the Popeye arm. Or she wants to kiss her, in front of everybody, and our team will make history and we will be remembered through the centuries and the millennia, amen. I know she wants to fix it, Carla.

'Stop it,' she says. 'Now.'

'I promised, Carla. I'm mathematically in the first ten, so I will get naked.'

'You'll ruin us all like this.'

'So why did you make me promise?'

'I just wanted you not to be scared! To think of something else. Something stupid.'

'I never was scared. You were.'

'What are you? Dumb?'

'If I don't take my clothes off, it'll bring us bad luck.'

Nadia slips her fingers under the leotard's Lycra, near her breasts. Both sleeves are now hanging like elephant trunks, coming out of her armpit. I would like to give a cashew to those elephant trunks.

'Let's pretend you're just adjusting your leotard, OK?' Carla says. 'I'll help you. It still won't seem quite real, but it might distract attention.'

'I want to get naked. A promise is a promise.'

Carla looks at Nadia with hatred. She grabs her arm and holds it tight, like my mum used to when I didn't want to follow her. I'd feel her fingers sink into my biceps and when she'd finally let go I'd have red marks on my skin. I don't think Mum knew how tight she grabbed me. But she did squeeze hard and it did always hurt.

Carla unrolls a sleeve and pulls it back onto Nadia's hand, her arm. Then she does the same with the other one. She crouches down as if to check the back of the leotard and does it with such confidence that I find myself staring at the leotard to see what's wrong with it. Nadia lets Carla finish. Her cheeks are no longer red and she doesn't look happy any more.

'You've ruined the magic, Carla,' she whispers.

Nadia walks near her, her head down, back to the bench. She puts her tracksuit back on. We all do the same. Alex and Rachele talk to some of the journalists. Then among themselves. They push Carla forward for some shots. For questions and handshakes. Carla smiles. We smile too.

At the end of the day, we are so stoked we've done so well in the competition that we try to forget the leotard episode together with all the other episodes and monsters that haunt us. I was perfect at the beam and got a luminous 14.60. I have even done better than Nadia on it, and this, today, makes me the team's second best at balancing on the beam, just after Carla. Maybe Rachele will really decide to put me forward for the national team selection. Shame about my landing at the bars, sure, OK, and shame about my left foot, which would just not stay still, but I have given my best and we have all given our best and that best was seen. My trimmed hair has helped; so has the forest and the snow. Carla is today's gold medallist, Nadia is in the top ten, and I made it to number twelve, which for me is great. It's more than great, it's a revolution. Maybe Benedetta will not be with the rest of us at the Olympics, and Anna needs to work more on her self-esteem, but hey, who doesn't? We are in a state of grace, we are all alive, Nadia hasn't stripped in front of everyone, and for now we cannot wish for more.

'One body, one heart,' we all whisper.

When Carla walks to the podium, to receive her gold medal, we are all receiving it with her. The crowd is cheering, and goes wild as she does her Popeye move. Despite Nadia's sad eyes, we scream out our happiness. We all hug, then we go to the stands to sign autographs for the young girls who want to be us. We pass around Carla's medal and we kiss it one by one. We also kiss the club's flag, then we hug Rachele. Alex hugs us too but I leave my arms down, like Nadia's empty leotard sleeves.

Lying back on the arena's benches, we glare at the Chinese and Russian girls like sworn enemies, but we are already imagining them far away again, faraway thoughts of a faraway future. They existed here, during this week, and they had a space in our minds and in our hearts for this week. They can now disappear again.

'Ladies and gentlemen, we regret to inform you that the Romanian gymnast Angelika Ladeci has gone missing,' the announcer says over the loudspeakers. Then repeats it in Romanian. 'Please report any sightings of her and be vigilant. I repeat, gymnast Angelika Ladeci – blonde, one metre forty-five – is missing.'

The Romanian team is sitting in front of us. Their coach holds her chin high; she still has the most neutral look I've ever seen in my life. Is she desperate? Is she OK? Is she even a person and not a machine? Each one of their athletes is strong and as a team they definitely proved themselves to be stronger than us, than most other teams. But it's true, without Angelika they don't have a star and we do have a Carla.

'Good girls!' Rachele says. And hugs us more. 'Not to worry, and let's get changed now, OK?'

I swallow twice, shift my foot twice, and drum my

fingers on my knees, but the number two is starting to get on my nerves. It looks like a number one, if I think about it properly. A mirror image, revealing itself to be too balanced. I try to bite my lip three times and run my hands through my hair three times. I resist for a few seconds, embracing the change, embracing the revolution, but I have to balance the accounts immediately, starting over with multiples of two and with the repetitions of two. After ten repetitions, I still feel that deep down the harmony has been disrupted by the series of threes.

More police arrive. The judges are shaking their heads and furrowing their brows. When an announcement is made over the loudspeakers that the boys' competition is postponed, Rachele tells us it's time to go back to the hotel and that they will let us know about Angelika and the boys' competition as soon as there is any news.

We get into our puffer jackets. We slip into our boots.

'Does anyone fancy calling home?' She adds, 'And having a starter, main course, dessert, and maybe even double dessert for dinner? We need to celebrate.'

Nadia and Carla look at each other, smile. Maybe they do fancy dessert. And they for sure want to celebrate.

'Love Romania,' Carla says. 'Will love it forever and ever. Amen.'

'Amen,' we all repeat.

'All fancy a hot shower now?' Rachele says.

I think of hot jets of water over my head, massaging my shoulders. I definitely fancy that. I'll turn the pressure up and stand under it for at least ten minutes, knowing that this day is nearly over, that the competition didn't kill me or destroy me. And that we are bringing home some gold and the whole of our team in one piece. Monday I'll be back to my fears, but today I can rest.

'I fancy the shower,' I say.

I cover my head with the hood and follow the team.

We step into the freezing cold and the snow under our feet is so soft that I feel like we are still on the mat, ready to jump. I smile, but the wind blows so hard I have to wipe away tears from the cold.

'Walk in a line behind me and don't disappear,' Rachele says. 'It's getting dark and we're worried enough about Angelika.'

'We're worried too,' says Carla, without sounding worried.

'In the meantime, keep your eyes peeled on our way to the hotel, OK?' Alex says.

'Let's keep our eyes peeled!' Carla bursts out. 'We're definitely going to be of help keeping our eyes peeled.'

She starts pretending to be something with sharp eyes and a fast-swivelling neck. A radar perhaps. Or a lynx. Rachele's teeth are chattering and I realize mine are too.

'I fancy a hot shower,' I say again.

'We know, hon,' Rachele says. 'You've said that already.'

It is still snowing hard and the teams and the police disappear in all that white. It has never been so cold and the snow is almost up to our knees. The two man-bears with the coats must be overworked by now, maybe not even laughing any more. I think that they might be my favourite people in the whole world.

Although I'm freezing, every breath reminds me that we have done well in the competition. And that the tournament is finished so I can stop visualizing the thousand different ways it could go. Tonight I will sleep deep and, once awake again, I will be able to think of other things. At dinner I will eat as much as I want, carbs, cheese, two desserts maybe, yes, definitely two, and tomorrow we'll go home and I almost look forward to it. I can finish a half-done puzzle with Dad. I can be their good mouse in the mousy house at least for a day or two.

'Let's hurry,' says Anna. 'It's freezing.'

Benedetta and Rachele pick up the pace. Carla follows, Alex by her side.

'You were amazing out there,' he tells her. 'You were the best by far.'

'Thank you. It felt great.'

'We are a great team,' he adds. 'One body, one heart.'

'I guess,' Carla says. And looks the other way.

I have to decide if I should walk slowly like Nadia or fast like all the others. But the other group has Alex in it, so I'm better off alone. I look at the sky and snow crystals fall into my eyes. There's about five minutes to go until dark.

'Martinaaa,' Carla shouts. 'Martinaaa,' she shouts again.

'Martinaaa,' and it is still Carla.

'What?' I yell, and run towards them.

One of the Romanian athletes is behind us, and falls in the snow. Tania the coach shouts at her, so we look. The girl is crying. The coach is very near her and pushes her to get up. See, Tania is not so unreadable. And she is officially not so sweet.

Carla comes to my side.

'Maybe she hits Angelika,' she says. 'She's so violent.'

'I guess,' I say. Mimicking her voice of just a few seconds ago.

Some teams remind me of those films with soldiers shouting in each other's faces. But maybe the Romanians are also acting, to look stronger and tougher, and this might be a scene they are putting on, just for us. Later, in secret, they will all laugh and hug each other.

'Do you think she ran away?' I ask Carla. 'Maybe her

physiotherapist touches her too. And that's why that gymnast is now crying.'

'You nutter. Maybe her teammate is crying because right now she hates Angelika,' Carla continues. 'She let them all down today.'

We are near the bridge and the police are switching on their torches to search the field ahead. A few beams reach all the way to where we are; other rays of light are like glow-worms lying on the buildings and the dark forest.

'God has helped us,' Cara says, 'Amen.'

'Amen,' we all repeat. And I am not sure if this guilt-soaked 'amen' will stick with us forever.

Nadia trots towards us. She is smiling and when I smile back, she winks at me. I copy her with my left eye only. But because of having to do things in sequences of twos, I have to wink again with the right one. I get mixed up, botch it, and feel sort of sad for myself.

'Now we slow down,' Carla whispers in my ear.

'We? Who?'

'Me, you, and Nadia.'

'But why?'

'Because we'll slow down, jog towards the darkness, then stop and hide for a few minutes. As soon as the coast is clear, we'll go and look for Angelika.'

My heart jumps. Like when I'm between a bar and the next, between galaxies, like when I'm with Carla and Nadia.

'Not only gold medallists and top-ten gymnasts, but heroes too. Wouldn't that be great?' Carla says.

'I guess,' I repeat.

'Stop doing that "I guess" thing.'

Ahead of us, Rachele is talking a mile a minute to Alex and they keep on saying 'Yes! Yes! Yes!' Anna laughs and when Alex shouts 'Yes!', I slow down. I slow more, as

Rachele recites again the list of the medals we got. They are walking fast because of the cold, and they are soon far ahead. Rachele turns round just once, and all three of us give her the thumbs up. She replies with the same gesture and seems content with that. I can still change my mind. If I don't want to follow Carla and Nadia, I just have to run towards Anna and I'd catch up with Rachele and Alex in a blink.

'Do you want to let her freeze to death?' Carla asks me when she sees me hesitate.

I shake my head. I want to be a hero and I don't want Angelika to freeze to death. I also don't want to join Alex or hear him say 'yes'. The police are here, the shovelling bears are here; how could we possibly be the ones that find her? And aren't Carla and Nadia afraid of wolves?

'So do you want her death to be your fault?' Carla adds.

'No. But I'm freezing.'

'Don't talk crap. I'll take care of you and will warm you up whenever you want.'

Carla, Nadia, and I slow down. Everyone disappears in seconds.

'Ten, nine, eight, seven, six, five,' Carla counts.

At four, we can still hear their voices. At two, the voices are gone. At one, Carla grabs our hands, and we run towards the nothingness. The snow muffles all sounds. The wind erases them forever. When we get a few dozen metres away, we crouch down in the dark. Carla and Nadia are still holding hands and I'm silently cursing my feet for going the wrong way, for not running towards Rachele, towards my warm shower and the double dessert. I need to pee, and in this posture, I am reminded of it every second.

'Beautiful night,' Carla says after a while. 'So romantic.'

'Lots of stars,' says Nadia. 'I also ordered this mega moon to celebrate your gold medal and our glorious finals.'

Carla and Nadia get up. We start walking back towards the gym and we border the forest. We bend down to make ourselves even smaller and even more invisible to the police torches that might catch us. We go down the valley, pretending to be snakes and ghosts, then we straighten up when we get to the bridge again. We walk more, slowly at first, then faster, and the rhythm of our steps on the metal is the same as that of our heartbeats.

While they have their backs to me, I try to send a text to Mum and Dad, without looking at the phone. I write that the competition has gone well. A hug, I write to Dad. Mouse of all Mouses. A kiss to Queen Mouse, I type. I put the phone back in my pocket and catch up with the girls.

'Snail,' says Carla. 'Tiny, lazy snail.'

My steps become their steps again, until Nadia stops halfway across the bridge. I think she might want to mock me or take the piss because she has seen me send the texts, and I am not obeying them or being fast enough. But then I realize she isn't even looking at me.

'It's freezing, stupid,' Carla says to her. 'Move.'

Nadia doesn't answer and doesn't move. I've had quite enough of her manias, her standby modes, and of this stupid idea of looking for Angelika. It is getting dark and we've been competing all day. Carla has given Karl up, we are back to being winners, and Nadia is still punishing her. Enough already.

'Nadia, your period will stop in this cold,' Carla says. 'The blood will freeze in your belly. Off we go.'

Nadia breathes in, then she runs towards the edge of the bridge. She runs as if she's going to vault over it, into the oncoming cars. My mouth falls open.

'Nadia!' I hear myself shout. 'Nadia!'

I look around, to see what she thinks will act as her uneven bar or her vault. She could grab anything and launch herself up to the starless sky. Carla and I won't be able to see her in the dark, but maybe a torch will light her up and then her fall will be spectacular. She'll probably choose to take her leave with a straight *Thomas*. She'll go up. Down. And we will hear a smash on the highway. Then, just silence.

I don't want to watch her die. I absolutely do not want to watch her die.

'Nadia!' Carla shouts.

I let out another scream and turn away. I count to two, maybe I don't even get to two, and from under us a lorry blows its horn and other cars hoot. I wait for the screeching of brakes. For the sound of her smashed body on the concrete down there. But the sound doesn't arrive. I hear another honk. If Nadia has jumped she will have caused an accident. The horns stop honking and I hear Carla take a run-up too. I turn round, with my eyes still closed. The Sunday of Revolution and Wonder is ending in a terrible way.

Then, ready to faint, to vomit, to scream, I open my eyes and Nadia is still there. She has stopped, on the verge of the bridge, her chest squeezed on the railing, the sky now black before her, and the vibrating echo of the horns now silent all around us. Maybe it was Carla snapping her fingers to break the spell, or pronouncing some kind of formula to undo the abra-cadabra. Maybe Nadia stopped before that and she never wanted to die.

'Dickhead,' Carla says.

Nadia turns round and smiles. She is panting. Her chest

is going up and down, lifting up her coat. Her breath is making a million tiny clouds in the air.

'What did you think I was going to do?' she asks.

'You scared me, fuck off.'

'You thought I was going to kill myself.'

'You wish, psycho.'

We start walking again. Carla's chin is trembling, but she pretends nothing has happened. That's what we always do, so we do it now too. We go down some steps at the side of the bridge and get near the forest. Our feet are in the snow, and the snow is up to our knees. Then our hips. I touch the tip of my nose and find a snowman's nose. It is a carrot now, so I touch it a second time to make it become my nose again.

'Stop that!' Carla says. 'You girls are fucking crazy. What's worse is that you don't even realize it.'

'My nose was a carrot for a second,' I say.

'Of course it was. Happens to me all the time.'

And she laughs, as we hear police sirens coming closer. We stay in the dark and we watch as some of the other teams and their coaches walk in line towards the hotel, their rooms, the heat, the hot showers, and the possibility of double desserts. I catch sight of the bears in their coats, who like us are looking around, and calling out Angelika's name. The policemen are saying to each other, 'We'll go this way. You go that way.' Karl, handsome but like a stiff plastic toy, goes past the police and towards the hotel. Nadia points deeper into the forest.

'That way?' I ask. 'Are you sure?'

'Yes, I am sure, Carrot Nose.'

Carla nods and we take a run-up, watching out for the teams, the police, everyone. We avoid their torch blazes and, faster than the light, faster than their steps and voices, we launch ourselves towards the trees. We get the giggles. But then we look around and can't see a thing. We switch on our phone torches.

'Where are we?' I ask.

'*Where are we?*' they whine, mocking me.

Carla grabs Nadia's hand and starts walking quickly into the woods, following the beam of her torch. Every bit of her reminds us that even out here, she is the boss. And even out here, she is our gold medallist. Not to give her any more satisfaction, I stop talking and promise myself I will never ask her for anything at all, ever, for as long as I live.

We reach the thickest part of the woodland and we hear voices shouting 'Angelika!' and others shushing them loudly, hoping to be able to hear her voice, her pleas for help. We walk along a beaten track where the trees are getting taller.

'I want to go back to the hotel,' I say, forgetting my promise to never talk again.

Carla points the torch at my eyes. My pupils contract so fast I feel them stinging.

'I want to go back to the hotel,' she says, copying me again, making my words sound stupid.

She keeps on walking, so I do too. To make it even clearer that she's mocking me, she takes her hat off and puts it back on twice and zips her jacket down and up twice. She says, 'Who am I, hey?' Nadia and I don't say anything so, after a few more tries, Carla stops having a go at me and starts playing with the torch's light. Nadia seems tired, more tired than me.

'Do you feel like you're going to faint?' I ask.

She doesn't answer. The week is almost over and Carla and Nadia want to fix things and first of all they need to get away from boring little Martina and go back to being just the two of them against everyone else. But why did Carla insist on taking me into the woods with them if they hate me so much? We'll all get punished for sure. Unless we really do find Angelika. Then we'll be forgiven and will be famous throughout the universe and make history. Us, the good girls. In the pictures Carla will do the Popeye arm. Nadia will bow. I will do the head stroking with the humble smile.

'It was the right thing to do,' we'll declare.

The forest gets darker and thicker and Carla stumbles on a tree root. We see her vanish behind a heap of snow as she lets out a scream. Nadia squeezes my hands. We walk towards Carla, but without her torch to help us, it's hard. I can feel Nadia's breath in my ears and I want to ask her again if she is about to faint. Her breathing is strange, like a dog's. I imagine her with a really long tongue, like a Doberman's. I'd give her water. Meat. We get to the tree root and step over it and as we lean down to look for her, Carla jumps on us from behind a little hill of snow.

'Woah!' Carla yells, and jumps up and down with her arms spread out and the torch pointing up under her chin. 'Woah!' she yells again.

'Fuck off!' I scream. 'You bastard!'

Nadia is furious. She pushes Carla and takes the phone from her. She storms off and starts walking away from us and we follow, Carla still giggling. I am getting over the shock so I feel like laughing too as the rush of fear has woken me up completely. After all, it isn't so bad to be strolling in the woods, or to be making jokes that scare us for a second or two, and this too is a good adventure, a good backdrop, one of many I will have in the future, all over the world. In forests, in hidden warm clean lakes where I will bathe naked, and in never-ending lands where I will live on my own. I need to learn how to build a house, and light a fire.

Nadia is walking faster and faster, and to keep up with her we almost have to run. The branches are low, snow weighing them down like they are sad. When we reach a clearing, Carla lifts her arms and from where I stand it looks like she is holding the mega moon Nadia has ordered for her in her hands, and she could touch it if she jumped high enough. Today she has won everything and today we can all believe anything.

'Let's go back to the hotel!' says Carla suddenly. 'We've been nice enough to Angelika the dog. Besides, I'm hungry and thirsty. And none of this is fun.'

Nadia has stopped by a tree. Carla goes to hug her and Nadia doesn't move.

'We really must make you better, crazy little one,' she tells her. 'You're in bits. And I'm bored.'

I picture Nadia in bits right there on the snow. A tooth. A finger. Bits of her eye and her head. A foot and all the single hairs from her eyelids laid out in a row against the white. Then, Carla lets out a scream and I hate that scream and can no longer stand it, her, or the jokes.

'I've had it,' I say. 'I'm off.'

I want to get under the duvet and listen to music. I want easy things, normal and warm. We are gymnasts, OK, our life is kind of hard and messed up, OK, but now we are really going too far. Here is where I draw the line. But then I see Carla put her hand over her mouth so I turn to look in the same direction. Nadia is crying and I can see Carla is shaking, so I screw up my eyes and look closer, until I see Angelika tied to a tree. Her face is hanging down and her hair is over her forehead. Beside her is one of the shovels of the bears with coats. She isn't moving. Her legs are buried in snow, her arms bound by ropes. Bandages actually, the kind we put on our hands and feet during training. The same ones the Chinese kid used to commit suicide in her shower.

Angelika, I think. *We've found you.* Her bound arms are actually just one arm.

My legs have turned to stone. And ice. I no longer know how to move them. But Nadia and Carla remain still so I grab one of my legs, then the other, and walk towards Angelika. I cannot stand her being there, alone, still and so cold. Most of all, the snow over her legs seems an unbearable torture. Are the legs two?

'Angelika?' I say. 'Are you OK?'

Carla follows me, her hand still over her mouth. Nadia is crying behind us and I want to stop her, for real, forever. Amen.

'Be quiet, Nadia!' I say. 'Shut up.'

I kneel and see that the snow has been falling on Angelika for so long that it's now up to her belly. I lift her head and look away immediately. I throw up. Carla and I shovel the snow with our hands, like dogs digging for a bone, then with the bear's shovel, and we pull her leg out.

'What's wrong with her?' Carla asks me, crying.

She can only look down. I'm the only one now looking at Angelika's destroyed face. Under my fingers I can also feel a crack in the skull. I throw up again and put my hands back on her. I lift up her face and Carla now looks too. The face is white. Blue. And broken.

'What the fuck is wrong with her?' she screams. 'Is she dead?'

I think of the wolves in the forest and of the words

tear her to pieces. I think of them with Anna's voice. Carla is retching but nothing comes up.

'Oh my God,' she repeats. 'Who did this?'

She sticks her fingers in the elastic bands, rips them with her teeth, and manages to untie Angelika and tries to hold her upright. Her face is scratched, there's blood on her cheeks. Part of one eye is bluer than the rest of her face. Some bits are missing. Under the snow, her hair is matted with blood, her nose covered in bruises and scabs.

'A wolf starts from the belly,' Anna had explained to us. 'That is what they like.'

I will absolutely not look at her belly. I don't want to touch it and I don't want to know. I look at my hands and Angelika's blood has not stained them. Maybe this is a dream. Maybe it's one of our rhymes and abracadabras, pure imagination.

'Her blood hasn't stained me, maybe we're in a dream,' I say out loud, and immediately regret letting out such idiotic words. I look more closely and half my jacket is covered in blood. My hands too are now stained. Everything seems darker; the moon has disappeared. So have our souls.

'Go and get the police!' I shout to Nadia. 'Go and get someone!'

But she doesn't move. And she doesn't look at me. She looks at Carla instead.

'Red red yellow blue – Coca-Cola Fanta glue – teeth straight feet straight – me me but it's you – blue pooh Fanta glue – I protect and so do you,' she says.

'For fuck's sake, Nadia,' Carla shouts. 'Not now! Go fucking get someone!'

'Red red yellow blue – Coca-Cola Fanta glue – teeth

straight feet straight – me me but it's you – blue pooh Fanta glue – I protect and so do you,' Nadia repeats.

Carla stands up, her legs shaking. She gets near Nadia. I cannot move. I cannot breathe and I don't want to be left alone in the forest with Angelika. Are these slashes from a wolf's paws and claws? Will the wolves come and eat my legs too? I try to look at her again. I see her mouth is full of sticks; near her are the scissors we used to cut my hair. I close my eyes again. *Picture her with sticks in her mouth*, I remember Carla saying to Nadia. I look at Nadia.

'You asked me to,' she is saying.

'What? What did I ask you?' Carla says. 'Shut up!'

'To put sticks in her mouth and spit in her eyes until she's blind.'

Carla takes a step back and looks at me, at Angelika. Then at Nadia again.

'Aren't you going to say anything, Popeye? I had to be as strong as you to win her over. Had to smash her head with that shovel first.'

Nadia copies Carla's Popeye move. Carla moves another step back, Nadia moves a step closer and pushes her. Then she says sorry.

'About what?' Carla says, slowly. 'What are you sorry for?'

'Pushing you? Just now?'

Carla starts crying harder. She is shaking her head now and huddling tighter inside her jacket. She is very cold now and I have never seen her as hunched.

'Keep your back straight!' our coach would tell her. 'You look like an old lady! Keep your belly in. Don't be such a drama queen.'

But there are no coaches here. It's only us.

'What have you done?' Carla mutters. Then she screams it again. 'What have you done?'

'I love you, Popeye.'

Carla screams more, as if something has cut her. She falls to her knees, sobbing so hard I can't bring myself to sob too. It's like she's doing it for everyone. Nadia pats her on the back. On the head. She looks proud, like when my cat offered me a dead lizard. The prey was for me. It was a present.

'I hit her head when she was running. I stabbed her with the scissors,' Nadia explains. 'I tied her up. The sticks in the mouth came after.'

'You make me sick! You are sick!' Carla says.

'I did it for you. For us and for the team. The wolves must have helped me too. Cute.'

I hold Angelika tight because it seems to be the only safe thing to do, the only place to be. I stay here even when Carla runs away and Nadia stands in front of me, watching Carla run away.

'Are you OK?' she asks me in her sweetest voice.

I nod and when she leaves, I hunker down deeper, and I pee. I wet myself and for a moment it feels warm, comforting, and the right thing to be doing. I am suddenly so tired I could lie down here and sleep, on Angelika's destroyed lap. I search my pockets. I want to call Mum, but can no longer feel my hands. It's probably the cold. Or the end of my life. My pee is now stinging under my trousers, behind my knees. I imagine Angelika dying and have to immediately stop. I imagine Nadia in prison. In front of the police.

'One day I will tell the police about Alex,' Nadia had told me and Carla a couple of years ago.

She had been the only one to come with me to Rachele

and that had clearly not worked. She had gone back to her alone, a few times, and that hadn't worked either. Carla had rolled her eyes even back then.

'Good girl, try that,' Carla had said. 'Let's see what silence will follow even then.'

'Would you really do it?' I had asked Nadia. 'Would you be brave enough to tell the police?'

'If I find myself with a gentle policeman, yes. Of course.'

I immediately thought that she would never find herself with a gentle policeman. Still, it felt better than nothing. It felt like something we could hope for. Hang on to.

'Thank you,' I had said.

'Why would you ever thank me?' She had laughed.

I scratch myself and Angelika's head slips and comes to rest against me. I straighten it and get up. If I leave, I am bad, but if I stay I will freeze. My feet are starting to ache, my face too. I slap my cheeks twice and it feels like I don't have cheeks. I have a hole there, like Angelika maybe has in her belly. I try to lift her up again, to hoist her over my shoulders. She is light, really light, but she is stiff and I cannot hold onto her. My feet sink in the snow under her weight and mine. I can't see anything, so I lay her down and cover her with my puffer jacket.

'I'll go and get someone,' I tell her, even if she can't hear me. 'I'll be back.'

I start running. It's snowing harder and I've had enough of this snow and of this running and falling. Of all these words, this pain, and all of this fear. I've had enough of this Sunday, of us. I clench my fists and don't feel a thing. Not only has my face gone numb, but so have my hands, and my heart. I feel myself running with my father's face in place of mine. When I was little my father used to still go and train. His saggy cheeks wobbled and he kept his mouth open. Every step rebounding all the way to his lips, every acceleration making him breathe faster.

'The cheapest sport in the whole world,' he used to say. 'You don't even need shoes.'

I'd watch him from the window, he'd smile at me. I had pictured him dying with that same smile on a thousand times. I had pictured him killing himself and leaving a suicide note with the words 'I'm happy' on it. Sometimes his note would have his handwriting, sometimes mine.

Tomorrow I will tell him it is over. My lies, his lies. I know he isn't happy. He knows I am not happy. I know he is scared and he knows I am scared. I feel his breath right in my ears and I chase it away with my hand.

As I run in the snow, feeling my feet about to give in, the hotel lights get closer and after my father's face falls from mine, I can still hear his steps behind me alongside Alex's, Angelika's, and Nadia's. Of all the coaches I've had to this day. Vittorio. Rachele. Their hands, their voices. Alex's hands, Alex's voice. All of the adults' voices of the world.

I come out from the woods to the front of the hotel and Carla is holding onto Karl. When she sees me, she moves away and runs over to Rachele. They are all out here, all probably still looking for Angelika. Carla is sobbing. Her back, shoulders, and head are shaking.

Nadia, still far in the distance, is walking in the snow towards them. Carla tries to look at her but can't and hides her face again between Rachele's breasts, in the shadow of that mega fringe of hers, now frozen with cold and terror. I know exactly what the smell is like so close to the coach and to her tits. The few times Rachele has held me I felt the same texture, the exact same smell of sweat, lotion, deodorant. Will Carla tell her? Or is the team, the competition, the Olympics, more important? Is Nadia's murder our murder?

One body, one heart.

The police are not following Nadia and nobody is going after her. Maybe Carla hasn't found the words yet. She holds on tight to her gold medal and cries harder. Alex hugs her. She pushes him away. I see a flash, then another one. Carla is now crying facing the cameras of the few journalists still here from the competition, resting only one side of her head on Rachele. Her mascara is running, making her black cheeks shine.

The shovelling bears with coats are standing perfectly still and like me they are now looking at Nadia, while the teams, in their coloured uniforms, assemble in the yard, the gel in their hair glinting in the dark. The police sirens fall silent, but the lights on the car roofs are flashing and change the colour of the snow, of the sky, of the faces of those who are closest to the road.

Of my face. Of Nadia's.

We go red. Then blue.

A memory of fireworks one stifling August fills my head. With Mum and Dad. We had climbed onto some old containers, Mum laughing as we pointed our chins to the sky to watch the colours explode. A terrible heat came up through my feet. I thought my shoes would melt. Mum kept saying, 'How nice it is here!' Dad held one of her hands in his, and mine with the other. At dawn, as we walked home, I lingered behind, watching as Mum stumbled, her heels cracked and bleeding.

'Best night of my life,' she had said. And as she said it again, her heels started bleeding more.

I feel sick and fall backwards into the snow. Nadia moves

a few more steps and takes her coat off. She stops and pulls off her shoes, her trousers. Carla turns around and the camera flashes turn with her and the teams have eyes only for Nadia now. She is taking off her jumper, her T-shirt. Rachele puts her hands over her mouth. I hate her. Why didn't she listen? Why didn't she stop our bodies and our minds from breaking? This is all their fault. I imagine Nadia's mother saying, 'My mistake has made a mistake.'

The flashes of light from the cars and the torches draw their blue and red lines on Nadia's skin. On and off again, like a lighthouse beam. Rachele is about to go to Nadia but Carla whispers something to her and our coach opens up her eyes wide. Carla has said it. What words did she use? Murder? Assassin?

The police lights make Rachele's face look even more monstrous.

I think of Angelika with bruises on her face, without a belly. And no one to protect her. Yesterday. Or ever. I think of her covered with my jacket and know she would not be happy to end her life under a rival team's flag. I have to tell someone where she is. I have to get her somewhere warm. And out of that flag.

I have to tell someone where we all are and get us all out of this flag.

Nadia takes a few more steps, five, maybe six. Then she stops, perfectly still and straight, her bottom sticking out like only ours do, her spine gleaming in the light. She looks like a child.

'I need to speak with a gentle policeman,' she says.

I hope the mega moon will fall on her head, our head, make her vanish – make us vanish – now, forever. Amen.

'Fall, moon,' I say out loud. 'Fall!'

But nothing happens.

Nadia pulls down one of the pink sleeves of her leotard, then the other, and rolls it all off. From behind, we see her naked and so tiny, on the snow that doesn't even seem cold any more. She kneels and becomes even smaller, a head and a few centimetres of the smallest back in the world, of the smallest body in the world, while everything goes quiet. There is silence, everywhere. We all stop breathing at once and seen from above we must look like we are posing for a photograph, so many of us and no movements, not a single foot shifting. Not a single breath.

Just click. Flash. Click.

My phone vibrates. Then it starts ringing with the usual ring tone, the one that makes me feel ashamed. I grab it and see it is Dad. I let it ring in my hand, and the name *Dad* keeps flashing on and off again. I don't know what to do with the phone and with the word Dad. When it finally stops, I put it back in my pocket. I look at Nadia, now completely naked in the snow, her pink leotard near her. I look at Carla crying and Rachele with that hand over her mouth.

I am cold. And I am very, very tired.

I turn around and go towards the hotel. I walk to the entrance, go past the bears with the coats who are not laughing anymore. They aren't moving either. It is possible everyone is on pause and I am the only one able to switch to play. If I shout, no one will turn around. If I cry, no one will comfort me.

'She hit her with your shovel. She tied her up. She put sticks in her mouth. And maybe a wolf ate her belly,' I tell the bears. 'But she'd been hurt too. And wolves ate our bellies too. Since forever.'

The bears don't look at me. Maybe I haven't even spoken out loud; my mouth has not opened and it probably is not even there anymore. I don't have the strength to check, so I don't run my hand over my lips or try to fix it. If I no longer have a mouth, there is nothing I can do about it and there is nothing I can fix.

In the foyer, I turn back one last time and watch as the police move towards Nadia. I really hope she finds the gentle one. I call the lift but don't wait for it. I take the service stairs and walk up to our room and look at Nadia's bed, her bag, the leotards. I sit on the mattress and switch on the bedside lamp. In the mirror I see a head of closely cropped hair and the face of someone who looks an awful lot like me but who surely isn't me. I switch the lamp off.

'People are disgusting,' Carla had said to Nadia last night.

It was just a few hours before, now I knew, Nadia had left the room, the war-hotel, and had chased Angelika in the woods during her run.

'They always have flaws. Spots. BO. Or they look pathetic from behind. If you stare up close, at their pores for example, or at their cracked enamel, everyone fails. That way nobody scares you anymore.'

'If someone is good but fails, they don't threaten you?'

'They only make me sick.'

'Angelika doesn't have spots,' Nadia had said. 'And she doesn't seem to fail.'

'Angelika is yellow. And she is a freak. Totally disgusting. Also, I hope she dies.'

We had laughed. Even though Angelika wasn't yellow at all. Even if we often felt like freaks and had spots too. And even if, as usual, we had brought in death. Carla had laid on top of Nadia and Nadia had said she liked it, because it must be pleasant to have someone's weight on you, legs on legs, skin against skin. It must be beautiful to let your back be loosened by someone you love. Thanks to their pleasure, I had felt the same pleasure and some of their love.

'Tell me your five favourite things in the universe,' Nadia had asked her.

'Gymnastics. You. The sea. Winning. I can't think of a fifth. Tell me yours.'

'Gymnastics. You. Mum.'

'Mum?' Carla had exclaimed. 'Did you really say Mum?'

Carla had repeated another million times, 'Mum? *Mum?*', pressing down on her more and more. Nadia, trapped under Carla, was laughing so hard she could hardly breathe. I laughed with them, trying to make myself heard, before closing my eyes and thinking of my five favourite things in the universe.

My first one too was still gymnastics.

Acknowledgements

No book is ever the work of one person alone. This one in particular is the result of many voices gathered over many years. It is also the result of many ideas of different people, who have looked at gymnastics and at our girls' week and lives – at this story – in a way that was often radically different from mine. *Corpo Libero* or *The Girls Are Good* was published for the first time in 2010: it began life as a film for the director Martina Amati. We never made that movie, but the story belongs to her as well, as does the vision: thank you. This story also belongs to a coach whom I worked with for a long time and who – despite his immense love for this sport and coaching – was no longer able to accept the terrible things he witnessed. He entrusted me with his secrets and with his thoughts. He handed me his pain and that of the girls to care for, always and forever, while also giving me

203

advice and his permission to expose some of the horrors he had seen. This book is also by all the gymnasts I have known and all those I have never met, but have observed and loved, from near and far, who have fallen and got up or, sometimes, did not get up again. The ones who enchanted me. Moved me. And broke me. Their voices – what I heard of those voices – are hopefully in these pages, and they have shaped and nurtured Martina's and the other girls' voices. Thank you. This story has now taken on a whole new dimension and meaning for me, thanks to all the gymnasts, whose names we now know, whose faces we now know, who – many years after the first publication of this novel, when all the horror was still being silenced – spoke loudly and forcefully, breaking through a wall that seemed indestructible. They have forged an immense revolution and we will always be grateful to them. Thank you, you are heroes.

This novel also exists thanks to those who have read, reread, written, and rewritten it with me hundreds of times for years: I am forever grateful to you.

To my editors: Alberto Rollo, who has been there since the beginning, to Linda Fava and to Gillian Stern who I hope will be there forever and are always my first and last readers. You are my allies and my teachers: thank you. To my Italian publishing house Mondadori who believed that going back to this story – years later – was right, and indeed, necessary. Thanks to Phoebe Morgan, my brilliant HarperCollins editor, who filled this new phase with energy, power, and magic: I'm very lucky you wanted this book. Elizabeth Sheinkman, my agent at Peter Fraser + Dunlop, who supports me, advises me, and laughs with me: thank you. Carmen Prestia, my agent at Alferj Prestia, who listens to my every idea and for every one of them has a better one: thank you. Ellie Game, who designed the stunning cover: thank you, I love it.

This story also exists thanks to the writers who are giving it new life in the TV adaptation: my forever sparring and shining partner Ludovica Rampoldi, the luminous and supernatural Chiara Barzini, and the very talented gymnast and writer Giordana Mari: you all improve the voice of everything, always, and fill the new life of the girls with light, wonder, and strength. I am in awe. Thanks to the unrelenting force and will of the producers: Nicola Giuliano, Carlotta Calori, Francesca Cima, and Viola Prestieri, along with the stellar Indigo Film team, Marica Gungui and Federica Felice. For more than ten years you have believed in these girls, and never gave up on them, and never gave up on me: thank you. To the wonderful directors Cosima Spender and Valerio Bonelli, who agreed in a second and a half to join us in this obsession, and make it their own: thank you.

To Leo and Elia, my loves, life with you is a glorious double backflip with three twists – crazy – but my favourite of them all. Thank you. One body. One heart.